SOUTH
AFRICA
AT WAR

SOUTH AFRICA AT WAR

White Power and the
Crisis in Southern Africa

RICHARD LEONARD

LAWRENCE HILL & COMPANY
WESTPORT, CONNECTICUT 06880

To the memory of my father

Published in the United States of America by
Lawrence Hill & Company, Publishers, Inc.
520 Riverside Avenue
Westport, Connecticut 06880

Library of Congress Cataloging in Publication Data

Leonard, Richard.
  South Africa at war.

  Includes bibliographical references and index.
  1. South Africa—Race relations. 2. South Africa—
Politics and government—1961-1978. 3. South Africa—
Politics and government—1978-   . 4. South Africa—
Foreign relations—1961-   . 5. Guerrillas—South
Africa. 6. Guerrillas—Africa, Southern. 7. Africa,
Southern—Politics and government—1975-
I. Title.
DT763.L46   1983   305.8′00968   82-23405
ISBN 0-88208-108-X
ISBN 0-88208-109-8 (pbk.)

1 2 3 4 5 6 7 8 9

Printed in the United States of America

CONTENTS

Preface		vii
Acknowledgments		x
1	From Police Repression to Military Power	3
2	The Black Struggle for Freedom	21
3	The War in Namibia and Regional Aggression	59
4	Military, Police, and Security Forces	98
5	Arms for Apartheid	131
6	The Propaganda War	161
7	The Total Strategy	198
8	The Crisis in American Policy	222
	Appendix A The Freedom Charter	242
	Appendix B Secret Propaganda Projects	245
	Appendix C The Crocker Documents	248
	Notes	261
	Index	275

Preface

For decades there have been warnings that South Africa is a tinderbox, ready to explode in a racial conflagration. These warnings have multiplied in the years since South African police killed hundreds of young protesters in Soweto and other black areas in 1976. A recent report, *South Africa: Time Running Out*, prepared by a Study Commission on U.S. Policy Toward Southern Africa and funded by the Rockefeller Foundation, concluded that violence in South Africa will "intensify and spread" unless real progress toward meeting black grievances is not made soon. Robert McNamara, former U.S. secretary of defense and president of the World Bank, echoed this theme in October 1982 when he told an audience in Johannesburg that South Africa could be "as great a threat to the peace of the world in 1990s as the Middle East is today" unless there were fundamental changes in its racial policies.

In fact, South Africa is *already* a country at war. Since the mid-seventies militarization and military conflict have become a central part of South African life. The conflict over South Africa's illegal occupation of neighboring Namibia has grown into a significant guerrilla war. Pretoria has become engaged in a pattern of aggressive intervention and attacks against other countries in an effort to enforce its hegemony throughout southern Africa. At the same time, South Africa's white minority government has been facing growing resistance by black South Africans against apartheid, both in peaceful protests and guerrilla attacks. Thus the future of South Africa and the strategic alignment of southern Africa in the decades ahead are being shaped by the conflicts that are underway now.

To insist that South African militarization and military conflict must be viewed as a central aspect of the current situation in southern Africa is not to say that it is the only important element. The military conflicts have grown out of and are intertwined with underlying political and economic factors. Nor does the focus on the military imply that what lies ahead will inevitably be a pattern of military escalation and all-out regional war. There was a settlement of the Rhodesian war in 1980 just when South Africa's military intervention was becoming more overt and extensive. A settlement (and independence) may yet be reached in South Africa's protracted war in Namibia. Nonetheless, military force, with South Africa as the dominant power, has come to play a main role in southern Africa. And final resolution of the region's confrontations can only come when there is an end to the fundamental conflict, which arises within South Africa.

Several incidents at the end of 1982 and in 1983 heavily underscored the future implications of the military's "Total Strategy." The first of these was a pre-dawn raid on Lesotho's capital, Maseru, by South African military forces. Approximately one hundred commandos, carried by five helicopters, launched an attack in which thirty South Africans, members of the African National Congress (ANC)—the standard-bearer of black resistance to apartheid—and twelve Lesotho citizens were killed. This "warning" by the South African government to its neighbors against harboring its opponents provoked a rare, united vote of condemnation by the United Nations Security Council.

It also brought retaliation by the ANC. One week after the Lesotho raid, at least four explosions ripped through South Africa's first nuclear power station, which is situated at Koeberg, only ten miles from Cape Town. In a statement issued in Dar es Salaam, Tanzania, the ANC claimed responsibility and declared that its military wing, *Umkhonto we Sizwe*, had carried out the sabotage for "all our fallen heroes and imprisoned comrades; including those buried in Maseru." At first the South Africans claimed that little damage had been done at the Koeberg plant, which is being built at a cost of more than $200 million by a French consortium, Framatome. Later, it was admitted that construction had in fact been set back by at least six months.

The conflict within South Africa reached a new stage of intensity on May 20, 1983, when a car bomb set by ANC guerrillas exploded on the street outside the headquarters of the South Africa Air Force and offices of South African Military Intelligence in Pretoria. Officials said 18 people were killed and 190 injured. Eight of those who died were said to be black, and almost half of the casualties worked in some capacity for the military. The South African military retaliated with an air raid on what were claimed to be ANC guerrilla targets outside Maputo, the capital of neighboring Mozambique. South Africa said that 61 people were killed, including 41 ANC members. However, reporters taken by Mozambican officials to the areas attacked said there was little evidence of current connections with the ANC. Mozambique said 6 people, including 2 children, were killed, and 26 were injured.

At a news conference in Nairobi, Kenya, ANC President Oliver Tambo said that the guerrilla attack was an escalation of the ANC struggle brought on by the South African raid in Maseru and by a series of assassinations of ANC officials. He said, "Never again, never again, are our people going to do all the bleeding, never again." And he asked reporters, "Don't you think that we have offered the other cheek so many times that there is no cheek left to offer?" Past ANC guerrilla actions had concentrated on sabotage attacks on strategic or symbolic targets. But a statement by the ANC office in Lusaka, Zambia, indicated a shift in policy. Saying that the conflict was caused by the "intransigence and violence of the apartheid regime," it warned that future attacks would be aimed at "an increasing number of those who have chosen to serve in the enemy's forces of repression."

The South African government claimed that the ANC bombing had been condemned by "all communities and every sector of political opinion" in the country. But correspondent Joseph Lelyveld reported in the *New York Times* (May 25, 1983) that among the black majority in urban areas, there was support for the ANC attack. A social worker said, "It is unfortunate that innocent civilians were involved, but the motive for the attack was very clear. The black fatalities are just a part of the larger sacrifices we as a nation have to face and accept."

"The people are jubilant," said a black with many political contacts. "They long ago gave up any hope for peaceful change. What they are saying is that the African National Congress is finally hitting real targets. That is why you are having crowds of blacks drawn to the street where the bomb went off. They want to see the place where a white man died." A teacher said, "You don't want to call the death of innocent people a good thing, but maybe some people will begin to realize now how valuable all human life is and take steps to negotiation." The Botha government's Total Strategy is not, however, aimed at fostering negotiations but at mobilizing all possible resources to defeat the ANC and maintain white dominance.

This study examines the South African crisis through a focus on the country's ongoing military conflicts and growing militarization, because this has become the dominant trend there and throughout the region. The first chapter describes how South African militarization, marked by the rise to power of former Defence Minister Pieter W. Botha, has taken root since the mid-seventies as a result of both internal and external crises facing the Nationalist government. The second chapter approaches the conflict in South Africa from the perspective of the growth of black resistance to apartheid, with the focus on the African National Congress. The aim of this chapter is to provide a basis for an understanding of guerrilla conflict in South Africa by placing it within the wider perspective of the history of African nationalism. This background stretches back through decades of peaceful protests after the formation of the white-ruled Union of South Africa in 1910 to its roots in African resistance to European expansion and conquest since the seventeenth century.

The war in Namibia against the South West African Peoples Organization (SWAPO) has become South Africa's largest conflict. As the war has escalated, South Africa's illegal rule over Namibia has become a harsh military occupation. The third chapter describes the Namibian conflict and how South Africa has extended it into neighboring Angola. This chapter also documents South Africa's earlier intervention in the war in Rhodesia, as well as its continuing military attacks and other pressures mounted against newly independent Zimbabwe and other neighboring countries. In its aggressive campaign of destabilization against the frontline states (i.e., the independent African countries closest to South Africa's borders) South Africa has used an array of tactics, including conventional military attacks, bombing raids, commando operations, sabotage, support for dissident groups, assassinations, and mercenary units.

The fourth and fifth chapters examine the foundations of South Africa's military power: its military and police forces and its arsenal of weapons. Despite the arms embargo imposed by the United Nations, South Africa has continued to build up its supply of arms and military equipment with the aid of Western sources. These chapters also reveal the limits of South Africa's military power, such as the strains on available white manpower and opposition to military service among young whites. They also show the limits to its claims of extensive self-sufficiency in arms production.

The sixth chapter describes another important weapon in the Nationalist government's arsenal, its propaganda machine, which has mounted an extensive international program attempting to manipulate the news media, politicians, and other public figures in the United States, Europe, Africa, and elsewhere. The South African propaganda apparatus was exposed in 1978 when it became a lever in a struggle for power within the National party. Nevertheless, Prime Minister P. W. Botha subsequently indicated that many of its operations would be continued.

These elements of South African power are the framework for the "Total Strategy" that now guides the Botha government. Chapter Seven analyses this Total Strategy. At bottom it is a military doctrine encompassing modifications in the structures of apartheid rule, large-scale militarization, and a readiness to use military force inside the country and throughout the region. This strategy is coordinated mainly by military leaders in the prime minister's department who have been trying to impose it on the entrenched government bureaucracy, the National party, and business leaders. It is a formula for maintaining white control in South Africa and reasserting South Africa's dominance in southern Africa.

The concluding chapter examines South Africa's conflicts in light of the new policies being pursued by the Reagan administration. The Reagan policy of "constructive engagement" represents an effort to formally establish southern Africa as a zone of United States influence and to stem Soviet involvement there. While expressing the longstanding U.S. position of abhorrence of apartheid, it clearly puts the emphasis on stability rather than black freedom in South Africa. Yet this stress on stability, on resisting Soviet influence in the region rather than on taking an effective stance against South African oppression and aggression that has brought it about, allows the Nationalist government to be the arbiter of change. It amounts to an acceptance of the Total Strategy and a de-facto alliance with Pretoria. These policies will not bring stability in South Africa, black freedom from apartheid, regional peace, or a lessening of Soviet influence. They point instead toward a deepening crisis and escalating conflicts.

Acknowledgments

In my work on this book the American Committee on Africa (ACOA) and its associated organization, The Africa Fund, have been important resources for my research. I am happy to thank friends and former colleagues there for their assistance. I am also indebted to others who gave advice and assistance on particular areas. Professor Thomas Karis of the Graduate Center of the City College of New York provided useful comments on Chapter 2. James Cason of *Southern Africa Magazine* was a source of assistance for Chapter 5 and in other areas. Karen Rothmyer gave useful advice on Chapter 6. Material from DEFA Research in London aided my research on several chapters, as did publications and research materials from the Episcopal Churchmen for South Africa.

I must thank my publisher, Lawrence Hill, for his interest and enthusiasm for the work, and his support and patience during preparation of the manuscript. Barbara Harmel provided valuable editorial advice concerning the organization of the book and helped to clarify the main themes. Carole Cook's editorial work on several chapters was also appreciated.

Finally, I must thank Laura for her support during this long project, and Peter and Daniela for bearing with their father's work on the book.

1 From Police Repression to Military Power

A SHIFT HAS TAKEN PLACE IN SOUTH AFRICA: a government anchored by police repression has become a government anchored by military power. The shift was ushered in by Pieter W. Botha when he succeeded J. B. Vorster as prime minister in 1978. Vorster had begun to build up South Africa's military forces, but he had relied predominantly on the security police to maintain white supremacy at home and on diplomatic maneuvers and a wide-ranging secret propaganda program mounted by his Department of Information to defuse international opposition to apartheid. Upon entering office, Botha stepped up the pace of militarization and brought military leaders into high levels of government to coordinate the "Total Strategy" for the country's future. The Total Strategy, designed to meet what is officially described as a mainly Soviet-inspired international onslaught against South Africa, is a program for mobilizing all the nation's resources for war.

The extent of the militarization was reflected in legislation enacted in July 1982 that makes all white men up to the age of sixty liable for military training and service. The total strength of South Africa's armed forces, including reserves, could be brought from the current level of almost 500,000 men to 1.2 million—out of a total white population of 4.5 million.[1*] In discussing the need for the new measure Defence Minister Magnus Malan declared that "it has become imperative that each citizen become involved, in one way or another, in the process of countering the onslaught which faces the country. The Permanent Force and the present number of National Servicemen are no longer capable of guaranteeing your safety."[2] However, while Malan and other South African leaders describe South Africa's situation in defensive terms, the strategies they have adopted have been aggressive ones.

South Africa's militarization has been a response both to the erosion

*Numbered footnotes will be found on pages 261-74.

3

of its strategic position in the southern African region and to the growing black challenge, including guerrilla attacks, to apartheid at home. The collapse of the Portuguese colonial empire in Mozambique and Angola in 1974, and then, six years later, of white minority rule in Rhodesia, made way for independent black governments. The new leaders of these countries have been committed to opposing apartheid and to giving all possible suppport to the black majority in South Africa. Inside South Africa, harsh police repression had been successful in eliminating most of the active black opposition to apartheid. But the police shootings of young protesters in Soweto in 1976 sparked a black student uprising that continued for months. This upsurge of black resistance was followed by the onset of guerrilla attacks within the country.

Further, while South Africa had been bolstered by an influx of Western corporate investment in the 1960s and 1970s, the country's international isolation deepened as a result of the brutal suppression of the Soweto protests. South Africa also came under greater pressure to end its occupation of neighboring Namibia.

The challenge to white domination thus emerged at many levels—black protest and guerrilla activity at home, new black governments opposed to apartheid on the borders, and intensified international pressures. The Total Strategy doctrine of the Botha government is an attempt to counter each of these, relying more heavily on military machinery than on the intelligence and police apparatus. This chapter focuses on the rise to power of Defence Minister Botha and the background to his government's decisions to implement a strategy by which modifications in the structure of apartheid are to be carried out behind a shield of aggressive military action.

South Africa's military buildup can of course be seen as an inevitable outgrowth of apartheid, which has generated bitter black opposition at home and throughout southern Africa. But behind the takeover by Botha and his military associates have been deep rifts within the National party, among Afrikaner leaders in several fields, and in the top echelons of the government bureaucracy. These tensions have centered on differences over strategies for maintaining white control and have also been marked by personal rivalries among top leaders. They also reflect the dramatic economic and political transformations during the more than three decades of Nationalist rule. Significant changes have taken place in the economic status of the Afrikaners, and this in turn has been accompanied by changed political perspectives within Afrikanerdom. There have also been important changes in the position of black South Africans which can be related both to their increasing militancy and deepening urgency among whites over the crisis in apartheid.

The National party that came to power in 1948 was the vehicle of Afrikaner nationalism, the political expression of the interests and attitudes of a large majority of Afrikaner workers, farmers, businessmen, lower-level civil servants, and professionals. After the defeat of the Afrikaner Republics in the Anglo-Boer War at the turn of the century and their incorporation into a united South Africa, Afrikaners found themselves in the bottom ranks of white society. English-speaking whites, generally better educated and trained, and with ties to British capital, dominated the social and economic structure. The leaders of the National party embarked on a campaign to weld the Afrikaner *volk* together and thereby to regain political power.

Under the guidance of the Broederbond, a secret society of select Afrikaner leaders, ideological cohesiveness to promote the *volk* through the National party was provided by Afrikaner churches, cultural organizations, and trade unions. A populist tone was adopted, reflecting the subordinate economic and political position of Afrikaners among whites. Local English-speaking capitalists and their allies, foreign investors, were castigated both for exploiting the country for their private gains and for promoting the "black peril"—the threat of whites being swamped by blacks.

After World War II, the issue of the "black peril" took on greater urgency. During the war the economy had expanded rapidly, creating a massive increase in the black urban population and work force as well as favorable conditions for new and more assertive forms of black political and trade union activity. The United party, then in power with General Jan Smuts as prime minister, was seeking a means whereby the black urban population could be incorporated permanently into the areas of the country which had been reserved for whites and become a settled labor force. The opposition National party claimed this portended the doom of "white civilization."

After winning power in the white parliament in 1948, the Nationalists imposed their own solution to the "black peril": the apartheid system. Blacks would be allowed into the white urban areas only as "temporary sojourners" and could stay only for as long as they were useful to the white economy. White employers would be assured of black labor through a rigid system of influx control, which enabled blacks to stay in white areas only if jobs were available. The passbooks blacks were forced to carry at all times under constant police surveillance insured that only "authorized" blacks could remain in the urban areas; the rest were to be endorsed out to their so-called homelands or Bantustans. Apartheid also provided for strict racial segregation in residential areas, the protection of white workers by reserving skilled categories of labor for them alone, and the prohibition of interracial sex and marriage.

The 1950s saw a rising confrontation between the two major political forces in South Africa: African nationalism and Afrikaner nationalism. Throughout the decade, peaceful protests against apartheid by the African National Congress (ANC) and other groups were met with harsh police reprisals. The Nationalists, among whose leaders were a number of Nazi sympathizers, branded opposition from virtually any quarter as communist-inspired treason. On March 21, 1960, a turning point was reached when the police opened fire on unarmed Africans protesting the detested pass sytem, killing sixty-seven and wounding one hundred and eighty-six in the black township of Sharpeville. In response to the ensuing protests, the government declared a state of emergency in which thousands were arrested and held without trial for months, and in which it outlawed the ANC and its offshoot, the Pan Africanist Congress (PAC).

Faced with the government's violence and sweeping repression, many black leaders and some of their white supporters felt that no alternative remained but to turn to sabotage and armed resistance. The ANC's long tradition of reliance on peaceful protest alone thus came to an end. The government responded by enacting harsh security measures. There was a sudden flight of foreign capital, but the economy was bolstered by strategic loans from American banks. By the mid-sixties, the hastily organized underground resistance of the ANC and the PAC had been crushed by police repression.

Once the threat from black opposition had been suppressed, confidence in South Africa's economy was restored and foreign investment began flooding back. Where Afrikaners had already benefited as businessmen, farmers, and civil servants through the 1950s as a result of state and political intervention through the National party, their positions improved even more rapidly under the boom conditons of the 1960s. In 1948 the percentage of private businesses owned by Afrikaners was 9.6 and of mining only 1.0. Afrikaners then had held only 16 percent of professional posts. By 1976, aided by state loans, subsidies, and other forms of government support, Afrikaners owned 20.8 percent of private enterprises, and 18 percent of the mining concerns. They occupied 38 percent of the professional posts by that date. Whereas in 1946 Afrikaners had an estimated one half the per capita income of English-speaking white South Africans, by 1976 they had achieved parity.[3] Their dominant position as managers and supervisory workers in the parastatal corporations and in the civil service contributed to this economic advance. Afrikaners were also moved into leadership positions in the Defence Force.

Nationalist rule and the apartheid system thus not only provided for further economic growth through the repression and control of blacks, but particularly enhanced the position of many Afrikaners, bringing substantial changes in their class position and their political attitudes. Whereas previously the interests of business had been seen as opposed to those of the traditional Afrikaner constituencies of workers and farmers, the new Afrikaners who are now in a position to influence policies have come to see capitalist growth (in which they now have a sizable stake) as one key to the country's survival. Private enterprise as well as the parastatal infrastructure to which it is linked have not only fueled white prosperity but also given South Africa its great economic power over the southern African region, which extends into the rest of the continent. Its gold and strategic minerals give South Africa international importance. The country's economic strength has enabled it to bear the sizable costs of imports of armaments and oil. A large proportion of local production of arms and military equipment is contracted out to private companies; this development and the expanding power of the Defence Force have brought closer ties between the military and business and have created more bonds between English-speaking whites and groups of Afrikaners.

The dynamic economy has become the basis of Afrikaner prosperity and the power of the Nationalist government. It has always been overwhelmingly dependent on black labor, but it now needs increasingly skilled black workers and the purchasing power of black consumers as well. By keeping the black majority politically powerless, relying heavily on unskilled migrant labor and forcing "superfluous appendages" (wives and children, the aged, the sick, and the injured) out to the Bantustans, apartheid provided high profits and kept black South Africans at the lowest economic levels. But the new Afrikaner stratum in business and government (known as *verligte*, or "enlightened," Afrikaners) has increasingly come to share the views of many English-speaking business leaders that, after three decades, apartheid in its raw form has become an economic and political—and military—menace. Despite the opposition of *verkrampte* (hardliner) Afrikaners, *verligtes* believe the structure of apartheid must be reshaped, both to accommodate the needs of business and to defuse rising black opposition.

The government of Prime Minister Vorster was based on the National party political machine and its traditional, *verkrampte*-oriented constituency. Vorster had served as minister of justice and police under the premiership of Hendrik Verwoerd, the charismatic architect of apartheid. As the minister responsible for law and order, Vorster had implemented the security measures that had crushed black opposition in the wake of the Sharpeville massacre. Upon his succession to prime minister he carried *verligte* support with him and also attracted some of the English-speaking electorate. At that time, too, he appointed his close associate, Security Police General Hendrik van den Bergh, to form and head a new security department, the Bureau of State Security (BOSS), which would coordinate and oversee all government intelligence operations.

Vorster, van den Bergh, and others in the government had old links to the most extreme wing of Afrikanerdom, the *Ossewa Brandwag* (Ox-wagon Sentinal) set up before World War II. This organization was strongly sympathetic to the Nazis. (Vorster and van den Bergh had been among those interned by the Smuts government during World War II on account of those sympathies.) Their plan for apartheid evolved along the lines set out by Verwoerd: blacks were to be accorded no rights in so-called white South Africa and were instead to be regarded as nationals of the Bantustans. But the evolution of apartheid took place in altered conditions: the growing split between *verligtes* and *verkramptes* and heightened domestic and international pressure against apartheid. A new strategy was needed to appease both the critics within and beyond the National party and the die-hards within Afrikanerdom.

In an attempt to offset the pressures against apartheid at home, Vorster promoted the program of Bantustan independence and also permitted minor steps to reduce racial segregation in public facilities. Abroad, he undertook semisecret diplomatic efforts with General van den Bergh aimed at gaining detente with several African governments. Among these were the Ivory Coast, Senegal, Zaire, and Zambia. The goal was to break down Africa's united front against apartheid by convincing these African states that racial conflict was being resolved in South Africa, and that Pretoria could offer advantageous economic relations as well as a secure bastion against Soviet influence in Africa. Acceptance by African countries could in turn be used to counter critics of South Africa in the West.

The Department of Information undertook a greatly expanded secret international and domestic program of propaganda as part of Vorster's attempts to neutralize opposition to apartheid from all quarters. The program included a wide variety of shady deals and "dirty tricks," involving millions of dollars, designed to buy media outlets, political influence, and friends for the Nationalist government in order to bolster the image of South Africa and challenge critics of apartheid. (These are discussed in Chapter Six.) The general tone of the new propaganda was epitomized by a statement made by Foreign Minister R. F. Botha to the United Nations Security Council in 1974: "I want to state here very clearly and categorically that my government does not condone discrimination purely on grounds of race or color. Discrimination based solely on the color of a man's skin cannot be defended and we shall do everything in our power to move away from discrimination based on race or color."[4]

Far from recanting apartheid, Botha's statement (with its careful use of qualifying words) reflected the Vorster government's effort to redefine the system in terms of "nationality" rather than race. Africans were to be classified into different "national" groups according to tribal or ethnic origin and as such would be "nationals" of independent Bantustans. At the same point Prime Minister Vorster also promised "startling" new developments in the country's apartheid policies if he were given six months to prepare them. The unrevealed surprises never appeared.

Events beyond the control of Vorster and his Information Department's efforts to win hearts and minds, and even beyond the power of BOSS, began to erupt by the mid-seventies. In the face of these events, Vorster's policies began to unravel. Externally, there were severe setbacks. The collapse of the Portuguese colonial empire in 1974 brought the Mozambique Liberation Front (FRELIMO) into power in Mozambique. In Angola, South Africa cooperated with the CIA to try to install a friendly government and prevent the People's Movement for the Liberation of Angola (MPLA) from taking power.The defeat of South Africa's invading forces in Angola by the MPLA with Cuban and Soviet aid led to stepped-up guerrilla activity in Namibia, where the South West Africa Peoples Organisation (SWAPO) fought to end South Africa's occupation. And on the diplomatic front, the launching of South Africa's first "independent" Bantustan ended in failure: the Transkei was never accorded international recognition as an independent state.

When police fired on protesting students in Soweto on June 16, 1976, a volcano of anger and resentment erupted among the black youth of South Africa. Inspired by the Black Consciousness Movement that had spread among black students in the 1970s, young blacks in segregated townships mounted open resistance for months against racism and repression. Hundreds were killed as the police countered protests with gunfire. (The official death toll was 451, but some estimates put the total at more than 1,000, with more than 5,000 injured.[5]) In their duration and intensity the protests were unprecedented: the younger generation was expressing the pent-up bitterness over the silencing of black protest in the fifteen years since Sharpeville. As the protests subsided, more than a year later, Black Consciousness leader Steve Biko died at the hands of the Security Police. The student upheaval and the death of Biko brought world-wide condemnation of the white regime. There could be no pretense that black South Africans accepted the new face of apartheid any more than they had accepted the system in the 1950s. It was clear that Vorster's plans for the evolution of apartheid at home and for gradually winning international acceptance were shattered.

At the end of 1976 there were indications that the Nationalist government could be facing further difficulties: several incidents pointed to the onset of ANC guerrilla activity, and this could only be aided by the wholesale police violence against young protesters. A police station was damaged in an explosion, and in another case two policemen were wounded by hand grenades while they were trying to make an arrest near the border with Mozambique. There were other incidents as well. Initially, as in the early 1960s, this was considered to be only a problem for BOSS and the Security Police. Early in 1977 Minister of Justice and Police James Kruger displayed a Soviet-made pistol, which he said had been seized by the police, in the white parliament and claimed that "urban terrorism is totally finished."[6] The 1977 Defence White Paper indicated that the "presence of troops under training" was being maintained full-time in areas on the country's northern borders to guard against insurgent infiltration, but there was no implication that guerrilla activity within South Africa was viewed as a serious future problem.

But the guerrilla incidents continued. In June 1977 three young men from Soweto fled from a police check and killed two whites in a garage on Goch Street in central Johannesburg. Two were caught, and it was revealed that they had left the country the year before in reaction to the killing of protesters by the police and had trained as guerrillas with the African National Congress. One of the youths, Solomon Mahlangu, was convicted of murder (though he had not fired on the men) and hanged. The Goch Street shootings jarred white South Africa. Guerrilla wars had undermined the Portuguese in Mozambique and Angola, and conflicts were simmering in Namibia and Rhodesia. But for most white South Africans these events were remote. Even the student protests were confined mainly to the black townships and hardly touched whites directly. And all the shooting was being done by the police. But the shooting of whites by black guerrillas in downtown Johannesburg was a startling event.

Paramilitary police patrols were stepped up along the borders, but guerrilla incidents continued. In November 1977 a bomb exploded at the new Carlton Centre, a modern office complex in Johannesburg. Seventeen people were injured. More police stations were bombed, and railway lines were sabotaged. Several black policemen known to be informers against the ANC were killed. Clashes took place between police patrols and guerrillas. By the spring of 1978 the government claimed that "91 trained and 594 untrained terrorists" had been captured by the police.[7]

The number of political trials mushroomed. At first, many involved charges of instigating student unrest, but increasingly they involved guerrilla activity: of trying to leave the country illegally for guerrilla training, of having returned as trained guerrillas with weapons, or of being responsible for specific guerrilla attacks. Brigadier C. F. Zeitsman, head of the Security Police, told television interviewers from CBS Reports, who had seen groups of police in camouflage uniforms carrying automatic weapons patrolling Soweto, that the ANC was spreading its underground network "all over the country. . . .They are everywhere."[8]

Police officials began giving shrill warnings to the public: one told a Johannesburg business group: "Check on your servant's bona fides, or those of your maid's husband. Don't give these terrorists a haven to hide in. Keep your eyes and ears open and bring anything unusual to our attention. . .they will not give up without a fight and we will have to overwhelm them in the streets or in their beds. . . ."[9]

With external and internal crises facing the Nationalist government it is not surprising that one main response by Vorster was stepped-up militarization. In part, this mobilization was aimed at supplementing the country's domestic police resources, which were under strain from the student protests and guerrilla attacks. But for the most part the military buildup was directed at external targets. Initially, the major cause for starting the military buildup was the invasion of Angola (during which reservists were called up for three-month tours) and the intensification of the Namibia war that resulted when the invasion failed. South African forces also began to secretly play a larger role in the war in Rhodesia. If, through a combination of military power and economic and diplomatic influence, Pretoria could check the advances made by African liberation forces in the region, then it would be easier to keep the lid on black unrest at home.

In 1977 compulsory national military service for white males was extended from one year to two years, and they were also obligated for additional Citizen Force or Commando active reserve duties for eight years. Through the 1977 Civil Defence Act, under which local authorities were required to establish Civil Defence units to mobilize those not actively engaged in the military or police forces, the government activated older men for local civil defense work. White women were encouraged to join both the Permanent Force and the Commando reserves; in 1978 national military service was extended to white women on a voluntary basis. For the first time women began to occupy Defence Force positions that had been reserved for men (these did not, however, include combat roles). The 1977 Defence White Paper also announced the goal of doubling the number of cadets, trained during high school for military service, to 200,000.

Special services and amenities were introduced for those in the military. The Johannesburg city council offered soldiers free use of public transport. Several hotels began giving special discounts to wounded soldiers and their families. National service-men became protected by law against being sued for debt. Hitchhiking was made easier for soldiers through a program known as Operation Safe Ride. In 1976 the government began selling National Defence bonds; the following year it added a Defence Bonus Bonds program which is run as a lottery.

In August 1977 the Soviet Union reported that its satellite photos showed evidence of South African preparations for a nuclear explosion in the Kalahari Desert. This observation was confirmed by U.S. satellite photos. The Nationalist government had enjoyed two decades of assistance in the development of nuclear technology from the United States,

West Germany, and other Western countries, ostensibly for peaceful purposes, but clearly this cooperation had also aided Pretoria in gaining the capability to produce nuclear weapons. The British and French communicated their opposition to any nuclear explosion to the South Africans, and President Jimmy Carter announced he had received Prime Minister Vorster's assurance that South Africa would not develop nuclear weapons and that the structures sighted were not erected for a nuclear test. Later, however, the South Africans denied giving such assurances. They said only that they were interested in peaceful uses of nuclear power, but gave no explanation for the structures in the Kalahari.[10]

A university lecturer writing in the *Cape Times* described the "war psychosis" he saw gripping the country, promoted by military propaganda of "mind-boggling and terrifying intensity":

> Switch on your radio and you are likely to hear some crooner urging you to buy Defence Bonds. During the pop program "Forces Favorites" you are treated to interviews with high-ranking officers in Pretoria and on the border.
>
> The newspapers—both Afrikaans and English—are falling over themselves to obtain and publish press releases about our military preparedness, and the South African Defence Force's many liaison personnel are only too happy to oblige. . . .
>
> The message is striking home. . .that the country is engaged in a low-to-moderate intensity war for which at present there is no end in sight; the chances are it will get much worse.[11]

The South African *Financial Mail* saw a growing "march of militarism" and concluded that "psychologically and in practice South Africa is being prepared for the gathering storm. . .digging in for the White Man's last stand—defiantly, tragically, suicidally," with the government able to "rake a growing number of businessmen, students, housewives, and even school children into the war effort."[12]

BOTHA AND THE MILITARY COME TO POWER

As the tempo of militarization increased, the National party reached a turning point with Vorster's impending retirement as prime minister in mid-1978. It was widely expected that his successor would be Cornelius ("Connie") Mulder, minister of the interior and information and a close colleague from the Nationalists' dominant Transvaal branch. Where Vorster had always been reluctant to implement changes that would strain Nationalist unity, Mulder was regarded as far less cautious. Like Vorster, Mulder favored predominant reliance on BOSS and the

Information Department, rather than on the military. But the crises of the mid-seventies had shown that urgent changes were needed even at the expense of the *verkramptes* and a possible National party schism.

In 1976 *Newsweek* magazine had reported that top BOSS officials felt that "drastic changes" were needed in the structure of apartheid, suggesting a federal structure of semi-autonomous "cantons," some black, some white, and some mixed, with common citizenship instead of the present divisions.[13] The proposed structure would certainly have retained most political and economic power in white hands, but could have permitted some black participation in a central government. BOSS denied the report, which implied a major revision of Bantustan policy; but after his retirement in 1978 General van den Bergh aired similar views to the press. In 1977 Mulder told a National party congress that it looked to him as though the country would become a one-party state and that he would welcome this.[14] He could well have expected to be its leader.

South African military leaders, however, had somewhat different proposals for the country's future, solutions which, unsurprisingly, emphasized the role of the military. There was talk of a "de Gaulle option," a takeover of government by reform-minded military leaders who would oversee socioeconomic changes while keeping both black resistance and white opposition in check within the country. In 1977 Defence Force chief General Magnus Malan, while claiming not to advocate military dictatorship, admitted that he saw a tension between the military's proposed strategy and a democratic system.[15] The strategy to which Malan referred was the "Total Strategy," which had been presented in the 1977 Defence White Paper and which he explained as a plan for state mobilization and coordination of all South Africa's resources to meet the threat of "total war."

Vorster's retirement set the stage for a struggle for power between Mulder, Defence Minister P. W. Botha, who was backed by the military, and *verligte*-oriented Foreign Minister R. F. Botha. The Information Department scandal—Muldergate—which involved charges of financial and administrative irregularities in the department's propaganda program, became the focal point of a wider struggle over power and future strategies.

Vorster and Mulder had wanted to limit the South African role in the 1975 invasion of Angola, and had opposed the strengthening of the invasion forces which Botha and military leaders had urged. There were also stories of risky military plans that had been stopped. Van den Bergh was said to have had his BOSS agents sabotage Defence Force vehicles which were ready to strike against FRELIMO forces soon after Mozambique became independent, thus preserving the detente policy being pursued by Vorster. At another point, Defence Minister Botha was said to have been ready to openly commit several hundred South African paratroopers to the Rhodesian war before the plan was halted.[16] The common theme of these reports is that, like Vorster, Mulder preferred to avoid overt military moves that would put South Africa openly in the role of an aggressor. Military attacks by South Africa could bring increased international pressures and support for the frontline states and the liberation movements, while risking being drawn into wider conflicts which could stretch the country's finite resources of white manpower and materiel. After the crises of the mid-1970s Voster had been trying a low-key strategy of edging toward settlements in the Rhodesian and Namibian conflicts which would bring in pliant independent governments which Pretoria could influence with its overwhelming economic and military strength without resorting to direct military intervention. This would give a breathing space to deal with the domestic crisis of apartheid.

From the point of view of South Africa's military leaders, however, the country had to use its military power aggressively throughout southern Africa for its strength to be credible to both its opponents and the rest of the world. The military claimed that the Angola intervention had not been a defeat, but instead that the limited South African force had fought well against numerically superior MPLA-Cuban forces having Soviet support. The invasion had been undertaken in tacit alliance with the United States and with the knowledge of several African leaders, and it was therefore not South Africa's fault that it had become politically and therefore militarily isolated. In addition, Prime Minister Vorster was reportedly the one who had decided to scale down the strength of the invasion force when a larger commitment could have brought success.[17]

For the military, the real blow to South African security had been the indiscriminate police shootings of protesting students, which brought black resentment and racial polarization to new extremes. Military leaders urged, as part of the Total Strategy, that major new steps had to be taken to give blacks a stake in the system and to reduce the most blatant forms of white racism, moves that Vorster had been unwilling or unable to take in the face of entrenched *verkrampte* opposition.[18] On Namibia and Rhodesia the military supported a strategy of giving strong military backing to "internal settlements" that would bring black faces into the governments but leave power in white hands. This would show that the liberation movements could be kept from winning power and that South Africa would maintain the security of its borders by forcefully asserting its influence through aggressive intervention in the region's conflicts. As with domestic reforms, military leaders could point to Vorster's political immobilization as a reason for failing to move more decisively militarily in Namibia and Rhodesia.

Beyond these divergent strategic perspectives there were also bureaucratic and personal antagonisms between the contending factions. Van den Bergh (a Mulder ally) was reported to have been angered by Military Intelligence in the early 1960s when it failed to pass on information to his Security Police units which could have aided in suppressing the sabotage campaigns.[19] With the formation of BOSS in 1968-69 van den Bergh was in a position to personally oversee and monitor all intelligence and security operations, including the military's. As Vorster's closest associate, he was able to keep a tight rein on the military leaders and Defence Minister Botha, who was viewed by some as "an unrestrained militarist whose perception of crisis resolution does not go far beyond the barrel of a gun," and an excitable "political epileptic."[20]

On the other hand, there was widespread resentment and fear of van den Bergh. While BOSS's main targets were clearly the African National Congress, the Pan Africanist Congress, and other groups actively resisting apartheid, it was felt even among Nationalists that, given BOSS's unrestrained powers and secret operations, van den Bergh could direct his organization with a free hand against opponents from any quarter. Two (unconfirmed) incidents are reported to have stirred Defence Minister Botha's anger against van der Bergh. In the early 1970s van den Bergh was said to have personally walked in and taken over the headquarters of Military Intellience for use by BOSS, and in 1977 Botha reportedly found that his telephone was being tapped by BOSS.[21]

Mulder's secret Information Department propaganda projects often entailed cooperation with BOSS. In some cases these operations strayed into the spheres of the Foreign Affairs Department and the Defence Department (see Chapter 6), and stories in the press about corruption in Information Department operations were apparently fueled by leaks from other departments annoyed by the secret maneuvers. Thus by mid-1978 Mulder was under growing pressure from the spreading scandal in his bailiwick. When Foreign Minister R. F. Botha failed in his bid for the National party nomination for prime minister, he threw his support behind Defence Minister P. W. Botha, who was able to narrowly defeat Mulder and succeed Vorster as prime minister.

Within weeks after P. W. Botha became prime minister the central role that the military was to play in his government became apparent. Van den Bergh had accompanied Vorster on important diplomatic missions, but when Botha met with Western representatives on Namibia in the fall of 1978 he was joined by Gen. Magnus Malan. In mid-1978 (at the time of van den Bergh's retirement) BOSS was renamed the Department of National Security (DONS) and made subject to parliamentary controls. Prime Minister Botha assured his direct control over the intelligence agency by taking the DONS portfolio. The first cabinet briefing on national security for the Botha government was not given by a DONS official, but instead by a top Defence Force general.[22]

Meanwhile Botha continued the military buildup started under Vorster. In 1978 the defence minister was granted the right to clear and patrol with martial law powers a ten-kilometer strip around the entire length of the country's borders. Along the northern border with Zimbabwe a unique border defense was begun with the planting of a fifty-foot-wide barrier of cactuslike sisal plants along a stretch of several hundred miles. The sisal rows were said to be mined in some areas and were being patrolled by Defence Force units, mainly Citizen Force reserves. There were also reports of secret landing strips laid out in the border areas and of stretches of rural roads which had been widened and straightened for use by the military as emergency runways.[23]

Soon after becoming prime minister, Botha toured the country's northern borders and announced that a committee would investigate border security. The committee's 1979 report related the security problem to the (white) depopulation of farms: of more than three thousand farms surveyed, 44 percent had no white occupants, though all were in white areas and had to be owned by whites. One district in the northwest Transvaal had 400 large cattle farms, but only 118 were owned by real farmers (instead of businesses or game farms) and only 20 percent had white occupants.[24] Prime Minister Botha warned that "a terrorist can walk from the Limpopo right through to Pietersburg without having to set foot on a farm occupied by whites,"[25] and one member of parliament called urgently for measures to aid farm security saying, "The terrorists must not be able to get at the bag of mealies a black worker has in his hut."[26]

In response to the survey the government announced plans to promote white repopulation of the border areas by offering interest-free and low-interest loans to young men with military experience to take up farming in key areas, a scheme that was to cost $100 million over a six-year period. As part of the program Deputy Defence Minister Coetsee called for a "ring of steel" to be forged around the borders by linking the new farmers into the MARNET (Military Areas Radio Network, a command and control network being set up around the country for local Commando units) and settling them in a string of fortified points. He also indicated that the Defence Force already maintained a permanent military presence in "priority regions" through a major base at Phalaborwa and four smaller training bases.[27] Legislation was passed in June 1979 to give farmers financial credits for keeping their property occupied and managed according to security guidelines to be established.

A complement to the security measures undertaken in white farming areas near the borders has been the Defence Force's Civil Action program to win black "hearts and minds" in strategic areas. By the late 1970s there was increasing publicity about Civil Action activities in Namibia and programs had also been started in border areas in KwaZulu and

Bophuthatswana. In the program services are offered by National Servicemen with a variety of skills, such as doctors, teachers, veterinarians,
and agricultural advisors. But the military impetus of the Civil Action
programs was reflected in the remarks of Brigadier C. J. Lloyd in 1979,
who said that if the "local population of border and rural areas did not
show loyalty, goodwill, and cooperation" despite the special services,
"we will have to move them out of the critical areas and resettle them."[28]
In the same year it was revealed that Soweto schools could be facing a
shortage of 350 teachers, and the government Education Department
offered to fill the posts with National Servicemen, a proposal which
drew strong opposition from black leaders.[29]

The 1979 Defense White Paper, reflecting the mood of urgency of the
Botha government, declared, "The military threat against the Republic
of South Africa is intensifying at an alarming rate and the country is
increasingly being thrown on its own resources to insure survival." It
referred to South Africa's increased "military responsibility" in Namibia
and also implicitly warned the frontline states of the costs South Africa
could impose for their continuing support for the liberation movements,
saying, "the terrorist organizations are beginning to pose a threat to
their host countries in Southern Africa. These countries will soon have
to choose between peace and development on one hand and continued
conflict and stagnation on the other."[30] This warning was an indication
of the more militarily aggressive regional strategy that the Botha government was adopting. It meant a bigger military buildup in Namibia
with the aim of carrying the war there into southern Angola. Botha was
also ready to give increased military aid to the Rhodesian regime and
to support its policy of launching major strikes into Mozambique and
Zambia.

To carry out this strategy South Africa needed manpower, and weaponry, too. The 1963 UN arms embargo had never been implemented by
France, and South Africa had also been able to get arms from other
Western sources as well (see Chapter 5). The UN Security Council passed
a strengthened, mandatory arms embargo in 1977, yet it was not long
before it became evident that it had loopholes and weaknesses. In 1979
Botha announced that the Defence Force had introduced several important new weapons, including an advanced, long-range 155-mm field
gun, high-speed missile patrol boats, an infantry rifle, and an air-to-air
missile. Botha claimed that all had been developed and produced in
South Africa and that South Africa had attained the self-sufficiency needed
to resist the mandatory arms embargo. Despite these claims, however,
observers noted that to a great extent the new arms were derived from
foreign technology and had involved cooperation and components from
foreign sources. This was most dramatically true in the case of the 155-
mm field gun, which was obtained, as a result of a wholesale violation

of the arms embargo, from the American-Canadian company Space Research Corporation. The missile patrol boats had come from Israel and included major components from other countries, and the infantry rifle was identified as being of Israeli design. The air-to-air missiles were seen as a product of cooperation with French arms producers.[31] Even with the continuing strategic foreign involvement in South African arms production and procurement, however, there was no doubt about the expansion of Armscor, the state-controlled arms agency. By the end of the 1970s Armscor had become one of the country's biggest industries, with a budget of more than $1 billion, almost 19,000 employees, and approximately 800 subcontractors in the private sector.[32] And it was still expanding.

There were other concrete indicators of South African militarization as well. Total defense expenditures rose from $933 million in 1974-1975 to $2.9 billion in 1979-1980. With the increased length of compulsory military service and stepped-up recruitment, the Defence Force had almost doubled in size during the same period, from some 270,000 men to almost 500,000. During the invasion of Angola and the intensification of the Namibia war Citizen Force reserves had been called up for three and even six months of active service. Three years later the Defence Force was continuing the call-ups, despite complaints about the economic problems caused to business and the personal difficulties of the reservists. Discussing the issue, a Defence Force general said, "Businessmen must realize we're fighting for our survival. I don't think there should be any doubt about that. So their commitment must increase. . . .This is a long-term problem—not short term. The sooner people realize this the better."[33]

There have been other problems as well. The Permanent Force (the career soldiers making up the core of the Defence Force) has had difficulties retaining skilled personnel, who have been attracted to private industry. There has also been resistance to military service among young whites, especially university-educated, English-speaking men. Scores of resisters to military service have sought refuge in Britain, the United States, Holland, Canada, and other countries. The London-based Committee on South Africa War Resistance (COSAWR) has estimated that in addition those who have chosen to leave South Africa, thousands of young white men are on the run from the military in South Africa for failing to report for reserve call-ups, for National Service induction, or for being absent without leave.[34] A further sign of difficulties was an investigation launched by the Defence Force to try to stop the bribery of clerks by parents of conscripts wanting their sons assigned to noncombatant units.

Another significant aspect of South African militarization has been the increased emphasis on recruiting blacks. The beginning of this effort goes back to 1972 when the Coloured Corps, which had been a non-combatant auxiliary unit, was given weapons training and made a part of the Permanent Force. The following year an African unit was formed for the Permanent Force, the 21st Battalion. In addition, South Africa began setting up small military forces for the "independent" Bantustans. In 1978 it was reported that 15 to 20 percent of the South African forces in northern Namibia were black; if the figures are accurate, these troops would include Namibian tribal units formed by South Africa, as well as black troops from South Africa.[35] In 1980 Defence Minister Magnus Malan announced that four new ethnically based black regional battalions were being formed to provide additional border protection and local security. They were being set up among the Swazis, Vendas, Shangaans, and Zulus, and plans were also mentioned for additional units in other parts of the country.[36] Recruitment of blacks for military service has been on a voluntary basis, but the introduction of compulsory military service for people of mixed race and for Indians became an objective for the Defence Force because of limits on white manpower and the limited number of black volunteers.

In 1979 it was reported that employees from factories in the Port Elizabeth area were being given voluntary military training focusing on protection of industrial sites and including the use of arms. Those taking the four-week courses included whites, people of mixed race, and Indians, but no Africans.[37] The following year the parliament passed the National Key Points Act giving the minister of defence the power to insure that installations designated as "national key points" are adequately protected. The owners of such facilities, which include factories operated by Western corporations, must institute the specified security measures at their own expense or face fines and a jail term of up to five years, as well as liability for the cost of government-provided security. The disclosure of any information regarding the security measures, as well as news reporting on any incidents involving security at the key points, is subject to military censorship, with fines of up to three years imprisonment for violations. The legislation permits the government to grant police powers to employees at the key points, including the authority to bear and use arms.[38]

Attention was focused again on South Africa's nuclear potential in September 1979 when a U.S. Vela satellite recorded a twin flash, the typical sign of a nuclear explosion, over the South Atlantic off South Africa. The Botha government denied that it was conducting any nuclear tests, although the CIA reported a South African naval task force had been in the area at the time, and it suggested to Congress that either South Africa, Israel, or both countries jointly could have set off a nuclear blast. The failure to detect fallout in the area led to speculation that a neutron weapon had been tested, and it was noted that South Africa's newly acquired 155-mm howitzers are capable of firing a neutron shell.[39] Although the Pentagon concluded that the satellite had recorded a nuclear explosion, a panel of scientists appointed by the White House to investigate the incident finally decided there had not been one, saying that the flashes probably had been caused by the satellite's collision with a meteorite.[40] Another satellite recorded a flash of infrared radiation over the same area in December 1980, but Pentagon analysts concluded that it had been caused by a meteorite entering the atmosphere, although speculation among U.S. intelligence officials about South African nuclear testing had been raised again.[41]

South Africa entered the decade of the eighties a country at war, within and beyond its borders. The military buildup that had begun in the mid-seventies had culminated with the military leadership in ascendency in the white government. The Total Strategy that is being promoted by Prime Minister Botha and Defence Minister Malan calls for coordinated government action in all areas in defense of white South Africa, domestically, regionally, and internationally. Malan insisted repeatedly that his approach was "80 percent political and 20 percent military," and Botha warned a National party congress in August 1979 that it must "adapt or die." Nevertheless, there was no doubt that, whatever the political strategies chosen by the white government to insure the "right of self-determination of the White nation" (as the 1977 Defence White Paper put it), they would be enforced with all the military power that could be mobilized.

2 The Black Struggle for Freedom

ON THE NIGHT OF JUNE 1, 1980, in coordinated attacks, guerrillas of the African National Congress struck an unprecedented blow against South Africa's strategic petroleum facilities. At Sasolburg, thirty-five miles southwest of Johannesburg, four reservoirs at the billion-dollar SASOL I oil-from-coal plant were destroyed, along with three others at the neighboring government-controlled NATREF refinery.* A third attack, at the SASOL II plant at Secunda, 150 miles north of Johannesburg, reportedly caused only minor damage. In a fourth incident, two bombs were found and defused at the recruiting office outside Johannesburg of the Fluor Corporation, the giant American construction company that is the main contractor for the SASOL progam. South African government officials put total damage in the attacks at $7.3 million.[1]

These events had significance for all South Africans. South Africa has no known oil reserves and is dependent on foreign imports and the oil-from-coal plants for its petroleum needs. The SASOL complexes are the largest industrial projects being undertaken in South Africa and represent an over-all investment in excess of $6 billion. They symbolize the financial and technical resources commanded by the Nationalist government in cooperation with western corporations, but they also reflect the vulnerability of a strategic sector of the economy that is of vital importance to South Africa's economy and mechanized military machine.

The military significance of the attack can be gauged from a feature on the SASOL Commando unit that appeared in *Paratus*, the magazine of the South African Defence Force, a year earlier, in August 1979. The ANC guerrillas had successfully eluded the highest-rated Commando unit in the country:

---

*SASOL is an acronym for South African Coal, Oil, and Gas Corporation; NATREF, for National Refinery.

21

When the men of SASOL Commando change their white coats for the uniform of the South African Defence Force, they become members of a specialist unit that, in times of war, will protect two of South Africa's national key points. The SASOL factory, where in a unique process fuel is manufactured from coal, and the Natref refinery are probably two of the most important installations in the country. The importance of the task of the Sasol Commando in defending these two key points cannot be overemphasized. The members of the Commando have no illusions as to the gravity of their responsibility. The fact that last year the Commando was evaluated as being the most effective Commando in the land is indicative of this.

Reactions to the sabotage give a picture of the political strategies behind the conflict in South Africa. The South African police minister charged that the attack had been masterminded by Joe Slovo, a white South African Communist party leader in Maputo, Mozambique, and that the Soviet ambassador in Lusaka, Zambia, had been involved. He warned that neighboring countries that harbored guerrillas faced military retaliation.[2] The *Rand Daily Mail*, South Africa's leading liberal newspaper, declared that "the country is now in a state of revolutionary war" and urged the Nationalist government to negotiate with the "true leaders of the black population."[3] ANC President Oliver Tambo stated:

We attacked these installations because of their strategic position in the South African economy. We have proposed sanctions and a foreign trade embargo as an alternative to the escalation of armed conflict in South Africa. This attack therefore is in the pursuit of the aims of a peaceful settlement, which can only come with the demolition of the structures of apartheid domination.[4]

The SASOL sabotage was the most dramatic in a series of attacks carried out since 1977, in the wake of the Soweto upheavals, mainly by the forces of *Umkhonto we Sizwe* (Spear of the Nation), the guerrilla arm of the ANC. The police and the military forces of the Nationalist government have been unable to contain the guerrillas, despite the stepped-up security measures being taken as part of the Botha government's Total Strategy. The targets have been mainly electric power and rail installations, police stations, and other government buildings. In one attack, guerrillas launched several rockets at the Defence Force's main military base, Voortrekkerhoogte, outside Pretoria. Officials claimed little damage was done, but like the sabotage at SASOL, the incident was important symbolically, for it showed the potential vulnerability of the heart of South Africa's military establishment.

At the time of the ANC bomb attack at offices of the South African

Air Force and Military Intelligence in Pretoria in May 1983, the ANC was known to have carried out more than 150 armed attacks within South Africa since 1977. The Pretoria attack was reported to be the eighty-eighth since the beginning of 1981, indicating the tempo of the attacks has gradually increased. It is also believed that the police and military authorities, since they have the power to withhold security information, do not always publicly report incidents not otherwise mentioned in the press or that they cover up guerrilla incidents by labeling them accidents.[5]

Another index of the extent of guerrilla and political activity within South Africa has been the continuing arrests, detentions, and trials. Up to the end of November 1982, for example, twenty-two security trials had been completed during that year in the white courts. Of the 30 people convicted, 24 were accused of being ANC members.[6] Three (Thelle Mogoerane, Jerry Mosololi, and Marcus Motaung) were convicted of high treason for participation in ANC attacks on three police stations and sentenced to death. They were hanged in June 1983 despite world-wide appeals for clemency. Three other ANC members who had been convicted in an earlier trial remained under death sentence. Charges of torture under police detention of defendants and state witnesses in security trials have become pervasive (see Chapter 4). The ANC has announced that it will abide by the Geneva Convention on the treatment of prisoners of war and has called on the Nationalist government to do the same.

The continuing guerrilla attacks and security trials substantiate the conclusions of South African lawyer Glenn Moss. After analyzing thirty trials involving politically motivated offenses during the period 1976-79, Moss concluded that the conflict in South Africa had reached the proportions of "a low-intensity civil war." He described the conflict as "structural in type. . .not a temporary aberation, or something incidental to the fabric of society."[7] To understand this widening conflict, it must be viewed from the historical perspective of European expansion and conquest in South Africa and of black protest against and resistance to white domination.

The roots of today's conflict go back to the first European settlement in South Africa. In 1652 the Dutch East India Company set up a refreshment station at the Cape, and within a few years conflict broke out between the Dutch and the local African inhabitants, the Khoikhoin. The Dutch set up farms on grazing land, and when the Khoikhoin disputed this, the Dutch took the land by force. Slowly, the Cape settlement expanded, and in the ensuing conflicts, the Khoikhoin and the neighboring San were killed, driven off the land, or forced into servitude. For many years the Cape settlement remained a small outpost of the Dutch mercantile empire (its population had reached about ten thousand in 1778). French Huguenots and Germans had joined the Dutch settlement. Slaves, brought from elsewhere in Africa and from Asia were a main source of labor. While there had been coexistence and commerce as well as conflict between the Europeans and the Africans, two guiding assumptions had taken root among the settlers: "Whites should be able to deal with slaves and other non-white dependents more or less as they saw fit. . .and all whites were entitled to as much land as they wanted without paying for it."[8]

By the time the British took over the Cape settlement in 1806 conflict with the Xhosa to the east had begun, again over land. Under British rule there was by the middle of the nineteenth century a transition in the Cape from racially based slavery and bonded labor to free labor and a nonracial franchise. Nevertheless, the Coloureds (people of mixed race—the descendents of the Europeans, the Khoikhoin, and the people brought to the Cape as slaves) and the Africans remained subordinate, and the tempo of European settlement and expansion increased.

The Dutch settlers chafed under British rule. The more liberal attitudes of Englishmen toward race and labor spurred the Great Trek, a series of migrations and conquests that took the Dutch toward the central and eastern parts of modern South Africa. This migration came at a time when the African societies in these areas were undergoing upheaval and revolutionary changes set off by the rise of Zulu military power. The Boers (farmers) wanted to occupy lands controlled by Zulus, but when the Boer leaders met with the Zulus, they were seized and killed. In the ensuing conflict, the Zulus, led by Dingane, suffered a terrible defeat at the Ncome River (Blood River), December 16, 1838. This was the initial victory in the complete European conquest of what is now South Africa, and it was, in many ways, a paradigm of what was to come. The Zulus came into conflict with both the Boers and the British, and their solidarity was weakened when some Zulus sided with the Boers. The British conquest depended on arms, supplies, and settlers brought to the Cape from Europe. The Boers wanted to escape British control, but still depended on arms and powder supplied from the Cape and Europe. These, in combination with the fortlike protection offered by stout ox-wagons, were the keys to victory over the Zulus. The British takeover and expansion of settlement were part of the building of a world-wide empire fueled by mercantile trade and then industrial capitalism. The Boers saw in their victory at Blood River a convenant with God, and their suppositions of white political and economic domination became linked in a Calvinist cosmology in which they viewed themselves as God's chosen people in Africa (therefore, *Afrikaners*—Africans—neither Dutch nor British) and black Africans as cursed descendants of the biblical Ham.

In the central and northern areas of modern South Africa the trekkers clashed with the Ndebele in a series of battles and laid claim to vast stretches of the region. The Afrikaner republics they set up reflected their racial attitudes: Africans and people of mixed race generally had no rights except as servants of whites; they could not own land, guns, or horses; and they had to carry passes. In the eastern Cape, the British subdued the Xhosa in a series of bitter wars and took over in areas where Zulu power had been diminished, founding Natal as a "white settlement." The British set up "locations" for Africans, imposed a system of indirect rule by selected chiefs and headmen, and demanded "hut taxes." The British also began bringing in indentured laborers from India in the 1860s to work on the sugar and cotton plantations in Natal, thereby establishing an Indian population in South Africa.

The discovery of diamonds in 1867 and of gold in 1884 led to increasing tensions between Afrikaners and British, but whatever their differences, the Europeans shared the belief that the African societies that remained independent had to be brought under white control, either by force or by the threat of force. There were more conflicts in the eastern Cape, until only the Transkei and the Ciskei remained as African reserves. The Zulu, led by Cetshwaya, administered a crushing defeat to the British at Isandhlwana in 1879, but British military power ultimately prevailed, and most of the remaining Zulu lands were then annexed for settlement by whites. In the north the Afrikaners were able to defeat the Pedi and the Venda by military force and by playing on African rivalries.

The Anglo-Boer War (1899-1902) was provoked by the British to assure their hegemony in southern Africa after the discovery of gold in the Afrikaner Republic ruled by Paul Kruger. Lord Alfred Milner, the British high commissioner for South Africa, said he aimed to secure "a self-governing white community, supported by well-treated and justly governed black labor from Cape Town to the Zambesi."[9] It was a white man's war (though Africans served with the British as noncombatants and African labor in the gold mines helped sustain the Afrikaner republics), and it was to unite South Africa as a white man's country. The British subdued the Afrikaners militarily, but could not extinguish the fires of Afrikaner nationalism.

By the end of the nineteenth century the African societies of South Africa had suffered military and political defeat at the hands of the Europeans, losing most of their lands and freedom. People of mixed race and Indians were also kept in subordinate positions. The modern South Africa that emerged has been described as a plural society, shaped by white and black alike and characterized by cooperation as well as conflict. But while there were forms of cooperation and a minority of whites who worked to aid blacks, the over-all context was one of white domination and exploitation enforced by laws made by whites and hence by coercion. Black labor on white farms, in white homes, in mines, and in factories went to advance white prosperity, not black. When they were not working for whites, blacks were generally restricted to tribal reserves or segregated townships or "locations."

In 1908 white representatives from the Cape, Natal, the Orange Free State, and the Transvaal drafted an Act of Union providing for a unified, self-governing state under British dominion. The Union barred blacks from the parliament and preserved only the limited black franchise in the Cape. This spurred four young African lawyers, headed by P. Ka Izaka Seme, who had earned a bachelor's degree at Columbia University and a law degree at Oxford, to call a conference of African leaders at Bloemfontein on January 9, 1912. Seme addressed the delegates:

> We have discovered that in the land of their birth, Africans are treated as hewers of wood and drawers of water. The white people of this country have formed what is known as the Union of South Africa— a union in which we have no voice in the making of laws and no part in the administration of them. We have called you, therefore, to this conference so that we can together find ways and means of forming *our* national union for the purpose of creating national unity and defending our rights and privileges.[10]

The new organization became the South African Native National Congress; subsequently, in 1925, the name was changed to the African National Congress of South Africa, or ANC. John Langalibalele Dube, a Zulu leader who had been educated in the United States, at Oberlin College, was chosen as the first president-general. The goal of the Congress, as a unified, national body, was to work for the end of racial discrimination and to promote African education and development. The first major issue the Congress faced was the Native Land Bill of 1912, which restricted African rights of land ownership or leasehold to reserves amounting to only 7.3 percent of the country's territory. The new white Union was thus legitimizing the dispossession and exclusion of Africans from lands taken during the white expansion and conquest of only a few years before. The Congress protested to the white South African government and even sent a delegation to appeal to the British parliament, but to no avail.

Over the next three decades the Congress functioned mainly as a forum for African opinion, where leaders could protest discriminatory measures and argue for Africans' rights. The ANC did not, however, operate as a true political movement trying to organize popular campaigns, strikes, or other resistance to discrimination, though it often endorsed or lent support when these developed. This began to change in 1940, when Dr. A. B. Xuma, a medical doctor, was elected ANC president. The next two decades saw major transformations in the ANC and in the political situation in South Africa. The changes can be related in part to economic and social changes in the country. The reserves were subject to overcrowding and soil erosion and received few funds for development, and so could not provide adequate subsistance for many inhabitants. More and more blacks were drawn to the urban areas where, despite increasing discrimination, the growing industrial and commercial economy offered greater chances for jobs and education. Moreover, in Africa and around the world, new movements to gain freedom from colonial rule were beginning to take shape. As a result, the ANC and the black political situation in South Africa today were decisively shaped by the young leaders and the new programs that emerged in the nineteen-forties and fifties.

In 1943 the ANC, in a statement on Africans' Claims in South Africa, reformulated the principles of freedom and democracy laid out in the Atlantic Charter from the perspective of Africans in South Africa. It also presented a Bill of Rights for Africans. In 1944 the ANC launched a national anti-pass campaign in cooperation with the Transvaal Indian Congress. The Youth League of the ANC was formed in 1943 by young members who were eager for more activist programs asserting a new Africanist perspective. Among the Youth League members were Nelson Mandela, Oliver Tambo, and Walter Sisulu. They were to become leaders of the ANC, and they remain leaders today. Mandela, who had studied law, came from a family of Tembu chiefs; other young leaders, many of whom were also entering professional fields, came from humbler backgrounds. The 1944 Manifesto of the Youth League declared that "Africanism must be promoted, i.e., Africans must struggle for development, progress and national liberation so as to occupy their rightful place among the nations of the world. . . ."[11] It condemned the white conquest of South Africa, white attitudes of domination, and the white pretense of benevolent trusteeship over Africans. The Manifesto announced the Youth League's determination to revitalize the ANC by forging African unity for the cause of national liberation.

In 1946 some 75,000 African miners struck, paralyzing the heart of the country's economy. The Chamber of Mines had ignored the grievances and wage demands of the African Mine Workers Union, which had been organized in 1941 by the Transvaal Branch of the ANC, together with members of the Communist party of South Africa (who were later charged with sedition by the Smuts government). The police drove the men back to the mines. Later, reports said that 9 miners were killed and 1,248 injured, but no official figures were ever released.[12] The following year Dr. Xuma took an important step toward formal cooperation with the Indian population by signing a pact with the presidents of the Natal and Transvaal Indian Congresses.

The 1948 white elections brought the National party to power. It was committed to implementing a program of apartheid that would assure white supremacy in South Africa. The Nationalists set about their project with such measures as the Population Registration Act (to formally classify people by race), the Group Areas Act (enforcing residential segregation), the Separate Representation of Voters Act (removing the remaining voters of mixed race in the Cape from the common roll), and the Immorality and Mixed Marriages Acts (outlawing interracial sex and marriage).

In the ANC the influence of the Youth League was rising. This was reflected in the election of Walter Sisulu as secretary general in 1949 and by the adoption of a Program of Action, which proposed using boycotts, strikes, civil disobedience, and a national work stoppage as forms of protest and mobilization. The program's goal of "national freedom" and the right of self-determination suggested the Africanist influence, and it also affirmed more traditional ANC goals of African representation in all governing bodies and the abolition of all racially segregated institutions. The first national work stoppage in South African history was initiated by the ANC on June 26, 1950, to protest the killing of nineteen Africans by police in a May Day demonstration. The date is now observed by the ANC as South African Freedom Day.

The Defiance Campaign was launched in 1952 by the ANC and the South African Indian Congress, with Nelson Mandela as chief organizer. Disciplined volunteers committed civil disobedience by openly defying apartheid laws. More than eight thousand people were arrested before the campaign lost momentum. This was a time of intensive mobilization, and the ANC's membership was estimated to have reached 100,000 (though the paid-up total was put at 28,900 in 1953).[13] The government, however, arrested many leaders of the campaign and convicted them under the Suppression of Communism Act. Dozens were banned— prohibited from engaging in political activities—and in some cases their movement was restricted.

The government's response to the Defiance Campaign showed, in the words that Mandela used before the ANC Transvaal conference in 1953, that there would be "no easy walk to freedom." He called upon local ANC branches to implement the "M-Plan": to start local cells to build membership and grass-roots support and to protect the organization from repression. The plan would enable the ANC to function if it was forced underground, but it was implemented effectively in only a few areas. Mandela declared that "a revolution is maturing in South Africa," and he linked it to the anticolonial and anti-imperialist struggle going on in Kenya and throughout the third world. At fault, he said, were the imperialist policies of the United States and its allies.[14]

In 1953 the ANC elected a new president, Chief Albert Lutuli, a teacher and Zulu leader. Police persecution continued, and Lutuli and others were soon banned. Professor Z. K. Matthews of the ANC proposed that a Congress of the People, open to all races, be convened to draw up a

"Freedom Charter for the Democratic South Africa of the future." The call for delegates to the congress was made by the ANC, the Indian Congress, the South African Coloured Peoples Organization (SACPO), and the Congress of Democrats, an organization of whites on the left. The South African Congress of Trade Unions (SACTU), a nonracial trade union body formed in 1955, also joined the Congress of the People.

To promote the congress and to collect local suggestions and grievances that would aid in formulating the Freedom Charter, meetings were held around the country. Then the Congress of the People was held, on June 25-26, at Kliptown, near Johannesburg. Some three thousand delegates, the large majority of them Africans, came from all over the country. Despite the threat of violence when armed police moved in to confiscate documents from the conference and the delegates, the Congress was peaceful. The Freedom Charter, which had been drafted prior to the congress by a committee of the organizing council, was presented and ratified by acclamation. Its preamble declares:

> We, the People of South Africa, declare for all our country and the world to know:
>
> That South Africa belongs to all who live in it, black and white, and that no government can justly claim authority unless it is based on the will of the people;
>
> That our people have been robbed of their birthright to land, liberty and peace by a form of government founded on injustice and inequality;
>
> That our country will never be prosperous and free until all our people live in brotherhood, enjoying equal rights and opportunities;
>
> That only a democratic state, based on the will of the people, can secure to all their birthright without distinction of color, race, sex, or belief;
>
> And therefore, we, the people of South Africa, black and white, together—equals, countrymen and brothers—adopt this Freedom Charter. And we pledge ourselves to strive together, sparing nothing of our strength and courage, until the democratic changes here set out have been won.*

The Freedom Charter expressed principles of a liberal, democratic character, calling for freedom and equality. Two sections ("The people shall share in the country's wealth" and "The land shall be shared among those who work it") reflected moderate socialist goals, the first time such aims were incorporated into an ANC program. But while the charter did not mark a wide departure from past ANC policies, the implications were far-reaching when considered in light of the course being charted

---

*The complete text of the Freedom Charter is given in Appendix A.

by the Nationalist government. As Nelson Mandela expressed it in an article published in 1956:

> The Charter is more than a list of demands for democratic reforms. It is a revolutionary document precisely because the changes it envisages cannot be won without breaking up the economic and political set-up of present South Africa. To win these demands calls for the organization, launching, and development of mass struggles on the widest scale. . ..[15]

The Freedom Charter was adopted by the ANC in 1956 and by the other congress organizations as well. Its importance lies both in that it was the basis of the multiracial Congress Alliance and because it has been confirmed as the democratic program of the ANC and its allies and supporters.

In 1955 the government announced that, beginning in 1956, African women would be required to carry passbooks. (Passbooks were already compulsory for men over the age of sixteen.) The ANC Women's League joined with the South African Women's Federation to organize protests around the country. These efforts culminated on August 9, 1956, in a protest by twenty thousand women at the governmental buildings in Pretoria. But the decree stood, and repression mounted. The largest police raids in the country's history had targeted some 500 people in September 1955, but the major blow fell in December 1956, when 156 people, including many ANC leaders, were charged as members of a Communist conspiracy to overthrow the state by violence. Those arrested (about two thirds were Africans) represented a wide spectrum of political opinion; some had been members of the outlawed Communist party, most had not. To the government, the Congress of the People and the Freedom Charter were the core of a treasonous conspiracy. The resulting treason trial—the number of accused was later reduced to 30— was to go on for five years until at last, on March 29, 1961, all defendants were declared not guilty. The chief prosecutor denied to an American observer that his aim was to gain the death penalty for anyone who was convicted; he only wanted to "jail the worst Natives" and curb the ANC. But, he added, "If any serious threat to white rule were to arise, the shooting of 5,000 Natives by machine guns would provide quiet for a long time to come."[16]

In 1957 the ANC approved a new constitution. It is often referred to as the Tambo Constitution because Oliver Tambo headed the drafting committee. It made no radical changes in the structure of the ANC, but it did grant more power to the national leadership, while allowing scope for initiative by by local branches. The aims and objects of the ANC were declared to be:

a. To unite the African people in a powerful and effective instrument to secure their own complete liberation from all forms of discrimination and national oppression.

b. To promote and protect the interests of the African people in all matters affecting them.

c. To strive for the attainment of universal adult suffrage and the creation of a united democratic South Africa on the principles outlined in the Freedom Charter.

d. To support the cause of national liberation and the right to independence of nations in Africa and the rest of the world.[17]

During the years 1958 and 1959 tensions which had been building within the Congress culminated in a factional breakaway. The new group, the Pan Africanist Congress (PAC), had coalesced around former members of the Youth League who wanted the ANC to follow what they saw as the true spirit of Africanism. They believed the ANC was being subverted by its alliances with groups from other races and groups influenced by Communists. The Congress Alliance and the Freedom Charter were the focus of their opposition. The younger leaders of the ANC (including Tambo, Sisulu, and Mandela) had also been Youth Leaguers, but they had come to believe that cooperation and unity among South Africans of all races were essential to the struggle for freedom. The open split came in November 1958 when an Africanist bid to gain the presidency of the ANC Transvaal branch failed. The Pan Africanist Congress was formally organized in April 1959. Robert Mangaliso Sobukwe, a lecturer in African languages at the University of Witwatersrand, was elected president, and Potlako Leballo, a teacher who had served in an African unit in the South African forces in World War II, was chosen national secretary. Leballo had been expelled from the Youth League and, later, from the ANC itself for disruptive activity.

The PAC contended that the multiracial approach of the ANC allowed for a disproportionate influence on the organizations by whites, people of mixed race, and Indians and inhibited the development of a liberatory national consciousness among Africans. Further, the PAC argued that the ANC aim of the unity of oppressor and oppressed, the dispossessors and the dispossessed, was impossible to achieve. The PAC sought a purely African society, which would be linked to the emerging African states to the north. Everyone who owed loyalty only to Africa and would accept democratic majority rule would be considered an African. They would form a United States of Africa, standing independent of Western colonial and imperialist interests and Soviet influence.

In response, the ANC charged that the Africanists had been a disruptive minority that was trying to slander and wreck the ANC and obstruct the freedom struggle by promoting racial discord and divisions.

It emphasized that, from its inception, the ANC had been dedicated to the goal of uniting the African people in the struggle for full democratic rights in a nonracial society and had long cooperated with all organizations, including Communists, that supported these aims.

The first PAC campaign, a boycott of businesses that refused to treat African customers with dignity, did not draw a large response, and efforts were shifted to planning an antipass campaign. People were called on to assemble at police stations and offer themselves for arrest on March 21, 1960. Around the country as a whole the turnout was not great, but at Sharpeville, near Johannesburg, perhaps 20,000 people gathered at the police station. The police opened fire on the crowd without warning. Sixty-seven people were killed, many of them shot in the back. As the PAC and ANC mounted protests at this brutality, the Nationalist government declared a state of emergency. It mobilized the armed forces and police, and then outlawed both the PAC and the ANC and arrested or detained more than 18,000 people. Both Sobukwe and Leballo were tried and imprisoned.

Sharpeville marked a decisive turning point, although for a while there was hope that the Nationalist government could be swayed by internal white opposition and international protests. At an All-in Conference in March 1961 Nelson Mandela emerged as a leading figure: he had been continuously restricted by bans since 1952 and had not spoken to public gatherings for almost a decade. The conference was to renew the ANC call for a national convention, urging a three-day nationwide stay-at-home if the call was rebuffed by the government. (The stay-at-home would be called on the eve of the white government's proclamation of the Republic of South Africa, marking the break with the British Commonwealth.) Mandela, faced with a warrant for his arrest, went underground. The PAC opposed the stay-at-home plan as a futile diversion. As the stay-at-home began, the government called out the police and military units and arrested thousands of Africans in massive raids.[18] After just one day, the stay-at-home was called off.

At the end of 1961 Chief Lutuli, the symbol of peaceful resistance to apartheid, was awarded the Nobel Peace Prize. Although he had been restricted to his village by a ban since 1959, he was allowed to go to Oslo receive the prize. In his address he implied that he accepted the need for armed resistance to apartheid: "Ours is a continent in revolution against oppression. And peace and revolution make uneasy bedfellows. There can be no peace until the forces of oppression are overthrown." He returned to South Africa and remained restricted by banning orders. In 1967 he was killed by a train near his home.

In November 1961 Umkhonto we Sizwe was formed by Mandela in cooperation with others in the Congress Alliance organizations. Their first sabotage attack was carried out the next month. Umkhonto aimed to use carefully planned sabotage to pressure the government and to show blacks that violence could be closely controlled and guided by political objectives and strategy. After Umkhonto started its sabotage campaign, Mandela left South Africa secretly to meet African leaders and take a military course in Algeria, and arrange for the training of Umkhonto cadres there. He also met with leaders of the opposition Labour party in London. Returning to South Africa, he operated underground until his arrest in August 1962.

Poqo (meaning "standing alone"), the armed movement linked to the PAC, was formed of loosely organized, semisecret local groups that were ready to attack whites—as well as blacks who collaborated with whites. Poqo supported the PAC ideologically, but it had no formal national leadership; it meant to promote African rebellion against white oppression and was ready to use indiscriminate violence as an antidote to the violence and terror whites used against Africans. While Sobukwe remained in prison for having organized the Sharpeville protest, Leballo had completed his sentence and left South Africa to go into exile. From neighboring Basutoland (now Lesotho) Leballo, claiming there were one thousand PAC cells, having 155,000 members, announced plans for a PAC-led revolution. In response, British police raided his office. He escaped, but mass arrests of PAC supporters in South Africa followed. By mid-1963 the PAC organization had been largely crushed; more than 3,000 alleged Poqo members had been seized, and 124 had been convicted of murder in the white courts.[19]

New security laws aided the government's moves against the ANC and PAC. The Sabotage Act, enacted in 1962, carried a maximum penalty of death, and included within its scope even such peaceful actions as those aimed at "disruption." The General Law Amendment Act (1963) allowed people to be detained incommunicado without trial. Sabotage, carried out mainly by Umkhonto, was becoming more professional and more damaging: more than two hundred incidents of sabotage were reported by mid-1963. In July 1963 police raided a farm in Rivonia, just outside Johannesburg, and arrested members of Umkhonto's high command. In the ensuing trial Mandela provided the framework for the defense in his opening speech. He reviewed the ANC's long years of peaceful protest, its aims, and the decision to form Umkhonto, and he concluded,

During my lifetime I have dedicated myself to the struggle of the African people. I have fought against White domination, and I have fought against Black domination. I have cherished the ideal of a democratic society in which all persons live together in harmony and with equal opportunities. It is an ideal which I hope to live for and to achieve. But if needs be, it is an ideal for which I am prepared to die.[20]

On June 12, 1964, the Rivonia trial ended. Nelson Mandela, Walter Sisulu, Govan Mbeki, Elias Motsoaledi, Andrew Mlangeni, Raymond Mhlaba (all of the ANC), Ahmed Kathrada (of the Transvaal Indian Congress), and Dennis Goldberg (of the Congress of Democrats) were found guilty and sentenced to life imprisonment. After "Rivonia" the police offensive continued. Thousands were arrested or detained (others left the country), and the underground organizations of the ANC and the PAC were virtually eliminated. Evidence began to mount that the police were using torture, including deprivation of sleep, beatings, suffocation, and electric shock on prisoners. As the first political deaths in detention were reported, police began to call them suicides. And official executions rose: between 1960 and 1965 some forty-five people were convicted of political violence and executed.

Umkhonto's sabotage campaign had heartened black South Africans, jarred the Nationalist government, prepared the ground for further guerrilla activity, and attracted international attention and moral support. But the sabotage, carefully planned by small groups, was not able to forge links with popular resistance or to hit important economic or military targets.[21] The underground organization had not been able to overcome the government's virtual state of siege and police-state methods. The ANC had also hoped that the condemnation of the violence and racism of apartheid by liberals in the West could be translated into concrete pressures against the Nationalist government. But efforts to promote economic sanctions were resisted by the Western countries. Instead, South Africa was soon being bolstered by increasing Western bank loans and investments. The arms embargo of South Africa passed by the UN Security Council in 1963 was only voluntary; it was ignored by France, in particular, and was soon being skirted by others. The newly independent African states lacked the resources to provide aid that could be decisive in a liberation struggle.

In 1966 the ANC resumed underground propaganda acitivities in South Africa, but its efforts to infiltrate small groups via Botswana failed. In 1967-68 the ANC joined with the Zimbabwe African Peoples Union (ZAPU) in sending small guerrilla groups into Rhodesia from Zambia in an attempt to establish routes into South Africa. But South Africa reinforced the Rhodesian forces with combat police, spotter aircraft, helicopters, and armored cars, and the guerrilla thrust was defeated.

These hard realities were the backdrop for the ANC conference held in April 1969 at Morogoro, Tanzania, where the organization's external headquarters had been established. At the conference Oliver Tambo was confirmed as acting president-general and Alfred Nzo, an ANC veteran who had suffered bannings, arrests, and long detention by the South African police, was named secretary-general. It was decided to welcome to ANC membership on an individual basis people of mixed race and Indians and "those white revolutionaries who show themselves ready to make common cause with our aspirations." However, the ANC leadership positions (the officers and national executive committee) would remain open only to Africans. A presidential council was established, and to guide strategic aspects of the struggle (with all races represented), a revolutionary council with Oliver Tambo as chairman and Dr. Yusuf Dadoo, a leader of the Indian Congress and the Communist party, as vice-chairman.

At Morogoro the ANC for the first time expressed its strategy in revolutionary terms, adopting a statement on the Freedom Charter, "The Revolutionary Programme of the ANC," and "Strategy and Tactics of the ANC," an analysis of the struggle in South Africa. In "Strategy and Tactics" the ANC path was defended against both those who would allege that its earlier programs were purely reformist and those who opposed the decision to take up arms. It rejected various views on guerrilla conflict, particularly the "foci" theory of "detonating" revolution through guerrilla attacks alone, as well as theories that special geography is necessary to guerrilla struggle, that a social crisis could lead to a sudden, decisive insurrection. It also found unorganized violence or individual terrorism unacceptable. Instead, it declared that "given certain factors, both international and local" guerrilla conflict could begin and would lead to all-out war and victory. "Strategy and Tactics" stressed the need to plan for a protracted conflict and emphasized the importance of "all-around political leadership" for mass mobilization and to guide the military struggle. The statement declared, "The main content of the present stage of the South African revolution is the national liberation of the largest and most oppressed group—the African people." But it indicated that the achievement of nonracial democracy in South Africa is viewed as the first step in a longer struggle toward a socialist society: "The perspective of a speedy progression from formal liberation to genuine and lasting emancipation is made more real by the existence. . .of a large and growing working class."[22]

"Strategy and Tactics" showed the determination of the ANC to mount a guerrilla war in South Africa, but that would clearly be a long and difficult process. South Africa's borders remained shielded by the Portuguese colonial rule in Mozambique and Angola, by the Rhodesian regime, and by South Africa's occupation of Namibia. Inside South Africa the kind of popular mobilization needed to sustain guerrilla activity was subject to severe police repression. It was difficult enough to carry out public protests, boycotts, or strikes; any kind of association with the ANC or the PAC would invite doubly harsh reprisals from the Security Police.

The growth of the Black Consciousness Movement (BCM) among the younger generation of black South Africans during the 1970s took place within this context. There was almost total elimination of public activity related to the ANC or PAC, and other forms of protest and opposition were silenced.[23] One specific focus of this movement was an inward-looking process of promoting black self-awareness and dignity in the face of white racism. The BCM initiated community projects in education, health, culture, and labor. These efforts were not specifically political: indeed, they aimed to transcend the blocked sphere of politics, while simultaneously politicizing Africans. The term "black" encompassed Africans, Indians, and people of mixed race, and was intended to refer not so much to color in a racial sense as to the unity of the communities oppressed by whites. Critical of white liberal paternalism, the BCM promoted independent black organizations and urged whites who opposed apartheid to work in their own communities against white racism.

The BCM grew in a loosely coordinated way. One key group in the formulation of BCM concepts was the University Christian Movement (UCM). The UCM was itself formed in 1967 as a nonracial, ecumenical body. Another component was created during the same period when black students split off from the National Union of South African Students, which had been the organization of liberal, English-speaking white students, to form the South African Students Organization (SASO) in 1969. SASO, in turn, was instrumental, in 1972, in organizing the Black Peoples Convention (BPC) as a coordinating body for a range of black consciousness groups. The BPC gained support from the South African Council of churches as well as from church and other organizations opposing apartheid in Western countries. Black consciousness groups were also set up among high school students, a key group here being the South African Student Movement (SASM), formed in 1972 in Soweto.

There were similarities, and important differences, too, between the black consciousness outlook and the Africanism of the PAC. Both perspectives emphasized the need to overcome the psychological ravages of white racism by asserting a positive self-image, as well as the need to break with white institutions; and both advocated noncooperation with apartheid institutions. However, black consciousness clearly included people of mixed race and Indians, whereas Africanism, though granting that people of mixed race were Africans and that Indians were racially oppressed, focused specifically on African identity and the political mobilization of Africans as a nation. Black consciousness retained a close link with Christianity (an important facet of the movement has been black theology: making Christian concepts relevant to the black struggle for liberation), whereas Africanism asserted the primacy of traditional African values. The PAC has sought to mobilize African nationalism in order to make white South Africa Azania, an African nation, whereas the Black Consciousness Movement has looked to a future state that is black-ruled, but nonracial, South Africa (or Azania). The Black Consciousness Movement clearly espoused nonviolence, whereas the PAC saw no virtue in nonviolence and was ready for violent confrontation. The Black Consciousness Movement was, and remains, diffuse. It is not wholly or exclusively political. The PAC has been a structured political organization.

The government's response to the renewed black activism and protest of the nineteen-seventies became increasingly severe. Some banned leaders left the country. Others, such as Steve Biko, carried on under tightening restrictions. In 1974 O. R. Tiro, who was organizing black consciousness activities from exile in Botswana, was killed by a parcel bomb believed to have been the work of the South African security apparatus. After a SASO and BCP rally in Durban supporting FRELIMO's victories in Mozambique, more than forty young leaders were detained, and there were subsequent reports of beatings and torture by the Security Police. Twelve persons were tried under the Terrorism Act, and nine were convicted and sentenced to five- and six-year prison terms. By the time of the Soweto uprising the Black Consciousness Movement had been hit hard by government repression, but its defiant message had been heard by a younger generation.

The immediate issue being protested by the 15,000 young people who marched in Soweto on June 16, 1976, was the introduction of Afrikaans as a medium of school instruction, but clearly the entire structure of white domination was at issue. FRELIMO's victory in Mozambique and the defeat of South Africa's invasion of Angola by MPLA and Cuban forces only a few months before had also inspired black South Africans. Armed police threw tear gas at the marching students; some accounts say the students retaliated with stones, others say that the police opened fire first. Several students were shot, but others stood their ground, countering bullets with stones. Then the young people swept through Soweto, stoning or burning administration buildings, beer halls, and other symbols of apartheid rule. In the following months the death toll mounted to more than four hundred, and thousands were injured and imprisoned. Nevertheless, student leaders were able to mount successful boycotts of schools and examinations, close beer halls, force the resignation of the Soweto Urban Bantu Council and Bantu School Boards, and successfully urge stay-at-home strikes and a Christmas shopping boycott. It was not until more than a year later, after the death of Steve Biko at the hands of the Security Police, on September 12, 1977, and a massive series of raids and arrests the following month, that the lid was finally put on the uprising. By this time, guerrilla activity, spearheaded by the ANC, was underway.

Another aspect of the 1976-77 uprising was the link forged between some members of the Black Consciousness Movement, including the SASM, and the ANC underground. ANC literature was circulating in the black townships, and there was an ANC influence among some students, though others claimed the ANC had not been active and criticized it for lack of support. It appears, however, that a majority of young people leaving South Africa at the time of Soweto and since sought to affiliate with the ANC. Baruch Hirson, in his book on the Soweto uprising and the black student movement says,

> . . .the ANC as an organization was not able to act directly in Soweto and, in recognition of the pre-eminent position of the SSRC [Soweto Students Representative Council], it made several attempts to persuade its leaders to work with its clandestine organization. These were rejected by the student leaders—or at least by the president at the time, and the ANC operated separately. At an informal level members of the SSRC executive, some of whom were. . .members of the ANC, sought advice from or worked with cell members.[24]

After Soweto, black consciousness groups continued their efforts in exile and in South Africa. In 1979 a new organization was set up, based in London: the Black Consciousness Movement of South Africa (BCM/SA). The BCM/SA was not a merger of black consciousness groups into a single organization, but rather a closer coalition to form an umbrella movement. The ANC criticized the move to form the BCM. However, in a speech in January 1980, Oliver Tambo made a strong appeal for unity among all the forces opposing white domination, adding, "It has become very clear to us that more dialogue is called for among us, the oppressed, to seek and find common responses to our common repression. . . ."[25] The BCM/SA held a conference in London in October 1979 which gave an indication of a new Marxist orientation. A report on the conference said that there was general agreement on the need for planning a socialist transformation within the context of liberation in South Africa. Blackness was defined in terms of economic exploitation, and the conflict with apartheid was viewed less as a matter of race and more of a consequence of capitalism and imperialism.[26]

After the suppression of the PAC/Poqo in South Africa, the PAC had set up its external headquarters in Dar es Salaam, Tanzania. However, with Robert Sobukwe remaining imprisoned (and, after 1969, confined to the town of Kimberley by a banning order), the leadership of Potlako Leballo produced a series of internal conflicts. Ideologically, the PAC adopted a Maoist stance, and was reported to have received aid from

China.[27] In 1968 a PAC contingent tried to infiltrate South Africa from Zambia via Mozambique, but it was intercepted by Portuguese colonial forces. Continuing PAC efforts at underground activity in South Africa were reflected in 1969 in the arrest and death, under police detention, of Imam Adullah Haroun, his body bearing the marks of torture. Police claimed that he was recruiting people for PAC military training in China under the guise of leaving for pilgrimages to Mecca. Several trials in the post-Soweto period indicated that the PAC still maintained an underground in South Africa aimed at promoting guerrilla operations. The principal trial ended in July 1979 in the conviction under the Terrorism Act of seventeen persons. The first accused, Zeph Mothpeng, aged sixty-six, was said to have been the PAC underground leader within South Africa.

The PAC did gain some new recruits from among the young people leaving South Africa in the wake of Soweto. Henry Isaacs, a former president of SASO who was elected to the PAC central committee in 1978, was one of these. Like the ANC, the PAC has been officially recognized by the Organization of African Unity and in 1974 was granted observer status by the United Nations on issues pertaining to South Africa. The PAC received assistance from the United Nations Development Program (UNDP) for education and vocational training programs in Tanzania amounting to some $730,000 in the period 1975-78, and planned to set up a new educational facility in Sudan.[28] Politically, the PAC has found some support in the United States and in other countries, particularly from black nationalist-oriented groups. The PAC is also reported to have received military training and support from Libya and from the government of Idi Amin in Uganda.[29]

The death of Robert Sobukwe in 1978 set off new conflicts within the PAC. Leballo's accession to the presidency was marked by the expulsion of more than one hundred members and the detention of others in Swaziland. In May 1979 Leballo resigned as president, and was replaced by a three-man council of PAC veterans. But in June one of them, David Sibeko, was shot and killed in Dar es Salaam, and another leader, Vusumzi Make, reported to the OAU that the PAC was in disarray, with two factions at war with each other. In October Leballo was expelled from the PAC for "reactionary and counterrevolutionary activities."

The continuing antagonism between ANC and the PAC, which began with the PAC breakaway in 1959, was further magnified by the repercussions of the Sino-Soviet differences over their approaches to Africa: the ANC has been associated with the Soviets and the PAC with the Chinese. In 1978 the ANC appealed unsuccessfully to the OAU to grant it sole recognition, pointing to the Angolan War as an example of the dangers of having more than one recognized movement. Instead, the OAU appointed a subcommittee to try to form a united front. In the years that followed, the PAC continued to be beset with dissension in its exile organization. It has not been able to carry out either popular mobilization or guerrilla operations within South Africa. In 1981 the PAC central committee chose John Pokela as its new chairman. He was a founding member of the movement and had recently left South Africa after thirteen years' imprisonment there. Since then the PAC claims to have restored organizational unity and normalized relations with the frontline states. In January 1983 Pokela met with Chinese premier Zhao Ziyang, who was visiting Tanzania, and the Chinese leader reaffirmed his country's support for the PAC. In May 1983 South African prosecutors dropped charges against nine defendants accused of conspiracy to commit terrorism and furthering the aims of the PAC after it appeared that police torture of defendants and witnesses would be exposed. But Joseph Thloloe, a prominent black journalist, and three others were given prison terms after pleading guilty to possession of PAC literature.

In contrast to the PAC, the ANC was able to recover from the setbacks of the 1960s and, after the Soweto upheaval, both to begin systematic guerrilla attacks inside South Africa and to reclaim its position as the central political rallying point for black South Africans. Despite the claims in the early seventies of South African intelligence officials that the ANC organization in the country had been eliminated, continuing arrests, deaths in detention, and trials, as well as the clandestine distribution of literature, leaflet "bomb" explosions, and other incidents, showed that the ANC underground efforts were continuing. By the mid-seventies several instances of arrests by the Security Police and subsequent trials gave an indication (through the lens of the South African security apparatus) of ANC underground activity prior to the Soweto protests. The ANC actions aimed at laying the groundwork for guerrilla action, and there had been contacts between the ANC and students involved in the Black Consciousness Movement. In 1977 twelve people were convicted in Pietermaritzburg on charges related to recruiting for ANC military training, and five were sentenced to life imprisonment. Both the accused and the state witnesses charged they had been tortured by the Security Police, and one person, Joseph Mdluli, who had been arrested in the case, died in police custody. In 1976 seven leaders of the National Youth Organization, a group formed for organizing high school students, were found guilty of inciting others to leave the country for ANC military training. In a major trial ending in 1978 six people with previous ties to the ANC were convicted of recruiting students for ANC military training and other offenses during the 1975-76 period. Defendants and witnessses again charged they had been tortured by the police.

The Soweto uprising and the police violence they were met with brought about a major shift in the black political climate in South Africa. Those events set the stage for ANC guerrilla action. The Vorster government and the police showed a new generation of South Africans, as well as the rest of the world, the depths of the racism and brutality underpinning the efficient "banality of evil" reflected in the daily workings of the bureaucratic and legal machinery of apartheid. Strategically, the façade of white invulnerability in southern Africa had been cracked by the collapse of the Portuguese colonial empire. South Africa's borders became accessible. For young South Africans the ANC provided a ready instrument: there was the opportunity for military training so as to be able to challenge the forces of apartheid with more than sticks and stones and also a structured program and political organization. In 1978 Brigadier C. F. Zeitsman, head of the Security Police, was claiming publicly that four thousand young South Africans had left the country, with three quarters of them joining the ANC and most of the others the PAC.[30] He also indicated that while the PAC had "little or no success" in launching guerrilla operations, "the ANC was another matter, with a far more sophisticated organizational structure and that the ANC accounted for most of the guerrilla activity in the country."[31]

Soweto and its aftermath served as a bridge connecting the younger generation of black South Africans, which had grown up in what was virtually a political vacuum, to the older generation, which had experienced the political turmoil of the fifties and early sixties and suffered the full brunt of government's repressive power. The ANC could offer the younger generation political and historical roots; specifically, it offered a political orientation centered on the Freedom Charter and an organization prepared for a long political and military struggle. At the same time, the young people had grass-roots experience: the black consciousness groups had been able to operate with relative openness, despite harassment from the police, in ways unavailable to the outlawed ANC, setting up community programs of different types and organizing meetings and conferences dealing with social and political issues.

In 1975, during the period when the ANC was working to try to expand its presence within South Africa, a bitter dispute came into the open. It ended in the expulsion of eight dissident members. The position of the expelled group was clearly another manifestation of the Africanist attitudes that had led to the PAC's breakaway almost two decades earlier. The dissidents opposed the decision taken at the Morogoro conference to open ANC membership on a nonracial basis and the adoption of "Strategy and Tactics." The central target of the dissidents' criticism was the South African Communist party, which they claimed was controlled by whites and had come to dominate the ANC at Morogoro. The ANC said the trouble had simmered for almost a decade and stressed that its strategy has been to work for black unity and to try to win over white South Africans who had come to oppose apartheid; the dissidents' attacks were said to represent racialism and anticommunism opposed to this long-standing position.[32]

This dispute raised once more the issue of relations between the ANC and South African Communists. The dispute has been argued from sharply differing perspectives over the years, and it is still a contentious one. After their election victory in 1948 the Nationalist government targeted the Communists as the subversive force behind resistance to apartheid. The Suppression of Communism Act of 1950 outlawed the Communist party of South Africa, and it equated even peaceful resistance to government policies by other organizations as illegally "furthering the aims of Communism." Since then, government prosecutions against the ANC and other groups have often included charges under the act, most dramatically in the Treason trial and the Rivonia trial, but in other cases as well. In terms of guerrilla conflict, both in South Africa and throughout the region, the standard government position has been that South Africa is facing a Soviet-sponsored "onslaught" that threatens not only white South Africa, but also the entire Western world. In addition, charges that the ANC has been dominated or unduly influenced by Communists have also been raised in critiques and polemics by conservative-minded Africans, South African Liberals, the Unity Movement of South Africa (from a Trotskyist perspective), the PAC (from an Africanist and Maoist perspective), and some black consciousness adherents.

The Communist party of South Africa was formed in 1921.[33] Although several African Communists rose to high positions in the ANC, the ANC resisted cooperation between the two organizations for a number of years. In 1946 Moses Kotane and two other prominent African Communists, J. B. Marks and Edwin Mofutsanyana, were elected to the ANC national executive committee. Kotane became treasurer-general in 1964 and was a key leader of the ANC external organization based in Tanzania until he suffered a serious stroke in 1968. J. B. Marks, who had led the mine-workers union, was to hold the post of chairman of the ANC national executive committee and national chairman of the Communist party at the time of his death in 1972.

With the passage of the Suppression of Communism Act, the leadership of the CPSA voted to dissolve the party rather than expose its members to prosecution after almost three decades of legal political activity. In the 1950s many who had been party members were active in campaigns against apartheid, working with the ANC and other Congress Alliance organizations. In 1953 the party was secretly reconstituted underground as the South African Communist party (SACP). Members of the SACP cooperated with Nelson Mandela in setting up Umkhonto We Sizwe and in its sabotage campaign, and several of those convicted at the Rivonia trial were or had been members of the party. The leading defense lawyer at the trial was Abram (Bram) Fischer, an Afrikaner, grandson of a South African prime minister, Oxford graduate, a successful lawyer, and a prominent member of the Communist party since the thirties. After the trial Fischer went underground when he and others were charged with membership in the outlawed SACP (at that point he was acting chairman of its central committee). He was arrested ten months later, sentenced to life imprisonment, and died in prison in 1975. Since the mid-sixties the SACP has operated in exile from London, and the distribution of its literature and arrests and security trials in South Africa all indicate that it has been able again to operate underground in South Africa.

The SACP is now led by Dr. Yusuf Dadoo, who was chosen as vice-chairman of the ANC's revolutionary council at the Morogoro Conference in 1969 and who became national chairman of the SACP in 1972 after the death of J. B. Marks. Dr. Dadoo, who is of Indian descent, was a leader of the South African Indian Congress. After Sharpeville, he left the country to work with the external organization of the SACP.

The current program of the SACP is "The Road to Freedom in South Africa," which was adopted in 1962. It declares that the party's foremost task is to work to "unite all sections and classes of the oppressed for a national democratic revolution to destroy white domination. The main content of this revolution will be the national liberation of the African people. . . ." This is the essential step toward the party's "supreme aim" of establishing a socialist South Africa. With these goals the SACP pledges its support for the Freedom Charter and the ANC and declares that there is no alternative but to meet the government's violence with armed resistance. The program, however, opposes undisciplined terror and supports nonviolent forms of opposition. It does not dismiss the possibility of a peaceful transition to democracy, but it views this as likely only with the growth of armed resistance. In terms of politics, the program declares the SACP's adherence to Marxism-Leninism and to the world Communist movement. The SACP has in general followed closely the policies and positions taken by the Soviet Union. However, it is clear that the party has been authentically South African, a part of the country's political fabric for more than half a century. At its dissolution, in 1950, the party had some two thousand members, three quarters of them African, but the central committee was composed mainly of whites. At the 1962 national conference it was reported that the majority of the delegates were black, and a predominantly black central committee was elected. In 1976 the party's journal, *The African Communist*, reported that the "overwhelming majority of the leadership and membership of the party is African."[34]

As regards the role and influence of Communists in the ANC, it is evident that the ANC policies as they have developed since the 1950s have in general had the strong backing of the SACP. But it would be an error to view them simply as a reflection of this. On such key issues as the Freedom Charter, the split with PAC, and the turn to sabotage after Sharpeville, the decisions had broad support within the ANC and among Africans. The main decisions reached at Morogoro, though made with the movement in exile and hardly able to operate within the country, appear to have been generally popular, and not simply imposed by SACP adherents. The nonracial membership policy was in harmony with longstanding ANC principles, and the decision to mount a protracted guerrilla war against apartheid became, a decade later, a reality with wide support among black South Africans. At the Rivonia trial Nelson Mandela discussed ANC links with South African Communists in response to prosecution charges, noting their close cooperation reflected the common goal of removing white domination, but not a complete community of interests. As the ANC Youth League member, he had at first been among those proposing to expel Communists from the ANC, but he had come to see the need for working with differing political groups for common objectives. He added that "for many decades Communists were the only political group in South Africa who were prepared to treat Africans as human beings and their equals: who were prepared to eat with us, talk with us, live with us, and work with us."[35]

The question of ANC-SACP relations is also covered carefully at various points in the comprehensive four-volume work *From Protest to Challenge: A Documentary History of African Politics in South Africa*. There the editors conclude:

> The intimacy of relations between non-Communist nationalists and Communists, in South Africa and in exile, made it difficult for many anti-Communist observers to recognize that African nationalists could hold their own. This was especially true for white analysts who assumed that in any such collaboration Communists—particularly white Communists—would dominate. . . .Despite the ANC's growing reliance on aid from Communist countries, the position of [independent African patriots such as Mandela, Sisulu, and Oliver Tambo] was strengthened by the fact that African Communists like Kotane and Marks were to an important extent also nationalists.[36]

Criticism of SACP ties with the ANC has also been voiced from independent Marxist perspectives, most significantly by a group that was expelled from SACTU in 1980. In the ANC's difficult post-Rivonia period, they have seen "petty-bourgeois tendencies within the ANC being merely reinforced by Communist Party influence and Communist Party-style bureaucratic methods."[37] A related problem, in this view, has been excessive attention given to guerrilla operations, with the result that the

ANC has not been adequately responsive to the upsurge of potentially revolutionary working-class ferment within South Africa.

On the opposite end of the political spectrum the recently created U.S. Senate Subcommittee on Security and Terrorism held five days of hearings in March 1982 on Soviet and East German involvement with the ANC and SWAPO and the degree of "control" Communists have gained in the movements. Most of the hearings were taken up by several witnesses who were former ANC and SWAPO members, with those from the ANC describing military training and education they received in Eastern Europe and links they had with the SACP. Senator Jeremiah Denton ended the hearings with the conclusion they had shown the Soviet's "support for terrorism under the guise of aiding struggles for national liberation" and that the evidence heard had indicated that the original purposes of the ANC and SWAPO have been subverted and the Soviets and their allies had gained "alarmingly successful control over them."[38]

ANC President Oliver Tambo recently responded to questions on these issues from the American press. In one interview he noted that the Freedom Charter, as the expression of the goals of the ANC, has been suppported by a broad cross-section of South Africans, including Communists, Christians, Moslems, and others, and that they were united in the ANC in the fight for a common cause. "The South African Communist Party supports and actively fights for the realization of the demands contained in the charter. It accepts the leadership of the ANC and therefore cannot but be an ally of the ANC as would any other organization that adopts the same position."[39] On the issue of military aid from the Soviets he noted that the ANC's decision to mount guerrilla resistance had been endorsed by the Organization of African Unity and by numerous United Nations resolutions, which have also appealed for international aid for the ANC. The ANC has sought aid from around the world, with varying responses:

> The supposed stigma of getting assistance from the Soviet Union has no meaning whatever in southern Africa. There would be no independence for anyone without those weapons. That's what ordinary people think. Where would we be without that assistance? Could we go to Washington?
>
> We are called terrorists. After seventy years, what would anybody do if the response had been murder, torture, life imprisonment? Who is a terrorist? Is it not the person who has been persecuting human beings simply because they are black?[40]

As the crisis and conflict in South Africa have intensified, there has been an increase in recognition and support on the international scene for the ANC and the anti-apartheid cause in general. With the exception of the principal Western powers, there is virtually world-wide support for the resolutions passed each year in the UN General Assembly aimed at mounting pressure against apartheid and support for the liberation cause. In 1974 the ANC and the PAC were granted observer status in all United Nations and international agency bodies dealing with questions relating to South Africa, whereas the Nationalist government has been largely blocked from participation in the activities of these bodies. The key to substantive United Nation action is, however, the Security Council, where the Western powers have, and use, the veto. Another world-wide forum for support of South African liberation is the Non-Aligned Movement.

The Organization of African Unity has been, since its inception in 1963, the African forum for promoting opposition to apartheid and support for South African liberation. The OAU countries, operating informally at the United Nations as the "African group," have played an important role in legitimizing and supporting the liberation struggle in the world body and its specialized agencies. The Liberation Committee of the OAU has the role of promoting and coordinating African and foreign assistance to the liberation movements. Its activities have been largely diplomatic: cooperating with UN agencies providing humanitarian aid for the movements and carrying out contacts with non-African states providing aid, such as the Scandinavian countries, the Soviet Union and other East European states, and China. In terms of the diplomatic and strategic aspects of the southern African conflicts the frontline states (Tanzania, Zambia, Mozambique, Angola, Botswana, Lesotho, Swaziland, and now Zimbabwe) have come to play a key role because of their direct involvement in the crises and because they have borne the brunt of political and economic pressures and also damaging military aggression from Pretoria. Nigeria, because of its economic weight and political commitment, has at a number of points been closely associated with the efforts of the frontline states.

The ANC has undertaken programs in education, health, agriculture, and vocational training and expanded them significantly to meet the needs of those leaving South Africa in the post-Soweto period. The Morogoro School Complex (including primary and secondary education, agriculture, and rural development) is being established in Tanzania, as well as the Solomon Mahlangu Freedom College at the same location, which is to accommodate up to a thousand students. An ANC Health Centre is also being set up at Morogoro, and vocational programs are operating in Zambia and Botswana. In addition to support for such projects from the socialist countries, educational aid has been provided by the United Nations Development Program, with $1.4 million allocated in the 1975-77 period. In 1977 the Swedish government donated $1.6 million to the ANC for humanitarian projects. Additional assistance has come from agencies of other governments—Denmark, Norway, the Netherlands, and Canada—as well as other United Nations agencies and a number of voluntary and nongovernmental organizations, including the World Council of Churches.[41] In Italy the Movimento Liberazione e Sviluppo promoted a scholarship program for ANC members, as well as a vocational training program in agriculture for refugees and a shipment of medicines; the city of Reggio-Emelia has signed a pact of solidarity with the ANC and in 1980 sent a freighter with supplies for the ANC, SWAPO, and the Patriotic Front. The Medische Kommittee Angola (Angola Medical Committee) of Holland raised all the funds needed for the construction of the ANC Health Centre, and the Holland Committee on Southern Africa sent $40,000 worth of emergency aid to the ANC for South African refugees in Angola. Other support groups have been instrumental in lobbying for aid from governments or private agencies.

In the diplomatic field the ANC has made important advances in Western Europe, gaining recognition as the representative of the people of South Africa from the governments of Sweden, Norway, Holland, Finland, and Ireland. An ANC representative was also granted an audience jointly with those of the Patriotic Front of Zimbabwe and SWAPO by Pope Paul II.[42] Through its office in London, the ANC has long had contacts with members of the British Labour party. In the United States the ANC has dealt over the years with liberals in Congress concerned with African issues and with administration officials during the Carter period. The Reagan administration has given priority to pursuing friendly ties with the Nationalist government. There is, however, growing concern about South Africa in the United States, as expressed in the formation of the Rockefeller Foundation-funded Study Commission on U.S. Policy Toward Southern Africa. The Commission's report, *South Africa: Time Running Out*, includes the recommendation that the United States expand contacts with black leaders in South Africa as well as the ANC and PAC.[43] A reflection of this recommendation and of the importance now accorded the ANC were meetings held in 1981 between Oliver Tambo and officers of the Bank of America, Citibank, Manufacturers Hanover Bank, General Motors, Ford, and General Electric, all of them companies having major involvement with South Africa.[44]

The growth of recognition and support for the ANC on the international scene does not, however, diminish the fact that the main arena of the struggle lies within South Africa. Here the increasing tempo of guerrilla attacks has been matched by an upsurge of open, public forms of support among black South Africans for the ANC and for the imprisoned Nelson Mandela. This has taken place in the face of the direct difficulties posed by the white security apparatus, and in spite of the many political problems created by the structures of apartheid. Historically, there have been differences and conflicts among black South Africans even though the dominant formula became white vs. black. Tensions among black South Africans are sometimes ascribed to the legacy of traditional historical patterns, but this view is incomplete and misleading. Black politics needs to be interpreted within the context of white conquest and domination, which shattered or twisted traditional institutions and imposed new ones. Thus the victorious whites manipulated the tribal structures of African societies in order to institute forms of indirect rule, and that has now been developed into the whole complex of Bantustan administrations. On the urban scene there has been the vast pattern of segregated townships for Africans, as well as for people of mixed race and Indians. To this has been added the pervasive pattern of forced removals of blacks—more than two million since 1948—from white areas and the vast system of migratory labor. The result has been a complex and difficult social and political terrain for those seeking to mobilize and unify black South Africans.

While virtually no black leader in South Africa would voice complete support for apartheid, there are those who have an economic and political stake in the system, and they say that the best hope for black improvement lies in operating within apartheid institutions. These include Bantustan leaders and administrations, those participating in the urban municipal structures, black civil servants, blacks in the police and military, and leaders of "parallel" segregated black trade unions operating within the orbit of white trade unions. A South African journalist has labeled them "system users,"[45] but their role goes beyond this: they are part of the apartheid system and often enforce it in strategic ways. Roughly half of the South African police are black, concentrated heavily in the lower ranks. The Bantustans have police and security forces that have been trained by whites, and in some cases are still commanded by them, and they cooperate closely with the South African police and military. In November 1981, for example, a Lutheran lay preacher, Tshifhiwa Isaac Muofhe, died in the hands of the Venda security police. He and others had been detained after an ANC guerrilla attack on a Venda police station. Four other Lutheran churchmen were hospitalized in Venda, reportedly having been badly tortured, after their detention by the Venda police in the same period. Gen. Charles Sebe, commander of the police and army of the Ciskei Bantustan and brother of its president, is described as having "embarked on a kind of holy war" against the black South African Allied Workers Union, which he sees as linked to the ANC. He was trained by the South African Security Police and is viewed as "the most conspicuous black on the side of the powerful South African security apparatus."[46]

There are others who have participated in apartheid institutions while voicing opposition, including, most prominently, Chief Buthelezi of the

KwaZulu Bantustan and his organization Inkatha, and to some extent the groups linked with Inkatha in the Black Alliance: the Coloured Labour party, the Indian Reform party, and also the Dikwankwetla party of the QwaQwa Bantustan and the KanGwana Bantustan government.

In varying ways these groups have been given an economic stake in South Africa's racially based economic system—either by the government or by private business. This, in substantial measure, explains their political stance.

Those groups and individuals peacefully opposing collaboration with apartheid and promoting resistance and protests against it have had a precarious existence to maintain in trying to operate openly in the face of government repression. This category has included mainly black consciousness groups, many of which were outlawed in 1977.

The newer groups, not outlawed, include the Azanian Peoples Organization (AZAPO), the Conference of South African Students (COSAS), the Writers Association of South Africa (WASA), the Port Elizabeth Black Civic Association (Pebco), and the Azanian Students Organization (AZASO). Not specifically aligned with the Black Consciousness Movement, and yet noncollaborationist, are the Soweto Committee of Ten, the Natal Indian Congress (NIC), the South African Council of Sport (SACOS), and the Federation of South African Trade Unions (FOSATU). These noncollaborationist groups have local roots and direct involvement in black community issues. They are able to operate publicly—within the limits of government repression—in ways that would be impossible for organizations having explicit ties to the ANC.

One of the most visible and controversial black leaders has been Chief Gatsha Buthelezi. He has vigorously defended his political position since the ANC openly criticized him, in 1980, for trying to stand between the white government and the widening black resistance to apartheid. Buthelezi had contacts with the ANC and had been able to use this in part to fend off criticism from black consciousness groups. His approach has involved building his own political organization, the Zulu-based Inkatha, now claiming a membership of 300,000, which is the dominant group in the Black Alliance. While attacking apartheid, opposing government-sponsored independence for KwaZulu, and warning of the need for fundamental change to avoid a "racial bloodbath," he has maintained frequent contacts with the white power structure, including Minister of Cooperation and Development Pieter Koornhof and major business leaders. He has also had meetings with prime ministers Vorster and Botha. While his political base has been built on his status as a Zulu leader, he has operated around the country, speaking frequently in Soweto and elsewhere to black groups and to white. Buthelezi has also been a frequent visitor to Western countries, meeting with top government officials and business and African-oriented groups.

In 1980 Buthelezi organized a commission to study the future of Natal Province, where some four million Zulus make up about two-thirds of the population and the KwaZulu Bantustan includes forty-one fragments of territory. The study, completed in 1982, proposes a unitary government, with the white minority given roughly equal power to that of blacks rather than majority rule. Buthelezi has hoped that, if approved by the government, it could be a formula for the whole country, but this prospect seems dim. His bitter conflicts with the Black Consciousness Movement and Dr. Nthato Motlana of the Soweto Committee of Ten have grown out of his use of his Zulu ethnic base and the Bantustan administration as his platform and his readiness to deal with white leaders. Buthelezi showed little support for students at the time of the Soweto uprisings, and he was subsequently stoned by youths at the funeral of PAC leader Robert Sobukwe in 1977. Dr. Motlana has denounced him as a "system Black."

Despite the size of its membership, Inkatha has not been mobilized on a mass basis for protests against apartheid, and Buthelezi has taken shifting positions on key issues. He has long opposed economic sanctions against South Africa, saying they would hurt blacks the most. But he retreated from this stance at the time of Soweto, and in an interview in 1980 his position was ambiguous:

> I think it is quite wrong to say I'm against disinvestment, because as a person committed to nonviolent change I must accept pressures on South Africa. I see it as harassment for the regime. But I see black people as the ones who bear the brunt. It is from that standpoint that I don't support it.[47]

He has enthusiastically backed the Sullivan Code, which called upon foreign corporations in South Africa to provide equal rights in the workplace for blacks, and he indicated that Inkatha would actively monitor their implementation. But in the same interview he could say only, "I must confess it is very problematic how one goes about that." Questioned about U.S. policy on South Africa during the Carter administration, Chief Buthelezi said only that he was disappointed that the United States did not offer humanitarian aid for black South Africans, but he did not call for any increased U.S. pressures on the government to end apartheid. While saying that he saw Nelson Mandela as "one of our leaders," that he had been the first to "mention his name" in public, and that he had talked to prime ministers Vorster and Botha about releasing him from prison, Buthelezi did not throw his personal weight or that of Inkatha behind the petition campaign for his release. Buthelezi's opposition to the school boycotts, in 1980, that spread to a township near Durban in KwaZulu alienated many young people among the Zulus. They resented his autocratic manner.

ANC criticism brought sharp responses from Chief Buthelezi and Inkatha officials.[48] Buthelezi said that the ANC was attacking him because they see that Inkatha "has as good prospects as anyone else of forming a government in this country," and he raised the threat of ethnic conflict among Africans, saying that "criticism" of Inkatha could lead to a "civil war situation among Black South Africans." His supporters, responding to charges that Inkatha has failed to attract support beyond its Zulu base, have answered that the ANC is dominated by Xhosas. The secretary general of Inkatha warned that Inkatha is "now prepared to shed blood when it comes to dealing with those people who make it their hobby to discredit and abuse Chief Buthelezi's stature as our leader." He also stated, "We don't see that there can ever be a black government in South Africa that can exist without the input of Inkatha and Chief Buthelezi."

Chief Buthelezi has also belittled ANC efforts to launch guerrilla attacks in South Africa. An Inkatha official commented, "The armed struggle has been going on for twenty years now, and other than a few bombings, nothing has happened." Yet the ANC attacks, while still limited, have had wide political impact, especially the SASOL sabotage. These comments ignore the extent of police repression and the military mobilization, extending to KwaZulu, that the ANC has faced.

While Chief Buthelezi has built his own political base and pursued contacts with white South African leaders and officials in the Western countries, it appears that he has been putting himself in position to take advantage of pressures mounted by the ANC and others who are taking a more militant path. Buthelezi has long paid tribute to the ANC and its goals, and in some ways, he seems to identify himself with Chief Lutuli. But Lutuli was a leader whose national stature was linked not to a Zulu political power base, but to the ANC as a unifying national organization. The strident remarks of Buthelezi and his aides about "civil war among blacks" and Xhosa control of the ANC appear to depart widely from the unifying role played by Lutuli, who supported and worked with the younger ANC activists in the 1950s and 1960s and with other groups in the Congress Alliance representing a variety of viewpoints, from those on the left to the Africanist-oriented.

The most significant political trend among black South Africans during the nineteen-eighties has been the upsurge of open public support for the ANC and its imprisoned leader, Nelson Mandela. This has developed even though the movement has been outlawed for two decades, even though membership or support for its aims has been a crime and all ANC literature, documents, and statements by its leaders have been banned. In the spring of 1980 the Johannesburg *Post*, a newspaper for black readers, launched a Free Mandela petition campaign that was also supported by other organizations. It was reported that 72,000 signatures had been collected by that September. Funerals for ANC guerrillas have drawn large crowds, as have security trials of those accused of ANC activity. The funeral in November 1981 of black lawyer Griffiths Mxenga, whose killing many attributed to the Security Police, was attended by 15,000 persons in what was desribed as "almost certainly the most blatant display of support for the ANC in two decades."[49] Bishop Desmond Tutu, chairman of the South African Council of Churches, openly predicted that South Africa would have a black prime minister within five to ten years—almost certainly Nelson Mandela. Support for the freeing of Mandela also came in the white press, including Afrikaner papers. The same papers also called for a national political convention—although the ANC has insisted that such a convention should be for the purpose of dismantling apartheid and forming a system of democratic rule. The editor of an Afrikaans newspaper that has advocated a dialogue with the "true Black leadership" privately told American reporters, "We believe we will have to talk to the ANC at some point, but we don't feel the time is yet right to print this."[50]

Of black South Africans polled in major urban areas by the Arnold Bergstraessen Institute in 1977, 44 percent indicated that Chief Buthelezi was their most popular political figure, while 22 percent indicated a preference for ANC leaders and 19 percent specifically cited Nelson Mandela.[51] Given that the ANC has been outlawed for years, and Mandela in prison, this was significant support. In addition, the poll did not include areas such as Port Elizabeth, which are traditional ANC strongholds. In 1979 polls taken for the Ciskei Commission Report among Xhosa-speaking Africans, as well as Zulus and Pedis in Soweto, indicated, as the Arnold Bergstraessen Institute polls had, that the ANC's political goal has overwhelming support: ". . . the notion of 'one-man one-vote' in a unitary state clearly has pride of place in the preferences of Africans all over South Africa. This for decades has been the goal of the ANC and the Black intelligentsia. . . ."[52] The poll also found a high level of discontent among Africans in urban areas—higher than after the Soweto uprisings—indicating that a "flashpoint" could touch off new disturbances and that there is fertile ground for protests, strikes, and even underground action.

Another poll, taken in August 1981 among six hundred and eighty-six black South Africans in Johannesburg, Durban, and Cape Town, found that the ANC was the most popular political organization.[53] The Africans were asked, "If you could vote for parliament today, which party would you vote for?" Forty percent chose the ANC, 21 percent Inkatha, 11 percent Azapo, and 10 percent the PAC (see Table 2-1). Again, the fact that the ANC and PAC are outlawed and that the poll

TABLE 2-1
AFRICAN PARTY PREFERENCES

If you could vote for Parliament today, which party would you vote for?

	ANC	INKATHA	AZAPO	PAC
BY CITY				
All respondents	40%	21%	11%	10%
Johannesburg	47%	20%	17%	8%
Durban	37%	31%	6%	12%
Cape Town	28%	5%	4%	13%
BY OCCUPATION				
Unskilled	29%	28%	9%	8%
Clerical & Skilled	48%	16%	14%	12%
Professional & Self-Employed	59%	8%	10%	16%
BY AGE				
16-25	46%	14%	21%	6%
26-39	40%	17%	10%	10%
40+	37%	31%	4%	12%
BY LANGUAGE				
Zulu	39%	31%	11%	12%
Other Nguni	33%	13%	8%	12%
Sotho	56%	8%	17%	4%

SOURCE: *Africa News*, November 2, 1981, based on a poll by the *Johannisburg Star*.

did not include Port Elizabeth or East London, both ANC strongholds, must be considered.[53]

The renewed public prominence of the ANC inside South Africa relates in part to its historical roots, stretching back to 1912, making it the oldest African nationalist organization on the continent, and older than the National party. Although the white government was able to outlaw the ANC and imprison its leaders or drive them into exile, the organization actually remained implicitly at center stage in South African political life in the years that followed. The ANC remained in a central position because the movement was kept alive within South Africa and in exile and, more important, because its program and leaders continued to have the support and represent the aspirations of most South Africans, i.e., a great part of the black majority, and some white South Africans as well. This is not to say that there has not also been support for other organizations and leaders, including the Black Consciousness Movement, the PAC, and the Unity Movement, and even some for those who have operated within the apartheid system, such as Chief Buthelezi and several other Bantustan chiefs. But the ANC and the goals expressed in the Freedom Charter of a united, democratic, nonracial South Africa have continued to have the broadest support among South Africans. This support has now carried over to the ANC decision to take up arms when both peaceful protests and the organization itself were outlawed. The increasing public support for the ANC has coincided with the increase in ANC guerrilla activity.

The reactions in South Africa to the settlement talks and elections in Zimbabwe in 1979-80 also reflected the new degree of public support for the ANC. The Rhodesian regime, despite extensive economic and military backing from South Africa, had been brought to the conference table by the pressures of guerrilla war and international isolation. The Patriotic Front leaders had long been excoriated by the South African government and in the South African press as criminal Communist terrorists. Robert Mugabe and Joshua Nkomo had spent a decade in the prisons and detention camps of the Rhodesian regime. But within a few months they were shown to be popular political leaders and skilled statesmen. When Robert Mugabe and the Patriotic Front overwhelmingly carried the elections, against initial Western and South African expectations, the message became clear to many in South Africa: Those who stand for genuinely popular political aspirations, who are willing to sacrifice and if necessary fight for freedom, can expect strong popular support. Those who operate within the racist system and ally themselves with the oppressors in power risk the repudiation suffered by Bishop Abel Muzorewa.

The pattern that has developed in the past several years, then, has been a related growth in ANC guerrilla activity and forms of popular support for the ANC within South Africa. As it has developed so far, the guerrilla operations of the ANC have differed from other conflicts in southern Africa. In Mozambique, Angola, and Zimbabwe, guerrilla activity was focused in the rural areas. Despite their superior firepower, the colonial and settler forces were forced to disperse their military operations over wide areas and, under a combination of protracted guerrilla attacks and international pressures, were finally worn down to the point where the African liberation forces were able to achieve political victories. The conflict in Namibia has been somewhat similar, except that SWAPO's operations have been carried out mainly along the long northern border areas. In all these conflicts there was political mobilization in the urban areas, but no extensive guerrilla operations. In South Africa, the ANC's guerrilla attacks have been carried out in both urban and rural areas, with the most damaging attacks being directed against oil-refining and power-generating facilities in urban areas.

It should be noted that there are similarities between the first sabotage campaign carried out by the ANC in the early sixties and the attacks now underway. In the sixties the ANC concentrated on economic targets and on symbols of apartheid, such as government offices. The attacks were carried out to damage property and avoid loss of life, with the goal of creating economic and political pressures. A rough plan to launch a full-scale guerrilla offensive was drafted but apparently never even discussed. Although the sabotage campaign crumbled after Rivonia, it is easy to forget two decades later that it had been quite extensive and that it was countered only by an all-out wave of repression by the Nationalist government.

In the period 1977-82 the ANC carried out mainly sabotage attacks in ways that avoided loss of life. There were, however, some attacks on police stations, members of the police, and police informants. In one incident, three guerrillas took hostages at the Volkkasbank (a major Afrikaner institution) near Pretoria and were killed in a police assault. The ANC said the hostages were taken after the guerrillas' plans had gone awry. In February 1983, seventy-six blacks were wounded in a bomb explosion at a government office in Bloemfontein. The ANC did not take responsibility for the bombing, though it is possible that an error by the guerrillas led to the many casualties. Oliver Tambo had warned in 1981, after a South African raid killed a number of ANC members in Mozambique and veteran ANC leader Joe Gqabi was assassinated, that the ANC was prepared to strike back at leaders of the white government. But the 1983 bombing of South African Air Force headquarters and Military Intelligence offices apparently marked a change in ANC policy. While the target was a military one, the attack caused many civilian casualties. The ANC warned that there would be future attacks on police and military personnel. The ANC has avoided attacks aimed at civilians. But the escalation reflected by the bombing indicated that more civilians could be casualties in future attacks.

Many different views on the conflict in South Africa can be found. Conservative analysts such as Lewis Gann and Peter Duignan stress the power and efficiency of the South African military and police and conclude that there are no prospects for a successful guerrilla challenge to apartheid at the present time.[54] Others have pointed to the great vulnerability of all white South African institutions that depend so entirely on black labor. "Every lorry on the highway is driven by a black. . . . A black man can go anywhere in Johannesburg as long as his pass is in order and he is servile in manner. . . . Every home is vulnerable, every skyscraper, every goldmine," writes journalist David Halberstam.[55] A journalist familiar with guerrilla conflicts writes that in South Africa, "Security experts realize that that a few crack guerrilla squads armed with 300 lbs or so of high explosives, detonated at strategic points throughout the country, could bring South Africa to its knees almost overnight."[56] A decade ago sociologist Heribert Adam suggested that as the economy has become increasingly dependent on skilled black labor, the structure of white domination could be broken by a massive general strike.[57] John Saul and Stephen Gelb, viewing the semispontaneous wave of strikes that developed in the 1979-81 period, interpret it in light of Rosa Luxemburg's concept of the "mass strike," not as a single event, but as a multifarious, extended process of working-class assertion. They see this as a potentially revolutionary component in the wider liberation struggle encompassing guerrilla attacks and various forms of popular mobilization and resistance.[58] They foresee that while black liberation will finally be won, the struggle will be long, difficult, and politically complex.

It should be noted that as potentially powerful as the black labor force is, there are many factors that can hamper its development into a revolutionary mainspring. While the oppression of apartheid is common to all, the conditions of black workers vary greatly. The most active elements have been among the skilled and semiskilled industrial workers, a significant, but relatively small and better-off sector of the working class. While in some cases strikes have been dramatically linked to the wider community struggle against apartheid, in others the more immediate concerns of wages and working conditions have been paramount. Observers from the labor movements in the West, such as the AFL-CIO, have also followed the growth of militancy among black South African workers and have been concerned to see it channeled away from revolutionary political directions and toward immediate trade union issues. The government's new labor legislation provides for recognition of black trade unions—and the machinery to monitor and control their activities. There is also police repression here: trade union leaders have been banned, arrested, and detained. In February 1982 trade unionist Dr. Neil Aggett, who was being held in detention without trial by the Security Police, was found hanged in his cell.

Tom Lodge of the University of Witwatersrand has concluded that the ANC's guerrilla activity has helped to enhance its role as a major force in South African politics. But he declares that the nonmilitary political aspects of the ANC activities in South Africa appear weakly developed and suggests that if its efforts continue to be focused mainly on the military, the movement may become more elitist.[59] Political mobilization and involvement in grassroots issues are clearly key aspects of the struggle for black freedom. But throughout the history of white rule such nonviolent activities have been ruthlessly suppressed. In some ways the ANC guerrilla operations seem to have opened opportunities for political action. As noted above, black reactions to the May 1983 bomb attack was widely sympathetic, and indeed the ANC has been criticized by blacks for its military restraint. The ANC has opposed militarism, terrorism, and unrestrained violence. Its strategy has accorded a central place to the guerrilla struggle, but stressed that this would be guided by the political leadership.

A 1981 report in the *New York Times*, apparently reflecting to some extent official South African sources, has described the ANC's sabotage successes as "a form of political graffiti," not causing any significant economic or military damage.[60] It suggests that through agents infiltrated into guerrilla ranks, the detention and torture of suspects, and rewards to informants the security apparatus has been able to contain the guerrillas. Thus the South African sources estimate that the ANC has trained fewer than 1,500 guerrillas and claim that it has not been able to set up a reliable underground structure within the country, so that guerrillas who are sent on forays into the country must then leave as quickly as possible.

However, aspects of these reports may be questioned. The continuing security trials reflect the degree of police pressure on the ANC underground and on open political and trade union work, but the guerrilla operations and popular mobilization have continued. It is obviously in the interest of the Nationalist government to claim that guerrillas operate only from neighboring countries and have gained no foothold inside South Africa. But the ANC attacks have been widely dispersed, often taking place hundreds of miles from the nearest border, and some have evidently been carried out with careful planning and knowledge of local conditions. This and the degree of open black support for guerrillas expressed at security trials and at funerals indicates that there exists an underground structure having popular support. The recent moves by the Defence Force to increase its forces virtually to the limit of white manpower, with one emphasis being on the strengthening of locally based Commando forces, is another indication of this. In Soweto and in other black urban areas police and military forces have conducted major sweeps and set up roadblocks: one correspondent has reported, "They're looking for weapons, explosives and Communist literature, and they'll search every inch of your car and your body to find anything that fits one of those categories."[61] Many police stations in black areas are now protected by sandbagged guard posts—a sign that local security is slight.

In 1982 a lengthy secret study by the CIA on the guerrilla conflict in South Africa was leaked to TransAfrica, the national black lobbying organization in Washington.[62] While referring to the ANC guerrilla actions as "terrorist activity," the report highlighted the growing influence of the movement. It stated that the ANC is gaining influence rapidly among students and trade unions, and because of the lack of significant reforms, blacks are coming to agree with the ANC position that whites will not give up the material benefits of apartheid until their "lives, property, and security are threatened." While asserting that the ANC had apparently not yet set up an extensive underground network, the study says the ANC is attempting to establish a permanent presence in South Africa. The Bantustans are seen as probably the main base for this. The importance to the ANC of a widespread underground inside South Africa relates to the white government's power to strike at the frontline states, which makes it impossible for the ANC to rely on big bases anywhere near South Africa's borders. However, it is not certain that the ANC will try to concentrate its efforts in the Bantustans. They are zones of poverty and discontent, but they are isolated from the economically and politically important urban areas where ANC influence has traditionally been strong.

The South African reports of the relatively small number of ANC guerrillas trained may be roughly accurate; there have been no reports of big bases in the frontline states or of South African forces clashing with large numbers of guerrillas, and the ANC attacks have involved only small groups. This makes the magnitude of Pretoria's military buildup all the more significant. It has been trying to tighten South Africa's military grip on Namibia and gain the wider objective of establishing military dominance over the entire region, but the essential goal remains police and military control within South Africa itself. This is what the ANC guerrillas are beginning to challenge. The guerrillas are able to operate successfully because they are a part of an encompassing political cause. Clearly, given the directions of the policies of the Botha government—and of the Reagan administration—military confrontation will have a central position in the South African conflict.

3 The War in Namibia and Regional Aggression

SOUTH AFRICA'S WAR IN NEIGHBORING NAMBIA has escalated since the mid-seventies to become by far Pretoria's largest conflict. South Africa provides no official figures on the number of troops deployed in Namibia, but the number cited unofficially in press reports has been 20,000 to 25,000. The South West African Peoples Organization (SWAPO), which has been fighting against South African rule in Namibia, has placed the figure much higher, at 100,000 troops by the early 1980s, an estimate that has been supported by reports from Western sources.[1] The South African military forces in Namibia include full-time members of the Defence Force's Permanent Force, National Service conscripts, reservists called up for three-month tours of duty, and in addition there are Namibians serving in the recently formed South West African Territorial Force. Early in 1982 Prime Minister Botha stated that it was costing South Africa $1 billion a year to maintain its presence in Namibia.[2] The South African escalation has involved not only an extensive military buildup within Namibia, but also a policy of carrying the war into southern Angola.

The war in Namibia has become a focus of international attention because of its increasing intensity and the protracted diplomatic maneuvering in the search for a settlement. But the conflict in Namibia is only a part of what has become a pattern of regional aggression, intervention, and destabilization by South Africa since the collapse of Portuguese colonial rule in Mozambique and Angola in 1974. Namibia was the base area for the South African invasion of Angola in 1975-76. Then the focus of regional confrontation shifted to Rhodesia, with the guerrilla forces of the Patriotic Front increasing their pressure on the white regime of Ian Smith. The Botha government reacted by giving increasingly open support to the Rhodesian forces, which, in destructive raids, carried the war into Mozambique and Zambia. The Rhodesian war ended suddenly with the Lancaster House settlement and the 1980 elections for the government of an independent Zimbabwe. The scene of major conflict then shifted back to Namibia and Angola. As ANC guerrilla attacks began to increase in South Africa, however, Pretoria put renewed pressure on other neighboring countries, including Mozambique, Zimbabwe, Botswana, Zambia, and Lesotho. South African pressure has taken a variety of forms, including straightforward military attacks, support for attacks by dissident groups such as UNITA in Angola and the Mozambique National Resistance (MRN) in Mozambique, sabotage and assassinations, and economic and political pressures. The frontline states' continued dependence, in varying degrees, on South Africa for industrial goods, investment, transport and communications links, food, and employment of migrant workers make them particularly vulnerable to South African pressure.

South Africa's war in Namibia and its aggression against the frontline states have the same goal. The Nationalist government has tried to restore the buffer that was lost by the collapse of Portuguese colonial rule and the Rhodesian regime by inducing or forcing the frontline states to withdraw political and material support for the ANC and other anti-apartheid forces in South Africa. An economic objective of reinforcing South Africa's economic dominance in the region is linked to this strategic goal. This, essentially, was what underlay the theme of the "constellation of states" proposed in 1978 by Prime Minister Botha. In Namibia the South Africans have fought to maintain their grip in an effort to ensure that the country becomes independent under a friendly government.

THE ILLEGAL OCCUPATION OF NAMIBIA

Under international law there is no ambiguity concerning South Africa's position in Namibia. In 1971 the International Court of Justice at the Hague, in an advisory opinion, held:

(1) that, the continued presence of South Africa in Namibia being illegal, South Africa is under obligation to withdraw its administration from Namibia immediately and thus put an end to its occupation of the territory;

(2) that States Members of the United Nations are under obligation to recognize the illegality of South Africa's presence in Namibia and the invalidity of its acts on behalf of or concerning Namibia and to refrain from any acts and in particular any dealings with the Government of South Africa implying any recognition of the legality of, or lending any support or assistance to, such presence and administration. . . .

It has been more than a decade since the court gave its opinion, yet South Africa's military grip on Namibia is now at its strongest. While engaging in protracted diplomatic contacts and negotiations, Pretoria has built up pro-South African political groups in Namibia, as well as local military and police forces and new administrative structures. While South Africa's strategic position in southern Africa is of prime consideration in the Namibian conflict, there are economic stakes as well.

Namibia is a large country with a population of about one and a half million, and whites, who for the most part retain South African citizenship, number fewer than 100,000. Its greatest asset is its mineral wealth. Namibia is the largest producer of gem diamonds in the world, and a monopoly of its diamond industry is held by Consolidated Diamond Mines, a subsidiary of the giant Anglo-American Corporation of South Africa. Namibia is also a principal African producer of base metals (such as lead, zinc, cadium, and lithium), with most of the production accounted for by the Tsumeb Corporation, which is jointly controlled by Newmont Mining Company and Amax, Inc., both American companies. Uranium has been the newest Namibian bonanza: the largest open-cast uranium mine in the world came into production at Rossing in 1976; by 1980 it was accounting for about one sixth of the West's production.[3] Rossing is controlled by Rio Tinto Zinc (RTZ), a British corporation, with South African and French interests holding other shares. The Namibian economy has slumped in recent years because of the decline in world diamond and metals prices as well as the war and political uncertainty, but its rich mineral resources are clearly a factor in the political equation.

The history of colonial rule in Namibia does not extend far back, but it has been marked by continual brutality. During the nineteenth century missionaries entered the territory and set up trading enterprises. In the 1880s Germany embarked on a belated campaign of colonization and moved into Namibia, then known as South West Africa. In 1904 the Hereros rose against the German colonists and were crushed: after a campaign of extermination, the destitute survivors were driven into the desert areas. The Namas rebelled, and were also defeated.

During World War I South African forces, on British orders, took over Namibia, and in 1920 the League of Nations conferred a mandate over Namibia to Britain, to be exercised by South Africa. Under the mandate South Africa assumed a "sacred trust" to promote the well-being and progress of the people of the territory. But under South African rule, more whites moved into South West Africa. They were allocated land in the rich farming and mining areas of the central plateau, whereas blacks were restricted in the main to tribal reserves or to urban "locations." Under the contract labor system men were recruited from the reserves to work in the mines, on farms, and at other jobs for local whites and the foreign mining companies. The system was rigid: breaking a contract was a criminal offense. With the onset of World War II the League of

Nations collapsed, and after the war South Africa refused to acknowledge that the newly formed United Nations had any authority over South West Africa. The former mandate was not included in the trusteeship system established by the United Nations. But in 1950 the International Court of Justice held that Namibia remained an international territory, that this status could not be unilaterally altered by South Africa, and that the United Nations should supervise South African administration of the territory. South Africa refused to accept the Court's opinion as binding and resisted United Nations efforts at implementation. The Nationalist government extended apartheid laws to Namibia and administered it as a virtual fifth province.

Meanwhile Namibian opposition to South African rule grew, and petitioners urged the United Nations to assume supervision of the territory and to reject South Africa's claims. In 1959 Africans in Windhoek, the capital, organized a peaceful resistance campaign against their forced removal to a new, segregated "location." South African police and troops opened fire on a protesting crowd, killing eleven people and wounding forty-four. A number of Namibian political groups were formed during this period. SWAPO, founded in 1960, emerged as the strongest, under the leadership of Herman ja Toivo and Sam Nujoma. South African rule moved into a new phase with the formal division of the country into eleven separate "homelands" for black Namibians on the basis of the 1964 Odendaal Commission report. Some 43 percent of the country, mainly the best agricultural and commercial areas, was reserved for whites. As had been the case before, South African rule in the African areas was enforced by chiefs and headmen appointed and paid by the government.

In 1966 the International Court of Justice narrowly decided that it could not rule on an appeal by Liberia and Ethiopia against South African rule over Namibia. After this decision the United Nations General Assembly voted to terminate South Africa's mandate and declared Namibia a direct responsibility of the United Nations. Further, it affirmed the right of the people of Namibia to self-determination and independence. The following year the United Nations established the Council for Namibia, aided by a commissioner, to secure the withdrawal of South Africa's administration and armed forces and to promote Namibian independence.

At this stage many Namibians felt that they could not rely on the United Nations alone to bring them independence. In September 1966 SWAPO launched its first guerrilla attacks against South African forces in northern Namibia. In 1967 South Africa brought thirty-seven Namibians, including SWAPO leader Herman ja Toivo, to trial in Pretoria under its newly legislated Terrorism Act. Observers for the International Commission of Jurists and the World Council of Churches cited evidence of torture of defendants and state witnesses. In 1968, thirty-four defendants were found guilty and nineteen were sentenced to life imprisonment on Robben Island. Herman ja Toivo told the court:

> We are Namibians and not South Africans. We do not now, and will not in the future recognize your right to govern us; to make laws for us in which we had no say; to treat our country as if it was your property and us as if you were our masters. . . .
>
> I am a loyal Namibian and could not betray my people to their enemies. I admit that I decided to assist those who had decided to take up arms. I know that the struggle will be long and bitter. I also know that my people will wage that struggle, whatever the cost. Only when we are granted our independence will the struggle stop.[4]

In the face of South Africa's continued intransigence the UN Security Council and the General Assembly declared South Africa's occupation of Namibia to be illegal, calling for its immediate withdrawal, and recognized the legitimacy of the Namibian struggle for freedom. In 1971, at the request of the Security Council, the International Court of Justice gave its advisory opinion, cited above, which declared South Africa's occupation of Namibia illegal.

SWAPO, in its bulletin (March-October 1971) *Namibia News*, assessed the Court's opinion and the course of the guerrilla struggle:

> It may seem futile to some, this never-ending battle on a small scale which has not liberated large areas within Namibia, nor led to irreplacable losses on the part of the enemy. However, what this war has done is of great value to us: it has reinforced the spirit of unity in Namibia. Our guerrillas are sheltered and fed by the civilian population to an ever-increasing degree. . . . Another result of our armed struggle is the insecurity it has created among the white population, in Namibia as well as South Africa. . . . This year the Opinion [of the International Court] was overwhelmingly in favor of the Namibian cause. Our question is: if our people had not, through the armed struggle, showed such a strong determination to fight for freedom, would the outcome. . . have been the same?. . . it is the armed struggle, which means heavy losses and great sacrifices from our people, which is the crucial and convincing indicator of the entire Namibian people's unbreakable determination to be free.

In December 1971 Namibia was paralyzed by a strike of contract workers. South African police reinforcements were brought into urban and mining areas, and when many of the workers demanded to be sent back to their homes in Ovamboland in the north, severe repression followed there. South African government army units were sent to Namibia, and the northern part of the country was sealed off. The workers did win modifications in the contract labor system, but more important, the strike was another powerful manifestation of national resistance to the conditions of South African occupation. By 1973 the South African Defence Force had taken control of counterinsurgency operations in northern Namibia with police units remaining in a supporting capacity.

After the International Court ruled, the Secretary General of the United Nations initiated contacts with South Africa on the Namibia question, but the Vorster government gave no clear indication that it was prepared to withdraw from the territory. In 1973 the General Assembly voted to recognize SWAPO as the authentic representative of the people of Namibia, and in 1974 the Council for Namibia enacted Decree No. 1, aimed at protecting Namibian resources and at putting pressure on South Africa and the companies mining in Namibia under South African rule. The decree holds that resources exploited in Namibia without the permission of the Council are liable to seizure and that those who disregard this clause will be liable for damage to the future independent government of the country. Protests developed in Britain on the issue after it was revealed in 1979 that uranium oxide from Namibia was being imported for use by Britain's Nuclear Fuels Corporation. Shipments of Namibian uranium were also reported to have gone to France and West Germany.

A new phase in the Namibian conflict developed when South Africa used Namibia as the base for its invasion of Angola in 1975-76. The MPLA victory bolstered SWAPO's position, and it was able to step up guerrilla operations in Namibia.

In 1977 five Western members of the Security Council (the United States, Britain, France, West Germany, and Canada) initiated contacts with South Africa that were aimed at arranging elections leading to independence in Namibia. The basis for the contacts by the Western five is Security Council Resolution 385 of 1976, which calls for free elections under United Nations supervision and control in a unified Namibia, steps by South Africa to withdraw its illegal administration, and other measures to transfer power to the people of Namibia. As South Africa continued to ignore United Nations authority over Namibia, the Western contact group drafted plans for the phased withdrawal of South African troops, the dispatch of a peacekeeping force, a UN-administered election (conducted by the South African authorities in Namibia) for a constituent assembly that would lead the country to independence. The Western plan was incorporated principally in Security Council Resolution 435 of 1978, and it remains the framework for continued negotiations on Namibia.

In coordination with the invasion of Angola, South Africa had initiated a military buildup in Namibia. Citizen Force and Commando reserve units units were called up, and these forces were not scaled down after the withdrawal from Angola. During this period it was estimated that the South Africa force in Namibia had reached almost 50,000 troops.[5] Several large military bases were constructed in the north, and a network of smaller ones, and it was announced in 1976 that a free-fire zone one kilometer wide would be cleared along the thousand-mile border with Angola and Zambia. This buildup did not succeed in stemming SWAPO's guerrillas, however. The call-ups of reserves for tours of "border duty" in Namibia continued, and in 1977 the initial period of national military service was extended from one to two years. Reports from South Africa gave varying views on the war, some minimizing the conflict and its demands on South African resources, and others pointing to its increasing intensity.

In October 1977, for example, a South African military correspondent concluded:

> In South West Africa, conflict is essentially of a low-level, protracted nature which the insurgents have geared for the purpose of wearing down the morale both at the front and at home . . . causing the public to question the reason why large bodies of men should be kept economically inactive in situations where very few of them ever make contact with the enemy.[6]

Other reports indicated a more intense conflict.[7] The director-general of the Defence Force told an audience in Johannesburg in the same month that South African forces were involved in about a hundred clashes a month with SWAPO. He added that Namibia was in "phase three" of a classic insurgency war; that is, open revolt, internal unrest, and open acts against the established system. SWAPO reported a large engagement in October 1977, when its forces attacked a South African base, killing 82 troops. South African accounts of the clash claimed 61 guerrillas killed with a loss of 6 South African men. The London *Times* reported in December 1977 that South African strategists believed that Ovamboland could be overrun in forty-eight hours if their forces were withdrawn.

The South African Defence White Paper of 1977 generally played down the magnitude of the war, but several comments indicated that there were strains: it noted the "considerable demands" placed on the medical services as a result of the Angola invasion and the war in Namibia. Two new military hospitals were reported under construction in South Africa, and medical care was described as "the most important single reason for the high morale" of South African forces. Shopping services for troops in Namibia could not always be made available because "it is naturally not advisable at times to move around certain parts of the operational areas away from established bases."[8]

Early in 1978 *Newsweek* magazine reported that South African bases were being attacked by SWAPO forces in units consisting of as many as sixty guerrillas using mortars and rockets. South African troops were said to be engaged in almost constant search-and-destroy operations, but were achieving a "kill ratio" of only two to one, considered inadequate in a guerrilla conflict.[9] South African journalist Gavin Shreve reported: "Soldiers and officers I spoke to . . . expressed a grudging respect for the growing efficiency of the SWAPO guerrillas. They admitted quite freely that the ordinary South African soldier doing a short tour of duty in the area was no match for the insurgents."[10] South African authorities discounted the report, saying they had no record of his having been allowed to visit the "operational area."

With white manpower resources limited, South Africa turned to the obvious solution—black troops. The first Namibian units were set up in the north largely on an ethnic basis: in 1974 the 31st Battalion, a San unit, was formed in West Caprivi. This was followed by the formation of similar battalions in Kavango, Ovamboland, and East Caprivi. In 1977 the 41st Battalion was formed on a multiethnic basis, including Damaras, Hereros, Tswanas, Namas, Rehobothers, and whites. Black units from South Africa were also being assigned to tours of combat duty in Namibia: elements of the Cape Corps Service Battalion (a Coloured unit) have served in Namibia since 1976, and in 1978 troops from the first African unit in the Defence Force, the 21st Battalion, were deployed in Namibia.

The escalation of the war and diplomatic pressures from the United Nations prompted Pretoria to begin belatedly to promote increased Namibian administrative autonomy and a local political alternative to SWAPO. After decades of enforcing white domination through racial and tribal segregation, Pretoria brought together the disparate groups it had fostered at the Turnhalle Conference in 1975. From this conference emerged the multracial Democratic Turnhalle Alliance party (DTA). The DTA failed to become the standard-bearer South Africa wanted it to be, and the reasons were soon evident. While the DTA was supposed to appeal to all Namibians, its leader was an Afrikaner farmer, Dirk Mudge. The political principle endorsed by the DTA is ethnic autonomy, which would essentially maintain the divisions set up by South Africa, leaving white power and privilege largely intact. In 1977 South Africa moved to give itself direct control over the political process in Namibia by appointing an administrator-general having the power to rule by decree. Pretoria also moved to annex Walvis Bay, Namibia's only deepwater port (which had not been included in the League of Nations mandate). It put the port under the jurisdiction of the Cape Province, a measure that was declared null and void by the United Nations General Assembly.

Events in 1978 demonstrated that South Africa was embarking on a "two-track" strategy: it continued negotiations with the Western contact group on a settlement, while at the same time it escalated the war and tried to build up pro-South African political forces in Namibia. This strategy allowed Pretoria to keep its options open: if conditions locally and internationally were favorable, they might allow a settlement that keeps SWAPO out of power. If not, South Africa would continue its occupation and the war. And if it is faced with stronger pressures for a settlement and an end to its occupation, South Africa has still maximized its political and economic influence over an independent Namibia in the future.

In April 1978 the Vorster government accepted the contact group's proposals for UN elections in Namibia, but soon afterward it launched a devastating airborne raid against a SWAPO camp at Cassinga in Angola. The South Africans claimed they were attacking SWAPO's main military headquarters, but representatives of the UN High Commissioner for Refugees and the World Health Organization confirmed that it was a refugee camp housing mainly women and children. More than six hundred Namibians were killed in the raid, and South Africa has continued to hold Namibians who were taken prisoner in that attack. But despite the Cassinga raid, SWAPO announced that it, too, would accept the Western plan.

At this point South Africa suddenly raised new objections. After Defence Minister Botha succeeded Vorster as prime minister, Pretoria carried out its own program of voter registration and then, in December 1978, its own Namibian elections for a national assembly. Not surprisingly, South Africa's chosen party, the DTA, won. Troops were used by the South Africans to promote registration, and DTA registration cards became the passport to jobs and pensions and medical treatment. In the elections black Namibians had to vote under the eyes of the South African-controlled tribal authorities and South African troops. And the ballot was not secret: voters had to put their registration numbers on the outside of the envelopes used for ballots.

The Muldergate scandal produced several stories concerning secret projects to promote the DTA. Two main Namibian newspapers were bought by a West German publisher prior to the elections, and their former editors charged that South African money had been used secretly in the takeovers. It was estimated that the DTA spent more than $5 million in the elections; it refused to reveal the source of its funds, but large amounts were said to have come from West Germany and South Africa.

The South African-run elections were widely condemned as a further defiance of UN authority over Namibia and as an illegitimate move to install the DTA in power. After the elections failed to gain international acceptance, South Africa announced again that it was ready to proceed with elections under the aegis of the United Nations. In early 1979, when UN personnel and UN armed forces were within weeks of arriving in Namibia to monitor a ceasefire between SWAPO and South African forces, South Africa suddenly pulled out of the plan. It claimed that the

United Nations had to monitor SWAPO forces in Angola and Zambia and that it had not agreed to having SWAPO forces at bases inside Namibia. With the breakdown of the election agreement, Pretoria moved to promote increased Namibian administrative autonomy with the DTA as the ruling party and to crush SWAPO's still legal political organization within the country. The new-formed national assembly, in which the DTA became the leading party, was given some legislative powers. More than fifty of SWAPO's leaders in Namibia were detained under new security measures, and a form of martial law, which had been in force in the northern war zone, was extended down to Windhoek, thus covering more than half the country. Identity documents were required of all inhabitants over the age of sixteen.

Pretoria also pushed moves by the DTA to start the repeal of racially discriminatory laws in Namibia, an essential political stance for the party in its efforts to gain legitimacy among the black majority in Namibia and internationally. Not surprisingly, racism has remained strong among whites in Namibia. The Namibian branch of South Africa's ruling National party has retained control over government bureaucracy in Namibia and resisted desegregation measures. Racist groups dedicated to maintaining white supremacy were also formed openly. One of them compiled a "death list" that included prominent black church leaders.

On the military front, South Africa unveiled a new counterinsurgency force, the Specialist Unit, which combines trackers with dogs, a mounted section, and troops with scrambler motorcycles. South Africa has also been using Civic Action programs in northern Namibia, in which men undergoing national military service provide a variety of civilian services when they are not needed to participate in military operations.

In September 1979 South Africa's programs of Namibianization took a major step when it was formally announced that a South West African Territorial Force (SWATF) was being formed. Preparations had been underway for two years. SWATF was based on the tribal battalions, and one multiracial unit, that the South Africans had already set up. Within the year the new Namibian military force was formally placed under the control of the South West African administration in Windhoek. Its budget, however, has been provided by South Africa, and South Africa's administrator-general has remained the executive authority in the territory. More important, the conduct of the war in Namibia remains completely in South African hands: the South African Defence Force is formally in charge of all areas where military operations are taking place. In addition, it was also indicated that South African troops could be seconded to the SWATF, an arrangement similar to that which had allowed South African widespread but discreet participation in the Rhodesian armed forces. Previously, only whites in Namibia had been required to undergo military service in the South African Defence Force;

blacks were recruited as volunteers. Then in January 1981 compulsory military service was extended to blacks, a move that not only drew considerable opposition, but also sent a wave of Namibian refugees of conscription age into neighboring frontline countries.

No official figures have been given for the size of the SWATF, but it is estimated to be about 20,000, half of them whites.[11] The formation of the SWATF represents a new phase in South Africa's defiance of international law, in that it is now compelling Namibians to fight Namibians. Moreover, the South African commander in Namibia specifically announced plans to increase the numbers of Namibians in the combat areas. Under the terms of the settlement proposed for the conflict, the SWATF, unlike the South African Defence Force, cannot be called on to withdraw from the country, even though it is dependent on the South Africans. A pro-South African military presence in Namibia is thus assured, even if the United Nations does assume control when a settlement is implemented.

At the end of 1979 it was announced that the South African Police units in Namibia would be restructured. The announcement foreshadowed the formation of the South West African Police in 1981. The SWAP remains linked to the South African Police, as training is conducted by the South Africans and many police operating in Namibia still belong to the South African Police. Some units of the police have played a major role for the South Africans in the war: they are heavily armed and operate with jeeps and helicopters and cooperate closely with the Defence Force in a paramilitary capacity. The South African Security Police has also been prominent in the conflict, operating in conjunction with the military to conduct political investigations, interrogations, and detentions. A quasi police unit, the Home Guards, operating in tribal areas, has been cited as playing an increasingly violent role. In 1979 an American observer from the Lutheran Church reported:

> There is no longer any semblance of order and the rule of law in Ovamboland. The 350,000 people are totally at the mercy of the arbitrary power of the South African Army and the Home Guards, comprised of young, black dropouts from Ovambo society . . . . These armed bands. . . are known for committing atrocities against their own people. South Africa now appears to be replacing some of its own units with Home Guards assembled from all parts of the country and from various tribes.[12]

THE INSTITUTIONALIZATION OF TORTURE

In defense of its role in Namibia South African officials have repeatedly claimed that their forces are in the country to protect Namibians from the violence and terrorism of SWAPO. It has been difficult for journalists to cover the conflict, since they have been able to visit the war zones in the north only with the permission of South African military authorities. However, there have been reports on the situation, such as that quoted above, which show that in response to the political support given SWAPO by Namibians, the South Africans have tried to enforce their authority through systematic violence and torture.

In 1976 the British *Guardian* published an account by Bill Anderson of torture by the South African forces in Namibia. Anderson, a South African soldier who had deserted in opposition to the war and sought asylum in Britain, described what happened to people who were suspected of links with SWAPO after they were picked up by counterinsurgency patrols:

> Torture began almost at once when the suspects were brought back. . . . Whenever the torture was going on either in battalion headquarters or in the open space behind, a crowd would gather to watch. I would not watch but every night I heard the screams. . . . The screams would go on until well after midnight. Officers boasted in front of me of using field telephones for electric shock torture to the genitals, nipples and ears. It was common knowledge that this was being done.
>
> I saw two suspects given water torture at the camp near Inahna. Their heads were stuffed into an ordinary iron bucket full of water and they were held under until they ceased to struggle. It lasted a good minute. I saw one large suspect who struggled so that five men had to hold him into the bucket.[13]

In June 1976 Anderson's battalian participated in a large-scale sweep. Orders were to kill people who tried to run away and bring in every male over the age of puberty. Anderson reported that about one thousand men were detained in the sweep, two hundred to three hundred by his unit: "All the arrested men were beaten, tortured and interrogated, without exception." Later, his unit was told that of the one thousand detained, forty were to be charged with "terrorism" offenses.

The South African Defence Force denied the *Guardian* report, but withdrew an offer that would permit an on-the-spot investigation when the paper asked for guarantees of its autonomy in such an undertaking.

In 1977 a group of lawyers in Namibia assembled sworn statements by twelve persons describing their torture at Oshakati Police Headquarters. These were subsequently included in a booklet, *Torture— A Cancer in Our Society;* published in Namibia and immediately banned by the South African authorities. The booklet concludes that "institutionalized torture. . . is proliferating in Namibia." It continues:

Institutionalized torture means that this practice is not casual or occasional, but that it is a generalized practice, so that people who are arrested under particular circumstances face a considerable probability that they will be tortured.

This is the case in this country, at least for people arrested under the security laws, in particular the Terrorism Act, either by the police or the South African Defence Force.

But torture is not only applied to political suspects, but also to those suspected of an ordinary misdeed, like minor theft.[14]

It is noted as well that complaints about torture at the hands of the South African authorities are not a new concern, but go back to the first appeal made to the South African Police in Ovamboland in 1967 by leaders of the Lutheran, Catholic, and Anglican churches there.

The sworn statements presented in the booklet were made by young men of school age, young women, a Lutheran pastor, and several older men, including a village headman aged fifty-one. The tortures described include beatings, water torture, and electric shocks.

In June 1979 Dr. Paul Wee, general secretary of Lutheran World Ministries in the United States, visited Ovamboland, the main war zone in northern Namibia, and reported:

> Although Namibia has been experiencing a gradual escalation of terror activities over the past two decades, creating a vicious circle which can only be broken by a political settlement, there is no doubt that the primary source of this escalation is the South African Army. The evidence of South African Army brutality among all segments of the population is so overwhelming, pervasive and capable of documentation that it makes a mockery of the South African Government's claim to be "responding to the request of the Ovambo people for protection."
>
> Some farmers, both black and white, have been subjected to violence by SWAPO units, causing a massive build-up of armaments in the homes of whites in Windhoek, Tsumeb, and other towns, but such activities are dwarfed by the constant, daily violence of the army. It is the South African Army together with units of the Home Guards which detain and beat students, hospital personnel and pastors, applying sand and electric shock torture to those accused of aiding SWAPO. It is these who are responsible for harassing, intimidating, blackmailing and bribing the population. It is these units which steal anything of value from the homes they raid. In the first instance, it is they who deserve the name "terrorists."[15]

While the Reagan administration pushed for a settlement on the diplomatic front, reports from Namibia indicate that the brutality of the South African forces and their Namibian recruits was continuing.[16]

A delegation of the South African Bishops' Conference stated after a trip to Namibia in September 1981:

> Reports of what occurs in the operational area indicate that it is commonly accepted that in searching out SWAPO guerrillas the Security Forces stop at nothing to force information out of the people. They break into homes, beat up residents, shoot people, steal and kill cattle and often pillage stores and tea rooms. When the tracks of SWAPO guerrillas are discovered by the Security Forces the local people are in danger. Harsh measures are intensified. People are blindfolded, taken from their homes and left beaten up and even dead by the roadside. Women are often raped.

A group from the British Council of Churches reported similar findings after a visit to Namibia in November 1981:

> The Security Forces maintain a region of arbitrary terror against which the local people have now no redress. . . . Church leaders told us that even when their members were willing to be indentified as complaining about Security Force atrocities there was no guarantee that they would be properly heard. . . . Again and again we were told, "These people are supposed to be protecting us. Against whom do we need to be protected? Would to God someone would protect us against these co-called protectors!"

The report also mentions that the South African forces drag the corpses of alleged "terrorists" behind their vehicles and exhibit them to their parents, to villagers, and even to young children in school.

Anglican Bishop Desmond Tutu, general secretary of the South African Council of Churches, visited Namibia in February 1982 and also cited the brutality of the South African forces against the local inhabitants, mentioning "the burning down of homes, the harassing and detaining of people, their torturing of them, raping women, killing them, laying landmines which they wanted people to believe was the work of SWAPO."

THE ESCALATING CONFLICT

At the end of 1979 international attention shifted to the settlement of the Rhodesian conflict. The results of the Zimbabwe elections in April 1980 were a blow to the South Africans. Guerrilla leader Robert Mugabe was elected as Zimbabwe's first prime minister, and the clear implication was that SWAPO and Sam Nujoma could win in the same manner if there was a settlement and elections in Namibia. Thereafter, diplomatic efforts toward a settlement came to a virtual standstill. In June 1980

South Africa launched its largest attack of the conflict—Operation Smo-keshell—one hundred miles into southern Angola. The three thousand ground and airborne troops clashed with Angolan forces, killed several hundred Angolan civilians, and did considerable economic damage. This attack heralded a new stage in the war, with the South African increas-ingly carrying the conflict into southern Angola and more openly at-tacking Angolans and the economic infrastructure of the region. The intrusions ranged from across-the-border raids by ground and helicop-ter-borne troops and air strikes and aerial reconnnaisance, to large-scale invasions. There has also been continuing South African support for UNITA (the National Union for the Total Independence of Angola), the movement which South Africa had backed in its original invasion and which has carried out sabotage and terror attacks in southeastern and central Angola.

In December 1980 the British *Guardian* published an account of a British mercenary, Trevor Edwards, who had fought with the Rhodesian forces and then gone to fight for the South Africans in Namibia.[17] Edwards was assigned to the 32nd "Buffalo" Battalion, which was made up mainly of Angolans led by foreign mercenaries. During the months Edwards fought with the battalion it operated almost entirely within Angola, carrying out search-and-destroy operations aimed at SWAPO and the local Angolan population. By Edwards's account, he left the battalion when he could no longer stomach the wanton killing and torture of civilians.

Although the South Africans had been claiming that the SWATF they were creating would be able to assume an increasing role in the war and even be able to defeat SWAPO on its own, the South African forces were actually being systematically strengthened, and the infrastructure of military bases, large and small, airfields, and roads was expanded. By early 1981 some Western sources agreed with SWAPO's charges that put the number of South African forces in Namibia at 100,000. With the United States elections over and Reagan elected, the Botha government was under less immediate international pressure to withdraw from Na-mibia. This relaxation was seen in talks at Geneva in January 1981: the South Africans demanded the inclusion of the DTA and other "internal" Namibian parties in the talks, which were soon stalemated. Dirk Mudge, the white leader of the DTA, said at Geneva that he would need up to two years before his party would be able to face SWAPO in a Namibian election.[18] This was a tacit admission that the South African side wanted the war to continue, but far more significant, it was an acknowledgment of SWAPO's political strength at a time when South Africa's military occupation was at its height.

It was clear that the South African escalation of the war had brought it no closer to military victory. South African commanders have told the press that they are operating in terms of "body counts." They claimed they killed 1,500 guerrillas in 1981 and set themselves the same goal in 1982, with a "quota" of 120 guerrillas a month.[19] There there is no way to verify such claims or to see whether the soldiers reporting the "bodies" distinguish between guerrillas and civilians, Namibian and Angolan. With SWAPO forces estimated at 7,000 to 8,000 it would appear that not even the most optimistic South African military leader could predict an early victory. South Africa provides no official figures on its own losses, but in 1980 casualties were unofficially put at about one hundred dead and six hundred to seven hundred wounded. Official notifications to families of soldiers rarely describe the circumstances of the deaths; moreover, many people believe that multiple casualties in any single engagement are dissembled as the announcements are staggered over a period of time. This serves to conceal the fact that SWAPO guerrillas have scored successes.[20]

Africa Now (May 1983) presented a report on the Namibia war by an unnamed informant interviewed by South African war resisters in London. The man, whose story was uncorroborated, claimed to be serving in a South African "medical intelligence unit" in Namibia. Captured SWAPO guerrillas and suspected SWAPO members, including women, were being tortured by the South African forces, he said. He charged that doctors participated in the torture, which included electric shocks and the use of various drugs. He also alleged that South African casualties were underreported, and his estimate indicated at least four hundred combat deaths and two hundred accidental deaths in 1981.

Despite the raids into Angola, border patrols, and heavy repression in northern Namibia, SWAPO attacks have continued. The guerrillas have been able to mine roads, mount ambushes, sabotage power lines and other installations, and carry out attacks on South African bases. On occasion they have infiltrated through the South African forces concentrated in the northern tribal areas and carried out attacks in the white farming areas to the south. While SWAPO cannot directly inflict military defeat on the South African military machine, they have, in classic guerrilla fashion, been able to raise the cost to South Africa of continued occupation of their country.

Once the openly friendly Reagan administration had taken office in 1981, the South African military command in Namibia indicated a change in tactics. Their forces would continue to strike into Angola in reaction to SWAPO attacks, but they would also, as a matter of policy, strike preemptively, even if this meant direct conflict with Angolan government forces. In August 1981 the South Africans launched Operation Protea, by far the largest of the war; mechanized columns with air support moved across the border from Ovamboland and struck as far as one hundred fifty miles into Kunene province. In the invasion, which lasted for several weeks, virtually the entire province came under South African control. Ngiva, the capital, and other towns were taken. South African ground and helicopter-borne forces struck in neighboring provinces as well. Angola charged that the South Africans had mobilized 45,000 troops along the Namibian border and that some 15,000 troops had taken part in the invasion, supported by tanks, armored cars, armored personnel carriers, 155-mm heavy artillery, helicopters, and fighter-bombers. The South Africans claimed to have killed a thousand SWAPO and Angolan troops and destroyed $200 million in war materiel, with a loss of ten of their own men. The UN Security Council convened to consider the invasion, but no action was taken, as the United States cast the sole veto against a resolution condemning South Africa.

This American reaction was an example of the "constructive engagement" policy promoted by Chester Crocker, Reagan's assistant secretary of state for African affairs. A Namibia settlement has been a focus of the Reagan policies, and in pursuit of this goal the Americans have offered Pretoria various concessions, such as relaxation in American enforcement of the United Nations arms embargo. The United States has demanded that a Namibian settlement should be linked with the withdrawal of the 15,000 Cuban troops in Angola, which have remained since the original South African invasion at the request of the MPLA to deter any major South African assault. The Namibia war has revealed the extent of South Africa's military power, built up despite the arms embargo, including Mirage fighter-bombers, helicopters, tanks, armored cars, heavy artillery and electronic equipment and transport vehicles of many types. Despite South African claims of near self-sufficiency, its arms buildup depended on supplies from Western sources, and this dependence continues in many areas. In addition, South Africa's highly mechanized forces are totally dependent on imports for supplies of gasoline and oil. South Africa has no oil of its own, and so, despite its multibillion-dollar oil-from-coal projects, it remains vulnerable to an oil embargo.

Under international law there are ample grounds, given the continued occupation of Namibia and attacks on Angola, for the UN Security Council to strengthen the arms embargo and to impose an oil embargo and stringent economic sanctions on South Africa. However, the approach of the Reagan administration has been to allow South Africa to use its military power to punish SWAPO and Angola. Other large-scale South African attacks in Angola have followed Operation Protea: in November 1981, March 1982, and August 1982.

Although the Reagan administration has been predicting that a Namibia settlement could be quickly achieved through its friendly approach to South Africa, the timetable has continued to be pushed back while negotiations and discussions go on. SWAPO has agreed to guarantees on property rights and civil liberties and to monitoring of its guerrilla forces at camps in Angola and Zambia. But both SWAPO and the front-line states opposed a voting plan put forward by the United States. Under this plan, which South Africa has accepted, each vote for representatives to a constituent assembly would be counted twice: proportionally with respect to the total vote gained by the different parties, and directly within the voting districts to effect the election of the top vote-getters. The plan was tabled in July 1982, and it was agreed that the settlement would use one or the other system of voting. For its part, South Africa dropped a long-standing objection that the United Nations should not supervise the elections. (The elections would, in any case, be conducted by South African officials—a major concession by the United Nations and SWAPO.)

In June 1982 South Africa formally raised the demand that Cuban troops be withdrawn from Angola as a condition for a settlement. This has become a new sticking point in the negotiations. Angola and Cuba have long insisted that Cuban troops could be withdrawn only when the threat of South African attack has ended, and this was reiterated in a formal joint statement in February 1982. There is, of course, no legal link between the question of South Africa's occupation of Namibia and the presence of Cuban forces in Angola. South Africa is under legal obligation to end its occupation of Namibia with no preconditions, and it has stood in defiance of international law and the world community on this issue since the revocation of its mandate by the United Nations General Assembly in 1966, an action confirmed by the World Court in 1971. The Cubans, on the other hand, are in Angola by invitation of a sovereign government. South African escalation has raised the war in Namibia and aggression against Angola to a peak. Pretoria has won concessions and inflicted heavy damage on Angola. But it has failed to defeat SWAPO militarily or politically, and the war has put military and economic strains on South Africa and deepened its international isolation. The question remains: Will the Botha government accept a settlement or continue its diplomatic delays and the war?

AGGRESSION AGAINST ANGOLA

Although Angola's southern border lies more than five hundred miles to the north of the nearest South African territory, Pretoria has, since 1975, invaded Angola and carried out a systematic campaign of aggression and destabilization launched from Namibia. In 1982 the Angolan government charged that South African forces had taken over an arc of territory extending 150 miles into southern Angola and set up two bases there. An article in the *New York Times* (July 19, 1982) said that Angola could be viewed as a critical piece on the chessboard of African politics as a "principal warrior in black Africa's campaign against white minority domination in South Africa" and because of its key role in supporting SWAPO's guerrilla war against the South African forces in Namibia. It has therefore emerged as South Africa's major foe. The conflict in Angola also casts the shadow of the Cold War over southern Africa, since the Marxist MPLA-Workers party government has been shielded from wider South African attacks by Cuban troops and its ties to the Soviet Union. The Reagan administration has charged that the Cuban forces represent illegitimate Soviet interference in the region and has demanded their withdrawal as a condition for United States recognition and for a settlement in Namibia. In addition, Angola has a geographically strategic position on the west coast of south-central Africa. It has a long border with mineral-rich Zaire and important resources of its own, including oil, diamonds, and iron ore.

Although South African military involvement in Angola goes back to the sixties, when it cooperated with the Portuguese colonial forces in the surveillance of the guerrillas, the present period of conflict began when the coup in Portugal in 1974 opened the way to Angolan independence. The United States and South Africa cooperated in backing the forces of the FNLA (National Front for the Liberation of Angola) and UNITA in an effort to defeat the MPLA. The MPLA had been the most effective movement in fighting the Portuguese. Although all the movements had regional ethnic roots, the MPLA was widely seen as the only one capable of forming an effective national government. John Stockwell, the head of the CIA's Angola task force at the time, has described the direction of United States policy, as it was guided by Henry Kissinger, in his book *In Search of Enemies*: "Clearly," he states, "the United States wanted this war."[21] While the United States was claiming to support cooperation between the three movements, it was actually doing the opposite. The Americans felt that the MPLA would become dominant in peaceful political competition among the movements. Through covert CIA action it set out to bolster the FNLA and UNITA militarily and politically so they could prevail over the MPLA. Stockwell spells out how the United States and South Africa initiated the pattern of military escalation in Angola, with the MPLA turning in response to Cuba and the Soviets for aid.

With Angolan independence scheduled by the new Portuguese government for November 1975, the FNLA attacked the MPLA in Luanda, the capital, nine months before, in February, but the MPLA countered the FNLA move and MPLA was able to win a loose control of much of the country in the following months, despite the initial allotment of $14 million in CIA aid to FNLA-UNITA and the intervention of Zairian forces as well. At this point, the South Africans began to supply arms and training to UNITA and FNLA forces at a base in northern Namibia. Then, in mid-October, South African forces invaded Angola: the column included 50 armored cars, artillery, and 1,000 troops. The column linked up with 1,000 UNITA men. Another 2,000 South African troops provided logistical support from the border; fuel and supplies for the column were provided by Lockheed Hercules C-130 transport planes and trucks, while light planes and helicopters gave additional logistical aid. South African Prime Minister Vorster decided to limit the size of the invading force, and chose not to use tanks or fighter-bomber aircraft. The South Africans wore Portuguese uniforms and were told to say they were mercenaries. South Africa also supplied forty military advisors to operate with UNITA forces in central Angola. While CIA links with the South Africans were not formalized, according to Stockwell, in practice "coordination was effected at all levels." Gen. van den Bergh, head of the South African Bureau of State Security, visited Washington twice during the conflict and met secretly with James Potts, chief of the CIA's Africa Division, which was overseeing the secret war.[22]

The South Africans, the CIA, and their FNLA-UNITA allies almost defeated the MPLA. The first South African UNITA column drove to the coast toward Luanda, capturing key towns as it went, while another column went into action with UNITA in west-central Angola. But more Cuban and Soviet aid began arriving for the MPLA. To the north the CIA-backed FNLA forces, aided by Zairian troops, launched their final assault on Luanda on November 11, 1975, the day of Angolan independence, as the MPLA was proclaiming the Peoples Republic of Angola in the capital. For the assault the South Africans supplied the FNLA with 5.5-inch artillery crewed by South Africans. The FNLA attack was repulsed only twelve miles from Luanda by a devastating rocket barrage by MPLA-Cuban forces. The South African coastal column continued to push toward Luanda, but it was checked a little more than one hundred miles from the capital, in mid-November.

The South African forces remained in west-central Angola, bringing in reinforcements and also sending a column to the east to control the Benguela railroad, while President Ford authorized the final increment of available CIA funds (which totaled $31.7 million for the secret war) for more arms and mercenary recruitment. But the CIA and South African secrecy unraveled. Captured South African soldiers were shown by the MPLA to journalists and to observers from the Organization of African Unity. The Senate Foreign Relations Committee cut through the cloud of CIA-generated propaganda and disclosed the clandestine CIA role. The U.S. Congress barred the use of United States funds in Angola, while the CIA continued to try to keep the war going. The South Africans, who were to spend $150 million on the Angola invasion, were politically exposed and isolated. Cuba and the USSR brought in substantial new aid for the MPLA and could justifiably say that they were responding to aggression by South Africa, the CIA, mercenaries, and Zaire. By the end of January 1976 the South African forces were in retreat, and they withdrew into Namibia on March 27.

The invasion had ended in a costly defeat for South Africa. While the Defence Force had not committed its full power, the failure nonetheless tarnished the myth of white invincibility. Vorster's efforts at diplomatic "detente" with conservative African states were undone, and South Africa's international isolation was deepened. The enthusiastic cooperation of the CIA and South Africa had led not to a public embrace and an official alliance with the United States, but to a Congressional shutdown of Kissinger's secret war. South Africa had not been able to install a dependent FNLA-UNITA in Angola. Now it had to contend with an MPLA government that was prepared to support SWAPO and the cause of southern African liberation.

The escalating war in Namibia after the defeat of the South African invasion of Angola was marked by continuing South African strikes in Angola. They have varied from across-the-border raids and reconnaissance overflights to major attacks. A key part of the South African strategy has also been continued support for UNITA. Because of the South African attacks and the threat of another large-scale invasion, Cuba has maintained a force of 15,000 to 20,000 troops in Angola at the request of the MPLA government. Stationed away from areas of conflict, they have been used to train Angolan forces and to guard the vital oil fields at Cabinda. Western diplomats have estimated that Angola has paid $50 million annually in overseas allowances for the Cuban troops and that $120 million a year is spent on Soviet arms.[23]

Ironically, Angola has been able to afford these outlays because of the earnings from oil exports from the province of Cabinda, where the Angolan government has continued the concessions originally granted by Portugal to Gulf Oil and Texaco. But despite the successful Angolan dealings with the American multinationals and the widely reported remark by Andrew Young, American ambassador to the United Nations under President Carter, that the Cubans were a "stabilizing force" in Angola, the Carter administration refused to recognize the MPLA government because of the Cuban presence. This was clearly traceable in part to wariness of a rightwing backlash domestically, though Carter officials probably were also hoping to appease South Africa and secure its cooperation on settlements in Namibia and Rhodesia. In Namibia, the result was instead to encourage South African intransigence and attacks on Angola.

The first large-scale South African attack on Angola after its invasion was the airborne assault on the SWAPO refugee camp at Cassinga, 150 miles north of the Namibian border, in May 1978. Mirage fighter-bombers strafed and bombed the camp, and paratroopers then overwhelmed the camp's defensive unit, killed fleeing inhabitants, and wrecked the camp's facilities. The Angolan government put the death toll at 612 Namibians, including 298 children, and 15 Angolans, with 689 wounded.[24] In coordination with the attack, South African forces also raided three Angolan towns near the Namibian border.

After the Cassinga attack, South Africa continued regular raids into Angola. Angolan President Agostinho Neto told U.S. Senator George McGovern in December 1978, "We are being attacked daily by the South Africans." If the attacks ceased, he said, there would be no need for the aid of Cuban troops.[25] The attacks included those by South African-backed UNITA, which was still operating in the central and southeastern areas of the country. A British journalist who visited UNITA forces during this period reported that they were in large part equipped with South African army uniforms and that their equipment, fuel, and food were being supplied by South Africa.[26] In July 1979, at the request of the Security Council, Angola submitted to the United Nations a listing of 193 South African acts of aggression dating from March 1976, ranging from violations of airspace and border provocations to ground attacks and bombings, with a total of 1,383 people killed and 1,915 wounded.

While the South African government continued stalling in the negotiations on Namibia with the Western contact group, it proceeded with its strikes into Angola. These included two major attacks, Operation Smokeshell in 1980 and Operation Protea in 1981. In addition to these large-scale attacks, Pretoria was also carrying out a "secret war" against the civilian infrastructure of the Angolan border region in an attempt to eliminate support for SWAPO. This was described by the British mercenary Trevor Edwards: "Our main job is to take an area and clear it. We sweep through it and we kill everything in front of us, cattle, goats, people, everything. We are out to stop SWAPO and we stop them getting into villages for food and water." He also described the torture of Angolans for information: "Sometimes we take the locals for questioning. It's rough. We just beat them, cut them, burn them. As soon as we're finished with them, we kill them." A twelve year-old boy was tied up to make his mother talk: "Then we played water polo with him, put him in this kind of dam and pushed him about, let him sink. Every so often we took him out. He wouldn't cry. He just wet himself. The mother didn't tell us anything. In the end we just left him in the water and he drowned."[27]

The South Africans used Edward's 32nd Battalion to capture the town of Savate, forty miles inside Angola, where Angolan government soldiers were based. After the battle a white South African intelligence officer and a black soldier claimed the town for UNITA. Edwards commented, "The point is that UNITA are a lot of crap. They hang around in the south-east where their tribe is and they can probably defend themselves, but they can't go out and take somewhere like Savate. We do it for them because it improves their bargaining position, gives them more talking power."

In February 1981 Angola hosted a meeting of an International Commission of Inquiry organized to investigate the extent of South African aggression against Angola.[28] The commission, headed by Sean MacBride, former Irish foreign minister and United Nations commissioner for Namibia, included former United States Attorney General Ramsey Clark among its members. The Angolan government reported that in the eighteen months from June 1979 through December 1980 there had been an intensification of South African attacks to the point where it was waging an undeclared war: 400 civilians and 85 Angolan soldiers had been killed in this period, and damages to the country from the time of the 1975 invasion were put at $7 billion. The Angolan military told the commission that while their forces could resist South African ground forces, the South African air force gave them superiority in their attacks against military and civilian targets. The brunt of the South African attacks fell in an arc of territory across the border from Ovamboland, with other raids sometimes hitting at more distant targets, such as the provincial capital Lubango, whose industrial area was badly damaged by a South African bombing in 1979. The commission also heard testimony from a former FNLA mercenary who had fought with the South African 32nd Battalion in operations in Angola before deserting to the Angolan side.

Under the Reagan administration, UNITA has been accorded high stature in the United States. UNITA leader Jonas Savimbi met with Secretary of State Haig and other high officials.[29] The Reagan administration's position on Angola goes beyond linking a South African military withdrawal from Namibia to a withdrawal of Cuban forces from Angola: it has also called for Angolan government reconciliation with UNITA as a condition for American recognition. South African support for UNITA has also been increased, and large areas of central Angola are reported to be unsafe for travel by road. Late in 1981 saboteurs attacked a strategic Angolan oil refinery in Luanda. UNITA claimed credit for the sabotage, but the Angolan government showed reporters and diplomatic observers grisly evidence to support their charge that South Africans were involved: found at the scene, they said, were the severed foot and a piece of scalp from the body of a white person.

Since the Reagan administration came into office, South African aggression against Angola has been increasing. The United States veto power in the UN Security Council has protected Pretoria from economic sanctions and other forms of concrete action by the international community. By July 1982 the Western contact group, led by U.S. Assistant

Secretary of State for African Affairs Chester Crocker, was claiming that intensive discussions with the South Africans and SWAPO had narrowed the ground on key issues and that a settlement was in the wind. Meanwhile, South African military actions have graduated from the secret war of the 32nd Battalion, which wore unmarked uniforms, carried Soviet weapons, and was made up of Angolan and European mercenaries, to the occupation and control of Angola's central border region by regular army forces.

While the Reagan envoys appear to be trying to get the settlement machinery "in gear" so that all parties will have to move ahead, the South Africans remain poised, ready for further escalation in Angola.

INTERVENTION IN THE RHODESIAN WAR

On April 18, 1980, the British colony of Southern Rhodesia became independent Zimbabwe. Robert Mugabe, who had long been described in South African and conservative circles in the West as a Communist terrorist, was chosen as Zimbabwe's first prime minister when his party, the Zimbabwe African National Union-Patriotic Front (ZANU-PF), gained a majority in the British-run parliamentary elections. ZANU-PF had played the leading role in the guerrilla war against the Rhodesian regime of Ian Smith. Zimbabwean independence came in the shadow of the threat of invasion by South Africa, and the Mugabe government still faces clandestine South African attacks and economic pressures. South African military and economic support sustained the illegal white-minority Rhodesian regime from its unilateral declaration of independence from Britain, in 1965, until December 1979, when, with guerrilla activity by the Patriotic Front spread through much of the country, the cease-fire for the Lancaster House settlement for elections and independence under British authority was signed.

The war for African freedom from minority rule cost more than 25,000 lives. Some 750,000 Africans in rural areas had been forced into strategic hamlets, 250,000 had fled to crowded urban townships, and another 250,000 had left the country as refugees. A quarter of the African population of Southern Rhodesia, seven million in all, was reported to be suffering from severe malnutrition when the war ended.[30] The heritage of white conquest and white rule remains strong in independent Zimbabwe. Its economy remains dominated by South African, British, and American interests, and a few thousand white farmers along with corporate investors with large estates account for a significant part of the agricultural production. Almost 70 percent of the country's capital stock was owned or controlled by foreign corporations, according to a study at the time of independence.[31]

South Africa was involved in the Rhodesian conflict virtually from the start. As early as 1967 South African paramilitary police with armored cars, helicopters, and spotter planes were sent to aid the Smith regime when the ANC of South Africa had briefly joined with the Zimbabwe African Peoples Union (ZAPU) in sending guerrillas into the country. South Africa continued to send its police forces to Rhodesia for counterinsurgency duty until 1975, when they were withdrawn as part of a diplomatic initiative. However, they left their equipment behind. Soon after, Pretoria was supplying helicopter pilots and technicians, military officers, and aid in the construction of five new military airfields under a secret program code-named Operation Polo. It was also revealed that South Africa had paid 50 percent of the Rhodesian defense budget for the 1975-76 year.[32] Even more significant than direct military support was South Africa's economic lifeline to Rhodesia, for South Africa refused to enforce the comprehensive economic sanctions voted by the Security Council against the regime at the request of Britain. South Africa was land-locked Rhodesia's largest trading partner, and South African companies functioned as middlemen for trade of all kinds, including arms, with third countries. Like South Africa, Rhodesia has no oil reserves, making petroleum products a critical commodity for its economy and military forces. The South African subsidiaries of British Petroleum and Shell (British), Caltex and Mobil (American), and Total (French) continued to supply petroleum products to Rhodesia, with the complicity of their parent companies and their governments.[33]

South African support for the Rhodesian regime was not unconditional, however. Conspicuous involvement in the conflict carried risks, and the long-term prospects for control by the white minority (only four percent of the population) were dim. Many Afrikaners, including Vorster and van den Bergh, had little sympathy for white Rhodesians, who had voted in 1922 to become a self-governing British colony rather than to join with South Africa. Therefore the Vorster government did put pressure on Smith at several points to move toward a settlement by holding up trade or aid. Nevertheless, when the Carter administration and the Callahan Labour government in Britain pressed for a settlement, Vorster dug in his heels, and in 1977-78 more arms from Western and South African sources began to appear in Rhodesia. These included Mirage III fighter-bombers, Alouette helicopters, Aermacchi Impala II strike planes, and Augusta Bell AB 205 "Huey" helicopters, which were used in attacks against Zambia and Mozambique as well as in the escalating conflict in Rhodesia. The Rhodesian military had previously been able to bring in South African soldiers as mercenaries by signing them up at bases in South Africa. But by early 1978 it was reported that the South African military was secretly deploying troop in southern Rhodesia from bases in South Africa and had other units working directly with Rhodesian forces.[34]

As guerrillas of the Patriotic Front alliance of ZANU and ZAPU became increasingly effective, in 1978 the Smith regime made an "internal settlement" with a group of black leaders, notably Bishop Abel Muzorewa, for black participation in the government. The agreement, however, left power in white hands. According to Eschel Rhoodie, the creator of the Information Department's propaganda war, South Africa channeled almost $1 million to Muzorewa's political party in a deal with an official of Allegany Ludlam Industries. This American corporation was the largest chromium mining concern in southern Africa and had interests in both Rhodesia and South Africa. Both the company and Muzorewa denied Rhoodie's charges.[35]

An important shift in South African policy came with the retirement of Vorster and the takeover by Defense Minister Pieter Botha as prime minister. The *New York Times* reported that Botha's close associate, Defence Force chief Magnus Malan, was "responsible for putting South African steel behind the Rhodesian defense effort," and that despite the United Nations sanctions "spare parts, aircraft, and sophisticated weapons became more available, on better terms, soon after Mr. Vorster was gone."[36] Vorster had been ready to back a Rhodesian settlement that would bring blacks into the government, but he wanted the South African role in diplomatic and military terms to be inconspicuous, in the fear that if Pretoria's involvement was too overt, the African and Western response would be negative.

In contrast, Botha and his generals felt that South Africa had to use its military power more openly for it to be credible, thus they gave strong backing to Bishop Muzorewa in the hope that a black leader in Rhodesia would legitimate South African military aid. When the Rhodesian regime held its own "internal" elections in April 1979, Bishop Muzorewa won easily. South Africa gave extensive logistic support for the elections, and reportedly left many aircraft and vehicles behind afterward. South African pilots were reported to be flying aircraft for intensified operation by Rhodesia's elite reaction-force troops, and there were major Rhodesian raids, supported by South Africa, against the Patriotic Front in Mozambique and Zambia. Prime Minister Botha announced his plan for a "constellation" of southern African states, a military-economic alliance that would include the Bantustans and independent African countries, with white South Africa as the central power. Rhodesia, with Bishop Muzorewa as its titular leader, was clearly slated to become a charter member of the constellation. A "senior Rhodesian official" claimed that South Africa had offered to back Muzorewa "to the hilt" with massive aid that would "radically alter the balance of the guerrilla war."[37]

Rhodesia needed aid urgently: the war was costing $1.5 million a day, and the government was virtually bankrupt. Bishop Muzorewa made it clear that he was ready to seek South African support and soon traveled there to meet with Botha. The key problem was political, however: to win diplomatic recognition from the new Thatcher government in Britain and from the Carter administration. But with power in Rhodesia still obviously in white hands, the country heavily dependent on South Africa, and the Patriotic Front guerrillas as strong as ever, Britain and the United States backed off. Under pressure from African and Commonwealth countries, Britain convened settlement talks at Lancaster House in September 1979, bringing the Muzorewa regime and the Patriotic Front to the table. The talks were punctuated by heaviest raids of the war. The Rhodesians attacked in Mozambique and Zambia, and South Africa openly threatened that it would be forced to intervene in Rhodesia. As the talks reached the final phase, Botha suddenly announced that South African forces were stationed inside Rhodesia on the border. Once the settlement was signed and election preparations underway, South Africa was finally forced to withdraw these troops. The British did nothing, however, to remove those South Africans who were already integrated into the Rhodesian military and police ranks. There were varying reports on the extent of South African funding for Rhodesia, but they all pointed to the same dependence: the *New York Times* put it at "more than 40 percent of the $2 million per day cost of the war"; the *Guardian* said it had reached the level of $67 million per month, while *Le Monde Diplomatique* stated that in 1979 Rhodesia had to borrow $580 million from South Africa, representing 16 percent of its GNP for the year.[38]

As the elections took place, South African leaders again stated that they were ready to intervene and mobilized a sizable force near the border. But the very magnitude of the ZANU-PF victory, together with Robert Mugabe's commitment to a moderate political course (he reportedly met on his initiative with South African Foreign Minister Botha and General Malan in Mozambique), brought South African restraint. The elections and Zimbabwean independence were an extraordinary triumph for the Patriotic Front, particularly ZANU-PF's guerrilla strategy, and a major political and military setback for Pretoria.

Even before Zimbabwean independence Robert Mugabe joined with the leaders of nine other southern African countries (Angola, Mozambique, Zambia, Zaire, Tanzania, Botswana, Malawi, Lesotho, and Swaziland) to form the Southern African Development Coordination Conference (SADCC). The goal of this diverse grouping (Malawi alone among African states has had diplomatic relations with Pretoria; and Lesotho and Swaziland are surrounded by South African territory) is to reorient regional trade, transport, and communications in order to lessen dependence on South Africa. Nevertheless, Robert Mugabe stressed that he would not seek direct confrontation with South Africa: like Mozambique, he pledged moral and diplomatic support for the cause of liberation in South Africa but indicated that Zimbabwe would not offer military aid or sanctuaries for operations against South Africa.

THE CAMPAIGN OF REGIONAL DESTABILIZATION

After the establishment of Zimbabwean independence, the war in Namibia and South African attacks on Angola became the main regional issue. However, by the end of 1982 it was clear that a wider regional crisis had developed. The settlement in Rhodesia had ended the Rhodesian and South African raids into Mozambique and Zambia. But with ANC guerrilla activity growing inside South Africa, the Botha government was gradually renewing its campaign of destabilization and acts of terrorism against the frontline states, with Zimbabwe added to the list of countries affected. Pretoria has used various tactics, including commando raids and assassinations targeting ANC members, military and logistic support for sabotage and terrorism by dissident groups, direct sabotage attacks, and economic pressures. The goal has been to strike at the ANC directly and indirectly, by undermining the frontline states economically, politically, and militarily to enforce their dependence on and subservience to South Africa. A related objective has been to show the West that the black-ruled states of the region are prone to instability and open to Soviet influence—this as a way to justify maintaining white dominance in South Africa. The frontline states have also had economic problems and political conflicts for which South Africa is not directly accountable. Nevertheless, many of the difficulties facing these countries can be linked to Pretoria's escalating campaign of destabilization.

In addition to having overwhelming military power, South Africa gains leverage in part from a legacy of nineteenth- and twentieth-century British colonial expansion, when roads and railways were pushed north from South Africa. Thus Botswana, Zimbabwe, and Zambia have traditionally relied on South African railroads and ports for shipment of much of their commerce. Lesotho is a small, mountainous country entirely surrounded by South Africa, and so is dependent on it for jobs for workers and for access to the outside world. Swaziland, sandwiched between South Africa and Mozambique, is almost as dependent. Mozambique, suffering heavy deprivation as a consequence of Portuguese colonial rule, has depended on South Africa to provide some 40 percent of the traffic that passes through its main port, Maputo. South African interests provided a majority of the loans for the giant Cabora Bassa dam in Mozambique (built just before the collapse of Portuguese rule), and South Africa buys most of its power. Alternative transport routes for the frontline states have faced various difficulties, mostly related to

South Africa. The Chinese-built TanZam Railroad, which links Zambia with Tanzania and the port of Dar es Salaam, was sabotaged during the Rhodesian conflict and has been hobbled by delays at the port and by maintenance problems. The Benguela Railroad, which extends from the port of Lobito in Angola through Zaire to Zambia, has been repeatedly cut by UNITA attacks. The main focus of the frontline states' SADCC group has been to develop Mozambique's railways, roads, pipelines, and ports so as to offer the inland countries shorter and more direct alternatives to South Africa for their commerce. Nearly $500 million in loans, mainly from Western sources, had been raised for these projects by 1982,[39] but Mozambique's transport infrastructure has been hit hard by sabotage by dissidents backed by South Africa. Therefore Botswana, Zimbabwe, and Zambia must continue to rely upon South African transport. Pretoria can use this dependence to apply economic pressures for political purposes.

In the case of Zimbabwe, in 1981 South Africa announced that it would end the preferential tariff agreements that were granted to the Rhodesian regime, and it ordered 20,000 Zimbabweans working in South Africa to return home at the end of their contracts. Pretoria also temporarily withdrew locomotives it had leased to Zimbabwean Railways and held up various essential commodities being shipped to Zimbabwe. Zimbabwe's relatively developed economy and strong agricultural sector offer the SADCC countries another kind of alternative to traditional reliance on South Africa, but Pretoria was clearly showing it could squeeze Zimbabwe. The Mugabe government has refused to recognize the Nationalist government diplomatically or to make formal ministerial agreements on economic matters, which it contends would amount to recognition. Mugabe's distrust of Pretoria was shown by his charge that the repatriation of Zimbabwean workers was a guise for infiltrating former members of Bishop Muzorewa's militia back into the country to launch attacks.

But the most serious conflict that has developed in Zimbabwe has been between the ZANU government and dissidents from Nkomo's ZAPU.* Tensions between the two parties first flared after independence

*This has roots that go back to the nineteenth century, when the Ndebele conquered what is now southwest Zimbabwe and made serfs of the Shona people. ZANU is largely Shona (making up some 75 percent of Zimbabwe's population), while ZAPU is mainly Ndebele. The central political issue in the 1963 split from ZAPU that created ZANU was similar to the ANC-PAC split in South Africa (with ZANU holding an Africanist position), but ethnic hostilities were a backdrop. In the war against the Rhodesian regime ZANU forces were based in Mozambique and received Chinese and North Korean backing. ZAPU was based in Zambia and had Soviet support, though Nkomo was known as a political deal-maker with closest ties to the West. The ZAPU-ZANU alliance in the Patriotic Front only partly bridged the differences between the movements.

in 1981 at a camp for former guerrillas, when scores were killed in fighting. Early in 1982 government raids discovered an arms cache at a farm owned by Nkomo. He was accused of plotting a coup and dismissed from his post of home minister. This prompted a number of ZAPU supporters in the new Zimbabwean army to desert, fearing a crackdown against them, and head for their home area in the southwest. Driven by a combination of economic hardship and political opposition, the dissidents, operating in loosely organized groups, were involved in attacks on white-owned farms and supporters of the government, robbery of road and rail traffic, and kidnappings. By the end of 1982 they were believed to number between three and five thousand and were held responsible for killing an estimated one hundred people. Regular military units were unable to curb the dissidents, and in January 1983 the government sent in the Fifth Brigade, an elite, 5,000-man unit trained by North Koreans and made up mainly of Shonas. At the same point Security Minister Emmerson Munangagwa claimed that South Africa was recruiting and arming thousands of dissidents to infiltrate Matabeleland and that there were at least four camps for them in South Africa, one having up to 5,000 men under arms.[40] There were, however, no reports from other sources to corroborate his charge. Soon the Fifth Brigade was being accused of waging a brutal pacification campaign against the dissidents, with men, women, and children said to be the victims of indiscriminate killings and torture. By March, it was estimated that several hundred to a thousand civilians had been killed, and the government was denying that its troops were responsible.[41]

While this internal conflict had reached serious proportions, several major incidents indicated that Zimbabwe had also been facing covert attacks from South Africa. In August 1981 explosions destroyed $30 million in munitions at an army base outside Harare (formerly Salisbury), the capital. In the same month, Joe Gqabi, a veteran ANC leader and the movement's representative in Zimbabwe, was assassinated in Harare. The national offices of ZANU-PF were destroyed by a bomb in December 1981. The following July saboteurs destroyed thirteen planes (including four new Hawk fighters from Britain) at Zimbabwe's main airbase, a significant part of the country's air force. Zimbabwe charged that South African agents were responsible for these attacks, but there was no direct proof. Then, in August 1982, Zimbabwean soldiers killed three white soldiers from South Africa twenty miles inside Zimbabwe's border with South Africa. A group of black soldiers accompanying them escaped back to South Africa.

The three soldiers were identified as former members of the Rhodesian Army who had joined the South African Defence Force. Their mission was said to have been to sabotage the rail line that runs through Zimbabwe to Mozambique's main port, Maputo. For Zimbabwe, this was conclusive evidence of South Africa's efforts at destabilization. South Africa ultimately acknowledged that the soldiers were in the Defence Force, but claimed they were on an unauthorized mission to free people at a detention camp. After this incident the *Sunday Mail* of Zimbabwe carried a report datelined Pretoria saying that unidentified members of the South African Defence Force, all formerly with the Rhodesian forces, told journalists they were angered that their dead comrades were being disowned by the South African authorities. They called the official story a lie.[42] They also said they had been involved in similar secret missions against Zimbabwe and Mozambique and that there was a special "destabilization center" at South African Defence Force headquarters that aimed at undermining neighboring countries.

Zimbabwe has, however, also been suffering economic dislocation from South African-sponsored attacks not within its own borders, but in neighboring Mozambique. Mozambique suffered considerable damage during the Rhodesian war because of its support for Patriotic Front guerrillas. The government put the number of Rhodesian attacks and incursions at 350, with 1,335 killed, $100 million in damages, and a loss of $500 million in trade and transport revenues from enforcing the UN economic sanctions against Rhodesia during the conflict.[43] The lost revenues were only partially compensated by international aid. Rhodesia also began backing an insurgency in Mozambique by a dissident group organized by right-wing colonialists who formed the MNR (Mozambique National Resistance), and South Africa took over patronage of the group after Zimbabwean independence. Western diplomats have supported the charge by the Mozambican government that the MNR is financed, supplied, and sometimes actively supported by the South African military.[44] A major goal of the SADCC group has been to reopen Mozambique's transport links with Zimbabwe in order to provide that country, as well as Botswana and Zambia, with an alternative to dependence on South African railways and ports for access to the outside world. But Mozambique's transport installations have become a main target of MNR attacks.

Several of the sabotage attacks claimed by MNR showed a sophistication that indicates a direct South African role. In October 1981 eight buoys marking the port of Beira were destroyed by mines, while inland saboteurs attacked the road, railway, and oil pipeline links of Beira with Zimbabwe. The oil pipeline, closed for fifteen years because of the UN sanctions against the Rhodesian regime, had been scheduled to reopen that December. A U.S. State Department official voiced the widely held suspicion: "This was a very professional job. . . . They [the MNR] had to have had South African help."[45] Although Mozambique and Zimbawe arranged to cooperate in operations against the MNR and Tanzania agreed to send two hundred military advisors to aid Mozambican forces, the attacks continued. The railway from Maputo to Zimbabwe runs close to the South African border and has been crippled by sabotage. The largest single attack in Mozambique was the December 9, 1982, raid on an oil depot in Beira. It caused some $35 million in damages. Much of the oil was destined for Zimbabwe.

In addition to these major attacks, MNR's activities spread greatly in 1982, affecting ten of Mozambique's twelve provinces. Road and rail traffic in many areas was attacked, government officials were murdered and mutilated, and several foreign technicians were kidnapped. There was even sabotage of the electric power lines from the Cabora Bassa dam to South Africa and of the rail line from Maputo to South Africa. Estimates have put the number of MNR supporters as high as several thousand, a sizable figure, but one that can be attributed both to material incentives provided by South Africa and the colonial legacy of distrust of the central government in remote areas. The FRELIMO government has acknowledged that in some areas there has been great discontent with the party, yet it is clear that with its history of ties to former Portuguese colonialists, white-ruled Rhodesia and now South Africa the MNR poses no legitimate political challenge to FRELIMO. A Western diplomat in Mozambique said, "If South Africa withdrew its support, the resistance would crumble."[46] But while South African involvement continues, the economic strain caused by the attacks has become increasingly severe.

A direct raid by South African forces into Mozambique was carried out on January 29, 1981, when commandos attacked three houses outside Maputo where members of the ANC and SACTU were living, killing thirteen and abducting three others. The South Africans claimed the houses were headquarters for ANC attacks inside South Africa, and invoked the invective of the new Reagan administration against "international terrorism." After the attack the Mozambican government expelled six Americans from the American embassy in Maputo, charging they were CIA agents who had been engaged in gathering information on the Mozambican armed forces and the ANC and had thus aided the South African raiders. In August 1982 Ruth First, a prominent South African activist and author and a member of the ANC, was killed by a letter bomb at a university office in Maputo. The letter carried the imprint of a project of the African Bibliographic Center in Washington, D.C., which is funded by the U.S. Agency for International Development; the publications of the Center are sent to Africa by U.S. diplomatic pouch and mailed locally. However, Mozambican officials blamed only South Africa for the assassination; and the police were reported to believe that the bomb was implanted without American involvement.[47]

For a number of years Lesotho's autocratic ruler, Chief Leabua Jonathan, has accused South Africa of harboring the opposition Basutoland

Congress party seeking his overthrow; the party, which charges Chief Jonathan with having illegally seized power, has denied links with South Africa. Since Lesotho declared its political support for the ANC in 1980, there have been an increasing number of small-scale border attacks. In 1982 two political figures were killed. Then, on December 9, 1982, the South African Defence Force carried out a sudden raid in Maseru, the capital, landing troops by helicopter and attacking houses in twelve separate areas. Thirty ANC members were killed, as well as twelve Lesotho citizens. South Africa claimed that the raid had thwarted ANC plans to launch major terror attacks in South Africa, but the South African representative at the United Nations claimed only one previous ANC attack as being linked to Lesotho. There are more than 11,000 South African refugees in Lesotho, including about 5,000 having some sort of political status.[48]

A few weeks later, only hours before the opening of a nine-nation SADCC conference in Maseru to formulate projects to promote regional economic independence from South Africa, the small city was shaken by a series of explosions that damaged a water storage installation. Credit for the attack was claimed by the liberation army of the Congress party, but it was seen as a blatant threat to the conference and its supporters among the Western countries, intended to show that South Africa has the power to bring any country in the region to its knees.

Botswana, bordering South Africa to the north, has long received refugees from South Africa, and in 1982 it openly complained of South African interference. Incidents cited included overflights by South African military planes from Namibia and attacks by South African agents against ANC members and other South Africans in exile. In Swaziland, ANC representative Petros Nyawose and his wife were killed by a bomb in June 1982. In South Africa there was speculation that this was a reprisal for a series of ANC attacks. Zambia suffered considerable damage from Rhodesian-South African raids during the Rhodesian conflict and has charged South Africa with conducting smaller-scale attacks along the Zambian border with Namibia. In 1980 South Africa was accused of involvement in a failed coup attempt against President Kenneth Kaunda.

The case of the South African-sponsored coup attempt against the socialist government of the Seychelle Islands in 1981 provides another example of aggression by Pretoria. The attackers, who included foreign mercenaries and South African military and intelligence men, came to the islands disguised as rugby players on holiday, but they were discovered at the airport and repulsed. Several were captured, and the forty-two others hijacked a plane and flew back to South Africa. Testimony by a captured intelligence agent and by the attackers' leader, the well-known mercenary Colonel Mike Hoare revealed the extent of official government backing for the attempt.[49] The men were put on trial in

South Africa because of international pressure. Hoare said the plan had been approved by the South African cabinet, and was supervised first by the National Intelligence Service and then passed to Military Intelligence. The men were provided with Soviet and Hungarian AK-47 rifles and Chinese hand grenades. Hoare also testified that he had informed a representative of the CIA in Pretoria about the plan, saying the United States was interested because of the strategic value of the Seychelles. Though not suggesting the United States had an active role, he admitted telling his men that the CIA had approved the plan.

Despite its escalating use of military force, South Africa has had diplomatic contacts of various kinds with the frontline states. While Malawi is the only African country to have recognized the Nationalist government, South Africa has had close contacts (including a customs union) with Lesotho, Swaziland, and Botswana growing out of their historic dependence. It was reported that a few hours before the South Africa raid on the ANC in Lesotho local security forces cleared the streets, an indication that the government had been warned of an impending attack.[50] Since independence, Mozambique has maintained contacts with South Africa on economic matters (particularly concerning traffic through Maputo) and other issues. In June 1982 South Africa announced that Mozambique's director of national security had asked for asylum after what was described as "a routine visit."[51] In December 1982 Mozambican officials met with South African Foreign Minister R. F. Botha to discuss the destabilization issue. Mozambique expressed its commitment to peaceful relations and mutual respect for sovereignty, calling on South Africa to do the same. Zimbabwe's contacts with South Africa have been more tense (perhaps a reflection of the extent of South African intervention in the Rhodesian war). The Mugabe government has rejected the idea of high-level economic agreements and bitterly denounced Pretoria's attacks and economic pressures.

Zambian President Kaunda, guided by his philosophy of Christian humanism, has engaged in dialogue with South Africa. In 1976 he met with Vorster in an effort to resolve the Rhodesian conflict. In April 1982 he met with Prime Minister Botha and General Malan, making an appeal for a Namibian settlement and for the release of Mandela and talks with the ANC. While Malan has described Zambia as a "Marxist satellite state" the meeting was held on friendly terms.[52] But subsequent escalating South African attacks in the region indicated Kaunda's appeal had failed. South African officials met, reportedly at their initiative, with Angolan officials in December 1982 and again in February 1983 on the issue of a Namibian settlement. Angola agreed to the talks even with South African forces occupying areas in the south, but apparently no substantive progress was made.

One analogy increasingly offered in South Africa both by supporters of Botha's policies and by its critics compares South Africa's regional strategy to that of Israel in the Mideast.[53] This has been prompted by the close relations which have developed between the two countries. As noted in Chapter 5, Israel has emerged as an increasingly important strategic partner of South Africa, supplying weapons technology and components, cooperating on intelligence matters, and, according to some reports, joining with South Africa in nuclear weapons development. Former Israeli Defense Minister General Ariel Sharon has visited both South Africa and Namibia, and there are reports that the Israelis advise the South African Army on antiguerrilla tactics. Thus the aggressive strategy of the Botha government in the region has been compared to that pursued by Sharon. Israel has occupied the West Bank, the Golan Heights, and southern Lebanon (and the Sinai before returning it to Egypt); South Africa occupies Namibia and controls a section of southern Angola. Israel has supported and armed the Christian militias as surrogate forces in Lebanon, and South Africa has supported and armed UNITA and the MNR. There has also been a confluence in South African and Israeli policies toward Zaire. Pretoria has had quietly friendly relations with President Mobutu going back to Vorster's "detente" strategy in the early seventies. Mobutu, a patron of the FNLA of Angola (headed by his brother-in-law Holden Roberto), cooperated with the United States–South African effort to defeat the MPLA. Zaire joined the rest of Africa in breaking relations with Israel at the time of the 1973 Arab-Israeli conflict, but Mobutu's attitudes toward Israel, where he received paratroop training, have evidently remained favorable. In 1982 Zaire reestablished ties with Israel after the return of the Sinai to Egypt, and one of General Sharon's last missions before resigning as defense minister was a trip to Zaire in January 1983. Several agreements were reached (with details remaining secret), including one for the training of Mobutu's personal presidential guard and its provision with $8 million in military equipment and a five-year program under which Israeli advisors are to restructure Zaire's 20,000 member armed forces and sell it arms and military equipment.[54]

When South Africa struck at the ANC in Lesotho the day after holding talks with Angola on Namibia, the South African Foreign Ministry noted, as one justification for the raid, that Israel had invaded Lebanon while negotiating with Egypt. In a more general way, supporters of the Nationalist government have defended its strategies by comparing them to Israel's, while critics refer to South Africa's leaders as Menachem Botha and General Magnus Sharon. The Botha government obviously welcomes the Reagan administration's friendly stance of "constructive engagement," but like Israel in its relations with the United States, the nationalists clearly intend to follow their own hard-line policies whether the United States approves or not.

Responding to questions about the regional situation in an interview in February 1983, Botha said that South Africa would agree to a non-aggression pact with any of its neighbors that would bar either country from allowing its territory to be used as a springboard for attacks against the other. Though far less sweeping than the "constellation of states" proposal he made soon after taking office, Botha's offer was similar to earlier ones made by his government and by Vorster before him. Calling the ANC "a small clique" controlled by the South African Communist party and through it by the Kremlin, Botha warned that while "the Communists are fighting us aggressively," through guerrilla attacks, South Africa would strike at neighboring countries.[55] He added that South Africa would consider aid from "anti-Communist" guerrilla forces, but would not comment on whether his government was already giving such support. Despite these threats, Botha called charges of regional destabilization by South Africa "another stunt by Marxist forces, by Moscow and their satellites." But Lesotho, Zimbabwe, Zambia, and Botswana have not had close relations with the Soviets, and the charges being made against South Africa have been supported by Western diplomats and journalists, and in some cases by hard evidence.

In private, South African officials have offered candid comments which directly contradict Botha's claims. Flora Lewis reported in the *New York Times* that while the South African government makes much of the " 'Soviet threat,' . . . when pushed for details, nobody seems to take it seriously except Washington. Even Jaap Marais, leader of the most extreme right-wing party, pooh-poohs a 'Soviet threat' and makes clear his concern is preservation of lily-white rule."[56] South African Defence officials admitted stepping up raids into Mozambique, Lesotho, and Angola and did not deny that the South African army retained control of a large part of southern Angola, despite public claims of withdrawal. Similarly, they admitted supporting and helping arm the MNR (though denying a direct role in their attacks). Other officials described South Africa's goal as "total elimination of 'all terrorist bases' " in the region, meaning not only ANC militants and SWAPO guerrillas, but also any agitation, propaganda, or other support of any kind in neighboring states for the black majority in South Africa. One, known as a moderate, said bluntly, "We want to show that we want peace in the region, we want to contribute and we can help a lot. But we also want to show that if we are refused we can destroy the whole of southern Africa."[57]

For Lewis the remarks of South African leaders confirmed charges by the frontline states that Pretoria is trying to make them submit to a "Pax Afrikaansa—enforcing permanent economic dependence and military vulnerability that will leave South Africa's regime unchallenged at home and easily dominant in the region." At the January 1983 SADCC conference in Lesotho, this was the overriding issue. Conference chairman

Peter Mmusi of Botswana noted, "It is not much use to develop ports and pipelines, roads and railways, and then to watch in silence as they are blown up." He also noted, referring to South Africa's occupation of Namibia and takeover of part of southern Angola, "Our forces do not occupy the Free State or ravage the Northern Transvaal."[58]

This comes back to the origins of the region's conflicts. The Nationalist government, through its illegal occupation of Namibia and the entrenched racism of apartheid, has left its victims with guerrilla resistance as their main recourse. South Africa claims the guerrillas represent a Soviet plan to take over southern Africa and strangle the West, but its attacks on neighboring countries have gone far beyond any kind of counterinsurgency tactics needed to counter guerrillas. The ANC has conducted some damaging sabotage attacks inside South Africa, but none of the countries on South Africa's borders has allowed guerrilla camps on its territory. To try to stop guerrillas from filtering across its borders, Pretoria can demand, or try to force, its neighbors to expel ANC members and refuse sanctuary to refugees from South Africa. But it is doubtful that this could stop the guerrillas and other forms of unrest and opposition in South Africa. The problem is within South Africa. Militarily and economically, South Africa is overwhelmingly powerful in the region. But politically it is weak and vulnerable. It is threatened above all by the black majority's determination to reject and resist apartheid.

The Reagan administration's policy of "constructive engagement" with South Africa has been aimed at achieving a Namibia settlement, reform in South Africa, and regional stability. Yet the Botha government has seized on this friendly policy and turned it into a carte blanche to assert its regional dominance through military muscle. Just before the Lesotho raid, a South African government broadcast referred to a "joint commitment" with the Reagan administration to "a Monroe doctrine for the region." This commitment recognized South Africa's "special responsibility" for maintaining stability in southern Africa, akin to the way the United States has sought to preserve stability in Central America.[59] The United States subsequently joined in a unanimous UN Security Council resolution condemning the raid (though insisting that the resolution refer only to the single "aggressive act" rather than to a pattern of South African aggression in the region, since that could be taken as grounds for wider sanctions against Pretoria). But within a few weeks the Reagan administration had, for the third time in less than a year, acted to relax its enforcement of the United Nations arms embargo against South Africa by reducing restrictions on the sale of American goods to the South African police and military.[60] The evident message from Washington was that while Pretoria sometimes overstepped reasonable limits in its military zeal, it remained America's main partner in the region.

NAMIBIA POSTSCRIPT, JUNE, 1983

As of mid-1983, negotiations on Namibia remain hung up on the issue of Cuban forces in Angola, an issue that the United States had tied to the Namibia question and South Africa had eagerly seized upon. In this stance the United States and South Africa stand virtually alone world-wide. Even the other Western countries in the contact group (with the possible exception of the Thatcher government in Britain) have regarded this approach as outside the ambit of the Namibia problem, which is South Africa's obligation to withdraw from the territory.

Within Namibia the political failure of South Africa's long efforts to build up an alternative to SWAPO became evident when it dissolved the DTA-dominated national assembly in January 1983 after only a few years' existence. South Africa thus resumed its direct rule in Namibia (although it had never actually loosened its full control over the country). South African military officials, particularly Military Intelligence, were reported to be behind this new strategy of trying to shape some sort of new alternative to SWAPO.[61] It is important to underline the central reason why South Africa has continued to resist a settlement: the *New York Times* (March 3, 1983) noted that SWAPO's "political ascendency has never seemed clearer" in Namibia. And though the South African military has claimed to have defeated SWAPO through its aggressive occupation of southern Angola, in early 1983 SWAPO guerrillas carried out their largest offensive of the entire conflict by infiltrating some eight hundred guerrillas into northern Namibia.

The South African reluctance to agree to a settlement is therefore clear. It would mean almost certainly that SWAPO would win in an election. This would mean billions of dollars in military costs, thousands of South African casualties, and years of effort will have brought only political victory by its opponent. It could bring a white conservative backlash against the Botha government in South Africa at a time when it is trying to restructure apartheid with its new constitutional proposals. It would mean that, even if SWAPO maintained curbs on ANC activity, South Africa's military defense/offense would be pulled back to its own borders.

The Reagan administration's strategy of insisting that Cuban forces in Angola stand as the main issue to be resolved for a Namibia settlement has significance in several respects. Most important, it represents a fundamental reorientation of the Namibia issue whereby South Africa's obligation to withdraw from the country is being subordinated to an attempt to place conflict within a context of a new regional realignment. Cuban forces would leave Angola and their role as a shield against South Africa would be replaced by an understanding whereby South Africa would withdraw from southern Angola and then Namibia and presumably end their backing for UNITA. Angola would no longer turn to the Cubans (and Soviets) for security, but instead would work out a modus vivendi with Pretoria. Thus the whole Namibia question, at least in this phase, has come to turn on whether Angola (and the frontline states with which Angola cooperates on regional issues) will accept this approach. There has been considerable diplomatic activity centering on this, with the United States evidently offering Angola full recognition, economic ties and other incentives. Angola has met with South African military officials on the issues. U.S. officials have had regular contacts with the Soviets as well: it can be presumed that the U.S. appeal is that Soviet restraint in southern Africa on Namibia could lead to better relations in other areas of global tension.

But the crux of the U.S. position has been that *Angola* must take the first step by assuring the withdrawal of the Cubans.[62] It is very unsure whether Angola and the other frontline states would accept this whole strategy, even with the incentive and assurances offered. They have suffered extensive damage at the hands of South Africa. Why should South Africa be granted concessions for carrying out its obligations to leave Namibia? The position of the United States is that there is no other way. South Africa cannot be forced to withdraw, the Reagan administration has claimed. Progress can only be made through compromise that deals with South Africa's regional concerns. If Angola proceeds and South Africa still stalls, then the onus will be clearly on Pretoria.

The problem with this policy is that it has twisted the Namibia question, shifting the responsibility from South Africa to Angola and the Cubans. It has sacrificed the right of the people of Namibia, who have suffered so much under South Africa's brutality, to independence with no preconditions. South Africa may well not want to allow Namibian independence regardless of the Cuban issue, given their failure to prevail over SWAPO. They have the ability to raise new issues and demands, to provoke new confrontations with Angola or other neighboring states. Responsibility for withdrawal from Namibia should be placed squarely on South Africa.

4 Military, Police, and Security Forces

THE SOUTH AFRICAN DEFENCE FORCE has, in common with other South African institutions, been shaped since 1948 by the apartheid policies of the Nationalist government and by the over-all strategic objective of ensuring, in the words of Prime Minister Botha, that "the principle of the right of self-determination of the white nation must not be regarded as negotiable."[1] In the simplest terms, this is reflected in the fact that the leadership of the Defence Force is now largely Afrikaner; and despite the recent stepped-up recruitment of blacks, the South African military forces remain almost entirely white.

In its present form the Defence Force incorporates elements from both the Afrikaner tradition of local Commando units (militia forces) and the British system of conventional forces. Historically, both types of forces were used in the conquest of South Africa's indigenous societies, although both Afrikaners and British used black forces as well. This they did either through alliances with African leaders or through various forms of recruitment of black troops, dating from the incorporation of black servants into Commando units in the first decades of Dutch enroachment at the Cape.

After World War II, when South Africa was still in the British Commonwealth, there was open military cooperation with Western countries, and most of the officers in the Defence Force were English-speaking. Under the Nationalists, however, Afrikaners were moved up in the ranks rapidly. Black South Africans had served with the South African forces in large numbers in World Wars I and II, in noncombatant roles, but these units were disbanded. After Sharpeville, in 1960, the Nationalist government began to build up the Defence Force, but the police still played the main security role.

Nationalist moves to temper the Afrikanerization of the Defence Force came only in the mid-seventies, when it became clear that the maximum mobilization of all sectors of the white population was going to be needed if South Africa was to assert its military power. Late in 1974 a high-powered committee of South African advertising and public relations men was established to design the 1975 Defence Force recruiting campaign. The mandate was to attract English-speaking recruits. It was noted that:

- 85 percent of the Army's permanent force staff were Afrikaners;
- 75 percent of the Air Force's permanent staff were Afrikaners; and
- 50 percent of the Navy's permanent staff were Afrikaners.

The Defence Force admitted that the special campaign was needed because English-speaking South Africans often felt detached from the military, sensing that they were "not wanted" and had little opportunity for promotions.[2] Prior to this change in policy, according to the South African *Financial Mail* (February 22, 1980), "It was not uncommon for an English-speaking officer to remain unpromoted for 17 or 18 years, and the result was that the cream of the Defence Force left in disgust." With the 1975 invasion of Angola and the escalation of the war in Namibia, the size of the Defence Force was nearly doubled, from an estimated strength of 269,000 in 1974 to nearly 500,000 in 1979 (see Table I). This heightened role for the military has become increasingly institutionalized since Defence Minister Botha became prime minister in 1978, bringing military leaders into coordinating positions at the highest levels of government.

The commander-in-chief of the Defence Force is the president of the Republic, though this is a largely honorific position. In practice, the executive function is exercised at the cabinet level by the prime minister and the defence minister. P. W. Botha retained the Defence portfolio when he became prime minister, but in 1980 he nominated his closest military associate, Defence Force Chief Gen. Magnus Malan, the architect of the Total Strategy, to be defence minister. General Malan's old position was filled by Gen. Constand Viljoen, formerly Chief of the Army. He, like General Malan, is a part of the new generation of Afrikaner military leaders. General Viljoen, a specialist in military hardware who enjoys action at the frontlines, is said to have played a major role in the attack on Cassinga and in other raids against Angola.[3] During his term as Defence Force Chief, General Malan reorganized the military structure, forming the Army, Navy, Air Force, and Armscor (the arms manufacturing and procurement agency) into a single bureaucratic structure that he called the Defence Family. Also, with the backing of P. W. Botha, he reduced the bias against English-speaking whites in the Defence Force, opened up more noncombatant positions to white women volunteers, and created units for black volunteers.

Military Policy

The scope of operations of the Defence Force is spelled out in the Defence Act of 1957 and its subsequent amendments. This provides for the Defence Force to be employed for the defense of South Africa or for the "prevention or suppression of terrorism" through operations in South Africa or in neighboring countries in the region. Therefore no specific declaration of war by the government is needed by the Defence Force to carry out military operations against other countries in southern Africa. The Defence Force may also be used within South Africa for "prevention of internal disorder," as well as for the protection of lives, health, property, and essential services, or for any type of police duties. Thus the parameters for military action are extremely wide, permitting the Defence Force to undertake a wide range of operations inside and outside South Africa's borders without the need for parliamentary authorization.

The 1982 Defence White Paper[4] describes the current policy framework guiding the Defence Force. The first section of the White Paper claims an "onslaught against South Africa" is being mounted by the Soviet Union through aid to "terrorist organizations such as SWAPO and the ANC and through "surrogate forces such as the Cubans." It is claimed that the Soviets are using all possible means to "overthrow the present body politic," including "instigating social and labor unrest, civilian resistance, terrorist attacks against the infrastructure of the Republic of South Africa and the intimidation of Black leaders and members of the security forces." Thus the whole pattern of resistance to apartheid is seen as being guided and promoted by the Soviets. It also charges that "subversive activity" is being furthered by some churches, supported by the World Council of Churches. The section concludes with a claim that South Africa could face the threat of conventional war mounted by the Soviets through aid to neighboring countries. This could represent an indirect appeal to Western countries for a relaxation of the arms embargo and for closer strategic ties.

The section on "Broad Policy" declares that South Africa has no territorial ambitions or intentions of aggression and that the Defence Force is a "peace task force." Then, however, the White Paper says that the country must be protected against any "internal or external revolutionary action" and that protection will include "offensive pro-active action." This phase refers to pre-emptive attacks and various types of destabilization carried out against the liberation movements and neighboring countries. (The following section on military operations says that "offensive defense is indispensable" for stability in Namibia.)

The policy statement then says that in order to support the civilian infrastructure of the country the Defence Force has become "increasingly involved in assisting other security forces and civilian organizations," a reference to the increasing number of counterinsurgency operations being undertaken in cooperation with the police. Future assistance will be concerned mainly with protection of "national key points" and other important areas, it is noted.

A significant new note is struck with the statement that "it is policy that all population groups be involved in defending the Republic of South Africa," which means "a Defence Force of the people for the people." This inspirational phrase marks a revision of apartheid principles (i.e., against arming blacks and relying on them for any significant military role). It is perhaps the most telling sign of the pressures that have been mounted against the white minority government by the spread of black resistance in all its forms. Naturally, the Defence Force will remain fully under white control. And the terminology "population groups" is used instead of "citizens," which would exclude blacks.

The policy statement concludes with several paragraphs on the need for the Defence Force to provide assistance to the "National and Independent States" (i.e., the Bantustans). It describes the programs for creating military forces in the "independent" Bantustans and the policy of setting up military agreements to form "joint management" bodies to promote cooperation "with the view to joint action." The goal is to encourage participation in a "Southern African military treaty organization against a common enemy." The "Black territorial units" being formed in the remaining Bantustans are to be the nucleus of their future Bantustan defense forces. These paragraphs reflect both the military's plans for the continued implementation of the Bantustan policy, a fundamental tenet of apartheid, and the need to build up their military forces for counterinsurgency operations.

The sections which follow describe the current military operations of the Defence Force. They reflect the escalation of its conflicts and how South Africa has become a country at war. In addition to the section on armaments supply (examined in Chapter 5), the other significant section of the 1982 Defence White Paper deals with manpower. A key statement says:

> It is in the national interest that the White male should no longer be utilized as the only manpower source. Therefore the SA Defence Force will be more and more dependent on other sources of manpower, such as White females and members of other population groups. . . .based on programmed development plans which extend to 1990.

The section on manpower goes on to describe the program to greatly expand the size of the Defence Force through plans not only to use the "new sources" of manpower but also by extending the length of military service liability and obligations for white men up to the age of sixty, depending on circumstances.

THE STRUCTURE OF THE DEFENCE FORCE[5]

The Defence Headquarters in Pretoria includes five staff divisions: personnel, intelligence, operations, logistics, and management services. The highest command body in the Defence Force is the Defence Command Council, which includes the chief of the Defence Force, the chiefs of the Army, Navy, and Air Force, the surgeon general, the quartermaster general, and the chief of staff operations. This body is charged with overseeing and directing all operations of the Defence Force in terms of the Defence Act of 1957 and its later amendments.

The Defence Planning Committee, which is charged with budgetary and procurement planning, includes, in addition to Defence Force leaders, executives from Armscor and representatives from private industry. The Defence Staff Council aids the chief of the Defence Force in coordinating the military. As noted, the Defence Force has been made into a unified, monolithic structure; the chiefs of the Army, Air Force, and Navy are responsible to the chief of the Defence Force, who in turn is responsible to the minister of defence. In addition to being the military commander of the Defence Force, the chief of the Defence Force is also the administrative head of the Department of Defence.

The Army

The Army is by far the largest branch of the Defence Force, accounting for more than 80 percent of its troop strength. The core of the Army is the infantry. There are eight battalions of white National Servicemen, one African battalion and one Coloured battalion (both part of the Permanent Force), and approximately one hundred Citizen Force battalions in reserve.[6] The South African infantry is highly mechanized and mobile, using armored personnel carriers, trucks, and other vehicles, as well as helicopters and transport aircraft. But although air and ground transport are heavily used in the guerrilla war in Namibia, many infantry operations (such as patrols) are still carried out on foot. The striking power of the Army is provided by a large force of armored cars (an effective weapon in the southern African context), a strong tank force assembled since the mid-seventies, and artillery, including advanced, long-range 155-mm howitzers. In addition, the Army operates in close coordination with the Air Force, which provides air support by helicopters and strike aircraft, reconnaissance, and transport and evacuation. In 1979 the deputy defence minister reported that for each National Serviceman on combat duty, 3.48 troops are required in supporting services (i.e., 78 percent of Army manpower is in support services and 22 percent in combat units).[7] For Army operations within South Africa, the country is divided into nine territorial commands, with each command allocated Citizen Force and Commando units.

The Air Force

The Air Force has four operational commands. The Strike Command includes the Air Force's main combat aircraft. Their missions include ground attack, interception, and reconnaissance. The Transport Command includes various heavy and light transport planes. The Light Aircraft Command undertakes low-level reconnaissance, liaison and transport, and evacuation. In addition to the regular operational light aircraft, there are thirteen Air Commando squadrons operating as reserve units. The members fly their own light planes for training exercises and, if called up, for combat purposes. The Maritime Command undertakes coastal and offshore patrols. It has helicopters for antisubmarine and other operations and has a squadron of strike aircraft. The Air Force operates in close cooperation with the Army. Helicopters play a particularly important role in this. Air Force operations, including attack missions and air defense, are coordinated by radar and communication units.

The Navy

The Navy is the smallest branch of the Defence Force. At the end of the 1970s it developed a new orientation, seen in the acquisition for its fleet of Reshef missile strike boats and smaller Dvora missile patrol boats. These ships can be used not only for coastal operations, but also for strikes against neighboring states. Other Navy ships include frigates, submarines, minesweepers, small harbor patrol boats, and a supply ship. The Navy was formed in 1946 with ships supplied by Britain, and through the Simonstown Agreement (1955) it operated in cooperation with the British and informally with NATO. A sophisticated surveillance and communications center at Silvermine, near the Cape, was opened in 1973. Constructed with Western equipment, it allows the surveillance of air and sea traffic on the west and east African coasts and over thousands of miles of the South Atlantic and Indian oceans. It was also reported to include communications links with the navies of Britain, the United States, France, and several other countries.[8] With Britain's termination of the Simonstown Agreement in 1975 and the passage of the mandatory United Nations arms embargo in 1977, South Africa indicated that security for the Cape shipping route would no longer be a priority. The Navy would concentrate on its regional concerns.

SPECIAL UNITS

The Reconnaissance Commandos

The Reconnaissance Commandos ('Recce') are the elite unit of the Defence Force. They are similar to the American Green Berets, the British Special Air Service, and the Rhodesian Selous Scouts. They are chosen through a rigorous selection and training program for unconventional missions of all types, including "dirty tricks." According to a South African commentator:

> The task of the reconnaissance commando is to paralyze the enemy by destroying its dumps, communications and other strategic targets using unconventional tactics.
>
> The members are trained to launch deep penetration operations and raids into enemy areas. This includes reconnaissance, sabotage, ambushes and similar actions aimed at causing chaos amongst enemy ranks.[9]

The Recces are recruited from all branches of the Defence Force and operate directly under the authority of the chief of the Defence Force, placing them outside the ordinary military command channels. Another South African commentator has noted that the Recces have a few British and American "specialists" (mercenaries) in their ranks.[10] It was reported that the Recces are recruiting black troops.

Paratroopers

The Defence Force has had two parachute battalions consisting of National Servicemen volunteers, but in 1978 it was announced that a larger Parachute Brigade was to be formed.[11] The Paratroopers are second only to the Reconnaissance Commandos as an elite force. They are able to play an important role in the Defence Force strategy of sudden attacks on targets in the frontline states and in counterinsurgency operations as well.

Marines

In 1979 the Navy announced the creation of the Marines to provide security for harbor facilities, backing up the police units of the Department of Railways and Harbors.[12] Training includes riot control, house-to-house searches, roadblocks, patrolling, underwater searches for mines and explosives, and bomb disposal. The Marines use a newly developed thirty-foot patrol boat called *Namacurras*, described as "the most heavily armed vessel of its type in the world," which carries up to three machine guns, other light arms, and other equipment. The first Marine unit deployed by the Navy was based not in South Africa, but at Walvis Bay, Namibia's only deepwater port.

South West African Territorial Force

In 1980 the Defence Force announced the formation of the South West African Territorial Force (SWATF) as the basis of a future Namibian national force. Aside from the goal of reducing the burden of the South African troops in Namibia, this Namibianization of the war has the political effect of bolstering the South African-supported political groups in Namibia and skirting the United Nations settlement plan, which has called for the withdrawal of South Africa forces from Namibia prior to elections. In 1981 the South African administration made it mandatory for all Namibians, black and white, to register for military service at age sixteen. The SWATF has been placed under the administrative authority of the South African-created administration in Namibia, but is operationally under the control of the South African Defence Force, and in military terms it is a part of the South African forces. According to the Defence Force, the SWATF numbers 20,000 troops, including the following elements:[13]

• Six regular, ethnically based African battalions of light infantry trained mainly for counterinsurgency;

• A conventional brigade with a regular interethnic motorized infantry battalion, a reserve armored car regiment, and a reserve artillery regiment;

• Twenty-six reserve "area force units" similar to the Commandos in South Africa;

• Support elements, training units, and headquarters formations;

• A mounted motorcycle and tracker unit called the 1st South West Africa Specialist Unit; and

• One reserve squadron flying light aircraft.

Civic Action Programs

The Defence Force has deployed hundreds of National Service troops with educational, professional, and technical skills in the combat areas of northern Namibia, as well as in KwaZulu and Bophuthatswana, to provide services to local areas. Civic Action programs have several functions. One is straightforward: to "win the hearts and minds" of the local people, providing them with incentives to cooperate with the Defence Force rather than with the political opposition or with the guerrillas. There are other aspects as well. Such programs permit the relatively unobtrusive introduction of military forces into local areas, and they can be used as a means for gathering intelligence.

Mercenaries

The presence of foreigners in the elite Reconnaissance Commandos has been noted. In addition, after the 1980 victory of the Patriotic Front in the Zimbabwean elections, the South Africans launched a recruiting drive among white Rhodesian forces; bonuses for signing up started at several thousand dollars for privates.[14] Virtually the entire Rhodesian Light Infantry is said to have joined, as well as officers from the notorious Selous Scouts and the Special Air Services. At the time of the elections 2,600 black auxiliaries recruited by the Rhodesian regime were said to have been in South Africa undergoing training, and efforts to recruit these troops were also expected.

The attack on the Republic of Seychelles in the Indian Ocean in November 1981 was carried out by a force of South African military men and mercenaries. A number of the fifty-two involved were foreigners (from Britain, the United States, and other countries) who were or had been in the Recce Commandos or other South African military units.[15]

In January 1981 the British *Guardian* carried Trevor Edwards's personal account of a year as a mercenary with the South African Defence Force.[16] His unit, the 32d Battalion, had been formed by South African military intelligence late in 1975 and comprised remnants of the Angolan FNLA force that had fought against the MPLA from its base in the Western Caprivi. The unit's principal assignment was to operate in southern Angola while posing as UNITA guerrillas and to clear out designated areas, destroying as much property as possible and attacking Angolan forces and civilians. Although the South African Defence Force officially refused to comment on Edwards's story, a senior staff officer in Namibia confirmed to a reporter from the *Financial Times* of London that there is a 32nd Battalion in the Western Caprivi. It is made up of recruits from Angola and commanded by "European and South African" officers. He also confirmed that they specialized in attacks in Angola, but he denied that they attacked civilian targets.[17]

Another report on the 32nd Battalion was provided in February 1981 by an Angolan, named Jose Ricardo Belmundo, who said he was a deserter from the unit.[18] The unit, according to Belmundo, included foreign officers and showed the high degree of South Africa support being given to UNITA. He also claimed that an American officer had fc ight with South African forces in Angola in 1975 and was responsible for setting up the 32nd Battalion.

It should be noted that in the South African context the role of foreigners in military and strategic activities goes far beyond that of a soldier of fortune who is hired to engage in special military operations. The South African military recruits white foreigners who come to reside in the country into its regular military forces at all levels, depending on their experience. And Armscor (the armaments agency), its subsidiary companies, and many private companies carrying out military or other strategic work, all seek foreigners having military, technical, or management skills for a wide variety of vital tasks for which South Africa lacks sufficient manpower or technical expertise. (A number of examples are mentioned in Chapter 5.) The roles played by foreigners in these strategic fields do not correspond to the conventional image of a mercenary, but they have been of great military importance to the Defence Force.

TABLE 4-1
SOUTH AFRICAN DEFENCE FORCE COMPONENTS

	GOALS 1981	ACTUAL 1977
IN FULL-TIME SERVICE		
Permanent Force	13.5%	7.0%
National Servicemen	12.5%	6.6%
Civilians	4.5%	3.1%
total	30.5%	16.7%
IN PART-TIME SERVICE		
Civilian Force	34.8%	54.9%
Commandos	34.7%	28.4%
Total	69.5%	83.3%
Grand Total	100.0%	100.0%
APPROXIMATE TOTAL STRENGTH (SEE TABLE 4-2)	500,000	370,000

SOURCE: Defence *White Paper*, 1977, p. xii.

THE SOUTH AFRICAN DEFENCE FORCE

The South African Defence Force (SADF) is made up of personnel in full-time and part-time service. Those in full-time service are members of the Permanent Force (as well as civilian staff) and those fulfilling the two-year National Service requirement. Those in part-time service (i.e., reserves) include members of the Citizen Force and Commandos who have completed their National Service requirement. In 1982 the active reserve period was extended to twelve years (from eight years), during which 720 days of training camp must be completed (a threefold increase), or an average of 60 days a year. Personnel are also liable to call-up to active duty at any time. The 1977 Defence *White Paper* noted that 25 percent of the members of the Citizen Force and the Commandos had completed their active reserve requirements and were therefore classified as "noneffective members." At that time they made up 21 percent of the Defence Force.[19]

The Defence Force has been engaged in an intensive effort to expand the size of its full-time forces (see Table 4-1). While increasing the ratio of full-time members, the Defence Force has also continued to expand in total strength (see Table 4-2). As of the end of 1979 it was estimated that the Defence Force had reached a strength of almost 500,000. This was larger than the combined forces of at least twelve African states in the sub-Saharan region. Among the nearby countries Angola's forces were given as 33,000 (with 20,000 Cubans); Zambia's as 15,500; and Mozambique's as 26,700; and Zimbabwe's as 34,000.[20]

The expansion of the Defence Force has been accomplished by several means. In 1977 compulsory National Service for white males was extended from one year to a maximum of two years. There has been an increasing effort to use white women in Defence Force positions, including the beginning of voluntary National Service by women. Since the early 1970s the Defence Force has gradually expanded the numbers of blacks in service. It now appears that the tempo of recruitment of blacks will increase, and it has been reported that compulsory National Service for people of mixed race and Indians is planned for 1984.[21] The Defence Force has also increased salaries and benefits for members of the Permanent Force in order to attract new members and reduce the turnover rate, but these measures have not been entirely successful and a number of difficulties were mentioned in the 1979 parliamentary de-

TABLE 4-2

DEFENCE FORCE STRENGTH, 1960-79 (ESTIMATED)

	1960	1967	1974	1977	1979
Permanent Force[1]	11,500	13,00	21,500	28,000	40,000
National Servicemen[2]	10,000	23,000	26,000	27,000	60,000
Citizen Force[3]	2,000	30,000	120,000	180,000	230,000
Commandos[4]	48,500	75,000	90,000	120,000	150,000
Civilian Employees	6,000	8,000	11,500	12,500	14,000
Total	78,000	154,000	269,000	367,500	494,000
Standing Operational Force[5]	11,500	42,000	47,500	105,000	180,000

SOURCE: *The Apartheid War Machine* (London: International Defense and Aid Fund, 1980).

NOTE: Official figures on the strength of the Defence Force are fragmentary. This estimate was prepared with documentation from the available official sources, mainly Defence *White Papers* and parliamentary debates. The International Institute for Strategic Studies' *Military Balance, 1980-81*, gives the total strength of the armed forces, *including police*, as 404,500, but this figure has been used since the 1978-79 edition, and so does not reflect the continuing expansion of the Defence Force since then.

[1]Full-time, professional core of the Defence Force, including some white women and several black units. [2]White males between age 18 and 25 serving their compulsory two-year period of initial military duty. [3]Mainly men who have completed their National Service; also includes older men serving as volunteers. [4]Volunteers and men serving active reserve period; local groups may include white women volunteers and black volunteers. [5]Estimated number of troops under arms.

TABLE 4-3

ESTIMATED GOALS FOR EXPANSION OF THE DEFENCE FORCE BY 1990

Permanent Force	50,000
National Service	65,000
Citizen Force	455,000
Commandos	420,000
Civilians	20,000
Total	1,000,000
Estimated Standing Operational Force:	200,000

SOURCE: Tables 4–1 and 4-2 and the 1982 Defence *White Paper*.

fense debates. The school Cadet program, which has been rapidly expanded, is another means of channeling added numbers into the Defence Force.

In 1979 the deputy defense minister told parliament of the success of the stepped-up mobilization: in 1977 there were six Citizen Force or Commando troops called up for service in Namibia for every one National Serviceman. By 1978 this ratio had dropped to one to one, meaning there was less strain on the active reserve forces.[22] However, there have been continuing surges in the call-up of Citizen Force and Commando reserves since then as a result of South African operations in the Rhodesian war and in Namibia and Angola.

The controlled reserves are former members of the Permanent Force, Citizen Force, and Commandos who have completed their service requirements. They are kept on nonactive reserve lists until age sixty-five. A particular effort is now underway to recruit nonactive members of the reserves into the rapidly expanding Civil Defence program.

Legislation passed in 1982 made registration for military service in the Commandos compulsory for all white men up to age fifty-five if they have not completed military service. They will be liable for call-ups for military training and service until age sixty. This could double the size of the Defence Force to one million or more by 1990, depending on the military's needs.

BLACKS IN THE SOUTH AFRICAN MILITARY

Considering that a large number of blacks serve in the Police, the Nationalist government has been slow to recruit them into the Defence Force. This now has a higher priority. Black South Africans were recruited in large numbers into the military during the two world wars as noncombatants. In World War II 45,000 South Africans of mixed race and 80,000 Africans served in the South African forces as transport drivers, stretcher-bearers, hospital orderlies, gunners, and sailors; many were wounded or taken prisoner, and 2,500 were killed.[23] They were demobilized after the war and then excluded from the Defence Force by the Nationalist government, although blacks continued to be employed in the Auxiliary Services (formerly the Bantu Labour Service). A 1977 amendment to the Defence Act allows the Defence Force to use members of the Auxiliary Services in combat capacities. This measure was apparently passed because of the Namibia war. In Namibia the Defence Force formed several ethnically based black battalions that were classified as members of the Auxiliary Services. An amendment to the 1979 Defence Act placed them under South Africa's code of military discipline.[24]

The first black unit created under Nationalist rule, the Coloured Corps, was formed in 1963. By 1967, 490 volunteers had completed training, and by 1972, the Coloured Corps was considered part of the Permanent Force and its members were receiving weapons training.[25] The Cape Corps Service Battalion, a reserve force, began taking recruits in 1975. After a year of training, members could apply to join the Permanent Force. Also in 1975 the first two hundred South African Indian volunteers began training in the newly established Indian Corps. The 21st Battalion, an African unit in the Permanent Force, was set up in 1974, the first volunteers being taken from the Bantu Labour Service. By 1979 the 21st Battalion was reported to have 515 men.[26]

In 1980 the Defence Force announced the formation of four new black battalions and described them as "regional units," with volunteers drawn from each area (thus making them essentially ethnically based). The regions lie along the northeast borders (with Mozambique, Swaziland, and Zimbabwe), and the battalions include Zulus, Swazis, Shagaans, and Vendas. It was subsequently reported that eight battalions were to be formed.[27] These new units reflect both the need of the Defence Force for more black troops and the expansion of counterinsurgency operations within the country. The fact that these units are ethnically based (rather than unified, as is the 21st Battalion) reflects both their regional function and the white government's continuing determination to promote tribal divisions among Africans. In 1978 African, Indian, and mixed-race members of the Defence Force were said to be 2.5 percent by the opposition Progressive Federal party.[28] Africans were reported to make up 1.3 percent of the Defence Force in 1979.[29] For the African majority, there has been no talk of compulsory military service, because all are considered to be citizens of the Bantustans. The situation was spelled out by Rear Admiral Ronnie Edwards, who is in charge of personnel for the entire Defence Force: "Every black [African] is potentially a citizen of another country. Then all blacks will belong to an individual state, which means the 21st Battalion will be a foreign legion." However, this view of their status is not shared by the members of the 21st Battalion who agreed with one member's statement: "We consider ourselves to be South African citizens, and we expect in five years time to still be."[30]

Officially, the Defence Force is "multiracial," but the different units are in fact racially segregated. The Africans in the 21st Battalion are not recruited on a tribal basis, and recruitment is done in the urban areas. The base pay for blacks in the Defence Force is 60 percent that of whites. In 1978 the benefits paid for service in the "operational area" (combat areas) were equalized. Black troops are said to be given the same food, barracks, and other facilities as white soldiers.

Stepped-up recruitment of Africans appears to apply to Army units only. Prime Minister Botha noted in parliament that the Army and the Navy were already "making extensive use of Coloureds."[31] (In 1978 the Air Force admitted two Indians and hoped to raise this number to 50.[32]) In 1978, when the 21st Battalion was first sent to fight in Namibia for a four-month period, it was commanded by white instructors, but there were plans to train African officers. In the same year the government announced that people of mixed race and Indians would be allowed to receive naval officer training.[33]

While the total number of black troops in the Defence Force remains small, they are particularly in evidence in the combat areas of northern Namibia.[38] Of course, the forces there include the tribally based units that South Africa has raised in Namibia. The first of these Namibian units were two black battalions formed in 1975 in Ovambo and Kavango. (Both regions fall within the operational area combat zone designated by South Africa.) In 1977 six more ethnically based units, each having up to 160 men, were set up. In 1974 South African forces had settled two thousand nomadic San people at a special "Bushman Centre" attached to a South African Army base in Caprivi. The men in this settlement were provided military training. By 1977, the South African commander in Namibia, Major General J. J. Geldenhuys, was saying that four units had already been trained. The "Bushmen forces," said to number several hundred, serve the South Africans as trackers and guides. They also provide information on survival techniques to South African forces under training.[34]

While it is a crime to discourage participation in the Defence Force, black South Africans opposing apartheid but still working within the system have not supported service in the military. When Defence Force officers suggested that "mighty Zulu warriors" could be expected to fight for South Africa, a spokesman for Inkatha, Chief Buthelezi's political organization, stated that they "would be first on the battlefield once there was something worth defending."[35] The South African Black Alliance (composed of Inkatha, the Coloured Labour party, and the Indian Reform party) has stated, "While blacks do not enjoy citizenship or share political power, it will not urge the black community to participate in the military defence of the apartheid regime."[36] Representatives accepting the government-sponsored Coloured Persons Representative Council and the Indian Council have endorsed voluntary service in the military.[37]

South Africa has also set up small military forces in the "independent" Bantustans. The Transkei had a battalion of 254 men trained by 1976, and there are plans to enlarge it by a third and train its members for conventional and counterinsurgency warfare.[38] In 1976 Chief Lucas Mangope of Bophuthatswana announced that he had asked South Africa to provide military training and that he was considering establishing a system of military service and a defense department for the Bantustan. Venda, which was made "independent" in September 1979, has an army of several hundred being trained by the South African Defence Force for antiguerrilla operations.[39]

The new emphasis by the Nationalist government on recruiting blacks for the military has been reflected in *Paratus*, the official magazine of the Defence Force. A steady stream of articles and stories on black units has stressed the importance of all "population groups" (they do not use the word "citizens") contributing to the defense of South Africa.

WOMEN IN THE DEFENCE FORCE

To help ease personnel shortages, white women are being actively recruited into the South African military. The Army Women's College was opened at George in 1971, and by 1978 the incoming class had more than trebled, to 500. The college trains women officers for positions in the Permanent Force, the Commandos, and Civil Defence. In 1978 women were permitted for the first time to register at the Defence Force military academy at Saldana Bay.[40]

A 1978 survey reported that the percentage of women in the Defence Force had increased from 0.6 percent in February 1973 to 7.0 percent in October 1978.[41] In 1979 voluntary national service was extended to women, the first group being trained at the Medical Service Centre in Pretoria. In the Air Force women are serving as air traffic controllers, operations/intelligence personnel, and radar operators. Those in the lower ranks serve as communications and telecommunications operators, administrative clerks, radio operators, military and navy police, and musicians. In 1977 the first all-women Air Commando squadron, with a woman commander, was created.[42] Although the women are trained for noncombatant positions, they do receive weapons training.

THE PERMANENT FORCE

The Permanent Force, the career core of the Defence Force, includes such areas as command, staff, training, specialist, and technical positions. Several of the Defence Force's black units are a part of the Permanent Force. The 1977 Defence *White Paper* spelled out as a goal the near doubling of the size of the Permanent Force by 1981 so as to constitute 13.5 percent of the Defence Force (see Table 4-1). The high rate of turnover has been an important obstacle to expansion of the Permanent Force. Between 1965 and 1975 the average period of service in the Permanent Force was only 6.45 years and the annual turnover averaged 15.5 percent. Recruitment of new members has not been a problem, however: in 1977, 8,000 applicants out of a total of 19,000 were accepted, and in 1978 it was stated that applications had risen by 80 percent over the previous three years.[43]

The problem of turnover in the Permanent Force was raised in parliamentary debate in 1979. One member, referring to the loss of specialists to private industry, declared: "Our helicopters must fly, our vehicles must move and our electronic equipment must function. . . .We are in a state of war and for the present we shall have to pay to retain particular services."[44] Other difficulties mentioned included "a considerable shortage of senior and junior staff members," high turnover among members of the Navy and the medical service, and "critical shortages in certain categories of Air Force flight personnel."[45]

A new plan introduced to attract those with skills from the private sector involves a "short service system" of one year in the Permanent Force, followed by assignment to Citizen Force or Commando units. Other measures to expand the Permanent Force have included recruitment of black South Africans, as well as white women.

In 1980 an article in the South African *Financial Mail* (February 22) discussed some key difficulties with the current system of reliance on a small professional force with the main military power supplied by the Citizen Force and Commando reserves. Sudden, large-scale call-ups of these forces have been needed for major operations, yet in these cases "the economy suffers seriously" from the loss of skilled white manpower. Further, such call-ups have also meant that "virtually everyone knows the Defence Force is on the offensive—so much so that reports of troop movements appear in foreign newspapers within days" even though the news is blacked out locally.

With the theme that "Blacks can add beef to the army" the article suggested two possible solutions to the problem of call-ups: opening the Defence Force to all races on an equal and nonsegregated basis and creating a special combat force of at least one division which could be "deployed speedily and silently without involving civilian families in repeated military activities." It also suggested that such a move could ease the problem of black unemployment. But despite the recruitment of more blacks and the strengthening of the Permanent Force, the obstacles to such moves in South Africa are great. Except for the pay incentive, it is doubtful that many blacks would fight for apartheid or that the Nationalist government would want to rely heavily on black troops.

NATIONAL SERVICE

National Service members are mainly white males between the ages of 17 and 25 who are conscripted or who have volunteered for compulsory military duty. They supplement the Permanent Force in forming South Africa's full-time military forces. In 1977 the period of National Service was extended from one year to a maximum of two years. Following National Service white men are required to serve twelve years as active reserves in the Citizen Force or Commandos. Men may volunteer for Citizen Force or Commando units, but still must serve the initial two-year National Service duty. The January 1979 intake of National Servicemen was 20,000 (there are two intakes each year, in January and June), the largest since World War II.[46]

As noted, the Defence Force is now accepting white women volunteers for National Service training, as well as people of mixed race and Indians. Whether compulsory National Service will be implemented for people of mixed race and Indians has become, of course, a very important issue relating to the Botha government's Total Strategy and the whole direction of its racial policies, and how these are perceived by people of mixed race and Indians.

The government would also like to draw even larger numbers of whites into compulsory National Service. The 1978 Citizenship Amendment Bill provides that foreign residents not older than twenty-five are automatically granted South African citizenship after two years and so become eligible for National Service. Those who decline the proffered citizenship immediately lose their resident permits. Between 1970 and 1978 more than 100,000 white immigrants registered for National Service, but there has still been resentment arising from a feeling that foreigners were avoiding military service.[47] The Defence Force established a new "complaints division" to deal with allegations of ill-treatment or sadism, problems often associated with those undergoing compulsory National Service. Reports in the press and in parliament pinpointed several deaths linked to harsh punishment.[48]

THE CITIZEN FORCE

The Citizen Force provides the majority of South Africa's trained military forces available for part-time service. It is made up of volunteers and conscripted men who have completed their two years of National Service. For twelve years they serve in the Citizen Force as active reserves, subject to call-ups for active duty for any period of time and liable for the completion of 720 days of training camp. Citizen Force units comprise regular elements of the Army, Navy and Air Force (whereas Commando units have been organized to serve at particular local areas and installations). Defence Force plans (see Table 4-1) called for a reduction in the percentage of Citizen Force units in the Defence Force from almost 55 percent in 1977, to about 35 percent in 1981, equal to the planned strength of Commando units. The 1977 Defence *White Paper* and the 1979 defense debate in parliament both mention shortages of officers, particularly senior officers, in the Citizen Force.

Also discussed in parliament was the burden that has been placed in recent years on Citizen Force reserves, particular infantry. They have been called up for active duty for the Namibia war for periods of three months, and in some cases six, per year, while being credited with only thirty days of training.[49] The problem has persisted even though the extension of National Service to two years was intended to ease this burden on active reserves.

Businessmen have been concerned about the economic disruption caused by the continuing call-ups of Citizen Force reserves. The *Financial Mail* has noted that in some instances men are called up with very little warning for three weeks of service only to find their tour extended to three months. The Defence Force has acknowledged the problem, but declared that businesses and families will have to accept that the situation "will get worse before it gets better."[50]

The lengthened period of active reserve duty of twelve years, begun in 1982, is intended to greatly expand the Citizen Force in order to lessen the disruptive impact of call-ups for training camps and military operations by spreading them over a larger number of men on reserve. The 1982 Defence *White Paper* states that under the new system the goal would be to have Citizen Force members called up for military operations only once every two years. Thus filling one full-time position for operations will require the call-up of ten Citizen Force members over a two-year period. Even with this new system, men in the Citizen Force will still be liable for emergency call to active duty at any time.

COMMANDOS

The Commandos are local Defence Force units modeled on the militias used historically by the Afrikaners. The Commandos have depended heavily on volunteers. In 1979 it was reported that approximately half of the Commandos were volunteers and that 70.7 percent of their officers were volunteers.[51] Like the Citizen Force, Commando groups include men who have completed their National service, but who are still liable for twelve years' active reserve and 720 days of training camp. It is apparent that the Defence Force is seeking to transform the character of the Commandos from what had been a relatively casual organization into an important component of the counterinsurgency effort. Commando groups are to be reorganized into offensive and defensive elements, with the offensive elements available for deployment outside of the local Commando's area.[52] The Commandos were to be expanded by 1981 to make up almost 35 percent of the Defence Force, equal in strength to the Citizen Force. Commando groups have been assigned to protect installations designated as "key national points" (such as factories, communications centers, power plants). There are even university Commando groups. In both rural and urban areas Commandos can be mobilized to cooperate with police and other military forces in counterinsurgency and other types of operations.

In 1978 the Defence Force authorized Commando units to recruit black volunteers for Army service in combat units; such volunteers will be required to serve on the border in Namibia after training. It was reported that the Johannesburg East Commando was establishing a platoon to "help and protect" the people of Soweto, and that soldiers of mixed race had been invited to joint Commando units in the Eastern Cape.[53]

Like those in the Citizen Force, Commando members still on active reserve have faced the difficulty of call-ups for three and even six month periods of active duty. In parliament there has been great concern expressed at the declining number of Commando volunteers in the rural areas. Another problem mentioned was shortages of vehicles and equipment at Commando camps.[54]

Under the new program launched in 1982 the Commandos are to be revamped and greatly increased in number. As in the case of the Citizen Force, the aim is to add greater numbers in order to spread the service obligation more widely. Under the new system white men who have not undergone military service will be obligated to register with the military up to age fifty-five and may be liable for service up to age sixty, depending on the needs of the Defence Force. The goal is to provide local military protection around the country that can be mobilized as demanded by the situation. It is a program that obviously anticipates the spread of guerrilla activity to many areas.

Civil Defense

South Africa has worked at a program to build up and strengthen its civil defense program. The Civil Defence Act of 1977 empowered provincial and local authorities to enact civil defense ordinances and recruit citizens for civil defense duties. The civil defense program is directly linked to and supervised by the Defence Force. Under the terms of the legislation, 636 civil defense organizations had been established by 1979, of which 131 had received an "A" preparedness rating from the South African Army. Approximately 173 more local civil defense organizations were to be established or reorganized.[55]

In parliament the deputy defense minister stated that "an intensive programme for training, exercises, and evaluation" of the preparedness of all civil defense organizations would soon be launched by the Army and that the goal was to have all local authorities establish civil defense organizations by the end of 1979. Civil defense groups can also be established by industries, businesses, schools, and universities, and they are open to men and women. The Civil Defence Act of 1977 empowers the minister of defence to proclaim a three month "state of disaster" in any area to provide assistance and protection and "to combat civil disruption. "Disaster" includes "any consequences arising out of terrorism."[56]

CADETS

The cadet system in South African secondary schools has been undergoing rapid expansion. In 1976, when it was reorganized, the system had 57,000 cadets. The 1977 Defence *White Paper* reported that the number had reached 100,000 and was expected to reach 200,000. By April 1978 there were reported to be 589 cadet detachments with 125,000 cadets and a budget of $40 million.[57]

The goal of the program is to feed youth into the military system: "The school cadet system goes a long way to preparing our youth for their National Service," *Paratus* noted in its November 1978 issue. The cadet program includes drilling, lectures on military concepts and counterinsurgency, and marching bands. Cadet detachments are being directly affiliated with Permanent Force and Citizen Force regiments, and young teachers are being called up during holidays for training as Commando officers. Girls have been made eligible for cadet training, and programs for girls have been set up at a number of schools. In 1978 it was reported that legislation was being prepared to extend cadet training to mixed race and Indian schools and that a government committee which included Defence Force representatives was surveying such an extension. In 1979 it was reported that the committee's report was being referred to the mixed race and Indian educational authorities for implementation. There have, however, been protests from both communities. The Indian Reform party opposed it as a step leading to compulsory military service for Indians, and the Cape Teachers Professional Association rejected the idea of a cadet system in Coloured schools, saying "Even if we foolishly accepted the cadet system, our children would reject it."[58]

In addition to the cadet system, Youth Preparedness programs have been introduced into the classrooms. These combine political indoctrination along pro-apartheid lines and the theme of preparation for conflict and war. Some white secondary schools in the Transvaal have started *Veldskool* outdoor camps for boys and girls which combine military-oriented physical activities and lectures on political topics, focusing on the menace of communism.[59]

THE SOUTH AFRICAN POLICE

According to the official South African Yearbook (1979), the South African Police (SAP) is a "semi-military organization constituted on a natioinal basis." The three branches—uniform, detective, and security—have as their functions the preservation of internal security and law and order, criminal investigation, and crime prevention. As the "first line of defence in the event of unrest. . .all members receive a thorough training in infantry drill and maneuvers."[60] As a national force, the South African Police are distinct from local municipal police and other police forces operating in the country.

In 1978 the police numbered more than 35,000, including 19,341 whites and 15,662 blacks. Black South Africans serving in the police included 12,990 Africans, 1,795 Coloured, and 877 Indians.[61] Blacks are concentrated in the lower ranks: figures on the number of commissioned officers in the police show there were 2,188 whites (in 1976) and 98 blacks (in 1978).[62]

In addition, there are two separate police reserve forces.[63] The Police Reserve is made up of former members of the police who can be called up in emergencies; it numbered 15,034 in 1978. The Reserve Police, on the other hand, is a voluntary citizen force made up mainly of people with prior police or military training. There are four different groups, operating in urban and rural areas and at important installations. They aid the police on a regular basis. Essentially, they assist with ordinary police duties, thereby freeing the police for more urgent tasks. The Reserve Police numbered 21,820 in 1978. In emergencies, the South African Police can mobilize a total force, regulars and reserves, of more than 70,000 men.

Until the 1970s the South African Police had the primary role in the Nationalist government's counterinsurgency operations. In the post-Sharpeville period they were used within South Africa, in northern

Namibia against SWAPO, and in Rhodesia against ZAPU, ZANU and the ANC of South Africa. But by the mid-seventies, as South Africa became a country at war, the Defence Force had in large part taken over these counterinsurgency operations. However, the police still play an important role in the Namibia war, and in South Africa they patrol the borders and urban areas. The Security Police, the third branch, combine the functions of political police, intelligence, and counter-insurgency.

The paramilitary role of the police was openly displayed during the 1976-77 student uprising. Police units wore camouflage uniforms, were armed with automatic rifles and shotguns, and used "hippos" (armored transport trucks). They were assisted by Air Force transport and reconnaissance aircraft.[64] In the years after Soweto, the police presence in black urban areas has continued to have a military cast, and a number of "crime prevention" operations have been carried out, some of them with the aid of Army units.

Several parliamentary measures have been passed to extend the powers and immunities granted to the police. The Indemnity Act of 1977 indemnifies the State and its officials (including the police) in respect to actions undertaken "in good faith. . .to prevent or terminate internal disorder." The act was applied retroactively to June 16, 1976, the day when police shootings of unarmed student protesters touched off the student uprising. The Police Amendment Act of 1979 contained several significant clauses. Clause two deepened the country's border zone from one to ten kilometers. Within this zone police may conduct warrantless searches of persons, vehicles, and property. If this measure is applied to the borders with the "independent" Bantustans, thousands of square kilometers in the heart of the country could come under its provisions. Clause three allows the state president to deploy the police inside or *outside* the country. Clause nine allows the "prohibition of the publication of untrue information" in connection with the Police Force. Similar laws previously passed cover publication of information on prisons and the Defence Force; the obvious effect is to muzzle press reporting on these areas, since the onus is placed on the publisher to prove there were "reasonable grounds" for believing any information published is true. Clause eleven provides for call-ups of Police Reserves for a total of up to 180 days a year.

In July 1978 the government announced that police were being assigned to three-month tours on patrol along the borders with Swaziland, Mozambique, Rhodesia, and Botswana. The aim was to stop guerrilla infiltration and prevent people from leaving the country for guerrilla training. In addition, police border posts were reinforced.

The increase in counterinsurgency operations has coincided with a continuing manpower shortage, and the police have expressed dissatisfaction with pay scales and conditions of service. In 1979 there were almost four thousand vacancies in the police, mainly for whites and Africans, and the police training colleges were far below capacity.[65] Under the terms of the 1957 Defence Act, National Servicemen can be assigned to the police for training and service; this was first done in 1975, and an estimated 1,000 conscripts are channeled annually to the police.[66] A 1979 article in the government's *South African Digest* (August 17) presented an account of the South African Police on counterinsurgency duty along the borders. There were photos of police on foot patrol, using infrared nightsight binoculars, and in a machine-gun nest:

> Although the danger involved in being a policeman is real and present everywhere, the demands placed on the South African Police serving on the border are definitely greater.
>
> Snipers, landmines, mortars and other weapons are among the threats to be faced daily as part of duty.
>
> Men of all races are specially trained at a centre outside Groblersdal in the Eastern Transvaal, where conditions and training are as close as possible to the real thing.
>
> After six weeks of rigorous training, the men return to their stations throughout South Africa and South West Africa to await call-up for border duty.

THE SECURITY POLICE

In the first years after the Union of South Africa was formed, police assigned to security matters (generally related to political and labor organisations) were detectives from the Criminal Investigation Division (CID), aided by informers. In 1947 they were formed into the Special Branch of the CID, which then, at an undisclosed date, became the Security Police.[67] The Police Amendment Act of 1955 (and subsequent legislation) extended police functions to include "preservation of the internal security of the Union" and empowered the Security Police to "undertake the covert collection of information. . .connected with sabotage, subversion, espionage, or any other matter relating to the security of the State."[68] South Africa's extensive security laws have given the Security Police powers of investigation (including the use of informers and "bugging" techniques), searches of persons and property, detention *incommunicado* without trial, and interrogation.

In 1963 Hendrik van den Bergh (later designated to form the Bureau of State Security, BOSS) was appointed head of the Security Police. In cooperation with the minister of justice, J. B. Vorster, and armed with new security measures, he set out to eliminate the underground campaigns of sabotage and other attacks launched after December 1961. As discussed in Chapter 2, there have been numerous complaints of torture and brutality by the Security Police, including the use of suffocation, electric shock, beatings, immersion in water, forced standing, and psychological torture.

In January 1980 there came to light a significant case showing that Security Police operations have not been restricted to South Africa itself. Then it was revealed that the deputy director of the Geneva-based International University Exchange Fund (IUEF), Craig Williamson, was an agent of the Security Police.[69] The IEUF, whose main support was Scandinavian government agencies, gave substantial assistance to Black Conscious Movement programs in South Africa. By the late 1970s educational projects of SWAPO, the Patriotic Front of Zimbabwe, and the ANC were also being supported through the IUEF. Williamson, who had administered IUEF projects while a student leader in South Africa, was hired by the organization after he had left the country in 1976 and was appointed deputy director in 1978. It was also revealed that an IUEF project in South Africa was set up by another former student leader, Karl Edwards, who was a BOSS agent.

Since 1963, at least forty-five persons are known to have died while under detention by the Security Police. The most infamous case was that of Black Consciousness leader Stephen Biko, who died in September 1977. Amnesty International, in its 1977 report, *Political Imprisonment in South Africa*, has declared, "The pattern that emerges, on examining the available evidence, is one of torture being used almost on a routine basis by the Security Police."[70] Targets of the Security Police have not been restricted to those who are believed to be linked to underground resistance; student, church, labor, and cultural organizations are also included: essentially, that is, any group that has seemed to be able to mobilize effective popular opposition to apartheid in any sphere.

Since 1967 the United Nations Commission on Human Rights has maintained an Ad Hoc Working Group of Experts to monitor human rights violations in South Africa, focusing on cases of torture and the deaths of detainees. The conclusion of the Working Group's report of January 1980 states:

> In the light of information which has come to its knowledge concerning accusations brought against police forces practising torture in South Africa, the Working Group concludes that the pattern has not changed, i.e. that torture by the Security Police is common practice and, moreover, that the Government seems to acquiesce in it and to cover it up by all possible means.
>
> It appears that several types of torture were systematically applied in all the cases brought to the knowledge of the *Ad Hoc* Group of Experts, in particular physical assault, electric shocks on the body,

standing upright for a prolonged period, wearing shoes previously filled with gravel, being compelled to remain in a half-squatting position for several hours, threats of death, deprivation of sleep and complete isolation with prohibition of communication with the outside world.

Although the charges of murder, torture and ill-treatment are generally rejected, the resemblance between the different statements concerning the methods of torture employed suggest that the allegations are true.

Furthermore, although a number of names of South African Security Police officers are regularly mentioned in the cases of alleged torture, the Group notes that in general, no steps were taken by the Government against these torturers.

The Group has been particularly struck by the concomitance of the acts of torture and murder committed by the South African police, especially since July 1976. It considers that these acts can constitute only a huge campaign of intimidation of African nationalists and that the attitude of the South African Government, which endeavours in almost every case to cover up the acts with which it is charged, can but lead to the conclusion that this is the true policy of South Africa.[71]

OTHER POLICE FORCES

In addition to the South African Police and its specialized branches, there are a number of other police forces operating in the country.[72]

The Railways, Harbours and Airways Authority Police are responsible for the security of the extensive installations of this agency, which have already been the target of sabotage incidents. In 1978 the South African Railways introduced a special engine unit, bullet-proofed, built to withstand land-mine explosions, and able to carry a land-mine detector to inspect the railway lines and other equipment.[73]

The Bantustan governments have police forces and guard units.

The mining companies and other large employers of migrant labour have their own company security forces and in some cases lock-up cells. Anglo-American Corporation is said to have a force of three thousand men equipped with tear gas and dogs. The services of security guard companies are available for smaller businesses.

The Military Police is responsible for searching for deserters, including those who have left the military for reasons of conscientious objection.

The inspectors of the Department of Plural Relations are armed and have the power of arrest and search without warrant. They operate under the authority of the local Administration Boards, which administer the African urban townships in "white" areas, that is, most of the black urban population of South Africa. Further, the Department of Plural Relations maintains finger-print records of Africans over age sixteen, and as of 1978, it reported it had 14,878,848 fingerprints on file.[74] It declared that the file was "absolutely essential" because it guarantees positive identification and provides protection against foreign infiltration.

The "squatter control" sections of the Divisional Council and other local Cape authorities have armed inspectors with the power of arrest and search without warrant. (They often carry concealed arms.)

The Community Councils that the government has been trying to set up in the African townships have been authorized to create guard units, and such a unit has been organized in Soweto in cooperation with the South African Police. Vigilante groups (Makgotla) have also cropped up in some townships. Though they have drawn criticism because of their brutality, they have nonetheless sought formal recognition by the white authorities.[75]

THE NATIONAL INTELLIGENCE SERVICE

The National Intelligence Service (NIS) was the designation given in 1980 to the organizational arm of the Department of National Security (DONS). DONS, in turn, was the successor to the Bureau of State Security (BOSS), which had been renamed DONS in 1978 when it was moved out of the office of the prime minister to become a new, separate government department. Prior to 1978 BOSS had been virtually synonymous with the figure of Gen. Hendrik van den Bergh, who, as director of the agency, had been the right-hand man of then Prime Minister Vorster. Van den Bergh and Vorster retired in 1978, when both were being linked in the press to irregularities concerning secret funds for the propaganda activities of the Information Department. Van den Bergh was succeeded by his assistant, Alexander van Wyck, and it was announced that there would be no changes in the agency's functions. But the newly appointed prime minister, P. W. Botha, took the new DONS portfolio himself and also retained the Defence portfolio. He has given priority to his military advisors and Military Intelligence.[76]

Van den Bergh had been a close friend of J. B. Vorster since their internment during World War II for pro-Nazi activities. After the war van den Bergh joined the police force, and when Vorster became minister of police in the Verwoerd government, van den Bergh was appointed (in 1963) head of the Security Police. When Vorster became prime minister, van den Bergh was retained as his special security advisor and assigned to organize BOSS.

BOSS's functions included the investigation of "all matters affecting the security of the State," as well as the correlation and evaluation of all information collected and its dissemination to other government bodies. BOSS also received an open-ended mandate to "perform such other functions and responsibilities as may be determined from time to time."[77] This effectively gave the agency the power to carry out covert operations. BOSS was freed of scrutiny by the country's Public Service Commission. Its funds, provided through a Security Services Special Account, were not subject to ordinary treasury and parliamentary controls.

BOSS was further shielded by two secrecy measures.* One law made it an offense to knowingly disclose any "security matter," and the other permitted government ministers to suppress any evidence, produced before courts or other bodies that is stated, by sworn affidavit, to be "prejudicial to the security of the State." Other legislation authorized taps on telephones and the interception of mail. BOSS was not, however, given such police powers as arrest, detention, and interrogation; these, in security cases, remained the province of the Security Police. BOSS was to receive, coordinate, and evaluate information from the police, Military Intelligence, and other government departments. It could also carry out its own intelligence operations abroad. The scope of BOSS's security operations, when interpreted most broadly, covered military, political, economic, social, educational, and psychological spheres as well as subversion, terrorism, sabotage, and espionage.[78]

In 1978, in testimony before the Erasmus Commission investigating the secret activities of the Department of Information, General van den Bergh stated that he had to know what went on in South Africa, "It does not matter what." BOSS had "many" secret projects, he said. The commission proceeded to expose his involvement in the projects and in the efforts to cover them up. Van den Bergh operated as a power behind the throne, and had considerable influence over Vorster. Van den Bergh testified: "Mr. Commissioner, I really want to tell you that I am able with my department to do the impossible. This is not bragging. I have good men, I don't have weak men. . . .I have enough men to commit murder if I tell them, kill. . .I don't care who the prey is. These are the type of men I have. . . ."[79]

There have been several cases which seem to bear out Van den Berghe's boast. One victim of an assassination was O. R. Tiro, exiled leader of the South African Student Organization (SASO). He was killed in 1974 by a parcel bomb in Botswana. In the same year John Dube, the deputy ANC representative in Zambia, was killed by a similar device at the Liberation Centre in Lusaka. ANC representative Joe Gqabi was assassinated in Zimbabwe in 1981, and Petros Myawose, the ANC repre-

*Clauses 10 and 25 of the General Laws Amendment Act of 1969, amended by sections 10 and 25 of the General Laws Amendment Act of 1972.

sentative in Swaziland, was killed by a car bomb in 1982. Ruth First, a prominent ANC member, was killed by a letter bomb in Maputo in 1982.

A number of reports spotlight London as a center of BOSS activity. In 1971 press reports and statements in the British Parliament charged that South African agents had been operating in Britain since 1966, spying on and harassing South African opponents of apartheid in exile and British anti-apartheid groups. The South African agents were apparently able to operate with impunity, and journalists suspected that they were being aided on an unofficial basis by Scotland Yard members.[80] In 1978 it was also alleged that BOSS had collaborated with a dissident faction of the British Secret Service in an effort to discredit the Liberal and Labour parties, which were seen as unsympathetic to South Africa.[81]

In 1979 journalist Gordon Winter, an admitted spy in London for the South African Security Police and BOSS for the previous sixteen years,[82] appeared on British television to charge BOSS involvement in the Jeremy Thorpe affair, in which the Liberal party leader was blackmailed, and in an attempt to frame Peter Hain, an effective campaigner against sports ties with apartheid. Winter charged that BOSS had murdered another agent, journalist Keith Wallace, who had been on the verge of admitting his activities. Winter also said he had given BOSS information on escape routes used by people fleeing South Africa and about arms smuggling into the country. The British television report stated that "people were killed because of his information."

In 1979 and 1980 the London *Observer* published three articles by South African BOSS agent Arthur McGiven. His articles gave details about BOSS spying on the parliamentary opposition in South Africa and in the frontline states, as well as the monitoring of anti-apartheid groups and political figures in Britain.[83]

The *New Statesman* published two articles (August 15 and 22, 1980) containing more information about BOSS spying in Britain. These were the work of another young South African, Ivan Himmelhoch. He had worked for BOSS from 1976 to 1979. While studying law in London he monitored anti-apartheid groups and reported secretly to BOSS at the South African embassy in London. He said that the post of first secretary in the South African embassy had been held successively by three men who were head of BOSS's operations in Britain.

In contrast to earlier reports, Himmelhoch claimed that BOSS was wary of surveillance of its activities by British intelligence. An article in the London *Observer* a few weeks later (September 7, 1980), citing unidentified intelligence sources, indicated that close British collaboration with BOSS was curtailed in 1976, after the BOSS campaign to smear Liberal party leader Jeremy Thorpe and anti-apartheid campaigner Peter Hain, and had since been limited to matters of "common interest."

CIA links to BOSS were said to be more "open," according to these sources. The CIA was prepared to pass on information to the South Africans on anti-apartheid activists in the United States in exchange for facilities in South Africa for American spying. For example, the article said the United States had planes based in South Africa to take reconnaissance photos over Africa. Copies of the photos were passed on to South Africa, but photos taken over South Africa itself were not. This arrangement—or the violation of it—was evidently reflected in an incident of early 1980, when the South African government expelled members of the U.S. embassy in South Africa. The Americans, it was said, had tried to spy on South Africa's nuclear facilities by using a secret camera mounted in the ambassador's light airplane. (In retaliation, the United States expelled two South African military attachés from Washington.)

The murder of Dr. Robert Smit, the South African ambassador to the International Monetary Fund, and his wife in 1977 gave rise to charges that Smit had uncovered massive currency smuggling by South African officials. These officials apparently had links to the Information Department scandals. Smit had been ready to disclose this information when he was murdered. The killers allegedly were West Germans (see Chapter 7). However, in 1980 a reporter for the *Sunday News Journal* of Wilmington, Delaware, charged that the CIA had helped BOSS to hire CIA-trained Cuban exiles to murder the Smits.[84] The article also claimed other instances of BOSS cooperation with DINA (formerly, the Chilean equivalent of the FBI). BOSS was said to have channeled CIA arms and money into Chile to back the 1973 coup against the Allende government and paid the assassins of Orlando Letelier, the Chilean exile leader who was killed by a bomb in Washington, D.C., in 1976, in gold Krugerrands.

John Stockwell, former head of the CIA Angola task force who resigned in protest against the agency's policies, describes a pattern of collaboration between the CIA and BOSS in his book *In Search of Enemies*:

> The CIA has traditionally sympathized with South Africa and enjoyed its close liaison with BOSS. The two organizations share a violent antipathy toward communism and in the early sixties the South Africans had facilitated the agency's development of a mercenary army to suppress the Congo rebellion. BOSS, however, tolerates little clandestine nonsense inside the country and the CIA had always restricted its Pretoria station's activity to maintaining the liaison with BOSS. That is, until 1974, when it yielded to intense pressures in Washington and expanded the Pretoria station's responsibilities to include covert operations to gather intelligence about South Africa's nuclear project. In the summer of 1975 BOSS rolled up this effort and quietly expelled those CIA personnel directly involved. The agency did not complain,

as the effort was acknowledged to have been clumsy and obvious. The agency continued its cordial relationship with BOSS.[85]

While not mentioned by Stockwell, investigative reports on the transfer of the advanced 155-mm Space Research Corporation howitzer from the United States to South Africa have indicated that the CIA could have had a key role (see Chapter 6).

The most significant BOSS link in the United States, however, was reportedly to Vice President George Bush. The semisecret visit of top-ranking South African military intelligence officials to the United States in 1981 resulted in a report that during the Nixon and Ford administrations General van den Bergh visited Washington frequently and "enjoyed close ties" with Vice President Bush, who served as CIA director during that period.[86] The Carter administration apparently wanted to limit such contacts and is reported to have refused van den Bergh a visa to enter the United States shortly before his retirement in 1978. A South African press report on this incident described General van den Bergh as a "close friend" of George Bush, and said, incidentally, that BOSS agents were stationed at South African diplomatic missions in the United States.[87]

From its inception BOSS had been tied to the political strategies of van den Bergh, Vorster, and Information Minister Mulder. They had formed within the Nationalist hierarchy the ruling faction that was seeking to assure the security of white South Africa through a strategy combining propaganda, secret diplomacy, and arms deals. The flavor of these efforts was described by British journalist Anthony Sampson:

> The secretive journeys of Mulder and Rhoodie, working closely with Gen. van den Bergh and BOSS, were often interlocked with military business, whether in Israel, Zaire or the Ivory Coast. Rhoodie, the polished playboy, mingled with arms dealers as well as newspaper owners. . . .And Van den Bergh's intelligence links were the key to many military bargains.[88]

With Prime Minister Botha favoring the Military Intelligence apparatus over NIS a new emphasis has also been placed on the State Security Council as the high-level coordinating body for security questions. In the past, such issues were likely to be settled by General van den Bergh and Prime Minister Vorster in private. But in spite of these changes and the scandals in the Information Department which brought some BOSS activities out of the shadows, the structure erected by van den Bergh apparently remains in place at home and abroad.

In 1979 Botha appointed an outsider head of DONS, Dr. Lukas Daniel Barnard, a young Afrikaner professor of political science. Reports on his academic background (he is the editor of a book and the author of twenty-five articles) indicate that Dr. Barnard's outlook combines a strong religious (Calvinist) orientation with a belief in the virtue of force in international affairs. In one chapter of the book he edited, *Conflict and Order in International Relations* (published in South Africa in Afrikaans), he argues in favor of South Africa's becoming a nuclear power and making this known as a deterrent, and declares, "The protection of the Lord's Kingdom on earth makes the use of the power of the sword a God-given task and calling."[89] Even the Afrikaner press expressed doubts about this unorthodox choice of a young professor whose work was not regarded highly in some academic circles. In many ways, however, Barnard's views apparently do express sentiments held by many Afrikaners, though these are framed in an abstruse academic style focusing on power politics and nuclear strategy. It is widely assumed by now that South Africa has already become a nuclear power. Just prior to his appointment, Dr. Barnard had traveled to Washington, D.C., where he was reported to have studied nuclear weapons strategy.[90]

Excerpts from other writings by Barnard published in the South African press indicate that while he says governments must cultivate the loyalty of their citizens to combat terrorism, his emphasis is on military power and its effective use. For example, he has advocated that South Africa set up highly trained antiterrorist units to act "lightning fast as a coordinated whiplash task force." His views on the international scene echo those of the right wing in the United States and Europe: he warns of aggressive Communist expansionism, the threat in the West of a "leadership crisis and undermining of moral guts," and a world that wants to "hide its spinelessness behind propagandistic talk of human rights and international morality."[91]

Events in 1982 indicated that the NIS was continuing secret foreign operations despite the preeminance of Military Intelligence in the Botha government. In October Daniel J. J. Opperman, a diplomat at the South African embassy in Washington, D.C., was reportedly asked to leave the country. He was said to have been the NIS station chief, but the U.S. State Department refused to comment on the case. TransAfrica, the black lobbying group, had reported that its offices were regularly broken into, with nothing taken. But a State Department source said Opperman was not "doing those break-ins." In London, another South African embassy employee, Joseph Klue, was asked to leave Britain in December after court testimony linked him to two men charged with planting explosives and breaking into the offices of the ANC and SWAPO.[92]

MILITARY INTELLIGENCE

Reports on the prominent position of Military Intelligence (MI) in the Botha government and its earlier tension with BOSS have been cited above. One incident that showed MI's importance was a secret visit to the United States by top-ranking MI officials in March 1981, less than two months after the Reagan administration took office. Among the five officials were Lieutenant General P. W. van der Westhuizen, the chief of Military Intelligence; Rear Admiral Willem N. du Plessis, assigned to the NIS; and Brigadier Nils van Tonder. These three were believed to be the top officials in MI.[93] The visit included meetings with Congressional members and staff, an official with the Defense Intelligence Agency at the Pentagon, a staff officer of the National Security Council, and American ambassador to the United Nations Jeane Kirkpatrick. When news of the visit began to leak out, the State Department (which has had a public policy of not permitting visits by military officers since 1962) claimed the men had failed to include their status on visa applications at the U.S. embassy in South Africa and had thus been given visas through an "oversight." The five were said to have been invited by the conservative American Security Council in Washington, but the South African *Financial Mail* concluded that the visit was to "discuss matters of common interest" with officials in the new administration and it was hoped it could be kept quiet.[94]

New York Times correspondent Joseph Lelyveld, commenting on cooperation on intelligence matters between the United States and South Africa, noted the "close cooperation" as late as the 1975-76 intervention in Angola by South Africa and the United States. There has "never been any suggestion that the Carter administration halted intelligence sharing with South Africa," although an American official said it developed an "adversary aspect" reflected in the expulsion of three American military attachés for spying, he reported. The Reagan administration's policy of "constructive engagement" evidently included a return to closer intelligence cooperation. Five months after the visit by the top MI officials, Defence Minister General Magnus Malan cited the visit as an example of the improved relations between South Africa and the United States.[95] General van der Westhuizen returned to Washington in 1982 as a part of a South African delegation dealing with Namibia, and he was included in Botha's delegation that met with President Kaunda of Zambia in May 1982.

The failed South African coup attempt against the government of the Seychelle Islands in November 1981 (see Chapter 3) provided additional confirmation of the primacy of MI. Mercenary leader Colonel Mike Hoare testified in a South African court that control of the operation had been taken away from the NIS and given to MI on orders from the prime minister's office. And, as noted above, he said he informed a CIA representative in Pretoria of the coup plans and told his troops that the CIA had approved the plans.[96]

THE STATE SECURITY COUNCIL

Because of Prime Minister Botha's determination to implement a "Total National Strategy," he placed greater emphasis on the State Security Council. The origins of this body are entwined with those of BOSS. During the mid-sixties, when the Nationalist government was gearing itself to combat the new development of underground and guerrilla activity, several national security bodies were set up,[97] but they proved inadequate. BOSS was then formed as the coordinating agency for intelligence and security. The State Security Council was established in 1970-71 to act in an advisory capacity on the information assembled and analyzed by BOSS. The Council consists of the prime minister, the ministers of justice, defense, police, foreign affairs, national security, the chief of the Defence Force, the police commissioner, the secretaries for foreign affairs and justice, as well as ministers and members of parliament coopted on an *ad-hoc* basis.

The role of the State Security Council is:

> Upon request of the prime minister, to advise the Government concerning the formulation of national policy and strategy in connection with the security of the Republic, the manner in which this policy or strategy must be carried out, and a policy to combat any particular threat against the security of the Republic; and to determine an intelligence priority.[98]

It appears, however, that under the government of Prime Minister Vorster this body was inactive, overshadowed by the close relationship that existed between Vorster and General van den Bergh. Under Botha, it is reported that the State Security Council has been given high status with coordination by military personnel (see Chapter 7).

5 Arms for Apartheid

SINCE 1963 SOUTH AFRICA HAS BEEN SUBJECT to an international arms embargo voted by the United Nations Security Council; in 1977 a new, mandatory embargo was passed with somewhat stronger provisions. Nonetheless, South Africa has been able to amass an arsenal of modern weapons in large part from Western sources during the two decades since the first embargo was voted. In addition to conventional military power, Pretoria now has achieved nuclear weapons capability. Because of the satellite sighting of a nuclear weapons test site in 1977 and of characteristic flashes in the South Atlantic in 1979 and 1980, South Africa is widely believed to have made and exploded nuclear weapons. Even without complete confirmation of the explosions, there is general agreement that South Africa could make nuclear weapons on short notice.

As a result of this build-up, the Nationalist government of South Africa's 4.5 million whites has virtually total military dominance over 24 million black South Africans, as well as some 50 million people of the neighboring countries in southern Africa. Using information from *The Military Balance* and *Jane's* publications, the South African *Financial Mail* compared South Africa's forces with those of other states in the region and concluded that "the South African Defence Force appears overwhelmingly stronger than the combined conventional forces of neighboring states—including the Cuban and East German forces in Angola."[1] Even if the forces of Nigeria, a nonnuclear power but the strongest military power in sub-Saharan Africa after South Africa, are added to those of the frontline states, South Africa still holds the edge in armaments. South Africa's military power is enhanced by an infrastructure of transport, communications, and modern industry unequaled in Africa and developed with the aid of corporate investment from the West. This pronounced military superiority has enabled the Nationalist government to play an offensive role in the region, as in the 1975-76 invasion of Angola, in the Rhodesian war, in the war in Namibia, and in the strikes against neighboring countries.

The significant issues concerning the South African military build-up have been the enforcement of the United Nations arms embargos, the sources of the weapons that it has acquired, the degree of South African self-sufficiency in arms production, and, finally, the development of a nuclear weapons capability. These issues are examined in this chapter.

THE EMBARGOS AND ARMS ACQUIRED BY SOUTH AFRICA

The 1963 arms embargo was passed by the United Nations Security Council (Resolution 181) during the turbulent period after the Sharpeville Massacre. At this time, repression and sabotage were escalating, and the call for total economic sanctions against South Africa was being raised. The operative paragraph of the resolution stated that the Security Council "solemnly calls on all states to cease forthwith the sale and shipment of arms, ammunition of all types and military vehicles to South Africa." In December 1963 a second resolution (182) appealed for compliance with the embargo and extended it to include "equipment and materials for the manufacture or maintenance of arms and ammunition in South Africa." A third resolution, passed in June 1964, reaffirmed the call to all states to enforce the embargo. In the Security Council, France abstained on the first and third resolutions; the Conservative government in Britain abstained on the first, but voted for the second and third. The United States had announced that it would impose its own arms embargo against South Africa a few days before the first resolution was passed and voted for all three.[2]

Both Britain and the United States declared that existing contracts for arms, parts, and maintenance would not be embargoed. Britain also continued to adhere to the 1955 Simonstown Agreement with South Africa, which is embodied in an exchange of letters that has never been fully published as a formal treaty. The agreement turned over to South Africa the Simonstown naval base, which had been run by Britain, and provided for cooperation between the two countries in defense of the Cape route. The statement by Ambassador Adlai Stevenson announcing the U.S. arms embargo included a loophole: the United States reserved the "right in the future to interpret this policy in light of the requirements for assuring the maintenance of international peace and security."[3]

The weakness of the 1963 embargo was, however, shown most clearly in the case of France: since the resolution only "called" on states to embargo South Africa and had no machinery for enforcement, France simply never adhered to it. In the next decade France emerged as South Africa's principal arms supplier (taking the place of Britain and the United

States). French companies provided a range of important weapons and signed licensing agreements for weapons assembly and production in South Africa. Among the weapons acquired by Pretoria have been Mirage III and F-1 fighter-bomber aircraft in various models; Panhard armored cars; Super Frelon, Puma, and Alouette helicopters; Transall heavy transport planes; three Daphne class submarines; and Milan antitank rockets. In reply to criticism of its policies, the French government stated on a number of occasions that its weapons were intended only for "external defense" and not internal repression, a distinction not made in the embargo resolution.[4]

Although the Italian government has claimed in response to questions raised in parliament that it was observing the embargo, Italy also became a significant source of arms for South Africa. Aermacchi of Italy supplied jet trainers with British engines (MB 326K, the Impala I) and strike planes (MB 326M, the Impala II) for the South African Air Force. Other aircraft supplied included Piaggo P-166 light transports (with American-made engines), and the American-designed Lockheed AL-60 and the AM-3C (both light planes with American engines) and Augusta Bell 205A "Huey" helicopters (a civilian model). These are of "dual use" (civilian and military), but were supplied to the South African military. Reportedly, Italy has also been South Africa's source of weapons provided to South Africa which were produced or reconditioned under American license, and therefore subject to United States and Italian export regulations. Among these weapons reported (but not confirmed) are M-109 155-mm howitzers and M-113A1 armored personnel carriers.[5]

Under the terms of the Simonstown Agreement, which was not terminated by Britain until 1975, Britain supplied South Africa with Bucaneer fighter-bomber aircraft, Wasp helicopters, and parts and maintenance for Canberra bombers and Shackleton patrol planes. South Africa also acquired weapons of British origin through other countries, including Centurian tanks (via India and Spain) and Tigercat antiaircraft missile systems (via Jordan). Britain has also supplied dual-use equipment to the South African military and police, such as a Marconi radar system, landrovers and trucks, and ICL computers.[6]

West Germany has had a role in the supply of military equipment and dual-use items to South Africa. The Transall heavy transport planes and Milan antitank rockets supplied by France are produced jointly with West German companies and should be subject to West German regulations. West German companies have supplied Unimog trucks and other heavy transport vehicles used by the South African military, as well as engines for missile boats. The South African factories used by the Sandok Austral company for the production of armored vehicles were reportedly constructed by West German firms. In addition, the West German company STEAG and other firms were involved in the South African pilot uranium enrichment program as a source of technology and specialized equipment. Since the ability to produce enriched uranium can provide South Africa with its own source of fissionable material for atomic weapons, such contacts have great military significance.[7]

A major violation of the arms embargo by the United States has been the supply to South Africa of one of the world's most advanced artillery systems: a 155-mm extended-range howitzer, which is capable of firing a nuclear shell. The howitzers were provided through the Space Research Corporation, which has headquarters in Vermont, straddling the American-Canadian border. (Additional details on this transaction are provided below.)

Italy is not the only country through which weapons of American origin have been transferred to South Africa. A similar transaction involving Commando V-150 armored personnel carriers was reportedly made through Portugal. There have been other unconfirmed reports that Lockheed F-104 Starfighters were supplied from West Germany and that North American F-51D Cavalier counterinsurgency strike planes were supplied from the United States. A number of dual-use items from the United States have been supplied to the South African military, such as Cessna light planes, Swearingen Merlin light transport planes, and IBM and other types of computers.[8] The United States has also been the principal source of nuclear cooperation with South Africa, conducted openly as a peaceful program.

In the years after the embargo was passed South Africa lobbied for formal military cooperation with NATO for the formation of a South Atlantic Treaty Organization (SATO), citing the need to protect the sealanes around the Cape and southern Africa as a route for strategic minerals to reach the West. While never formalized, South Africa did succeed in establishing links with NATO officials and NATO countries, most significantly through Project Advocatt, a sophisticated military surveillance center to monitor ship and air traffic built underground at Silvermine near Cape Town and said to be able to withstand atomic attack. Silvermine was opened in 1973 with radar, communications, and computer equipment supplied by West German, British, American, French, Danish, and Dutch companies. The NATO codification system for this equipment was provided to South Africa. Silvermine is reported to be able to monitor ship and air traffic south of the Tropic of Cancer (the southern limit of NATO's area), in the Indian Ocean as far as Bangladesh, south to Antarctic, and across the South Atlantic to South America. Silvermine is reportedly linked to the Royal Navy in Britain, to the U.S. Naval Base in San Juan, Puerto Rico, and also to Argentina, Australia, and New Zealand.[9] In 1974 South Africa set out to triple the capacity of the Simonstown Naval Base—to a capacity of forty to fifty ships—far beyond its own needs, and it has since been urging Western navies to utilize these facilities. In 1973 NATO's governing council instructed the Supreme Allied Command, Atlantic (SACLANT) based in Norfolk, Virginia, to prepare contingency plans for military operations off southern Africa, although it was said in response to questions that these plans did not involve defense of or cooperation with South Africa.[10]

THE ARMS EMBARGO OF 1977

Although the limitations of the 1963 arms embargo became apparent within a brief period, the Western countries resisted calls to strengthen the embargo until December 1977. The 1977 embargo came at a particular political juncture, after the failure of the South African and CIA intervention in Angola, after the Soweto shootings, and after the death of Steve Biko while in police hands. The new embargo served the Carter administration and the Callahan government in Britain in several ways. Both governments were committed to playing active roles in southern Africa, and the embargo put some additional pressures on Pretoria to promote settlements in Zimbabwe and Namibia and reforms at home. It also alleviated pressures from African states that were asking full economic sanctions. At the time it was passed, the Western powers had refused to accept a stronger arms embargo resolution in the Security Council and instead offered a weaker version.[11]

The main operative paragraphs of embargo resolution 418 (1977) stated that the Security Council:

1. *Determines,* having regard to the policies and acts of the South African Government, that the acquisition by South Africa of arms and related materiel constitutes a threat to the maintenance of international peace and security;

2. *Decides* that all States shall cease forthwith any provision to South Africa of arms and related materiel of all types, including the sale or transfer of weapons and ammunition, military vehicles and equipment, paramilitary police equipment, and spare parts for the aforementioned, and shall cease as well the provision of all types of equipment and supplies, and grants of licensing arrangements, for the manufacture or maintenance of the aforementioned;

3. *Calls* on all States to review, having regard to the objectives of this resolution, all existing contractual arrangements with and licences granted to South Africa relating to the manufacture and maintenance of arms, ammunition of all types and military equipment and vehicles, with a view of terminating them;

4. *Further decides* that all States shall refrain from any co-operation with South Africa in the manufacture and development of nuclear weapons.

Under resolution 421 (1977) the Security Council established a committee to examine the implementation of the embargo and study ways for it to be made more effective.

Like the 1963 embargo the new embargo could be effective only if strictly enforced by all countries, and like the earlier one the weaknesses and loopholes soon became apparent. The statement that "the acquisition of arms by South Africa" threatens international peace and security avoided calling South Africa itself the threat, for that could have been grounds for imposition of full economic sanctions; it also avoided calling the *supply* of arms to South Africa such a threat. There is no definition of "arms and related materiel" in the resolution, and the embargo asks only that countries "review" contracts and licensing arrangements with South Africa. It does not then stipulate that they be terminated. This loophole is important, given Pretoria's efforts to set up such agreements. Rather than banning all nuclear cooperation, only cooperation in the "manufacture and development of nuclear weapons" is curbed. Clearly, South Africa's current acknowledged nuclear weapons capability clearly owes a great deal to the years of peaceful nuclear cooperation with Western countries. The committee set up by the Security Council to oversee the embargo has limited powers—to gather information on enforcement and to study ways to make the embargo more effective—but no monitoring or enforcement role. Therefore, under the terms insisted on by the United States, Britain, and France, while the embargo was made "mandatory" on all countries, considerable leeway in interpretation and enforcement remain to individual states.

In light of this, it is not surprising that reports continue to appear concerning the supply of arms and military equipment to South Africa. The chairman of Armscor, the South African arms procurement and manufacturing agency, publicly stated that in 1980 about a quarter of South Africa's spending for arms—or $500 million—was being spent on imports.[12] Reports on the supply of arms to South Africa have been summarized in the 1979 and 1980 reports of the Security Council's Arms Embargo Committee, and additional information was presented by groups from a number of countries at a seminar in April 1981 sponsored by the UN Centre Against Apartheid. In addition, the role of a privately organized clearinghouse for information and protests on the supply of arms to South Africa has been played by the World Campaign Against Military and Nuclear Collaboration with South Africa, based in Oslo, Norway. Among the reports received by the Security Council Committee on the Arms Embargo have been the Space Research Corporation 155-mm howitzer deal, the shipment of British Centurian tanks to South Africa from India via Spain, and the shipment of Belgian FN rifles and 12,000 tons of unspecified arms to South Africa on a Spanish ship in 1978.

TABLE 5-1
RECENT DELIVERIES OR ORDERS OF WEAPONS FOR SOUTH AFRICA

ORIGIN	WEAPON AND TYPE	DATE	COMMENTS
France	AS-12 air-to-surface missile	1974-79	1488[1] delivered; deliveries reported continuing
France	Milan antitank missile	1979[1]	Reported on order
France	Mirage-50R jet fighter	1979	Reconnaissance version on order
France	MM-38 Exocet ship-to-ship missile	1976	36 delivered
Israel	Corvette	1979	
Italy	Aspide/Albatros ship-to-air and ship-to-ship missiles	1979	Three systems reported on order for Israeli corvette
Italy	M-109 self-propelled 155-mm howitzer[2]	1977-79[1]	200[1] reported delivered; deliveries continuing
Japan	Survey ship	1976	1 delivered
Spain	Centurion main battle tank	1979[1]	60[1] reported delivered
United States	Cessna light aircraft[3]	1979[1]	80[1] reported delivered

SOURCE: *Yearbook of World Armaments and Disarmament, 1980* (Uppsala, Sweden: Stockholm International Peace Research Institute, 1980)

NOTES: [1]Figure unconfirmed. [2]Made under U.S. license. [3]Export licensed for civilian use only.

The 1980 Arms Trade Register compiled by the Stockholm International Peace Research Institute (SIPRI) listed a number of deliveries or orders of arms for South Africa. The listings show that in a number of cases orders for weapons have continued to be placed or that deliveries have continued to be made despite the 1977 embargo. The SIPRI 1980 listing is shown in Table 5-1.

SOUTH AFRICA'S ARMS INDUSTRY AND THE ISSUE OF SELF-SUFFICIENCY

Armscor

In 1964, after the imposition of the first United Nations embargo, the Nationalist government established the Munitions Production Board, which was subsequently changed to the Armaments Board and modeled after the French D.M.A. (Delegation Ministerielle pour l'Armement). This board was given responsibility for weapons procurement, research, testing, maintenance, and inspection. The Armaments Development and Production Corporation of South Africa (Armscor) was established in 1968 as a parastatal corporation with an initial government investment

TABLE 5-2

ARMSCOR'S EXTERNAL PRODUCTION BY PRIVATE CONTRACTORS

Armored vehicles
Operational vehicles (heavy and light trucks, four-wheel drive vehicles)
Vessels
Radar and computers
Telecommunications
Weapon electronics
Maritime technology
Electronic warfare

SOURCE: Department of Defence, Republic of South Africa, *White Paper on Defence and Armaments Supply, 1979,* p. 23.

of $150 million. It was to take over the state-owned arms factories, which had been run by the Armaments Board, and was empowered to build new factories and other facilities and to control the manufacture or acquisition of arms and the stockpiling of strategic materials.[13] Defence Minister P. W. Botha stated at the time that the government welcomed offers from foreign companies suggesting the joint establishment with local companies of arms factories in South Africa. He added that foreign "know-how" could reduce South Africa's arms research costs and that Armscor would facilitate links between local and foreign arms producers.[14] In 1976 Armscor was merged with the Armaments Board to form the Armaments Corporation of South Africa. The new agency retained the Armscor acronym.

The chairman of Armscor is Pieter G. Marais, a successful sheep farmer who holds the rank of colonel in the Commandos. The sixteen directors of Armscor and its subsidiaries are appointed by the state president. Their identities are secret, although directors are drawn mainly from the military and from private industry. The annual report of Armscor is secret; it is not published in the white parliament. In 1979 Prime Minister Botha appointed John Maree to a three-year term as executive vice chairman of Armscor. He had the responsibility of running the agency on a day-to-day basis. Until his appointment Maree had been the executive director of Barlow Rand, a manufacturing conglomerate and one of the country's largest companies. Earlier in his career, he had attended Harvard Business School.[15]

Maree's appointment was regarded as symbolic of the close working relationship that had been fostered between Armscor and private industry. It has been Armscor's policy to use private corporations as much as possible as contractors and subcontractors for the weapons, components, and military equipment being produced within the country. Manufacturing by Armscor's subsidiaries is undertaken for particularly strategic items or when production by private companies is uneconomical.

TABLE 5-3
ARMSCOR'S SUBSIDIARIES

ATLAS AIRCRAFT CORPORATION (manufacture, maintenance and design of aircraft)
ELOPTRO (electro-optical systems)
KENTRON (missiles, missile systems, gun sights, and periscopes)
LYTTLETON ENGINEERING WORKS (rifles and artillery)
NASCHEM (fills and assembles large calibre ammunition)
MUSGRAVE (high-precision arms components, hunting and target rifles)
PRETORIA METAL PRESSINGS (rapid-fire and small-arms ammunition)
SOMCHEM (propellants, explosives, rocket propellant systems, and rockets)
SWARTKLIP PRODUCTS (hand grenades, pyrotechnic items, commercial ammunition)

SOURCE: *Financial Mail* (South Africa), December 5, 1980; *Salvo* (Armscor house magazine, South Africa), 1978-79 issues, cited in *The Apartheid War Machine* (London: International Defence and Aid Fund, 1980), p. 16.

South Africa's spending for weapons and military equipment, both imported and locally produced, has expanded tremendously since the first UN arms embargo was passed. In 1966 South Africa spent $35 million on armaments; by 1980 the figure was about $2 billion (R1.43 billion). In the 1981-82 year Armscor spent slightly more (R1.54 billion), though the dollar value dropped to $1.4 billion.[16] In 1982 Armscor's total assets were $1.17 billion (R1.30 billion).[17] It had become the third largest industrial enterprise in the country, and officials claim South Africa is the largest weapons manufacturer in the southern hemisphere.[18] When Armscor was established in 1968, it employed 2,200 workers; in 1982, Armscor had 29,000 workers, and arms contractors in the private sector employed another 76,000 people.[19]

Like all industries in South Africa, Armscor and its subsidiaries rely to a significant extent on black workers. At the end of 1978 Armscor reported that of its total of 18,975 workers, 42 percent were black. The breakdown was 10,982 whites; 4,770 Africans; and 3,223 people of mixed race.[20] Armscor maintains that employees from all "population groups share the same conditions of service, salary scales, and benefits." It can be expected, however, that, as elsewhere in South Africa, black workers are concentrated in the lower ranks.

Self-Sufficiency

In terms of the arms embargo, at least as significant as South Africa's imports of complete weapons have been the licensing and coproduction agreements to assemble or produce weapons of foreign design in South Africa. This is done using varying quantities of foreign-supplied components in combination with locally made parts. The proportion depends on the capabilities attained by local industries and on the government's priorities. Especially since the 1977 embargo, South Africa has clearly been working to maximize its self-sufficiency by trying to promote local production of components and parts for the weapons being produced in South Africa. Although this has been accomplished in some areas, even Armscor officials indicate that self-sufficiency has not been achieved, nor is it fully attainable.

In 1966 it was reported that 70 percent of the $35 million spent on weapons was spent on arms from overseas.[21] A decade later, in 1977, Defence Minister P. W. Botha told the parliament that 57 percent of South Africa's arms and military equipment came from overseas sources.[22] In 1980 Armscor chairman Piet Marais said that of Armscor's $2 billion budget for the year, 25 percent, or $500 million, would be spent abroad.[23] He said that South Africa had "thwarted the brunt" of the arms embargo. In 1982 he claimed that only 15 percent (or $210 million) of the budget valued at $1.4 billion would be spent on imports.[24]

The efforts at self-sufficiency go back to the period of the 1963 embargo. By 1965 the defense minister was reporting that South Africa had obtained 120 foreign licenses to manufacture weapons locally.[25] One of these early agreements was made with Panhard of France, which licensed production of its AML armored cars. At first, they were produced with major components supplied from France, but by the late seventies South Africa had reached the stage where practically all the components could be supplied locally[26] and the Panhard cars had become a mainstay of the South African arsenal.

The West German Anti-Apartheid Movement has reported that the plants for the production of the armored cars by the South African company Sandock Austral were constructed in cooperation with the affiliates of the Thyssen Industries of Essen, West Germany, which were also said to have supplied component parts for production of the South African Panhards.[27]

In 1964 South Africa made an agreement with Aermacchi of Italy for the production by the government's Atlas Aircraft Corporation of the MB 326K (known in South Africa as the Impala I), a jet trainer which can be armed for a ground attack combat role. The MB 326M (the Impala II) is a full ground-attack version developed by Aermacchi and Atlas, with the initial four airframes supplied from Italy in 1974. It is now reported that Atlas is largely self-sufficient in the production of the Impala II, including the Rolls Royce Bristol Viper II engine.[28]

In 1976 Atlas Aircraft began the production of the C4M Kudu single-engine light plane derived from the Lockheed AL-60 of the United States, produced under license in Italy by Aermacchi, which had previously supplied the planes to the South African Air Force. Similarly, the slightly larger three-seat, single-engine AM 3C (which can be armed with rockets, bombs, napalm, and machine guns) has been produced by Aermacchi in Italy. It was licensed for production in South Africa by Atlas

Aircraft under the name Bosbock; in 1974 forty were imported for assembly. Local production was to begin the following year.[29]

For more advanced combat aircraft South Africa has relied on imports of various models of the French Dessault Mirage III fighter-bomber. Such imports began in 1963 and continued through the early 1970s. In 1973-74 agreement was reached for the local production in South Africa by Atlas Aircraft of the Mirage IIIs. During the same period, South Africa bought forty-eight of the more advanced Mirage F-1 fighter-bombers. Thirty-two of the planes were partially assembled by Atlas. By 1976 it was reported that Atlas would produce "at least" one hundred of the Mirage F-1s. Some reports indicate that Atlas has been able to produce the F-1 with locally made components except for the engine, but more comprehensive studies indicate that the F-1s have been assembled mainly from imported components.[30]

The Ratel armored personnel carrier, developed by South Africa in the mid-seventies, has been described as a combat vehicle designed and built entirely locally. Whatever South African military sources may say, *Jane's Weapons Systems* described the Ratel in 1979-80 as being similar in appearance to the French Berliet VXB; its armament is similar to that used on French armored personnel carriers, and it is powered by a diesel engine—although local production of diesel engines in South Africa has only just begun.[31]

The Cactus surface-to-air missile, which entered the South African arsenal in the early seventies, relied on French cooperation: South Africa reportedly supplied the financing and some scientists for the project, while the missiles were constructed in France by Matra and Thomson-CSF.[32]

In 1979 Prime Minister Botha announced to parliament that South Africa had added several important new weapons to its arsenal. These, he said, had been locally developed and produced. From what is known about the new weapons, however, his claims were exaggerated.

The "G-5" 155-mm howitzer, which is a significant new weapon for South Africa, is the product of Armscor links with the Space Research Corporation of the United States and Canada. In this large-scale violation of the arms embargo, Space Research supplied the shells, gun barrels, technicians, and testing equipment to South Africa in the 1976-78 period. South Africa therefore acquired the technology and components for its new advanced howitzer from Space Research. Armscor was able to arrange for production of the "G-5" by Cementation Engineering, a South African subsidiary of Trafalgar House, the large British conglomerate that owns the Cunard Line and the *Daily Express* newspapers. Cementation is supposed to manufacture mining equipment. Special lathes for producing the shells were imported from CIT Alcatel of France, and equipment for filling the shells from Rheinmetall of West Germany.[33]

The missile patrol boats announced by Prime Minister Botha were widely identified as Israeli Reshef patrol boats. Three of the boats were reported to have been built in Israel, and three in South Africa. (Six more are to be built in South Africa.) The Reshef is said by the West German Anti-Apartheid Movement to be based on West German designs; more significantly, the key components are reported to be of foreign origin, including the diesel engines (from West Germany), the Gabriel surface-to-surface missiles (from Israel), the cannons (made by OTO Malara of Italy, with shells from Canada), and the radar-jamming and decoy systems (from the United States).[34]

The missile patrol boats are armed with surface-to-surface missiles known as "Skerpioen" in South Africa, but they have been identified as Israeli Gabriel IIs. *Jane's* has noted that while it is not known whether there are facilities to make the missile under license in South Africa, the limited number suggests that only imports from Israel are used.[35]

The new South African "V3" air-to-air missile was said to be an advance on the French Magic, designed and built by Matra, which had been used to arm South Africa's Mirage fighter-bombers.[36] South Africa has collaborated in the past with French companies in missile projects; but whether the design and manufacture of these missiles are South African is not known.

The new "R-4" infantry rifle being introduced for the South African army is reported to be a copy of the Israeli Galil assault rifle.[37]

Another new weapon announced subsequently by the South African military was a 127-mm truck-mounted multiple rocket launcher, reported to be a locally developed and manufactured. *Jane's* notes, however, that the rockets are similar to the Working Bee 6 system made in Taiwan, which, like Israel, has been cooperating with South Africa in the military field.[38]

In 1981 a new chemical plant owned by the Armscor subsidiary Somchem was opened. It will produce rockets and explosives for bombs. At the opening a Somchem spokesman said that two countries had "assisted" South Africa in setting up certain of the manufacturing processes for the plants, but he did not name them.[39]

These examples show how South Africa's self-sufficiency on arms production has been overstated. In addition, one must take into consideration that the private industrial sector, which as Armscor officials themselves have stressed is relied on for the bulk of Armscors's contracting, has been dominated by foreign corporations. Let us see how.

The 1979 Defence *White Paper* specifically cited the "enthusiastic assistance of local industry" in meeting the challenge of the arms embargo. The private sector, it indicated, was especially important in determining the growth of self-sufficiency in arms production.[40] At the same time, Armscor's chief executive John Maree declared: *"The only way we can arm*

South Africa is to make use of all available resources, including the talents of the private sector" (emphasis added).[41]

In 1982 Armscor's spending for domestic arms procurement was allocated approximately 70 percent to private companies, and 30 percent to Armscor's own subsidiaries.[42] During the 1977-78 fiscal year Armscor placed 5,636 contracts directly with private companies, and the number of these companies was put by Armscor officials at approximately 800.[43] It is clear that the role of the private sector in arms manufacturing has grown. This can be gauged when the recent figures are compared with those for 1973, when it was reported that 50 percent of the expenditures for arms were paid to some 200 private contractors and subcontractors.[44]

The stimulus to one local industry has been described by the South African *Financial Mail*:

> Armscor's most dramatic boost to local manufacturing capability has been in micro-electronics. Armscor contracts for communications equipment, missile guidance systems, radar and minicomputers have been behind the establishment of most micro-electronic manufacturers in South Africa.[45]

Other examples were provided by the Ratel armored car, which has a suspension system and gearbox designed and made in South Africa for local conditions, and by Iscor (the parastatal steel company), which had acquired the capability to make vacuum-cast armor and (gun)barrel steel.

There have been gains in the ability to produce equipment and materiel for the military as a consequence of contracts offered through Armscor. But some of this gain is, at the least, illusory. Often, the local supplier includes key foreign involvement, either directly or in less visible positions, such as minority partners and sources of technology or among suppliers of components and parts to be used in conjunction with locally made ones. The electronic industry provides but one example of this continuing dependence. As a consequence, according to Armscor chairman Pieter Marais, the replacement of imported parts and components was "still a high priority, especially in electrical and mechanical products," but that Armscor and its private contractors had "succeeded in transplanting a lot of technology." In addition, the *Financial Mail* noted:

> Fears have often been voiced that Armscor relies heavily for supplies on foreign-controlled firms. It is known that it encouraged the takeover last year of Racal Electronics [a British corporation dealing in military communications equipment]. But several suppliers have taken steps to blot out foreign connections, and Marais reckons that "there's no company controlled from overseas that does a lot of work for us."[46]

Nevertheless, in electronics, even the South African-controlled companies are highly dependent on foreign supplies. As one South African industry analyst put it:

> At the present time, regardless of sanctions, the great majority of all [electronics] equipment and components required by South Africa are directly imported. For the future, the proportion of local manufacture will certainly increase but the vast majority of the technology will continue to come from overseas.[47]

Through distributorships, South African companies have access to a wide range of electronic components from the United States and other countries. Despite the embargo, advertisements for military-specification items sold by American companies appear regularly in South African journals.[48] Among the major Western electronics companies having investments in South Africa are General Electric Corporation of Britain, General Electric (U.S.), Westinghouse (U.S.), AEG-Telefunken (West Germany), Siemens (West Germany), Sperry Rand (U.S.), Philips (Netherlands), and ITT (U.S.).

The South African motor industry, with sales estimated at $2.3 billion (approximately the same as electronics) in 1981, also plays a strategic role for the South African military and for the economy as a whole. Vehicles supplied to the South African military and police include trucks, four-wheel-drive vehicles, and police vans. The foreign corporations involved include General Motors (U.S.), Ford (U.S.), Leyland (Britain), and Daimler-Benz (West Germany).[49] The South African government has long promoted self-sufficiency in the motor industry through local-content regulations: requirements as of 1980 were 66 percent local content (by weight) for autos and 50 percent for light commercial trucks.[50] It is noteworthy, however, that these guidelines are not being applied to heavy and specialized vehicles of the kind used by the military.

The strategic role of the motor industry in South Africa was highlighted in 1978 when a secret memorandum from General Motors' South African subsidiary was released by the American Committee on Africa. The memo revealed that GM plants in Port Elizabeth had been designated "key national points" in terms of 1966 Civil Defence legislation. It also outlined contingency plans for operating under conditions ranging from "civil unrest" to "national emergency" with security provided by GM Commando units and, if necessary, by regular military forces. It noted that GM has supplied vehicles for the South African armed forces, and that a refusal to continue to do so could raise doubts among government officials about the company's "motives," leading to a loss of government business and thereby threatening the company's viability; under emergency conditions it was assumed that operation of the plants would pass under full government control.[51]

In the late 1970s, in cooperation with Daimler-Benz of West Germany and Perkins Diesels of Britain, South Africa launched the Atlantis Diesel project. The goal was to set up the first plant for the production of diesel engines in South Africa, and so promote self-sufficiency, for this engine is the vital component of heavy vehicles and other motorized equipment of many types. Even the Atlantis diesels will, however, use key imported parts.[52]

In 1981 it was reported that the Eaton Corporation (U.S.) was planning to enter into a joint venture with the government's Industrial Development Corporation to set up a gear and axle plant to make components for heavy trucks. The object was to serve the needs of the South African military. In 1981 it was reported that two local South African companies would be producing American Rockwell Corporation axles and West German truck axles respectively, but with only partial local content.[53]

In addition, major Western corporations have played a role in other South African industries important to the drive for military and strategic self-sufficiency, including iron and steel, chemicals, and rubber. Two other industries have extreme military importance to South Africa: oil and nuclear energy.

Although the countries that have long assisted South Africa's nuclear development have insisted that their cooperation has involved strictly peaceful purposes, there have been clear signs that South Africa's nuclear military potential is taken seriously by these same countries. This was apparent in the public warnings addressed to South Africa in 1977 by the United States, Britain, and France not to proceed with a nuclear bomb test when ostensible preparations in the Kalahari desert were sighted by satellites.[54] Since 1976 the United States has held up delivery of enriched uranium for the Safari I research reactor in South Africa as part of an effort, so far unsuccessful, to persuade Pretoria to sign the Nuclear Non-Proliferation Treaty. (Former Interior Minister Cornelius Mulder warned in 1977, "If we are attacked, no rules apply at all if it comes to a question of our existence."[55]) Given the Western record, which shows more than two decades of nuclear cooperation with South Africa, the responsibility for the Nationalist government's nuclear weapons capability must also lie with the West.

Major foreign assistance to South Africa's nuclear programs have been provided by the United States, West Germany, and France, beginning as early as the 1940s.[56] In 1965 Allis-Chalmers, an American company, designed and built a research reactor, Safari I, for South Africa, and the United States has since supplied 231 pounds of highly enriched (weapons grade) uranium for the reactor, through deliveries were later halted. More than 155 American nuclear experts have been sent over the years to assist South Africa's nuclear program, and 90 South African nuclear scientists had completed assignments in the United States by mid-1977. Other South Africans have been trained in West Germany and France.

The key to South Africa's nuclear weapons threat lies in its uranium enrichment program. The pilot plant was put into operation in 1976. While the Nationalist regime has claimed its enrichment process is "unique," the African National Congress and the West German Anti-Apartheid Movement, relying on documents taken from the South African embassy in Bonn, have charged that the process is an adaptation of the "jet nozzle" method developed in West Germany; hence South Africa's program must have been aided by the West German government and government-controlled research institutes. The West German government denied these allegations, but the groups responded with further documentation of their charges. In January 1978 Dr. A. J. A. Roux, president of the South African Atomic Energy Board, indicated that there had been exchanges of nuclear scientists with West Germany, and that STEAG, a company controlled by the West German government, "had cooperated with South Africa in the field of uranium enrichment from 1973 to September, 1975, with a view to the joint construction of a commercial enrichment plant."[57]

South Africa is also constructing a nuclear power station at Koeberg, near Cape Town, which is being built by a French consortium. The West German Anti-Apartheid Movement, noting the high cost of the project (more than $1 billion) and South Africa's plentiful supplies of cheap coal, has charged that the Koeberg project is serving to camouflage supplies, of a military nature, that are imported for the commercial enrichment plant, and that other major South African projects are serving the same purpose.[58] It is also noted that the power station will produce large amounts (1,000 pounds per year) of extremely poisonous plutonium. The lack of strict international safeguards raises the possibility that this could be diverted and reprocessed by South Africa for nuclear weapons use.

CHEMICAL AND BIOLOGICAL WARFARE

In 1963, at a time when South Africa was beginning an intensive weapons research program in response to the international arms embargo, the London *Times* and other British papers reported the disclosure by Professor le Roux of the South African Council of Scientific and Industrial Research that work was being done on the development of the poison (nerve) gases Tabun, Soman, and Sarin.[59]

More recently, South Africa's chemical and biological warfare potential was described in an article appearing in the *Cape Times* (June 23, 1978). That article, based on information from a government publication produced for the military and for civil defense groups, declared, "Any future conflict will certainly be a no-holds-barred affair and the South African

Defence Force is prepared for germ, gas, and chemical attacks on the military and civilians." While the article stressed South Africa's defensive preparedness, it pointed out, "The advantages of biological warfare are becoming increasingly apparent as its possibilities have increased and the cost of other weaponry becomes prohibitive." The South African Navy is reported to have a biological and chemical warfare defense school.

According to a report in *Africa Now* (May 1983) a soldier in the South African Defence Force has told South African war resisters in London that the Defence Force is developing shells carrying nerve gas for its 155-mm howitzers. The soldier, whose name was not revealed, also alleged that the South African military is conducting research on biological weapons that could be targeted specifically on black populations.

OIL: A STRATEGIC VULNERABILITY

Any consideration of South Africa's self-sufficiency must take into account the country's vulnerability to oil sanctions. This has been extensively documented by British economists Bernard Rivers and Martin Bailey in a report for the United Nations Centre Against Apartheid.

South Africa has no known reserves of petroleum and has had to import most of its oil requirements. The local oil is supplied by SASOL I, an oil-from-coal plant. SASOL II will be able to meet only 12 percent of the country's needs when it is in service. South Africa has had a crash oil stockpiling program, and it is estimated that these stocks could be stretched to last for two years in the event of a complete embargo but that well before then there would be wide economic and social disruption. Rivers and Bailey conclude, therefore, that "oil sanctions probably represent the most effective form of external pressure that could be exerted on South Africa."[60] South Africa's military forces depend on mechanized weapons and equipment of all kinds (planes, helicopters, tanks, armored cars, armored personnel carriers, trucks, landrovers, and jeeps), all of which depend on petroleum products.

The refining of imported crude oil and the sale of petroleum products in South Africa is dominated by five major Western corporations: Caltex, Mobil, British Petroleum, Shell, and Total. The South African government controls one main refinery (NATREF) which accounts for roughly 15 percent of the country's main refining capacity. However, under existing legislation, the government can, in a national emergency, take over the facilities of the private corporations. Oil has been defined by the government as a "munition of war," and, as such, information concerning its supply is subject to official secrecy laws. South Africa has been subject to an oil embargo by the Arab OPEC countries since 1977, and in 1979 the new government of Iran, which had supplied 90 percent of South Africa's oil, joined the embargo. Oil has reportedly come from Bahrein, a British-controlled territory in the Middle East and from spot-market deals, some involving elaborate secrecy measures, including switches of the itineraries, names, and ownership of tankers, and even the scuttling of ships following deliveries to South Africa. A formal international oil embargo could be instituted by the UN Security Council—if approval for it were to come from the Western powers.

CHESTER CROCKER'S EVALUATION OF SOUTH AFRICAN SELF-SUFFICIENCY IN ARMS PRODUCTION

Just prior to his appointment as under secretary of state for African affairs in the Reagan administration, Chester Crocker made one of the most thorough examinations ever of the South African arsenal, the question of South African self-sufficiency in arms production, and the effects of the arms embargo. Crocker's studies included discussions in South Africa with Defence Force and Armscor officials as well as current and former employees of Armscor subsidiaries. Although South Africa has attained substantial self-sufficiency in some weapons, Crocker pointed out that its ability to produce these items could be challenged by stronger enforcement of the 1977 arms embargo to bring a cutoff in "critical components" and "highly specialized raw materials needed in arms manufacture." He said, "Bearing in mind the critical importance of just one or two unavailable components in a complex weapons system, it is by no means certain that self-sufficiency can be achieved without long lead-times that would be needed to duplicate foreign technology—sometimes by hand."[61] Therefore the arms embargo, enforced more strictly, *does* have the potential to undermine even those areas of weapons production where South Africa claims to have achieved self-sufficiency. Crocker concluded that, given Pretoria's policies and the current situation, the combination of local production using local designs, foreign-licensed production, and "embargo evasions" offers "a *moderate but growing* level of self-reliance" (emphasis added).[62]

According to Crocker, the items that South Africa is able to produce from local or modified foreign designs with largely local content are the following: armored vehicles; mine-clearing devices; artillery; most types of ammunition and explosives, sighting devices; communications equipment; some missile types; and some types of naval and aircraft instruments. The first category cited by Crocker included weapons and military equipment that South Africa is able to produce from local or modified foreign designs with largely local content. It is important to note that this category does not include many of South Africa's most important weapons and that even in these items self-sufficiency is not total.

The second category of weapons and equipment listed by Crocker comprises licensed items "incorporating imported designs and components as well as some local modifications and locally duplicated components": light utility aircraft; helicopters; combat aircraft; missile patrol boats; and some missile types.

A third category of weapons includes those in which "major investments are being made to design, develop, and produce local models, possibly based on foreign models but not dependent on imported components. These are upgraded versions of utility and ground attack aircraft, armed and transport helicopters, modern tank and field guns, avionics equipment, and updated targeting and homing devices for missiles.

According to Crocker, South Africa is *not* undertaking the local production of several types of weapons and equipment, and would therefore remain dependent on imports of these: long-range maritime reconnaissance aircraft; advanced fighters and fighter bombers, beyond the Mirage F-1s already in production under license; heavy modern tanks; advanced avionic and ECM (electronic countermeasures) technology; ships larger than the missile patrol boats; and possibly small submarines.

Crocker's conclusion, therefore, that South Africa's self-sufficiency is "moderate but growing" should be underscored. There was some confirmation of this in a *Washington Post* article in April 1981 reporting on South Africa's expectations of closer ties with the United States during the Reagan administration:

> There are also some hopes that the United States will unilaterally lift a mandatory arms embargo imposed by the United Nations in October, 1977. Although the government boasts that the boycott has not hurt it has even spurred its own arms industry, it would like to buy some sophisticated weapons and fighter planes.
>
> The South Africans also want to be able to buy a number of items the United States has unilaterally embargoed [for sale to military and police agencies], such as computer spare parts, police equipment and planes for reconnaissance and sea rescue.[63]

ENFORCEMENT OF THE ARMS EMBARGOS

As noted, one significant violation of the arms embargo involved the Space Research Corporation. In this case the SRC had provided South Africa with one of the most advanced artillery systems in the world.

The violation was discovered during the Carter administration, but the response to the discovery left many serious questions. The Justice Department brought charges against the SRC, and two chief executives pleaded guilty to charges of violating U.S. arms export laws. They were fined and given short prison terms. When the case was raised in the UN sanctions committee, American officials stated that the investigation and the guilty pleas showed the effectiveness and utility of the 1977 arms embargo.[64] In fact, the case illustrated a serious breakdown in enforcement of the embargo by the United States and other countries.

A study of the Space Research case by the staff of the House Subcommittee on Africa released in March 1982 summarized the extent of the embargo violation:

> Between April 1976 and September 1978, Space Research Corporation of North Troy, Vermont, broke the U.S. and U.N. arms embargos against South Africa by selling and shipping to the South African Government approximately 60,000 155-mm extended-range artillery shells, at least four 155-mm guns including three advanced prototype guns, a radar tracking and firing range instrumentation system to follow and measure the paths of fired projectiles, and a number of artillery sights, lights and mounts. Almost all of this equipment was acquired in the United States from U.S. Army-owned plants and supply stocks in Scranton, Pennsylvania, Watervliet, New York, and Aberdeen, Maryland, and from a variety of private firms. SRC also violated the embargos by exporting technology to South Africa. SRC personnel traveled to South Africa to assist the Government in setting up and operating artillery test range facilities (including advice on design of propellants and firing techniques) and in establishing its own 155-mm gun and ammunition manufacturing capacity. SRC also entered into manufacturing license agreements with the South African Government for both the guns and the ammunition. In return for SRC's services, South Africa paid SRC approximately $19 million which the company assigned to its principal creditor, the First Pennsylvania Bank.[65]

The report concluded that the case shows that "there is a 'non-system' of enforcing the arms embargo in the U.S. government." Although the United States has had "a *policy* of embargoing arms to South Africa since 1963, the relevant U.S. government agencies have thus far failed to adopt *procedures* to effectively implement the embargo." The report cites the role of a CIA operative in recommending to Armscor officials that they could obtain superior 155-mm artillery from Space Research and states, "At the very least, this episode suggests serious negligence on the part of the Agency. At most, there is a possibility that elements of the CIA purposefully evaded U.S. policy." The Office of Munitions Control of the U.S. State Department is the primary monitor of U.S. arms exports, yet the office had misapplied its own regulations in wrongly advising Space Research that it might be legally possible to ship artillery shell forgings out of the United States without any arms export license.

The two central recommendations made by the report are that the government should take significant steps to strengthen enforcement procedures of the embargo and that the House and Senate intelligence committees should investigate the possible roles of those affiliated with the CIA in efforts to evade the arms embargo in this case.

Richard Moose, assistant secretary of state for African affairs in the Carter administration, insisted in Congressional testimony that "no officer in the executive branch knowingly was engaged in some scheme to help get weapons technology or weapons to the South African government." However, the former head of the CIA's Angola Task Force, John Stockwell, has stated that if the CIA had been actively involved in facilitating the Space Research deal, it would have had to work through the State and Defense departments and that the assistant secretary of state for African affairs and "most likely" the secretary of state—at the time, Henry Kissinger—would have to have known about it.[66]

Another area of reported arms embargo violations involving the United States and other countries is the transfer of weapons built in the United States or under American licenses to South Africa by third countries. When charges of such deliveries were first raised in Congressional hearings by economist Sean Gervasi in 1977, they were called "false and tendentious" by the State Department, which insisted that the United States had "observed this embargo faithfully": allegations that the United States had "assisted South Africa in building a stockpile of sophisticated weapons" were false. In a reference to the disposition of U.S.-licensed weapons by third countries, it was asserted that "permission to sell such weapons to South Africa is never granted."[67] These denials did not actually meet the allegations directly, since such weapons could have been illegally transferred to South Africa without formal American approval; such transfers would not necessarily involve the United States in "assisting" South Africa in any active sense, but rather in neglecting to *enforce* weapons-transfer regulations. The effectiveness of the American enforcement of its regulations against weapons transfers through third parties is not in fact so certainly established, since the State Department has admitted that, while checks are made with embassies, foreign governments, and sources in South Africa, "This is obviously not a foolproof method."[68] In light of this admission and the continuing documentation in authoritative sources, such as the *Military Balance*, of third-country transfers of arms to South Africa, it appears that there have been failures in American enforcement of the embargo. Rather than vaguely worded denials, an adequate response by the United States government in this situation would be a specific case-by-case report detailing the investigations conducted.

A related area of arms embargo enforcement concerns components that are incorporated into weapons being supplied to South Africa. The Reshef missile patrol boats, which Israel has supplied, are a prominent example. They reportedly contain components from several countries. The provision of such components also constitutes a violation of the arms embargo, but so far action has apparently not been taken by any of the governments involved in this case.

A *New York Times* columnist claimed in March 1981 that the Reagan administration was considering granting permission to Israel to export its Kfir fighter-bomber aircraft to South Africa.[69] Such a transfer would be a breach of the embargo by Israel, the United States, and any other countries supplying components for the Kfir. In this instance, the American component is the jet engine.

Another case involving components of American origin concerns the Lockheed Hercules C-130 heavy transport planes supplied to the South African Air Force just prior to the 1963 embargo. The United States allowed Lockheed to continue the supply of spare parts and maintenance as an exception to the 1963 embargo; when the 1977 embargo was passed, the flow of supplies was supposed to cease. A U.S. official agreed that South Africa is "obtaining spare parts from somewhere"[70] for the C-130s, yet, although the disposition of parts of the C-130 by domestic or foreign suppliers comes under U.S. export controls, the United States offered no prospect of an investigation to determine the source of continuing supplies to South Africa.

While the export of American commodities to the South African military, police, and apartheid agencies was restricted under the 1978 Carter administration regulations, the United States has continued to allow the sale of a variety of "dual use" items to other South African government departments as well as to private buyers in South Africa. Among the items known to have been put to military use in the past are light aircraft, computers, and electronic equipment. The United States has also supplied a significant number of commercial transport and passenger planes to South Africa, including the Lockheed L-100s operated by Safair and more than forty Boeing aircraft of different models for South African Airways, including five 747s. These planes can be a valuable military asset for the transport of troops and equipment. The United States has informed the United Nations embargo committee that it monitors the use of dual-use items through the embassy in South Africa, yet in 1977 Congressional testimony a Commerce Department representative admitted the difficulty in doing this, saying that "enforcement is a difficult matter in this area. Extraterritorial questions raise difficulties not only with respect to South Africa but other countries as well."[71] In its 1981-

82 and 1982-83 editions, the *Military Balance* includes the Lockheed L-100s in its listings of the South African Air Force reserves. Both General Motors and Ford admitted that their South African subsidiaries have continued to sell vehicles to the South African Defence Force through the government's central purchasing agency, saying that the parts and components used have either been made in South Africa or have not been imported from the United States and therefore they did not violate the Carter regulations.[72]

The examples cited here (particularly the Space Research case) raise a number of questions about the effectiveness of the enforcement of the arms embargo by the United States. Nonetheless, Richard Moose, then undersecretary of state for African affairs in the Carter administration, asserted at a House subcommittee hearing in April 1980: "U.S. law and regulations pertaining to the arms embargo are clear and categorical, penalties are specified, and enforcement has been systematic and rigorous. No system is foolproof, given intent to violate the law, but the U.S. government has taken its responsibilities regarding the arms embargo with the utmost seriousness and will continue to do so."[73]

Although Moose asserted that the arms embargo and the U.S. restrictions on sales to the South African police and military constituted significant examples of American pressure, he also said that "South Africa has beaten the UN arms embargo by building the world's tenth largest arms industry, and other governments, rightly or wrongly, believe that South Africa has nuclear weapons."[74]

While stressing the importance of the arms embargo, Moose would say only a few words publicly about South Africa's weapons sources. He was asked several times to provide that information, but would do so only on a classified basis. In fact, there was and is considerable unclassified information available to the public on the issue. And while pointing to the capability of South Africa's arms industry, Moose declined to endorse the conclusions of the 1978 study by Senator Dick Clark about the source of that capability: "The net effect of American investment in South Africa has been to strengthen the economic and military self-sufficiency of South Africa's apartheid regime."[75]

American-South African cooperation on intelligence matters and South African links with NATO are not compassed by the terms of the arms embargo, but they are indicators of United States policy. Secretary Moose stated that the administration would not "comment publicly on intelligence-related issues." But in September 1980 *Newsweek* magazine reported: "Although relations between Pretoria and NATO members are in tatters, South Africa unofficially reports to the West on Soviet ship movements. Recently, South African photographs gave U.S. experts their first look at a Soviet warship with its missiles uncovered, and Washington showed its gratitude by alerting Pretoria that a pair of Soviet submarines were stealing around the Cape."[76] Another indication of South Africa's continuing NATO contacts was the private visit of South African Foreign Minister R. F. Botha with NATO Secretary Joseph Luns in Brussels in November 1980; according to one report there had been at least two other visits between the two in recent years.[77]

The statement of the Defense Department representative who joined Secretary Moose at the Congressional hearings was brief and sketchy to the point of being misleading in its description of the South African military and its activities. The size of the Defence Force was put at only 72,000, which was less than half that of the standing operational force and a small fraction of its total strength, since there are reserves, of some 500,000. While he noted that the Defence Force was "well equipped," he made no mention of the arms embargo or of any details about the weapons in use. The discription of South Africa's military activity was low-key, with no account of the tremendous militarization, the Total Strategy, the central role of the military in the Botha government, or the beginning of counterinsurgency operations against the African National Congress. The pattern of South African intervention and agression against the frontline states was simply called "activities," and the escalation of force especially against Angola, and the brutal effects of the war in Namibia were skipped over. He did not mention South Africa's nuclear weapons capability.[78]

The guarded approach of the Carter administration officials at these hearings indicated a wariness about charges of a failure by the United States and other countries to strictly enforce the arms embargo and of describing the situation in ways that could have created added pressures to close arms embargo loopholes or to initiate economic sanctions.

In contrast to the reluctance of Carter administration officials to discuss publicly military issues concerning South Africa, Chester Crocker, as noted, wrote in considerable detail about precisely this area prior to his appointment as assistant secretary of state for African affairs in the Reagan administration. While critical of what he terms "the conspiracy theory of South African military strength," he did accept in large part the charges of those who condemn the West's failures to enforce the embargo. He said, "There is little doubt, as critics of Western arms export policy charge, that substantial amounts of hardware and related technology have been purchased by Pretoria through various channels."[79] He also spells out the kinds of channels that have been used:

. . .unreported third party transfers, loopholes in embargo procedures, and the import of "dual" (civilian or military), used equipment or equipment readily converted to potential military use. . . .Several hundred licensing and coproduction agreements were signed with various Western countries. . . .Equally significant, formal controls on arms exports (where these existed) were not extended to a large array of items of obvious military value: communications, electronics and radar systems; information processing equipment; civilian aircraft; and sophisticated engineering technology.[80]

Crocker also cited likely examples of continuing trade in "items of clearly military application: marine diesel engines and communications gear from Germany, British-designed jet engines and avionics, Israeli missile components and electronic technology, French and Italian components and spares for aircraft and armored vehicles under pre-1977 licenses and co-production agreements."[81] He notes "evidence of continued local assembly since the embargo of a number of French and Italian aircraft and helicopter models and Israeli patrol boats" for which license and coproduction agreements were apparently signed prior to the 1977 embargo. He also declared that "it is safe to assume that the secondary market" (i.e., through corporations, arms dealers, and governments) is "considerably more extensive than public reports would suggest. He describes the means employed:

> . . .it is often possible to disaggregate the component or technology in such a way to "bury" it in trade data as a nonmilitary transaction. South Africa is still able to purchase used or reconditioned end-items [weapons or equipment] from a government or through the private arms market. Although such deals are intended to be covered by the embargo, they are less traceable because the seller is not the original producer and intermediaries can be used to camouflage the transaction.[82]

Crocker concluded that even with strict American adherence to the embargo (and the one major case he does *not* discuss is Space Research) the commercial and political interests of "European, East Asian, and Israeli firms and governments make it likely that some technology and components will continue to flow to South Africa."

Although he confirms embargo violations and loopholes, Crocker chided those who he says have seen a Western "conspiracy" to arm South Africa, saying that in large part the arming was done with relative openness for a decade by France and Italy, who did not adhere to the embargo. He said that enforcement of the embargo gradually became tighter up to passage of the 1977 embargo, when South Africa had grown increasingly isolated politically. But while he made light of the idea of conspiratorial policies, Crocker himself served on the National Security Council during the Kissinger era, when the policy options in NSSM 39 (National Security Study Memorandum 39) to secretly "tilt" U.S. policy more favorably toward South Africa were being implemented.

Crocker said that the 1977 embargo had not weakened South Africa militarily or brought changes in its policies, and that at most it had defused African pressures for economic sanctions, allowed the West to distance itself diplomatically from South African policies, and spurred South African military self-sufficiency. The implication is that expectations for an effective arms embargo have been unreasonable or unwarranted. Nevertheless, his analysis shows that with pressure from African states, UN committees, and anti-apartheid groups, the embargo has been partially effective and that South Africa's military resources and self-sufficiency, while considerable, are still constrained by the embargo. From his considerable research on the topic, Crocker is certainly aware of ways that the embargo can be strengthened. Instead, the "constructive engagement" policies he has pursued with the Reagan administration have led in the opposite direction.

Writing in *Foreign Affairs* in 1980, just prior to his appointment, Crocker declared:

> Western governments have made it clear that they have not desired to participate in the defense of white minority rule. Adherence to the UN arms embargo and the U.S. refusal to use South African defense facilities are symbolically important ingredients of policy; they should be continued in the absence of major polical change, barring a dramatic deterioration in the geopolitical situation facing the West in adjacent areas.[83]

The qualifying words are significant: that the embargo was described only as "symbolically important" indicated that vigorous enforcement and proposals to close loopholes would not be seen as priorities. Proposing the option of unilaterally dropping the embargo showed a readiness to disregard its status as a binding commitment under international law.

Relating to enforcement of the arms embargo under the Reagan administration, in two cases in 1981 the U.S. Customs Service arrested people allegedly preparing to sell arms to South Africa (small arms in one case and Bell UH-1 helicopters in the other).[84] In May 1982 the *New York Times*, in an article dealing with the general problem of illegal arms exports, reported that federal officials, commenting on the export controls, said, "The system frequently breaks down. . . .There's little anyone can do if a buyer misrepresents a shipment's final destination or simply labels arms as something else."[85] The article also cites Britain, South Korea, and Israel as countries with significant arms trades open to illegitimate buyers.

At hearings of the House Subcommittee on Africa in December 1982 the State Department representative responded to the subcommittee staff report's recommendations for strengthening enforcement procedures for the arms embargo against South Africa, citing examples of the Department's recent efforts to improve enforcement. While the measures fall far short of the report's suggestions, they do indicate that the administration accepted the basic finding by the subcommittee staff that enforcement of the arms embargo had been inadequate. The State Department representative also cited ten seizures of illegal shipments to South Africa by the Customs Service as part of Operation Exodus to control exports of U.S. arms and technology.

In terms of the provisions of U.S. export regulations on South Africa, the Reagan administration systematically relaxed the policies of the Carter administration, which banned all sales from the United States to the military and police. In a series of three revisions (in March and September 1982 and January 1983) the Reagan administration moved to end the ban on all but the most sensitive nonmilitary items.[86] As of the latest revision, the only items barred for export to the South African military and police (aside from weapons and other specifically military equipment) are commodities controlled for national security, nuclear nonproliferation, or crime control reasons, as well as automotive vehicles, "watercraft," parts and accessories for these, and tires. Export licenses are still required for aircraft and helicopter sales and for computers for the five government departments directly enforcing apartheid laws.

Looking at specific cases,[87] there have been a number of examples of products being approved for export to South Africa which can clearly provide military or other strategic support for the Nationalist government. Two powerful computers, a Control Data Cyber 170/750 and an Amdahl 470/V7, were approved for export to the government-run Council for Scientific and Industrial Research (CSIR), which does research in many fields, including military-related research. The Control Data computer is large enough to be used for code-breaking and nuclear research. Although the United States required assurances that the computers would not be used in the military or nuclear fields, verification can be difficult. In addition, the Commerce Department approved the export of two Sperry computers to the Atlas Aircraft Corporation, an Armscor subsidiary producing military aircraft. One was approved under Carter and the other under Reagan.

In another case, export was approved in 1982 for six Beechcraft Super King 200C planes to the South African Air Force for use as air ambulances. A decision by South Africa on which company to buy the planes from remained pending. In April 1982 the Commerce Department authorized the sale of 2500 electric shock batons (for crowd control) to private buyers in South Africa. This authorization was subsequently described as "an honest mistake" by the administration.

In 1982 it was revealed that since May 1980 (during the Carter administration) the Commerce Department had approved five export licenses to South Africa's nuclear agency for such equipment as vibration test equipment, computers and multichannel analyzers, and hydrogen combiners—all items that can be used in a nuclear weapons program. After a delay, approval was also given for export of Helium-3, which can be converted to tritium and used in the production of nuclear weapons. In September 1982 it was also reported that the administration was considering an application to export a large hot isostatic press, which can be used to produce certain components of nuclear weapons. (Applications to export these devices to Israel, India, and Taiwan have been turned down in the past.) At the end of 1982 a decision was also pending on whether to allow the supply of enriched uranium from the United States to fuel South Africa's Koeburg reactor, which has been embargoed since 1976 because of South Africa's refusal to sign the Nuclear Non-Proliferation Treaty. Earlier in the year the United States had not raised objections to the supply of enriched uranium for the reactor by a Swiss affiliate of an American company.

Although the Israeli government has declared that it abides by the arms embargo, the cases cited above indicate that Israel has become an important source of arms for South Africa. Some of these dealings may be justified on the grounds that they stem from license agreements dating to before the 1977 embargo, but this in no way diminishes the fact that the Israeli government has chosen to pursue a policy of collaboration with apartheid. Furthermore, other recent reports point to even wider and more open collaboration with South Africa. A 1979 study for the U.S. Defense Intelligence Agency (reported in the *New York Times*, June 28, 1981) stated that nuclear cooperation between South Africa and Israel is only a part of an intensive pattern of military and economic ties that have developed between the two countries and Taiwan as well. In 1981 Israel's economics minister suggested in a speech to American and European businessmen that Israel could act as a proxy for the United States in the sale of arms to South Africa and other countries.[88] A report in May 1982 on Israeli supply of arms to Argentina stated that according to Israeli officials South Africa was the leading recipient of Israeli arms.[89] Israeli Defense Minister Sharon made a ten-day visit to the South African forces fighting in Namibia late in 1981. According to the *New York Times* military correspondent, he indicated that South Africa needed more modern weapons, a view said to be shared by U.S. and NATO analysts.[90]

France was reported to have cancelled the delivery of submarines and corvettes being built for South Africa after the 1977 arms embargo was voted. But in 1981 it was reported that South Africa was likely to be the first customer for the new French maritime patrol plane, the Transall C. 160S.[91] Although the Socialist government has said it would end the supply of arms to repressive and racist governments, it has also said it would honor all arms orders placed with the previous administration.[92]

Given the magnitude of such South African orders, involving such important weapons as Mirage III and F-1 fighters, Alouette helicopters, and Crotale missiles, this is a significant loophole. It appears that France will continue as a major military collaborator with the Nationalist government. According to one report, Israeli technicians in South Africa have been maintaining planes of French origin (Mirages) with parts supplied to Israel by France. The repairs are said to reach a level of complexity at which the manufacturer would normally be called in.[93]

The British computer company ICL, one of the main suppliers of computers for the South African market, has provided a computer for the South African police. The British government (which owns 25 percent of ICL) has stated that the computer does not fall within the scope of the arms embargo and therefore it cannot halt such exports.[94] Similarly, Plessey of Britain has supplied a combined civil and military radar air control system to South Africa and trained South Africa military personnel in Britain to operate it. The system also includes a Digital Equipment computer of American origin. Although the system is of a sophisticated type that allows South Africa to monitor aircraft in neighboring countries and guide its aircraft on offensive missions in the region, the British government has claimed it could not halt its delivery because it is not a specifically military system. As noted above, Cementation Engineering, the South African subsidiary of Trafalgar House of Britain was the company that acquired, through Armscor, the technology and financing to produce the "G-5" 155-mm Space Research Corporation howitzer in South Africa. Trafalgar House denied any knowledge of this activity by its own subsidiary.

It was reported in 1982 that South Africa had placed orders for corvettes to replace its frigates and that the new ships would be built locally and that the South African Navy also wanted to build submarines. Again, however, foreign support is needed for these projects: the *Rand Daily Mail* interpreted the remarks of Admiral Ronnie Edwards on these plans as "a reference to South Africa seeking international partners in building warships, particularly the submarines."[95] At the opening in 1981 of a new chemical plant owned by the Armscor subsidiary Somchem, a Somchem spokesman said that two countries had "assisted" South Africa in setting up the plant.[96] The plants produce rockets and explosives for bombs.

The surprise presence of Armscor at an international arms sales exhibition in Athens in October 1982, where it displayed the G-5 howitzer (the product of the Space Research Corporation deal), raised a number of new issues. Pretoria has launched a major drive to break into the international arms market: the goal is to increase arms sales from about $9 million in 1982 to about $135 million within two years, mainly through sales of the G-5 and the new self-propelled model, the G-6.[97] Experienced

Western arms salesmen may be brought into the new marketing branch that Armscor has set up. Armscor is said to have potential customers in Africa, Latin America, and the Far East. This move by Pretoria poses a major challenge to the arms embargo. It represents an effort to break out of the isolation imposed by the embargo, openly gaining contacts and legitimacy in the arms field, and of course to earn money. Foreign sales can also aid South Africa in achieving economy-of-scale in arms production, which is obviously difficult, given the limited size of the Defence Force.

In the five years since the UN Security Council passed the 1977 arms embargo, it has become clear that its provisions need to be strengthened. A number of countries have been disregarding the embargo or using its loopholes to continue to justify the supply of arms and military equipment to South Africa. The Security Council committee set up to monitor enforcement of the embargo and consider means to strengthen it has not had a substantive meeting since 1981. The problem of enforcing an effective arms embargo cannot be separated from the crisis and conflicts in southern Africa. South Africa has escalated its war in Namibia, invaded Angola, and struck in various ways against other neighboring countries. For the Western powers on the Security Council not to agree to strengthen the embargo is to lend support in very real ways to South Africa's defiance of international law and aggressive strategies. Despite its claims of considerable self-sufficiency, Pretoria remains dependent on foreign supplies for many aspects of its armaments program. Action is urgently needed to strengthen the arms embargo and to promote effective enforcement by individual countries.

6 The Propaganda War

IN 1978-79 THE NATIONALIST GOVERNMENT OF SOUTH AFRICA was rocked by an unprecedented upheaval: a scandal that exposed a secret international campaign of propaganda, political manipulation, and "dirty tricks" mounted by the Information Department. The scandal became known as "Muldergate" (after Cornelius P. Mulder, the minister of information, and the similarities to the Watergate affair in the United States), and it grew into a major struggle for power within the National party. The pivotal figure in the scandal was Eschel Rhoodie, who had been appointed secretary of the Information Department by Mulder in 1972. He had been the architect of the secret campaign.

There were three main aspects to the Muldergate scandal. First, there were charges that Rhoodie and several associates had lavishly spent Information Department funds for their own benefit. Second, there were allegations that the *Citizen*, a major daily newspaper started in Johannesburg in 1976 with a strongly pro-government stance, was secretly funded by the Information Department with the approval of Mulder and Prime Minister Vorster. And third, there were the revelations of scores of other secret Information Department projects conducted both inside South Africa and around the world. As a result of the scandal, Mulder, who had been expected to succeed Vorster as prime minister, was swept from power and resigned from the National party. Rhoodie, fearing prosecution, fled South Africa and revealed many details of the secret projects to journalists.

The scope of the Information Department's secret campaign is shown by a summary published in June 1979 by a South African newspaper: in addition to extensive projects within South Africa itself, the operations had reached into at least thirteen countries on five continents. There were allegations of payments to politicians, political organizations, and trade union leaders in the United States, Britain, Japan, and other countries. A network of front organizations had been set up and a variety of

161

publications and other media outlets were established or taken over, including newspapers, news and photo agencies, and business, trade, and travel magazines. Other deals involved buying houses, apartments, and land.[1]

According to Eschel Rhoodie, the South African government spent about $100 million on these projects during the five years from 1974 through 1978. At the time of his resignation in June 1978 a second five-year plan having a budget of $250 million, or $50 million per year, was said to have been formulated.[2] This phase was, Rhoodie claimed, to have focused on the media with the aim of secretly taking over major newspapers (such as the *Guardian* or the *Observer* in Britain), television stations in London and Washington, and a large British publishing house.

The Muldergate scandal unfolded in a few articles in the South African press in late 1977 and early 1978. The articles alleged that Information Department officials had spent extravagant sums on trips abroad. Thereafter, the issue mushroomed, and leaks to the press reflected the political infighting.[3] When asked to account publicly for the money spent, Rhoodie refused, but revealed for the first time that his department was administering a secret fund. Vorster offered the public assurances that "irregularities" were being investigated; in fact, the BOSS officials charged with the investigation were actually trying to keep a lid on the affair, for their agency was involved in it. By mid-1978, Rhoodie had been forced to resign and the Information Department had been renamed (it became the Information Service of South Africa) and placed under the Foreign Affairs Department.

Journalists then turned their attention to the *Citizen*. Mulder and Vorster denied in parliament that the newspaper had received secret government funding, but the controversy over the *Citizen* grew. Mulder narrowly lost the National party nomination as Vorster's successor to Defence Minister Pieter W. Botha in August 1978. In November, Judge Anton Mostert, originally appointed by Vorster to investigate foreign exchange violations, released documents showing that the *Citizen* had been financed and controlled by the Information Department.

Prime Minister Botha refused to accept Mostert's findings and appointed his own commission, headed by Judge Rudolph Erasmus, to investigate the Information Department. In December 1978 Rhoodie left South Africa and went into hiding when it appeared that he might face prosecution for failing to account for the use of secret funds. He surfaced in Europe at various places and was said to have forty-one tape cassettes and stacks of documents dealing with the secret projects, some implicating members of the Botha government in the "irregularities" under investigation. One source said that he had a list of six hundred secret projects that were being planned.[4] Despite his threats that he could bring down the Botha government with his revelations, Rhoodie did not succeed in trading silence for immunity from prosecution. He offered his information to major news organizations, reportedly for $200,000, but then withdrew the offer. He did give an account of the secret projects in an interview with BBC-TV in March 1979, and in August *Elseviers* magazine in Holland published an extensive account by Rhoodie in four installments.[5] Interviews with Rhoodie in Ecuador were used by South African journalists Mervyn Rees and Chris Day for their book *Muldergate*,[6] based on their press coverage of the scandal in South Africa.

By June 1979 the Erasmus Commission had issued three reports: these implicated Vorster and Mulder in misleading parliament about the secret funding of the *Citizen* and laid responsibility for extensive financial irregularities on Rhoodie, Mulder, General van den Bergh, and several collaborators. Vorster resigned from his honorary position as state president, and Mulder was forced to resign from parliament and left the National party. (Van den Bergh had retired in mid-1978.) While keeping secret the details of many of the Information Department operations, the commission did provide background on some projects in South Africa, the United States, and Europe, particularly the links to American publisher John McGoff. The commission accepted Botha's contention that he was not aware of the disposition of funds provided for the secret projects from the Defence Department's secret Special Defence Account, which was under his control as defense minister. Those implicated by the commission charged, however, that Botha had known what the funds were being used for and that they had been made scapegoats.

The Erasmus Commission reported that there were at least 160 secret Information Department projects and that the department had gained a stake in forty-nine private companies. But while charging official misconduct, the commission did endorse the propaganda campaign, recommending that 68 of the projects be continued, 56 of these in secrecy.[7] It described the Information Department's efforts to take over a large British publishing company, Morgan Grampian, as "a bona-fide effort to gain a foothold in foreign media with the object of promoting South Africa's interests."[8] Even as the commission presented its final report, there was little confidence within South Africa that the full story had come out. An opposition leader in parliament complained that there was continuing talk of "millions stashed away in steel army trunks. . . numbered bank accounts. . . and farms in Paraguay. These rumours and whispers are going up and down the corridors of power in Pretoria and are discussed in every restaurant and cafe."[9]

In August 1979 Rhoodie was arrested by French authorities at a resort on the Riviera and extradited to South Africa for trial. He was convicted in October 1979 of five counts of fraud for diverting $70,000 in secret Information Department funds for his own use. A year later the appeals court reversed the conviction, stating that "in executing his instructions to wage a psychological and propaganda war, Dr. Rhoodie would have had to act unconventionally." The court accepted in evidence a secret document showing that Rhoodie had made payments to two major publishers who were trying to buy a British newspaper covertly on behalf of the South African government, thus accounting for the funds at issue in the case.[10]

Rhoodie charged that he had been made a scapegoat for the Information Department scandal by the Botha government and accused his former collaborators, Vorster and Mulder, of responsibility for the scandal. There were other indications that the political conflicts behind the scandal were not over. Copies of a draft of the final report of the Erasmus Commission, leaked in November 1980, were said to have many revisions, implying that Prime Minister Botha had tailored the report to indict Vorster for covering up the *Citizen* project and to clear himself.[11]

HOW THE PROPAGANDA WAR WAS LAUNCHED

The Nationalist government's efforts to promote a favorable image in the West and to cultivate opinion leaders abroad certainly did not originate with Eschel Rhoodie. Political scientist Galen Hull, in a useful bibliographic essay,[12] has documented programs undertaken in the United States by the Information Department in the nineteen-fifties and sixties. But it does appear that Rhoodie is justified in his claim that he wanted to dramatically expand and transform these activities by launching a "propaganda war."[13] He was well trained for such a war.

Eschel Rhoodie and his brothers, Nic and Denys, were sons of a prison warder. They all joined the South African Information Service in the fifties and subsequently earned doctorates in social science at the University of Pretoria. Eschel Rhoodie served with the Information Department in New York in the early sixties, and was transferred to The Hague in 1966. During these years he established a close friendship with Mulder, who was to become information minister. Rhoodie claims—though there is no corroboration—that the seeds of the propaganda campaign were planted in his mind by Americans he believed were linked to the American Central Intelligence Agency (CIA),[14] in particular by a man named Brown (not otherwise identified). An American businessman introduced Brown to Rhoodie as an expert on the media. Brown, and others whom Rhoodie said he met through him, are said to have described to Rhoodie how the CIA operated to influence politics and the media, telling him that in order to have influence with the media it was necessary either to own the media or to "own" the top people running them. They suggested infiltrating student and political movements to establish ties to future leaders and financing groups in order to "take them over," according to Rhoodie. These ideas for aggressive manipulation of the media and political groups struck a responsive chord in Rhoodie. He felt that people in the United States had a distorted image of South Africa and that South African diplomacy and information activities were too stodgy.

After Rhoodie got the Information projects underway, two Americans became linked to them who reportedly also have had ties to the CIA— Richard Mellon Scaife and Beurt SerVaas. Scaife is a scion of the wealthy Mellon family of Pittsburgh, which has controlled the Gulf Oil Corporation and the Mellon Bank. Scaife's link to the CIA was reported to be his ownership between 1973 and 1975 of World Forum Features, a London news agency identified in the British press and in the *New York Times* as a CIA front organization having the mission of planting pro-American stories in the European press. In 1977 Scaife bought newspaper publisher John McGoff's majority share in the *Sacramento Union* and subsequently became a director of McGoff's Panax Newspaper Corporation. McGoff, cited as a major figure in the Information Department's secret operations in the United States by the Erasmus Commission, allegedly bought the *Sacramento Union* with secret funds from South Africa.[15] Scaife declined comment to Karen Rothmyer, a journalist investigating these issues.[16]

Beurt SerVaas is chairman of the Curtis Publishing Company in Indianapolis, which publishes the *Saturday Evening Post*, edited by Cory Jane SerVaas, his wife. SerVaas served in the Office of Strategic Services (OSS) in World War II and subsequently in the CIA. He is said to be an old friend of former CIA director Richard Helms.[17] The SerVaases traveled to South Africa in 1976 and then made other visits, and the *Saturday Evening Post* carried a number of articles dealing favorably with South Africa. Beurt SerVaas met Rhoodie, Mulder, and other figures involved with the Information Department projects and was identified by the Erasmus Commission as an overseas investor in the *Citizen* and as being involved in several secret projects. He also reportedly chartered a jetliner from Thor Communicators (an Information Department front) during a two-week trip to South Africa with former Texas governor John Connally.[18] According to the *Indianapolis Star*, which launched a three-month investigation into SerVaas's South African involvement, a number of people caught in the Information Department scandal in South Africa felt that SerVaas's CIA background played a role in his South African activities. SerVaas, however, called the statements "ridiculous," saying that he "had no. . . CIA business or covert reporting business or propaganda business, nor. . . any personal business dealings with Rhoodie."[19]

Commenting on Rhoodie's claim that his propaganda war had been inspired by his CIA contacts, the South African *Rand Daily Mail* raised the question of whether the CIA was "aware of some, if not all" of the secret projects.[20] The reports concerning Richard Mellon Scaife and Beurt SerVaas add substance to that question.

Rhoodie's third book, *The Paper Curtain*, published in South Africa in 1969, hinted at the secret campaign he launched a few years later. In the book Rhoodie argued that South Africa was being isolated by a "curtain" of lies and Communist propaganda playing on a hypocritical obsession against apartheid in the West. It called for a dynamic campaign using unorthodox and even illegal means to break through the curtain and gain support for South Africa abroad. Rhoodie claimed that one source of distortion was the warped impressions gained by foreign commentators who knew no Afrikaans and so read only the English-language press—that is, in the South African context, the opposition press. This was the rationale that was later used in the setting up of the pro-Nationalist *Citizen*. Rhoodie also suggested in this book that the government should not try to "sell the unsellable," trying to defend apartheid, but rather stress the "positive" aspects of the country.[21]

In 1971, Information Minister Mulder appointed Rhoodie as his special advisor in order to implement a more aggressive program. In 1972, despite the opposition of older officials, he became secretary of the Information Department. In 1973, he suggested starting a secret propaganda fund and launched some experimental projects in the United States, France, the Scandinavian countries, and Africa. Rhoodie says he traveled extensively, talking to politicians and journalists in many countries, and that he commissioned Richard Manville, Inc., a New York public relations outfit, to survey the attitudes of politicians and opinion leaders in sixteen countries toward South Africa. The survey cost some $500,000.[22]

In 1974 Rhoodie convinced Mulder and Prime Minister Vorster of the need for a large-scale secret program having a firm five-year plan. The idea was said to have been approved by Vorster and then by a "committee of three"—Vorster, Mulder, and Finance Minister Nico Diederichs. The large sum of money required could be concealed only by using the secret Special Defence Account (an account set up for the procurement of foreign arms and military equipment and not subject to normal governmental audit or public parliamentary review). With the approval of Defence Minister Botha, it was arranged that the Bureau of State Security (BOSS) would act as "banker" for the secret propaganda funds.

Rhoodie has said he told his associates he wanted to mount "a propaganda war" in which "the normal rules no longer apply" and that he wanted approval for—if necessary—"large-scale bribery": "If it is necessary for me to purchase a sable coat or a mink coat for an editor's wife, I should be able to do so. If it is necessary to send a man on holiday to the Hawaiian Islands with his mistress for a month, then I should be able to do so."[23] The repertoire to be used by Rhoodie would also include "dirty tricks" to counter groups and individuals who opposed apartheid: "If certain organizations, for example, were out to arrange an anti-South African rally or were trying to get companies to withdraw investment in South Africa, we would perhaps send out notices and documents cancelling the meeting so that the other party wouldn't know what was going on.[24]

It was not long, however, before Eschel Rhoodie's penchant for dramatization violated the secrecy that was supposed to surround the new campaign. He was soon telling the *Rand Daily Mail* that, because of his new initiatives, he could see a time when "50 or 60 percent of the Department's methods would be 'hidden.' "[25]

That from the beginning Eschel Rhoodie had in mind not only a propaganda campaign, but also secret political programs and "dirty tricks," was underscored by the program's links with BOSS. Not only did BOSS handle the funds for the secret projects, but General van den Bergh was personally involved in some of them, such as the efforts to promote "detente" with African states. Rhoodie, even with his far-reaching plans, was a junior member of Vorster's inner circle, as reflected by General van den Bergh's comment to the Erasmus Commission that he had taken Rhoodie under his wing when the latter was appointed secretary of the Information Department.

The counterpoint to the Information Department's links with BOSS, however, was the friction and rivalry that developed between the Foreign Affairs Department and the Defence Department, which became a focal point of the inner party struggle over the successor to Prime Minister Vorster in 1978. Rhoodie's secret operations often impinged on the sphere of the Foreign Affairs Department, and on some occasions, according to his own accounts, he undertook informal and unorthodox diplomatic moves. There were military aspects to the Information Department's activities as well. Mulder's trip to Washington in 1974 included a meeting with a Pentagon official. His contacts with West German industrialists and politicians had important strategic payoffs in deals relating to South Africa's nuclear program. Rhoodie is said to have "mingled with arms dealers as well as newspaper owners," and one of his business colleagues has claimed that Rhoodie once asked him if he could buy spare parts for the French submarines in South Africa's fleet.[26]

Despite the political upheavals of Muldergate, some of the operations launched by Eschel Rhoodie have been continued. As noted, the Erasmus Commission recommended that 56 projects be continued secretly and 12 openly. In 1980 the head of the South African Information Service, A. Engelbrecht, criticized Rhoodie's operations, saying that giving "a rand or two" to groups that promote South Africa could hardly be considered a "project" and claiming that only one really substantial project of Rhoodie's had been continued. He did, however indicate that the use of lobbyists, seminars, and conferences initiated by Rhoodie was being continued abroad in an open fashion. He said that Rhoodie's revelation of the secret projects had been "crippling" to his agency's work because many who had collaborated with Rhoodie now refused to work for South Africa. He admitted that some "collaborators used by the former department are still being used."[27]

Scraps of information about the secret projects continue to leak out in South Africa. It has been reported that several projects involved arms purchases abroad, but because of strict military censorship specific information uncovered by reporters in South Africa cannot be printed in the local press.[28] In another case, Rhoodie claimed that an unnamed American who had received $430,000 in secret funds had traveled to South Africa to account to the government for what he had done to earn the money.[29] There were also reports in South Africa that an unidentified news agency aimed at Arab and African states had been bought as one of Rhoodie's projects and had since moderated its previously negative attitude toward South Africa.[30]

One of the most important organizations promoting South Africa abroad—the South Africa Foundation (SAF), a private, nonprofit organization founded in 1959 and supported by corporate and private contributions—was not directly affected by the Information Department revelations. The foundation was not linked to the Information Department in the material that was made public, though it has long been viewed by critics of apartheid and others as a front for the government.[31] The foundation dissociates itself from official policies, urges more rapid reforms, and criticizes racial discrimination and social intolerance in South Africa. But it supports the over-all political framework of the country, increased corporate investments in South Africa, and South Africa's international strategic interests. The South Africa Foundation has representatives in London, Washington, Bonn, and Paris and promotes regular contact with government officials, businesses, and the media; it produces several publications and also sponsors tours to South Africa.

Although the Information Department had been unsuccessful in 1975 in a bid (allegedly by John McGoff) to buy the Washington Star, South Africa gained a new advocate in Washington, D.C., in 1982 when the Washington Times was launched by the Unification Church of the Rev. Sun Myung Moon. Many of the Washington Times's top management and staff have had links to McGoff (who serves on the newspaper's editorial advisory board) or have been known to be sympathetic to the South African government.[32] This has raised questions of whether, beyond having a conservative stance naturally favorable to Pretoria, there has been some form of secret South African support for the paper.

(Further details about this paper are included below with the descriptions of McGoff's activities.)

The Foreign Affairs Department has openly established two important new projects in Washington. In 1980 the South Africans hired the law firm headed by former Senator George Smathers and former Representative James Symington to act, as registered foreign agents, as lobbyists and legal advisors for the South African embassy. Smathers and Symington are Democrats with top contacts in Washington in and out of the government. Symington stated that because they believed South Africa was trying to achieve a "new order and a just and stable society," they would oppose boycotts and sanctions against South Africa. They were "proud and anxious to proceed and perform" for their clients. It was reported that the firm had a one-year contract for $300,000 running from April 1, 1980.[33] On the Republican side, South Africa was able to hire the law firm of John Sears, a former presidential campaign manager for Ronald Reagan, to engage in similar lobbying. In addition, several American veterans of the Rhoodie era moved into posts in the Reagan Administration. Most prominent was lawyer Donald de Kieffer, who joined the office of the U.S. Trade Representative; until 1979 he had been South Africa's chief lobbyist in Washington. Prominent Republican lawyer Thomas Shannon was appointed a presidential assistant for public liaison; his law firm had initially employed de Keiffer, thereby earning more than $880,000 in fees from South Africa over five years. Another lawyer, Marion Smoak, was appointed to work on African affairs at the State Department; his firm was hired to lobby for the South African-sponsored DTA administration in Namibia. Jay Parker became one of President Reagan's few black advisers; he was a paid representative for the Transkei in 1977-78.[34]

To a surprising extent, therefore, figures in Washington who had been associated with secret or semisecret projects initiated by Rhoodie have become part of the Reagan administration, and at the same time the South African Foreign Affairs Department and the Information Service have set up the significant new projects cited above. This situation is a reflection of changes that have taken place in South Africa and in the United States. In the mid-seventies, after Soweto and the death of Steve Biko at the hands of the South African Police, the Nationalist government was on the defensive. In the eighties the Botha government's claims of change and reform in South Africa have made it easier to gain a hearing in the United States and other Western countries. Furthermore, South Africa has found a receptive audience for its shrill rhetoric about a Soviet threat in Africa, and for the related themes of South Africa's key role as a supplier of strategic minerals and the military importance of the Cape of Good Hope vis-à-vis the Persian Gulf and Africa. The Reagan administration's emphasis on confrontation with the Soviet Union around the globe and its concern for sources of raw materials seem to mesh conveniently with the issues stressed by Pretoria.

Described below are Information Department projects, including both those known to have been implemented and those alleged but not confirmed. There are several sources for this list, including investigative press reporting, the reports of the Erasmus Commission, and the accounts given by Eschel Rhoodie. However, gaps and questions remain. While individual cases (such as that of the American publisher John McGoff) have come under scrutiny—the House Subcommittee on Ethics had a brief investigation—there have been no major governmental investigations into the South African propaganda war as a whole in any of the countries that were its targets, even though concerted South African efforts to influence political and public opinion are still being made.

INFORMATION DEPARTMENT PROJECTS IN SOUTH AFRICA

The Citizen

The sponsoring of the *Citizen*, a daily newspaper, was the largest single secret project undertaken by the Information Department. It cost the government $36.8 million between 1976 and 1978.[35] It was an internal project by which the Nationalist government created its own mouthpiece in South Africa to support its policies and to counter the critical voices of the English-language press. The aim was to generate more backing for the Nationalists among white South Africans and to influence foreign reporters and commentators who were seen to rely on the English-language press.

The origin of the *Citizen* project lay in a failed attempt by the Information Department to take control secretly of South African Associated Newspapers (SAAN) in 1975. SAAN has been controlled by several major mining companies, including Harry Oppenheimer's Anglo-American Corporation, and the papers, particularly the *Rand Daily Mail*, have long been critical of apartheid and so were a thorn in the side of the Nationalists. In a plan devised by Rhoodie and General van den Bergh a group of businessmen would buy up two million SAAN shares to obtain a controlling interest. The South African businessmen were Jan Van Zyl Alberts, who figured in a number of other projects, and Louis Luyt, who had made a fortune in the fertilizer business. (Alberts was among those interned during World War II for pro-Nazi activities by the United Party government. The Erasmus Commission concluded that his mishandling of $18 million in secret Information Department funds pointed to "theft and fraud," and the South African *Financial Mail* called him apparently the "most corrupt" of those involved in Muldergate.[36]) There were also two foreigners involved in the bid for the SAAN shares: West German Axel Springer, owner of one of the largest publishing empires in the world, and American publisher John McGoff. In 1976 McGoff was asked about his role in the bid for the SAAN papers by U.S. Senator Dick Clark, chairman of the Senate Foreign Affairs Subcommittee on Africa. McGoff called the *Rand Daily Mail* a "radical" paper and said that if the bid had been successful, he would have acted to make its editorial stance more conservative.[37]

Some $13 million were to be put up for the shares, and the money, apparently, was to come in toto from the secret Information Department funds. However, the takeover bid was blocked by a group of Johannesburg businessmen.

The alternative was the creation of the *Citizen*. Louis Luyt was made the nominal publisher, but the entire $13 million needed to set up the newspaper came from the Information Department. The true source of the money was made clear in the "contract" between Louis Luyt and the Information Department, which was marked Top Secret: it provided for an editorial charter drawn up by the Information Department that editors were to sign and follow. According to paragraph d (viii):

> The paper supports the broad objectives of the present elected government in respect of separate political development of the black population and the white population [i.e., apartheid] of the Republic of South Africa as well as the anti-communist and security legislation of the Republic of South Africa.[38]

Within a year the *Citizen* was reported to be running deficits at the rate of $460,000 a month. To meet these expenses, Luyt got another infusion of Information Department money.

The *Citizen*'s finances increased friction between Rhoodie and Luyt, and in early 1978, when there were louder rumblings in the English-language press about the Information Department, nominal ownership of the *Citizen* was transferred from Louis Luyt to Jan van zyl Alberts and Hubert Jussen (from Holland) and a group of foreign investors.*[39] Jussen was chairman of *To the Point* magazine (which was receiving major Information Department funding), and Alberts, among his other roles, was the managing director. However, when Judge Mostert's investi-

---

*Foreigners named in the deal were later revealed to be Dr. Otto von Hapsburg of Lichtenstein; Beurt SerVaas, the chairman of Curtis Publishing Company in the United States; and David A. Witts, of Dallas, Texas, a lawyer and former member of the Texas State Legislature.

gation revealed in November 1978 that all the funds for the *Citizen* had come from the Information Department, it appeared doubtful that any of the new "owners" had any real stake in the paper; the owner remained the Information Department, and the South African government continued to carry the paper's losses, to the tune of almost half a million dollars a month.

In the fall of 1978 the new government of P. W. Botha appointed a commission to liquidate the holdings of the Information Department. In December it was announced that Perskor, an Afrikaans-language newspaper company would take over the *Citizen*, paying for it only a nominal sum.

To the Point

To the Point, a weekly magazine, was started in South Africa in 1971 by Hubert Jussen, a Dutch businessman. Later, *To the Point International* was established in Amsterdam to provide international distribution. Eschel Rhoodie, who had met Jussen when he was stationed in Holland with the Information Department, held the post of deputy editor-in-chief of the magazine for almost a year, until September 1972, when he was appointed secretary of the Information Department. Jan van zyl Alberts was the managing director. One of Rhoodie's first moves in the Information Department was to order some thiry thousand subscriptions to *To the Point*, paid for by the Information Department, for world-wide distribution to influential people, especially in the United States and Europe. By Rhoodie's account, the value of the subscriptions over the six years between 1972 and 1978 was $12 million.[40] The magazine did not openly support apartheid, but stressed instead the strategic importance of South Africa to the West. *To the Point* ceased publication in 1980.

Afripix (Johannesburg)

Afripix was a news photo agency set up by the Information Department in 1978 as a subsidiary of Hortors, Ltd. Within six months of its formation, it was claimed Afripix was serving 360 major communications outlets in ten countries, including the *New York Times*, the *Washington Post* and the *Chicago Tribune*.[41]

The *Rand Daily Mail*, reporting the disbandment of Afripix (June 27, 1979), noted that American publisher Beurt SerVaas had been listed on the Afripix letterhead as a director of the company.

Pace

The Information Department launched the magazine *Pace*, a glossy English-language monthly aimed at black readers in South Africa, in 1978. It is said to have attained a circulation of about 200,000.[42] In June 1979 the Writers Association of South Africa (WASA), a black organization, charged that *Pace* was linked to the Information Department and excluded its reporters from a commemoration of the Soweto uprising. *Pace*'s editor denied the charge and claimed that the magazine's orientation was anti-apartheid.

Within a few weeks, however, Rhoodie revealed to *Elseviers* magazine that *Pace* was an Information Department project, and that the publisher had an agreement with the department whereby the magazine would not openly defend apartheid, and would stress the virtues of peace, order, and capitalism and condemn political violence and communism. By August 1979 *Pace* was up for sale, and its staff had been given notice.

Films and Theatres for South African Blacks

This Information Department project involved Andre Pieterse, a South African well known in the international film industry and a former vice-president of MGM International.

According to Pieterse the goal of the project was to "build theatres, produce ideological films, and distribute international films which would be acceptable to our black people."[43] There are few movie theatres in the black urban townships, and the film diet permitted by government censors and offered by white distributors consists mainly of low-grade, outdated Westerns. The Information Department, recognizing that films are a popular and powerful cultural medium, planned to modernize films and theatres for blacks under government control.

The Information Department provided Pieterse $950,000 for the first year. But faced with delays, he used the money for a film of his own called *Golden Rendezvous*. Chemical Bank of the United States also loaned $3.9 million for the film, which turned out to be the most expensive ever made in South Africa (it cost $5.5 million).[44] It was a box office failure.

Film Industry for South African Blacks

In addition to the deal with Pieterse, the Information Department had a three-year program with an $8 million budget, managed by Jan van zyl Alberts, to make feature films about and for black South Africans.[45] In connection with this project a news service, Afrimirror, was to be established and a studio complex was to be built in Johannesburg. A listing of secret projects for 1978-79 includes "Bantu Film Productions" and "Distribution of Films to Black Population." (See Appendix B, items 6.17A and B).

Southern African Freedom Foundation

In November 1978 the director of the Southern African Freedom Foundation (SAFF) admitted that the organization was an Information Department front and that Rhoodie had been responsible for its creation. This project is among the eight that the Botha government decided to transfer to the Department of Foreign Affairs and to fund openly. Founded in 1976, SAFF had a budget of $164,000 in 1977-78; this was to be increased in 1979-80 to $258,750.[46] SAFF publishes literature, holds conferences, and sponsors visits to South Africa. It hosted a South African visit in 1978 by arch-conservative Meldrim Thompson, then governor of New Hampshire. In 1979 it was reported that the organization was hosting Major General Richard Cooper and Major General J. Milnor Roberts, both members of the U.S. Reserve Officers Association, on a two-week trip to South Africa.[47]

The Christian League of Southern Africa and Encounter

The Information Department supported the strongly anticommunist Christian League of Southern Africa in order to counteract programs against racism and apartheid of the World Council of Churches and similar programs sponsored by national churches of the West. For the 1978-79 fiscal year, the League was funded with $325,000 from the Information Department, and offices were to be set up in Washington, D.C., and London. The group's publication, *Encounter*, was revamped, and its circulation goal was set at several tens of thousands of copies.[48] The league's leader, the Reverend Fred Shaw, denied receiving the money.

It was also reported that American publisher John McGoff was another contributor to the Christian League. He is said to have donated $26,000 in 1977.[49]

Dr. Christian Barnard

Dr. Christian Barnard, the famous heart surgeon, had an "invaluable" role in improving South Africa's image around the world, according to Rhoodie, through his contact with top political leaders and public figures. Rhoodie claimed that, initially, Barnard's trips abroad were made at his own expense, but later were paid for by the Information Department. Barnard was a particularly valuable asset since he claims to oppose apartheid and is not a supporter of the government—yet he has supported the government's repression of peaceful opposition, accepts the division of the country along racial lines, and is militantly opposed to any forms of outside pressure on South Africa.

In 1979 it was reported that Barnard had given a South African official a list of people overseas to be "neutralized or eliminated" as threats to South Africa. When this was revealed, he denied he meant they should be murdered: he had only given one or two names of those he thought "should be put out of the way." But, he insisted, the government should "stop at nothing" in dealing with "enemies of South Africa."[50] Rhoodie pointed to one instance in which Barnard had acted effectively: in 1978 exiled South African editor Donald Woods was trying to convince George Meany of the AFL-CIO to support a trade union boycott of South Africa. Barnard agreed to contact Meany to counteract Wood's influence.

Anti-apartheid groups in the United States, citing Dr. Barnard's association with the Information Department and his statements about "eliminating" people seen to be threats to South Africa, have indicated that they will call upon the federal government to deny him visas for future visits. It was noted that Dr. Barnard had been in the United States twice in 1979 alone.[51]

OTHER PROJECTS IN SOUTH AFRICA

Thor Communicators and Homerus Finance Corporation

Thor Communicators was set up by Rhoodie in 1974 as a public relations company in South Africa, but it functioned only as a front for Information Department activities and as a conduit for funds—mainly for the *Citizen*. Homerus Finance Corporation was set up to replace Thor as a a conduit for Information Department funds.

Hortors, Ltd.

Hortors, a large South African printing and publishing company, was bought by businessmen David Abramson and Stuart Pegg in 1977 for $6.18 million. The source of their funds was the Information Department. Hortors was used to start *Pace*, a magazine for blacks in South Africa, and Afripix, a news photo agency.

Ecumenical Organization Bureau (Operation Manel)

This project was set up to counter the programs of the World Council of Churches and other church groups in opposition to racism and apartheid. The churches' campaign against American investments in South Africa, according to Rhoodie, had begun to show "alarming results."[52] The organization was set up in 1974 with the cooperation of leaders of the Dutch Reformed Church in South Africa in order to provide contacts with church groups around the world that disagreed with the position of the World Council of Churches. A visitors' program was established, and documents were produced for international distribution. The Information Department reportedly channeled a total of $150,000 to the Bureau, and for 1979 a further grant of $60,000 was approved.

Foreign Affairs Association

The Foreign Affairs Association (FAA) had been set up in the spring of 1975 when the Information Department discovered that the regulations of the U.S. Congress forbade members of Congress to accept trips paid for by foreign governments. To circumvent this restriction, FAA was founded under the supposed sponsorship of five Afrikaner millionaires and given a budget of $575,000. It paid for a number of Congressional visits and held conferences on strategic resources. The director of the FAA, Cas de Villiers, gained notoriety during Muldergate when it was revealed he had used secret funds for personal junkets and for affairs with women.

After disclosures that it was receiving 70 percent of its funding from the Department of Information, the Foreign Affairs Association was closed down, in November 1978.

Afri-Comix

Another secret project aimed at black readers in South Africa allocated $2.5 million to comic books. The comics were supposed to stress the importance of separate cultural backgrounds (thus supporting apartheid) and of law and order. The vehicle for the project was *Afri-Comix*, which was printed in South Africa by Xanap, a subsidiary of John McGoff's Panax Newspapers. According to Rhoodie, the comics were abandoned in 1977 in favor of *Hit* magazine, but he also showed journalists a copy of a letter by Mulder providing for a secret allocation of $460,000 for the 1978-79 fiscal year for comic publications intended for South Africa and Namibia.[53]

Hit

Hit, a monthly English-language magazine for black readers in South Africa, was started in April 1977 by the Information Department. The front man for the operation was Jan Van Zyl Alberts.

The Mmabatho Herald (Bophutatswana)

The *Mmabatho Herald*, which began publication in September 1978 in Bophutatswana, an "independent" Bantustan, was another Information Department project aimed at black readers. Rhoodie claimed that the Botha government was continuing the secret subsidy of the paper at an annual cost of $100,000. The newspaper is published by the Craft Press, which was controlled by John McGoff's Panax Newspapers.[54]

Institute for the Study of Human Rights (University of South Africa)

The Institute for the Study of Human Rights was revealed by Foreign Minister R. F. Botha to be one of the eight Information Department projects that would be continued and funded openly by the Foreign Affairs Department. The Institute was set up at a cost of $200,000 to invite selected foreign visitors in an effort to provide a favorable image of human rights in South Africa.

Institute for Strategic Studies (University of Pretoria)

The Institute for Strategic Studies, founded with Information Department funds, was continued with the overt support of the government under the aegis of the Department of Foreign Affairs. It was to receive $11,500 as a subsidy in the 1979-80 fiscal year.[55]

Center for International Politics (University of Potchefstroom)

The Center for International Politics received secret Information Department funding, but it was to be openly supported by the Foreign Affairs Department in the future. In the 1978-79 fiscal year it received $28,750, and in 1979-80 it was to be given $51,750.[56]

Institute for the Study of Plural Societies (University of Pretoria)

The Institute for the Study of Plural Societies, set up and funded by the Information Department, was headed by Eschel Rhoodie's brother, Dr. Nic Rhoodie. It was identified by Foreign Minister R. F. Botha as an Information Department project that would continue to operate with open government funding: $120,000 was provided in the 1978-79 fiscal year, but no money was budgeted for the 1979-80 fiscal year.[57]

Gary Player

In March 1979 South African golfer Gary Player admitted that he had been paid by the Information Department to play host to groups of prominent American businessmen on golfing holiday in South Africa. Such trips were organized in 1974, 1975, and 1976, when campaigns against American corporate investment in South Africa were becoming increasingly active. Top executives came from Chrysler, Boeing, Ford, and the Bank of America, and Player was paid $30,000 for his services, according to Rhoodie. Player announced, "I'm proud to have been able to be of assistance. I am prepared to do something like this for any party as long as it is to the advantage of the country."[58] The golfing excursions for businessmen were reported to be continuing, now underwritten by the Afrikans Merchant Bank of South Africa.

Prescon Business

Prescon Business, a financial news service published in Johannesburg, was owned by the Information Department. It was to receive $44,000 in 1978-79.

News Photo Agency (Johannesburg)

One of Rhoodie's first projects after taking over as Information secretary was to start a news photo agency in Johannesburg. The agency (not identified) was able to place photos in sixty leading magazines in Europe, according to Rhoodie. The director was also able to attend meetings of the Organization of African Unity and relay information to Rhoodie and to the Bureau of State Security.[59]

Valiant Publishers (Johannesburg)

Valiant Publishers was completely funded by the Information Department. It sells its own books, in South Africa and abroad, and imports books having a conservative viewpoint. The project was said to have cost $650,000. In 1978-79, Valiant was to get $190,000.

South African Grand Prix

The South African Grand Prix was organized in 1976, 1977, and 1978 with the aid of the Information Department in the form of financial guarantees funneled through the *Citizen* as $200,000 in extra prize money for the winners.

Information Department Moves Against Chief Buthelezi

The South African *Daily News* (March 19, 1979) reported that the Information Department had attempted on several occasions prior to 1977 to undermine Chief Gatsha Buthelezi of KwaZulu. At the urging of the Department of Plural Relations and Development, which was said to appreciate Buthelezi's cooperation in their "attempts to develop the homeland," the efforts were halted.

South Africa Book Fair Proposal

A large international book fair was planned for early 1978 to attract to South Africa publishers and authors from all over the world. It was to be secretly sponsored with $500,000 from the Information Department. The plan was not carried out, because a British author who was to be organizer withdrew, fearing such secret involvement of the South African government.

The Smit Murders

In November 1977 Robert Smit, a National party candidate for parliament, and his wife were murdered in their home. Smit, an economist and former South African ambassador to the International Monetary Fund in Washington, was reportedly on the verge of disclosing information concerning large-scale currency smuggling from South Africa. There were rumors of a link between the murders and the Information Department's secret projects. In 1979 a retired judge of the South African Supreme Court announced that his client, a former South African Airways pilot, would testify before the Erasmus Commission that two assassins from West Germany were paid $35,000 each and flown by private plane from Britain to South Africa to murder Smit.[60] An American reporter charged in 1980 that the murders had been carried out by Cuban exiles recruited by South Africa's BOSS with the aid of the CIA (see Chapter 5). In South Africa the murders remain officially unsolved, and the motive has never been established.

INFORMATION DEPARTMENT PROJECTS IN THE UNITED STATES

The South African Connections of John P. McGoff

John P. McGoff started his newspaper career as a small-town publisher in Williamston, Michigan. Aided by contacts with the Information Department, he acquired a chain of newspapers and made his own personal fortune. He became a close associate of Rhoodie, Mulder, and other Information Department figures and a strong promoter of South African policies both in his publications and in contacts with leaders of the Republic party. McGoff had a personal acquaintance with former President Gerald Ford going back to Ford's days as a representative in Congress, and he is said to have had contacts with Richard Nixon. An idea of his personal views on South Africa can be gained from remarks he was quoted as making at a seminar in Houston sponsored by the Information Department to promote business with South Africa. He called the Carter administration officials "gutless jackals" for their policies on southern Africa and he added, "I'm sick and tired of seeing our friends thrown to the dogs for the sake of appeasing leftists and minorities at home."[61]

McGoff's main business enterprise was Panax Newspapers, Inc., which, in 1980, published six daily and sixty-one weekly newspapers in Michigan, Florida, Texas, Virginia, Indiana, and Maryland. According to the U.S. Securities and Exchange Commission, McGoff increased his personal share in Panax from 4 percent in 1973 to 40 percent in 1979, a controlling interest that is estimated to have cost $2 million.[62] This was the period in which McGoff allegedly received secret funds from the Information Department. One of the directors of Panax was Jan van zyl Alberts, who acted as a front man for the Information Department. Panax owned 40 percent of a printing company in South Africa, named Xanap, which put out Afri-Comix (see above); and one of Albert's companies owned another 30 percent. Panax also owned an interest in the Craft Press in South Africa, which published the *Mmabatho Herald*, a secretly funded Information Department operation. McGoff was said to be a director of another South African company, named Lotandanya, which owned a number of apartments in a Cape Town development where Rhoodie's Information Department front Thor Communicators also had apartments. McGoff was named as a co-owner of a 420-acre game farm, known as "Copenhagen," in the eastern Transvaal, along with Mulder, van zyl Alberts, and Eschel Rhoodie and his two brothers.

The Bid for the Washington Star

The bid to acquire the *Washington Star* was the Information Department's largest project in the United States. The aim was to use the newspaper as a conduit for South African propaganda in Washington, D.C.[63]

According to Rhoodie, McGoff discussed the project in South Africa with Mulder. He also met with Prime Minister Vorster. The expected cost was placed at $25 million: McGoff was to put up $15 million and the South African government $10 million. In 1974 the project was begun, and the South African funds were transferred via the Information Department's secret Swiss conduit, Thesaurus Continental Securities Corporation. McGoff had set up his own private company for the bid, the Star Newspaper Company, so that he would not have to reveal the identity of his backers. But the owners of the *Star* doubted that McGoff actually had enough money, and so they sold the paper to another bidder.

The Sacramento Union

After the failure of the bid for the *Washington Star*, McGoff bought the *Sacramento Union*, a daily paper in California. According to the Erasmus Commission, $10 million in South African government funds were used to do this.[64] But according to an account in the *International Herald Tribune* (March 22, 1979), McGoff paid only $8 million for the *Union*, and used the remaining funds to buy other small California papers. In 1977, McGoff became involved in a lawsuit in California that would have forced him to disclose the source of the funds used in the purchase. To avoid such disclosure, he sold a majority interest in the paper and repaid to Rhoodie $5 million of the original advance. The buyer of McGoff's majority interest in the *Sacramento Union* was Richard Mellon Scaife, of Pittsburgh. Scaife became a board member of Panax.[65]

United Press International Television News (London)

Another project in which McGoff allegedly used secret Information Department funds was the 1975 purchase of a half interest in United Press Television News of London. The money, $1.35 million, was transferred through the Thesaurus Continental Securities in Switzerland to McGoff's private company, which was renamed Global Communications.[66] The shares were purchased from Paramount Films; other shareholders were United Press International (U.S.) and Independent Television News

(U.K.), each having a 25 percent share. McGoff was thus able to buy a controlling interest in the company, thereafter known as UPITN.

UPITN is an important international television news service, selling its material to television stations in many countries, though the United States constitutes its biggest market. Of the American television networks, ABC Television has the closest ties to UPITN, but NBC has also arranged to use their material.[67] The president of UPITN, Roderick W. Beaton, claimed that McGoff "made no attempt to influence the editorial content of UPITN." But McGoff was able to appoint Clarence Rhodes, who had held a top position with Panax Newspapers, Inc., manager of UPITN. According to Rhoodie, they were able to include films on South Africa in the packages of materials distributed world-wide: Rhodes had interviewed Prime Minister Vorster, he added, and that interview was sold to stations in many countries. In the wake of the disclosures of the Information Department operations in 1979, Independent Television News bought McGoff's share in UPITN.

The Bid for the Trib (New York)

In 1977 McGoff tried to buy control of *The Trib*, a conservative newspaper that survived in New York City for only two months during 1977-78, a move that was uncovered by journalist Karen Rothmyer.[68] Leonard Saffir, publisher of *The Trib*, discussed the sale with McGoff and others at Panax Newspapers in the fall of 1977. The impetus came from Richard Mellon Scaife, who was associated with McGoff in the *Sacramento Union* project. Saffir then met twice with Gerald Zoffer, who says he is an investment broker and who writes under the name of Matthew Conroy for the *News World*, the New York paper put out by the followers of the Reverend Sun Myung Moon. According to Saffir, Zoffer told him the South African government wanted a stake in *The Trib* and could disguise its involvement. Saffir quoted Zoffer as saying, "We have a way—John McGoff. He will make the actual investment."[69] Zoffer called Saffir's account "total nonsense," but he was revealed to have had regular contacts with the South African mission in New York. In further contacts between *The Trib* and Panax officials, it was stated that an outlay of $5-$10 million for *The Trib*'s budget would be "no problem." Later, as the secret projects began to be exposed, Saffir was informed that McGoff was no longer interested in the deal.

The Washington Times: A Secret South African Role?

The *Washington Times*, a daily newspaper started by the Unification Church of the Rev. Sun Myung Moon in Washington, D.C., in May 1982, has a number of links with McGoff's operations and South Africa.[70] The editor and publisher, James Whelan, served from 1977 to 1980 as the vice president and editorial director of McGoff's Panax Corporation and then became editor of the *Sacramento Union*. His background as a reporter in Latin America for twenty years has prompted questions about ties to the CIA. Jeffrey P. Green, marketing director of the *Washington Times* and Joseph J. Gross, its business consultant, both previously worked for Panax, and Green is South African. Contributing columnist Allan C. Brownfeld once served as Washington correspondent for a number of South African publications, including *To the Point* magazine, which was backed by the Information Department. Executive editor and columnist Smith Hempstone was for many years an associate editor of the *Washington Star* and has long been supportive of South Africa. After traveling around Angola for ten days with South African-backed UNITA, he wrote an article for *Reader's Digest* ("Angola: Where the West Can Still Win," February 1981) urging American support for UNITA. Carlyle Reed, associate publisher and general manager, was publisher of the *Sacramento Union* before McGoff bought it and was part of a delegation to South African ceremonies attending "independence" for the Transkei in 1976. (The Ford administration had followed a policy of nonrecognition.) William Rusher, like McGoff a member of the *Time's* editorial advisory board, is publisher of the conservative *National Review* and a long-time supporter of South Africa. In the mid-sixties he was co-chairman of the African-American Affairs Association (AAAA), which had close links to the Rhodesian regime's information office in Washington.*

Soon after it began publishing, the *Washington Times* stated in an editorial that it was "totally opposed to South Africa's apartheid." But it argued that the country's democratic institutions, despite racist restrictions, offered more hope for freedom than would their violent overthrow, and that geopolitical strategies and South Africa's mineral wealth had also to be considered in weighing the situation there.[71] Even with this moderate tone, however, there has been no doubt of the paper's firm support for the Botha government. And its links with McGoff have raised the question of possible secret support from South Africa.

As noted above, the Erasmus Commission indicated that McGoff never returned more than $5 million of the secret South African funds provided to him, and the South African government did make it clear that, despite Muldergate, it would continue to mount secret propaganda operations. For its part, the Moon organization has a well-known history of trying to buy political influence (notably the scandal involving the Korean CIA and buying of influence in the late seventies), and it has cooperated openly with individuals and foreign governments sharing its anticommunist doctrines. As early as 1977, a connection between McGoff, the

---

*In a 1978-79 listing of secret Information Department projects the AAAA was slated to receive $13,000 (see Appendix B).

Moon people, and South Africa had cropped up when McGoff was considering buying the *Trib* in New York (see above).

Finally, it is clear that the *Washington Times* is meant to serve an ideological purpose. It is not a journalistic enterprise of a conventional sort. This is underlined by the fact that the *Times* has been a money-losing venture. Its costs for the first few months alone were estimated at up to $12 million, and it had not accepted any advertising to provide revenue.[72]

Federal Investigation into McGoff's Role

McGoff was first officially mentioned in South African government investigations in November 1978. Judge Anton Mostert reported that McGoff had received South African government funds to finance his bid for the *Washington Star*. McGoff responded with a statement saying that the charge was "utter nonsense."[73] The investigations continued in South Africa in the carefully contained forum of the Erasmus Commission; in the United States the Justice Department stated that an investigation was underway, but that the "allegations are just a little vague" to warrant a full-scale probe.[74] By June 1979 the final report of the Erasmus Commission stated flatly that McGoff had bought the *Sacramento Union* and United Press International Television News with $11.3 million in South African government funds, that $6.3 million of these funds had not been repaid, and that it was not yet clear whether the South African government had a claim to the money remaining in McGoff's hands.[75] And Florida records revealed that a Miami Beach house used by McGoff was actually owned by the Information Department's Swiss conduit, Thesaurus Continental Securities.[76] Yet the Justice Department (under Carter) still took no decisive action.

In July 1979 McGoff broke his silence on the issue. He told the Associated Press, "I am not now or ever have been an agent or a front for any foreign government, including the Republic of South Africa."[77] The charges he faced included failure to register as a foreign agent (with a maximum penalty of a $10,000 fine or five years' imprisonment) as well as violations of foreign exchange regulations and federal tax laws. The Securities and Exchange Commission investigated McGoff's dealings and referred the matter to the Justice Department. The Justice department presented its findings to a grand jury which, as of July 1983, had taken no action.

Beurt R. SerVaas and the Saturday Evening Post

Beurt R. SerVaas, chairman of the Curtis Publishing Corporation in Indianapolis, which publishes the *Saturday Evening Post*, has been named in connection with several Information Department projects. There have also been questions raised about his past ties to the CIA (as noted earlier). After SerVaas was mentioned in reports in the South African press and by the Erasmus Commission, the *Indianapolis Star* published, in March 1980, an investigative report on his ties with South Africa.[78] SerVaas told reporters he first traveled to South Africa in 1976 at the expense of the Information Department after the Curtis Publishing Corporation had been invited to send a representative to make a tour. Rhoodie claimed, however, that SerVaas had gone to the South African consulate in New York and said he wanted to go to South Africa. Mulder said he first met SerVaas "many, many years ago" at a luncheon in Pretoria and met him "quite often" during other visits since. SerVaas claimed he had traveled to South Africa only four times in all and met Mulder only twice.

What is indisputable is that between 1976 and 1980 the *Saturday Evening Post* published seventeen articles and editorials about South Africa and the Nationalist government, all of them favorable. Some of the articles were actually paid advertisements; two were written by Rhoodie, and one was composed by Gordon van der Merwe, a South African who had worked with *To the Point* magazine and Afripix. In 1978 the *Post* set up a Cape Town bureau, its only foreign office. The Erasmus Commission cited SerVaas in connection with several secret Information Department projects. He was identified as an overseas investor in the *Citizen* and a director of Afripix. He was also named in South African court documents as a backer of an investment plan that allegedly misused stock in ESCOM, the national electrical utility. The plan was promoted by businessman David Abramson, who was a front man for the Information Department.

Gerald Ford's 1976 Presidential Campaign

One of the most sensational charges to come out of the Information Department scandal was the allegation in the *Sunday Express* of Johannesburg (March 25, 1979) that former President Gerald Ford's 1976 presidential campaign had received $3.9 million in secret funding from the Information Department. The newspaper gave no source for its charge, and it did not reveal the channels by which the money moved or how such a large sum could have been used secretly to support the Ford campaign. Robert Visser, general counsel for Ford's campaign, called the allegation "preposterous."[79] Since the maximum individual contribution permitted by law in a presidential campaign was $10,000, disguising an infusion of such magnitude would have been extremely difficult, though it is conceivable the support could have been given indirectly, through special interest groups concerned only with certain issues. Though Rhoodie stated that "we didn't make payments to the politicians" in the United States, he did imply that South African funds were channeled to politicians through front organizations and third parties.[80]

At any rate, Ford did have dealings with South Africa on several occasions. In 1974 an important breakthrough in the level of official contacts between South Africa and the United States came with the visit of Mulder to Washington, D.C, which included a meeting with Ford, then Vice President. Rhoodie claimed that the meeting had been arranged by John McGoff. In 1975 and 1976 the Ford administration, carrying out policies shaped by Secretary of State Henry Kissinger, cooperated with the South African invasion of Angola in the clandestine CIA intervention aimed at defeating the MPLA. The intervention failed, but the South Africans certainly would have had every reason to want Ford to win the 1976 presidential election. In 1979 Ford gave a speech on relations between the United States and South Africa at a seminar in Houston for the South African Foreign Trade Association and the SenBank of South Africa. SenBank paid Ford $10,000, but according to Rhoodie the bank was reimbursed by the Information Department. Ford's speech was used in a special supplement on South African in *Business Week* magazine (October 1979). That supplement was also secretly underwritten by the Information Department.

The Defeat of Senator Dick Clark of Iowa

In 1978 Senator Dick Clark of Iowa was chairman of the Senate Foreign Relations Subcommittee on Africa and a strong critic of apartheid. According to Rhoodie, the Information Department provided $250,000 to aid the campaign that year of conservative Iowa Republican Roger W. Jepson, and that aid was instrumental in the November 1978 defeat of Clark. Documentation of Rhoodie's claims was supposedly included in material he offered to news organizations for $200,000. (No one accepted Rhoodie's offer.) Senator Jepson denied the report, but the *New York Times* reported that "the record of the Clark-Jepson campaign disclosed a pattern of involvement by South Africans and people strongly supportive of South Africa."[81] It was also reported that the South African funds were used to support a mass door-to-door distribution of right-wing pamphlets by anti-abortionists who were opposing Clark.[82]

The Defeat of Senator John Tunney of California

Another electoral victory was claimed by Rhoodie through the allocation of money to the senatorial campaign of S. I. Hayakawa in 1976. Senator John Tunney of California went down to defeat in his bid for reelection.[83]

Bid to Influence Governor Jerry Brown and Other Operations

The South African press reported on other efforts by the Information Department to gain influence in California, by unspecified means, with top aides of Governor Jerry Brown, in anticipation of a presidential bid in 1980. A former associate of Rhoodie's told Anthony Sampson of the *London Observer* that the Information Department's California plans were "mind-boggling," and that if they came to light they would "wreck South African-American relations." It was also claimed that the Information Department came "within a whisker" of buying a television station in California.[84]

Jimmy Carter's Campaign for the Presidential Nomination in 1976

According to Rhoodie, the Information Department, through a third party, arranged a contribution of nearly $20,000 to the 1976 New York State primary campaign of Jimmy Carter in his effort to win the Democratic nomination for President.[85] Rhoodie also said that the Information Department had cultivated contacts in the Carter camp prior to his election in order to temper his policies toward South Africa.

OTHER PROJECTS IN THE UNITED STATES

Sydney S. Baron Associates, New York (Codename: Red Baron)

In 1976 the Information Department engaged Sydney S. Baron Associates, a prominent New York public relations company with close ties to the Democratic party. While this was nominally a secret project, aspects of it soon became known, both because Baron organized a number of public projects relating to South Africa and because organizations or individuals acting for foreign governments must register with the Justice Department as foreign agents. The *New York Times* (March 28, 1979) described Baron as "one of the largest" of the twenty registered lobbyists and agents for South Africa in the United States.

Among the key projects organized by Baron Associates for South Africa were private conferences on United States-South African relations. They were meant to attract American business leaders. At a conference held in Rye, New York, in 1977 former Treasury Secretary William Simon spoke as a stand-in for Henry Kissinger: he was paid $10,000 for his effort. Such conferences were said to be sponsored by the South African Foreign Trade Association and the SenBank of South Africa; Rhoodie said the expenses were reimbursed by the Information Department. In June 1979 another conference was organized by Baron, this time in Palm Springs; it was publicly sponsored by the South African government. The featured speaker was Gen. William Westmoreland, who was paid $4000. In 1979 it was revealed that the South African Foreign Affairs Ministry would continue to use the services of Baron Associates, and $650,000 was budgeted to pay them in the 1979-80 fiscal year. That amount was equal to what had been budgeted secretly for Baron by the Information Department.[86] In 1980 the contract was cancelled.

Among the activities undertaken for South Africa by Baron and listed with the Justice Department were a luncheon and reception for Finance Minister Chris Heunis, a meeting between Dr. Christian Barnard and AFL-CIO president George Meany, and lobbying in Congress to oppose the Tsongas Amendment, which would have halted Ex-Im Bank guarantees for investments in South Africa.[87] In 1977 L. E. S. de Villiers, who had been deputy secretary of the Information Department under Rhoodie, joined the Baron office; he was later appointed president of the Baron affiliate in South Africa. The affiliate acts as the advertising sales representative of the *New York Times* and other companies.

It appears that Baron put together the special South African financial and economic supplements published in *Business Week* magazine in 1976, 1977, and 1978; Rhoodie said that the advertisements of South African companies appearing in the supplements were secretly paid for by the Information Department at a cost of $300,000.

De Kieffer Associates (Washington Lobbyists)

The hiring of Washington lawyer Donald de Kieffer as a lobbyist was another Information Department project that was soon known, since de Kieffer's activities on behalf of South Africa were immediately evident. (He had registered as a foreign agent with the Justice Department.) Between 1973 and 1978 the South African government had a contract with the law firm of Collier, Shannon, Rill and Edwards (and later Scott). It was this prestigious Washington firm, having links to the Republican party, to which de Kieffer belonged. In 1978 de Kieffer formed his own firm and continued to work on behalf of the South African government. Eschel Rhoodie stated that through the fiscal year ending March 31, 1979, the Information Department had paid $1 million for these lobbying services.[88]

Another aspect of South African lobbying activities in Washington was reflected in a report in the *New York Times* (March 23, 1979) saying that in recent years about fifty Congressmen or Congressional staff members had made trips to South Africa that were subsidized by the South African government.

The Sports Boycott

An international sports boycott of apartheid has been an effective protest against South Africa's policies. To counter the boycott, the Information Department set up a Committee for Fairness in Sports to place ads in major Western papers in favor of sports ties with South Africa. The 1978-79 budget was $180,000. Richard Lapchick, head of ACCESS (the American Coordinating Committee for Equality in Sports and Society), has been a key organizer of protests against sports contacts with South Africa. In February 1978, while working on a campaign against South African participation in Davis Cup tennis competition in the United States, he was attacked in his office and badly injured by two assailants. They concluded the attack by carving the word "niger" into his abdomen. Both before and after the attack Lapchick received telephone threats against himself and his family. An indication of a possible South African link came later in the year when, at a meeting held in New York by the South African Information Department with journalists from South Africa, one official mentioned "the destruction of Richard Lapchick" to a correspondent as an example of the success of his department's programs.[89] Lapchick continued his work with ACCESS, but anonymous threats and harassment have continued.

The Atlantic Council

A listing of Information Department projects for 1978-79 shows an allocation of $336,000 to establish a head office for the "Atlantic Council" in London and branch offices in South Africa and the United States (see Appendix B). Rhoodie claimed this project was suggested by Professor John Hutchinson, a conservative who teaches in California. Hutchinson allegedly told Rhoodie on a visit to South Africa that he wanted to form an organization to counter the influence of the Council on Foreign Relations.[90] There is nothing to show how far the Information Department project developed or whether Hutchinson was actually involved.

Influence on United States Trade Unions

Rhoodie claimed that substantial payoffs were made to American labor leaders to oppose a planned week-long boycott of trade with South Africa. The *London Observer* noted that "there seems little doubt that a sum in excess of $100,000 was distributed among [American] labor leaders."[91]

INFORMATION DEPARTMENT OPERATIONS IN BRITAIN AND EUROPE

Thesaurus Continental Securities Corporation

The Thesaurus Continental Securities Corporation, (a subsidiary of the Union Bank of Switzerland) functioned as a key conduit for Information Department funds to a number of important projects. Thesaurus was organized as an established subsidiary of the Union Bank of Switzerland, one of that country's biggest banks. According to the *Sunday Times* of Johannesburg (July 29, 1979) Dr. Bruno Saager, the chairman of Thesaurus and a former general manager of the Union Bank, was personally involved in the funneling operations. His experience with South Africa goes back to the 1950s, when he took the lead in forging Swiss financial links with South Africa, culminating in the switch of the bulk of South Africa's gold marketing from London to Zurich in the 1970s. From the *Sunday Times* account, it appears that Dr. Saager was not a passive participant in the secret projects: he reportedly signed a letter containing false information that enabled Eschel Rhoodie to conceal the Information Department's funding of the *Citizen*. He is also said to have arranged loans for the Information Department that were not authorized by the South African Treasury or Reserve Bank. Among the Information Department projects in which Thesaurus was involved were:

- The $13 million used to start the *Citizen*.
- The $4 million provided to Thor Communicators, an Information Department front company.
- The transfer of Information Department funds in the takeover of the British publishing company Morgan Grampian.
- The $10 million provided to American publisher John McGoff for his attempt to buy the *Washington Star*.
- The transfer of funds used to buy control of Hortors, Ltd., a South African printing company.

Bruno Saager retired from the Union Bank when the Information Department scandal began to break.

The Club of Ten (Operation Sparrow)

In 1978 retired British judge Gerald Sparrow confirmed that the Club of Ten, for which he had been the public organizer from 1973 to 1975, was a secret project of the South African Information Department. Since 1973 the mysterious Club had placed expensive advertisements for South Africa in major Western newspapers. Although supposedly a campaign paid for by wealthy South African businessmen, the project was financed and created by the Information Department. Sparrow said he was drawn into the project in 1972 when he was preparing a tourist book for the Information Department and South African Airways. In 1975 he was replaced by British journalist John Boddie. Rhoodie stated that, from 1973 to 1979, the Information Department spent about $1 million on Club of Ten advertisements in major papers, including the *Washington Post*, the *New York Times*, the *London Times*, and important papers in Canada, Australia, Germany, France, and the Netherlands.

The Morgan Grampion Publishing Group (Britain)

In 1976 the Information Department provided South African businessmen David Abramson and Stuart Pegg a $1 million interest-free loan and loan guarantees to finance the takeover of the Morgan Grampian

Group, one of the largest publishing companies in Britain. (Morgan Grampion owned forty-one magazines, mainly dealing with technical fields, and four newspapers.[92]) Through this deal the Information Department became involved in a number of other takeover moves. Abramson and Pegg attempted to buy *City* magazine in Britain, but failed. In France, they succeeded in buying the Nouvelle Société de la Presse (see below). Two other ventures failed: attempts to buy *Drum* magazine and the prestigious financial publication *Investors Review* were thwarted. But the takeover of Hortors, Ltd., the large South African printing and publishing company, was linked to the Morgan Grampian deal.

The Morgan Grampian operation was such a rapid success that Abramson and Pegg ultimately accepted a takeover bid that yielded them a profit of more than $4 million. They split the money with the Information Department.

British Politicians and Disruptions of Anti-Apartheid Activities

It was reported that the Information Department was able to buy the services of two Labour party members in parliament to report on activities of anti-apartheid activists.[93] The British *Guardian* (July 26, 1979) noted that one project, "G48," of the Information Department referred to "Parliamentary activities—Britain" and included $12,000 for 1978-79. This was to finance visits to South Africa. Rhoodie also claimed the Information Department distributed copies of a petition that was virtually identical to one being used by the British Anti-Apartheid Movement, but to discredit the organization, it used Marxist terminology.

German-South African Association (Deutsch-Sudafrikanische Gesellschaft) and Other Projects in West Germany

West Germany has been an important area of Information Department activities, and the main vehicle for these has reportedly been the German-South African Association, which claims a membership of several thousand. The founding of the Association was reportedly promoted by the Department of Information, which used it to channel $575,000 to a public relations company in Bonn.[94] The company's main task has been to promote visits to South Africa by West German members of parliament and to produce German-language publications issued by the Foreign Affairs Association (the Information Department front based in Pretoria). The South African Foreign Affairs Department disclosed in 1979 that it would continue to fund a project in West Germany at a rate of $580,000 annually for 1977-78 and 1979-80 (apparently the same public relations company).[95]

West Germany—General

The Lutheran Church in West Germany has been a particular target of Information Department efforts to end its support for the World Council of Churches and its program to combat racism. Between 1970 and 1977 there were more than fifty special advertising supplements placed in major West German newspapers to promote economic ties with South Africa, as well as specifically political ads placed by the South African embassy or by the Club of Ten, the Information Department front based in Britain. Another organization in West Germany, Transa, has promoted white immigration to South Africa with the cooperation of the Federal Labor Exchange. Two important pro-South African voices in West Germany have been publishing baron Axel Springer and conservative politician Franz-Josef Strauss, said to be a regular visitor to South Africa.[96]

La Nouvelle Société de la Presse (France)

In 1977 South African businessmen David Abramson and Stuart Pegg were able to buy a controlling interest for the Information Department in the Nouvelle Société de la Presse, a French publishing firm that publishes the Gault et Millau guidebooks and a half-dozen magazines, mostly tourist publications. The aim was to start political magazines, but the project collapsed. When Abramson and Pegg liquidated their French holding, the Nouvelle Société de la Presse went bankrupt, in December 1978, leaving $1 million in debts.[97]

Stichting Beheerscentrum (Foundation Control Center) (Netherlands)

Stichting Beheerscentrum was the vehicle for various pro-apartheid activities. Up to June 21, 1977, the Information Department had provided this organization with a total of $125,000 for "actions. . .aimed at creating confusion in the anti-apartheid movement."[98] According to Rhoodie, he managed to bribe a prominent member of the anti-apartheid movement in Holland through the center, a claim supported by anti-apartheid activists there.

In 1974 the center undertook to publish a bogus issue of Peace Journal, an annual put out by an interdenominational organization, containing articles favorable to South Africa.

While there was no formal coordination among the various Dutch groups favoring South Africa, the center was a focus for other groups and individuals. Some of the important groups are the Dutch-South African Society, the Netherlands-South African Working Community, the Legion of Ex-Servicemen, the periodical African Express, the Jan van Riebeeck Society, No Church Money for Violence (opposing activities of the World Council of Churches), and the Committee for Consultation on South Africa.

African Development Magazine (Operation Hippo)

African Development was first published in 1973 in South Africa by the Information Department. In 1976 the magazine was transferred to London because postal connections were better; and the editor, who held a British passport, was better able to travel to most African countries. Rhoodie estimated that the Information Department had spent some $225,000 on the magazine up to the beginning of 1976.

OTHER PROJECTS IN BRITAIN AND EUROPE

Drum International (Britain)

Rhoodie wished to control a magazine distributed in Africa. Using his stake in Morgan Grampian as a base, he tried to buy *Drum International*, which markets magazines in Nigeria, Kenya, Tanzania, Zambia, and South Africa, but the owner withdrew from the deal at the last moment.

Investors Chronicle (Britain)

The Information Department narrowly missed acquiring the *Investors Chronicle*, an authoritative British financial magazine. The purchase of $1.5 million worth of shares in the publication had been approved by Prime Minister Vorster, who then forgot to authorize the money for it in time, according to Rhoodie.

Investors Review (Britain)

After having failed to take over the *Investors Chronicle*, the Information Department did succeed in buying a fifty percent interest in the London financial publication *Investors Review*.

The Attempted Takeover of West Africa Magazine

Information Department front men Abramson and Pegg stated that by using $200,000 in secret funds and an Israeli businessman as a front, they were able to make a deal for the purchase of the influential magazine *West Africa* (published in London).[99] At the last minute, however, the deal fell through. The management of *West Africa* denied that the Information Department bid ever succeeded, but the staff was dissatisfied with this explanation of events. The editor and several others therefore resigned.

Foreign Affairs Research Institute (London)

Rhoodie described the Foreign Affairs Research Institute in London as one of "various institutions with interesting, neutral names" that were founded with Information Department funds.[100] The institute vehemently denied the allegation. The Johannesburg *Sunday Express* (June 10, 1979) claimed also that Information Department payments were made to British politicians involved with the activities of the Foreign Affairs Research Institute.

French-South African Chamber of Commerce

Citing the importance of French-South African commercial ties, Rhoodie said that he had urged the formation of the French-South African Chamber of Commerce.

French-South Africa Society

The French-South Africa Society was to be given $144,000 in secret funds, according to the Information Department's 1978-79 listing (see Appendix B). Rhoodie claimed that he had helped set it up.

Université Libre

Rhoodie said that he donated $20,000 to students for the transformation of *Université Libre* into a monthly magazine carrying positive articles on South Africa.

French-South African Friendship Society

Rhoodied reported that he had founded the French-South African Friendship Society and provided with it with $200,000 of Information Department funds.

Institute for the Study of the Modern World and Le Monde Moderne

The Institute for the Study of the Modern World and its publication, *Le Monde Moderne*, were set up in Paris to provide a source for "authoritative and scientific" reports on South Africa, according to Rhoodie.

France Eur-Afrique

France Eur-Afrique, a monthly magazine published in Paris, was controlled by the Information Department.

Bids for Paris-Match and L'Express

It was reported that the Information Department tried, unsuccessfully, to take over *Paris-Match* and *L'Express*, two prominent French weeklies.[101]

Campaign Leaflets

During the French general elections of March 1978, leaflets were distributed smearing former French Premier Jacques Chirac. These were said to have been the work of South African agents.[102]

Foundation for Social Studies (Holland)

The Foundation for Social Studies, an international academic organization founded in 1969, has published the magazine *Plural Societies*. The magazine, distributed world-wide, carries articles dealing with societies made up of differing ethnic groups and cultures. A major production of the foundation is the five-volume series *Case Studies on Human Rights and Fundamental Freedoms, a World Survey*, which has been distributed to academics, scientists, university libraries, and other institutions in the Netherlands, Britain, and the United States. One of the editors of the studies is Nic Rhoodie, brother of Eschel Rhoodie. He is chairman of the Sociology Department at the University of Pretoria, and head of the Information Department-funded Center for the Study of Plural Societies there. *Case Studies* has been distributed by the prominent Dutch publisher Martinus Niijhoff, which has denied being responsible for its publication. For 1978-79 *Case Studies* was to be allocated $60,000 by the Information Department and *Plural Societies* $25,000 (see Appendix B).

Activities in Scandinavia

A copy of an Information Department letter authorizing $11,500 for secret projects in Scandinavia for 1978-79 was produced by Rhoodie in an interview.

Establishment of Norwegian Political Party

The Information Department promoted the formation of a conservative political party in Norway. The party won four seats in the Norwegian parliament in 1973. According to *Le Monde* (March 23, 1979), the group, known as the Party Against Taxes and Bureaucracy, disappeared in 1977, but Rhoodie stated that the party continued under the new name Progressives.

PROJECTS IN AFRICA

Funding for the Democratic Turnhalle Alliance in Namibia

It was reported that the Democratic Turnhalle Alliance (DTA) spent more than $5 million on the December 1978 "internal" elections run by South Africa in Namibia. The DTA won. It refused to disclose the sources of its funding, though it was believed that substantial amounts came from West Germany and that other funds (said to be at least $1.2 million) came from South Africa. Rhoodie said that the Information Department had helped to finance the DTA.[103]

Namibian Newspapers and Political Funding

In 1978 the former editors of two newspapers in Namibia (the *Windhoek Advertiser* and the *Allgemeine Zeitung*) charged that the German publisher who had bought their papers was actually serving as a front for the Information Department.[104] Dieter Laurenstein, the publisher, denied the charge, but it was noted that the new editor of one of the papers (which backs the South Africa-supported DTA in Namibia) is a former reporter for the *Citizen*, which was the Information Department's main project in South Africa.

Operation Cherry (Namibia)

Operation Cherry used a Navy ship to cruise the Namibian coast broadcasting radio propaganda against SWAPO. A ship was used in order to prevent pinpointing the source of the broadcasts. The budget for 1978-79 was to be $100,000. A related project cited by Rhoodie distributed color slides, brochures, and color comic books. The artwork for these was prepared by a New York-based public relations firm, Richard Manville, Inc.

Operation Chicken (Rhodesia)

Operation Chicken allegedly involved financial support of almost $1 million for Bishop Abel Muzorewa and James Chikerema of the United African National Congress. According to Rhoodie, the operation was conceived by and implemented with the aid of an official of Allegheny Ludlam Industries. That American company, the largest exporter of chromium from southern Africa and with substantial interests in Rhodesia and South Africa, denied the allegation. (The project is described in greater detail in Chapter 3.)

Operation Playboy (Seychelles)

A tourist trip by Eschel Rhoodie and his associates and their wives to the Seychelle Islands, off the east coast of Africa in 1977 was one incident that drew comment in the South African press when stories about Information Department corruption began to leak out. By Rhoodie's account, the trip was really part of a secret project, Operation Playboy. That project was aimed at influencing James Mancham, the prime minister of the Seychelles. Mancham was said to have agreed to arrange landing rights for South African Airways and to resume normal diplomatic relations with South Africa, including trade and tourism links, and to have provided political information on the OAU. South Africa provided a Belgian printing press (at a cost of $60,000) for his election campaign, along with cash for his political party, Mancham later told the South African *Sunday Express* (August 8, 1979). The plans went awry when Mancham was overthrown in a coup in 1977, but new plans were set in motion to reinstall him. In November 1981 an attack was made by a military and mercenary force from South Africa to try to overthrow the government of Prime Minister Albert René of the Seychelles, but was foiled. (See Chapter 4 for additional details.)

Other Moves toward Detente with African States

General Van den Berghe of BOSS was closely involved in other efforts at detente and secretly visited Zaire, Gabon, Tanzania, Zambia, and the Central African Republic, according to Rhoodie. He claimed that South Africa had provided secret technical and agricultural assistance to these countries. It is known that South Africa carries on trade and other business contacts (some secretly) with a number of African states. Prime Minister Vorster met with Liberian President W. R. Tolbert, in Liberia, but Tolbert refused further dialogue after the Soweto killings. Vorster met with President Kenneth Kaunda of Zamiba in 1977 as part of an unsuccessful South African push for an "internal settlement" for Rhodesia. Rhoodie also said that South Africa set up two large farms in Gabon and Zaire, the one in Zaire on land belonging to President Mobutu.

Mobutu was said to have been ready to put $2 million into a French-language magazine for Africa: South Africa would contribute $500,000, and the printing and distribution would be done in Paris. The *Sunday Express* of South Africa (June 10, 1979) said the plan never came off because (among other things) Mobutu could not produce the necessary money.

Another African detente project involved arranging an air corridor for South African Airways flights to and from Europe; since 1960 the airline had been barred from flying over the rest of the continent. Permission was given by Zaire, the Central African Republic, and Gabon. The last links were to be the Sudan and Egypt, but the project was abandoned because Vorster decided to discontinue plans for meetings with leaders in North Africa and the Middle East.

Television News Service (Nairobi, Kenya)

Setting up a television news service in Kenya was one of Rhoodie's first projects. An American producer was put in charge. When the operation became successful, films on South Africa were also included in the packages being sold to foreign television stations. It appears in the 1978-79 list of projects with an allocation of $24,000 (see Appendix B).

Operation Wooden Shoe (Senegal and the Ivory Coast)

In 1974 Prime Minister Vorster made an important breakthrough in his efforts to promote "detente" with selected African countries: accompanied by General Van den Berge of BOSS, Eschel Rhoodie, General M.

Geldenhuys, and other officials, he flew to the Ivory Coast for talks with President Felix Houphouet-Boigny. It was reported that at the talks landing rights were arranged for South African Airways at Abidjan and that the South Africans also met representatives of Senegal, Gabon, and Zambia. In interviews, Rhoodie took credit for setting up the talks through secret meetings with President Leopold Senghor of Senegal and then with Houphouet-Boigny. Contacts with the Ivory Coast continued with another official visit in 1976 by Rhoodie and Mulder, and there were also arrangements made for Ivory Coast officials to travel to South Africa. After the 1976 Soweto uprising Senghor's attitude was said to have hardened against the Nationalist government; however, Houphouet-Boigny is said to have maintained his belief in dialogue.

Links with Israel

Using personal contacts and avoiding formal diplomacy through the Foreign Affairs Department, Rhoodie claimed, he, General van den Bergh, and Mulder traveled to Israel "many times" to prepare the ground for Vorster's 1976 state visit.[105] The visit was considered a diplomatic breakthrough for the Nationalist government. It had military overtones as well. One stop on Vorster's tour was the aircraft factory where the Israeli Kfir fighter aircraft are manufactured. Exactly how much credit should go to Rhoodie for the strengthening of South Africa's ties with Israel is unclear, for the record of economic, diplomatic, and military contacts actually goes back to the 1973 Middle East war.

South American Press Articles

A public relations man in Buenos Aires was paid $140,000 between 1974 and 1978 by the Information Department to get articles favorable to South Africa published in the nine most important newspapers in South America.

Payments to Members of Parliament in Japan

A payment of about $200,000 in secret Information Department funds was reportedly made by General van den Bergh to two members of the Japanese parliament who had close connections to the trade union movement there.[106]

7 The Total Strategy

WHEN P. W. BOTHA BECAME PRIME MINISTER IN 1978, the military buildup he had promoted as defense minister was already underway. But with his political opposition within the National party on the defensive, Botha was in a position to start implementing the Total Strategy that he and Magnus Malan, chief of the Defence Force, had advocated for defending South Africa against what is described as the "total onslaught" being mounted against it. To understand this Total Strategy, however, it will be helpful first to review the backgrounds of the men responsible for it. Although he served for more than ten years as defense minister and presided over the large-scale buildup of the Defence Force and Armscor's arms procurement and manufacturing capabilities, "Piet Wapen" ("Pete the Weapon," as Botha was nicknamed) does not have a military background.[1] Pieter Willem Botha was born in 1916 in the Orange Free State. He did not finish his university studies. Beginning his political career with the National party at the age of twenty, he rose in the heirarchy in the Cape. His mentor was Dr. D. F. Malan, also from the Cape, who became the first Nationalist prime minister in 1948 and presided over the introduction of apartheid measures. Botha became National party leader in the Cape Province, was appointed interior minister in the Verwoerd government in 1958, minister of community development and racial affairs in 1961, and then defense minister in 1966. He retained the defense portfolio after becoming prime minister, but turned it over to General Malan in 1980. Though known as a hot-tempered militarist, Botha established a reputation as a competent administrator and an experienced political operator who enjoyed party infighting. Because he has his base in the Cape, he has been considered an outsider and distrusted by the National party majority of the Transvaal branch. While Botha had been viewed as a hard-liner on racial issues, as prime minister he has adopted a rhetoric that is markedly *verligte* in tone, a reflection of the military's Total Strategy.

The major influence on Prime Minister Botha's political and military thinking has been a younger generation of Defence Force leaders, particularly Magnus Malan, who, in 1976, at the age of forty-six, became the youngest chief of the Defence Force in the country's history. General Malan, who is said to have provided Botha with lists of books on military affairs to read, has clearly been the architect of the Total Strategy. General Malan's own background illustrated the importance of the new Afrikaner generation in business and government and its interest in reshaping traditional Nationalist doctrines.[2] General Malan comes from a prominent Afrikaner family: his father was an academic who, as a strong Nationalist, went on to become speaker of the House of Assembly and also chairman of the Volkskas bank, an early pillar of Afrikaner capitalism. Magnus Malan chose a military career and advanced quickly as the Defence Force itself was being Afrikanerized under the Nationalist government, but he also retained his personal and political links to the Afrikaner power structure: the Broederbond, the church, and business. His attitudes remained staunchly Nationalist, but of a new variety, influenced by the economic liberalism of business and a conviction that the future of the Afrikaners can be assured only by a restructuring of white rule.

General Malan's military background includes considerable experience in guerrilla conflicts and counterinsurgency operations. He has been involved in the wars in Namibia and Rhodesia, the Portuguese colonialist struggles in Mozambique and Angola, and the guerrilla conflict that has begun in South Africa itself. In the early sixties he was attached to the French forces fighting in Algeria and witnessed the deep conflicts that war produced within French society. He also studied with the U.S. Army, taking the regular Command and General Staff Officers Course at Fort Leavenworth, Kansas, in 1963. He is said to be a close observer of the military and political policies of the Israelis and the Nationalist Chinese on Taiwan and to maintain close contacts with their military establishments.

A report in the South African press identified a main source of the Total Strategy concept advocated by Botha and Malan as a slim, little-known book by a French general, André Beaufré, titled *Introduction à la Stratégie*.[3] In speeches military leaders and government officials have paraphrased passages from the book describing modern war as "total," carried on not only in the military sphere, but in all fields, including the political, economic, diplomatic, cultural. This view draws, of course, on such classic military sources as Von Clauswitz and Mao. Beaufré describes the implications for modern military planners and calls for a "total strategy" coordinated throughout all fields of government policy. The book describes various types of conflicts, including the kind of protracted guerrilla war South Africa now faces.

One of the clearest general statements of the Total Strategy in South Africa appeared in the opening section of the 1977 Defence *White Paper* under the heading "National Security." The White Paper states that "Russia has maintained a multi-dimensional campaign against the West" since World War II. "Consequently we are today involved in a war, whether we wish to accept it or not." The *White Paper* goes on:

> It is therefore essential that a Total National Strategy be formulated at the highest level. The defence of the Republic of South Africa is not solely the responsibility of the Department of Defence. On the contrary. . .[it] is the combined responsibility of all government departments. This can be taken further—it is the responsibility of the entire population, the nation* and every population group.[4]

The *White Paper* mentions that the United States found it necessary to have "coordinated action planning by all government departments" in support of world-wide strategic objectives after World War II (and that this led to the formation of the National Security Council). It states that South Africa established the State Security Council in 1971 to fill a similar function of formulating the "total national strategy" for national security. The Total Strategy is then defined as:

> . . .the comprehensive plan to utilize all the means available to a state according to an integrated pattern in order to achieve the national aims within the framework of the specific policies. A total strategy is, therefore, not confined to a particular sphere, but is applicable at all levels and to all functions of the state structure.[5]

The section concludes with a listing of fourteen aspects of national security that are included in the formulation of a total strategy:

- Political action
- Military/paramilitary action
- Economic action
- Psychological action
- Scientific and technological action
- Religious-cultural action
- Manpower services
- Intelligence services
- Security services
- National supplies, resources, and production services
- Transport and distribution services
- Financial services
- Community services

---

*In South African terminology, "the nation" means, of course, only the "white nation."

- Telecommunication services

While the *White Paper* cited the key role of the State Security Council in formulating the Total Strategy, this body had actually been relatively dormant after its creation. The origins of this body are linked with those of BOSS.[6] During the mid-sixties the Nationalist government was gearing up to combat the new development of underground and guerrilla activity; several national security bodies were established (a State Security Committee and then an Intelligence Coordinating Committee), but these were apparently not considered adequate. BOSS was formed in 1968-69 as the coordinating agency for intelligence and security. The State Security Council was established in 1970-71 to function at the highest level in an advisory capacity on the information assembled and analyzed by BOSS. The Council included the prime minister, the ministers of justice, defense, police, foreign affairs, national security, the chief of the Defence Force, the police commissioner, the secretaries for foreign affairs and justice, as well as other ministers and members of parliament co-opted on an *ad hoc* basis. It appears, however, that in the Vorster government the State Security Council was not active and that its functions were performed on an informal basis by Vorster and General van den Bergh of BOSS. With P. W. Botha in office, the Council was activated to play a central role in formulating the Total Strategy, under the guidance of the Department of the Prime Minister. The process was described in the 1979 Defence *White Paper*:

> At the national level the Cabinet is assisted by the State Security Council (SSC) and its executive agencies to fulfil duties concerning the national security of the Republic of South Africa. The Department of the Prime Minister is responsible for management at this level by issuing guidelines, total national strategy directives, and total national strategies concerning national security. The national strategic planning process is conducted by the State Security Council with its Work Committee and Secretariat and fifteen interdepartmental committees of the State Security Council while coordination of the executive function is carried out by a National Joint Planning Centre.[7]

Within this bureaucratic structure the military has been given a prominent coordinating role by Botha. One commentator noted: "The South African Defence Force. . .takes part in a wide range of interdepartmental meetings, regardless of topic."[8] Various other examples were cited by another.[9] A senior commerce official is said to have complained to a Western diplomat that he had to waste too much time teaching "the generals" the intricacies of exchange control regulations. Among those attending a cabinet meeting on the sensitive subject of Bantustan consolidation (i.e., juggling land allocations to make the fragmented Bantustan areas more homogeneous) was General Malan. An investigation of the impact of apartheid laws in Capetown's District Six, an area where black residents have been being removed so that it can be turned over to whites, was apparently assigned to Military Intelligence. In 1980 a Defence Force document came to light detailing a plan to offset opposition criticism in parliament of the defense budget on such issues as the unequal burden borne by the infantry in the Namibia war, conscientious objection, unlawful hunting of game by soldiers, pay problems, and difficulties in recruiting blacks for the Defence Force because of pay advantages given to white soldiers. It was also reported that Defence Force officers had met with officials of the South African Broadcasting Corporations to stress the need for more "sabre-rattling" films for television. [10]

It is important to note that the Total Strategy being promoted so vigorously is a concept which calls for a bureaucratic structure as a mechanism for the effective coordination of policies. The major issue for the Botha government, beyond the obvious pattern of militarization, is the choice of policies to be pursued. In several key areas, Botha has attempted to reorient both apartheid policies and the stance of the National party. The first has been that of government relations with business, traditionally a zone of cleavage between Afrikaner and English-speaking elites, but one in which the growth of Afrikaner business has narrowed differences. Other major areas are the policies of apartheid and the question of the political structure of the government.

In November 1979 Botha dramatically demonstrated his interest in forging ties to the business sector by bringing his entire cabinet to an unprecedented meeting in Johannesburg with three hundred business and industrial leaders, including several blacks. In his speech he stressed his government's belief in free enterprise and promised to relax state controls. He also used the occasion to propose a "constellation of states" for southern Africa that would include white South Africa, the Bantustans (independent or not), and the other countries of the region. While these were similar to the "detente" proposals offered in the Vorster era, Botha stressed the importance of business in this plan to turn the region into a bulwark against Communist expansion. An economically powerful South Africa could offer increased investment, technical aid, transport, emergency food supplies, and, of course, military security. The other countries would gain wider markets and an enhanced supply of labor. Most important, they would play a security role by curbing the liberation movements. The constellation plan envisaged economic cooperation and integration as leading to forms of political integration. Countries that rejected the South African embrace and supported the liberation movements could expect economic pressure and military retaliation. When the constellation plan was offered, it was obvious that an independent

Zimbabwe headed by Bishop Muzorewa could be a keystone; instead, Robert Mugabe triumphed in the elections held only a few months later. While the constellation proposal has been kept alive, particularly with reference to the Bantustans, it has gained no support in the region. Instead, on April 1, 1980, nine countries of southern African joined in the Southern Africa Development Coordination Conference to promote economic independence from South Africa.

One basis for business ties with the Botha government is founded in the military's close ties to private industry through the Armscor arms manufacturing and procurement system. Sixteen business and professional men sit on the board of Armscor and its nine subsidiaries, and in 1978 the parastatal had almost six thousand contracts with eight hundred private suppliers. In 1979 Afrikaner businessman John Maree was seconded from the giant conglomerate Barlow Rand to become Armscor's chief executive. Botha has expanded the ties by appointing thirteen top business leaders,* Afrikaners and English-speakers, to a reconstituted Defence Advisory Board having a watchdog role over the Defence Force and the arms industry.[11]

In addition, directors of top companies were appointed to the new Presidential Council and to the Public Service Commission, which had been controlled by the Civil Service. Finance Minister Owen Horwood, who had also served in the Vorster government, moved to promote increased investment from the private sector, contain expansion of public spending, and free exchange controls. A Competition Board was set up to attack monopolies and cartels in various sectors.

Another significant aspect of the Botha government's efforts to forge closer ties with the business sector has been the various measures taken or proposed to reshape apartheid policies in several fields. Traditional apartheid policies limited black access to education, training programs and apprenticeships and to semiskilled and skilled jobs. As a result, severe strains have developed in the industrial economy because of a shortage of skilled workers. At the same time, these policies have long provoked black anger at unemployment and at the denial of opportun-

---

*Those appointed were A. M. Rosholt, chairman of Barlow-Rand, a manufacturing conglomerate; Basil Hersov, chairman of Anglo-Vaal, operating in mining and industry; Willem J. de Villiers, chairman of General Mining and Finance; Frans Cronje, chairman of South African Breweries and Nedsual (in finance) and eighteen other companies; Gavin Reilly, deputy chairman of Anglo-American Corporation; Richard John Goss, executive director of South African Breweries; Chris Saunders, chairman of Tongaat Sugar, a conglomerate, and Huletts Corporation; Ian Mackenzie, chairman of Standard Bank and six other companies; Richard Lurie, president of the Johannesburg Stock Exchange and Protea Holdings; Johannes G. van der Horst, chairman of Old Mutual (insurance); Frederick J. du Plessis, chairman of Trust Bank and managing director of Sanlam (insurance); Johannes A. Hurter, chairman of Volkskas bank; Jacob Wilkens, president of the South African Agricultural Union.

ities for advancement. The sensitivity of the architects of the Total Strategy both to the difficulties facing South African business and to the security problems posed by black resentment was illustrated in the remarks of General Malan at the annual meeting of the Volkskas bank in 1980.

> If there is a single factor that will have a retarding effect on the country's continued growth, it is the shortage of skilled workers.
>
> This shortage of skilled manpower in turn gives rise to unemployment amongst the unskilled. According to the latest estimate, considerably more than 100,000 posts are vacant at the moment, owing to the lack of trained workers. Problems that are very closely interwoven are: population growth, the creation of work, and training. . . .
>
> The way in which the community deals with its economic problems is not isolated from other areas, and a high level of economic development, employment and training will play an important part in improving the security situation. These issues involve not only the market-economy core of South Africa, but in particular the underdeveloped periphery, in which is to be found the internal center of gravity of the threat to the prevailing order in South Africa.[12]

Expectations of rapid changes were also raised by the minister for cooperation and development, Dr. Pieter Koornhof, in his frequent assurances that far-reaching transformations would be underway. In August 1980 Koornhof, who has been nicknamed "Promises" by Africans, told the National Press Club in Washington, D.C., "I say to you that apartheid, as you know it in the United States, is dying in South Africa."[13] In the same month, he wrote in the *New York Times*, "We will not rest until racial discrimination has disappeared from our statute books in South Africa."[14] While these claims were similar to some made earlier by the Vorster government, the military leaders' zeal to implement the Total Strategy appeared to ensure action.

Prime Minister Botha himself added to the sense of change through a campaign to effect a new attitude toward blacks, particularly among the *verkramptes* in the party. When a senator complained at the 1979 National party convention about the elimination of segregated lines at a local post office, Botha angrily criticized the *verkramptes*. They were "happy to be served hand and foot in their homes, but if they had to share a post office line then blacks had to disappear." Calling for whites to give others respect, he referred to the black volunteers who were serving in the military in the fight against "communism and terrorism." "Must I denigrate them?" he asked.[15] Comments of this sort—along with his widely quoted warning that whites must "adapt or die"—flew in the face of traditional Nationalist claims that apartheid segregation is designed to reduce racial friction. Botha termed the segregation of public

facilities insulting and dangerous. He also suggested that the laws pro-
hibiting interracial sex and marriage should be repealed, but made no
move to repeal them. In addition to appealing for changes in white
attitudes, Botha, described in one press report as "moving like a white
tornado," made a tour of all the non-"independent" Bantustans, and
an unprecedented visit to Soweto. He also met with Anglican Bishop
Desmond Tutu, the head of the South African Council of Churches and
a vocal opponent of apartheid.

The new rhetoric of the Botha government created wide expectations,
at least among whites, of important changes. For many whites the pace
of change has in fact appeared to be rapid, enough to oust the hardline *verkrampte* wing from the National party. But for black South Africans
the picture has been different. The general direction of the changes Botha
has advanced for the restructuring of apartheid has been toward solid-
ifying the relatively better-off position of a minority of blacks (basically
those people of mixed race, Indians, and Africans who are permitted to
live near white urban areas) while at the same time strengthening the
basic framework of apartheid—the Bantustan system. The result is that
for a majority of black South Africans hope for improvement in economic
and political status is receding, not advancing.

Under Vorster, the ideological basis of apartheid began to be reformulated. The original racial doctrines, grounded in a philosophy of
"white supremacy" became increasingly difficult to maintain in the face
of black resistance and international condemnation. Botha has vigorously pursued the new ideological approach in which racial segregation
is viewed as a positive form of preserving "national" and "cultural"
distinctions. Thus the claims by Koornhof in the United States that
apartheid "as you have known it [as a racial doctrine] is dying." Now
Africans may be allowed to wait in post office lines with whites, or go
to a restaurant or a nightclub that has applied for permission to serve
blacks. But they may still do so only if their passbooks are in order (if
they have permission to be in "white" areas). The principle that blacks
should only be allowed in "white" areas to work for whites is, in fact,
being maintained. Africans continue to be deprived systematically of
their political status as South African citizens under the program of
"independence" for the Bantustans, which has continued under Botha.
Venda was given that status in 1979, and the Ciskei in 1981.

Other overriding concerns of the Botha government have been the
various moves toward economic liberalization and the military buildup.
In some ways these different goals can be seen as relatively harmonious,
but in other respects they are not. For example, businesses have been
glad to have the shortage of skilled workers eased by measures that
allow blacks entry into more skilled jobs, but the continuing call-ups of
young whites for military duty have been disruptive and caused concern.

Similarly, the growing number of skilled black workers can only augment black pressures for full political participation and rights, and these will have to be controlled and dealt with in some way. Therefore the task of the Total Strategy as it is being carried out by the military planners in Botha's Prime Minister's Department is to coordinate policies in all areas to minimize and control conflicts and friction. A picture of the direction of the Total Strategy as it relates to the key aspects of apartheid can be gained by examining the specific measures introduced and their impact.

In the field of labor relations the government ended "job reservation" in 1979. Under this system, various categories of jobs in the industrial sector had been reserved to specific groups—in the main, the more skilled positions went to whites. In that same year parliament passed the Industrial Conciliation Amendment Act, which provided for government recognition of black and nonracial trade unions. The act allowed them to negotiate legally binding contracts and also granted unions the right to strike. But official recognition was made contingent on registration by the government, and that can be denied arbitrarily. Strikes are considered legal only after a lengthy arbitration procedure. Other measures by the Botha government have allowed blacks to enter apprentice programs in selected trades and permitted companies to include blacks in training programs of all types, including those at the managerial level. The Labor Relations Act of 1981 provided for the registration of nonracial trade unions and allowed migrant workers to join unions. But the act also outlawed political activity by unions; barred dues checkoff by unregistered unions lacking government permission; mandated that all unions submit detailed reports to the government on their structure, officials, and financing; made it illegal for unions to pay strike benefits during illegal strikes; and provided for a fine of up to R500 and a year in prison for illegal strike activity.

Complex legislation was introduced in October 1980 to modify the conditions under which Africans have been allowed to live and work in white urban areas. Under Section 10 of the Bantu (Urban Areas) Consolidation Act of 1945 and its later amendments, Africans have had to qualify under various restrictive criteria to remain in white urban areas for more than 72 hours to live or work. These include having lived in the area since birth or continuously for fifteen years, having worked for the same employer for at least ten years, or being the child of a qualified person under age eighteen. Spouses and relatives are not included in Section 10 authorizations. Permission to reside in the segregated townships outside the white urban areas has been a sought-after goal for Africans, since permission means access to better-paying work in the white industrial and commercial sectors. Other Africans working in the white urban areas are migrants on eleven-month conracts (to assure that they never gain designation under Section 10) living in single-sex hostels or those who commute by the day or the week, often over long distances, from outlying black settlements in "white" areas or Bantustans. Then there are the "illegals'—workers, spouses, or relatives of those with Section 10 authorization who violate the pass laws by staying in in the white areas without authorization stamped in the passbook that all Africans over sixteen years of age must carry at all times. The magnitude of the influx of illegal residents into the white urban areas can be gauged by the common estimate that half of the more than one million people believed to be living in Soweto are there illegally.[16]

The proposed legislation would have repealed the Urban Areas Act and thirty-five other racial laws while incorporating some of their provisions. It appeared to offer those "insiders" with Section 10 qualifications more secure status as permanent urban residents in "white" South Africa, while making conditions more difficult for illegal residents. Study of the complex measure revealed, however, that they would actually jeopardize the status of qualified residents by leaving authorization to remain in white areas entirely to the discretion of the white government bureaucracy. (Even those qualifying under Section 10 have faced expulsion to the Bantustans if they are found to be "idle or undesirable" or "redundant," and whole black communities have been liable to removal to other areas or the Bantustans as part of the continuing implementation of apartheid or simply slum clearance. As a result of protests from blacks and whites in the opposition, the legislation was withdrawn, but the government did institute a fine of up to R500 for those found to be employing illegal black workers.

In August 1982 the government introduced new draft legislation dealing with the same issues, but on even tougher terms. The proposed Orderly Movement and Settlement of Black Persons Bill would reduce the time that blacks might remain in urban areas (including the segregated black townships) without official authorization from 72 hours to 17—the period between 5:00 A.M. and 10:00 P.M. The penalty for sheltering persons illegally present during the hours of curfew created by the bill would be up to six months in jail and a R500 fine for first offenders. The maximum fine for employing an illegal black worker would be raised from R500 to R5,000 (some $4,350) and a year in prison. While the new measure would thus create extremely heavy penalties for unauthorized blacks found in the urban areas, it would grant "permanent urban resident" status to those blacks who are authorized residents, the section-tenners or "insiders"—the first time such a designation has been offered. There are no official statistics on the number of authorized black residents in the urban areas, but it is thought to be roughly a fifth of the black work force,[17] or some 1.4 million adults and a total of some 4 million if children are included. The bill would still provide a loophole for the white government to withdraw the "permanent resident" authorization if it was found that those concerned did not have "approved accommodation."

In 1979 Botha set up a new body, a one hundred-member Presidential Council. The members were appointed by the prime minister and included whites, people of mixed race, and Asians. Africans were not included, and the council was given an advisory role only. Because of these limitations, and because their communities were granted no role in appointing members of the council, the main mixed race and Indian political parties, the Coloured Labor party and the South African Indian Council, both rejected participation in the new body.

The formation of the Presidential Council was the first step in the Botha's more far-reaching goal of a "new constitutional dispensation" for blacks. In the political vocabulary of the Total Strategy, the Council would offer "co-responsibility" and "power-sharing" while still allowing "self-determination for whites." On these lines, the issues debated within the National party have concerned whether some kind of parliamentary role should be offered to people of mixed race and Asians and whether they might be included in a cabinet. There has been no question of offering such new arrangements to Africans at this point, however. Under the schema of apartheid, all Africans are to become foreigners, citizens of "independent" Bantustans, and have no political role within South Africa.

In May 1982 a committee of the Presidential Council presented a long-awaited report with proposals for a new governmental structure. The proposals called for limited parliamentary representation for people of mixed race and Indians (but offered no precise format for this) and for inclusion of representatives of both groups in the cabinet. The report labeled the new arrangement "segmentary autonomy," whereby racial groups would legislate on limited matters affecting their own affairs.

The report also proposed a major new role for the president. He could be elected by the white parliament, the mixed race and Asian representatives perhaps having a symbolic role, and have greatly expanded, authoritarian powers. The president would serve a seven-year term and have the power to dissolve parliament and to appoint and dismiss the prime minister and the cabinet. At present, the president, the head of state, is appointed by the prime minister. The position is largely an honorific.

The committee suggested that Prime Minister Botha could install a new president and appoint black members to the cabinet, so setting the new system in motion before opposition could arise among right-wing whites or blacks. The report stressed that the new system would "not in the least disturb existing power arrangements" among racial groups whereby "obviously enough" the white minority are dominant. While asserting that the goal was the creation of a democratic system, the report declared that the African majority could not be included because of their "cultural differences, relative numbers, conflicting interests, and divergent political objectives."[18]

In August 1982 Prime Minister Botha presented a version of this proposal to the National party convention. Under his plan a new parliament made up of three separate bodies—one each for whites, people of mixed race, and Indians—would replace the present all-white parliament. The white president would have the wide powers described above, and the Presidential Council would be transformed from an advisory body into an upper house of parliament, and have power over the three racially constituted chambers of parliament. As in the earlier council proposals, the African majority was excluded from the plan. White right-wingers opposed Botha's plan, as expected, as a radical step toward racial integration. Leaders of the Coloured Labor party and the South African Indian Council did not endorse it either, despite the lure of cabinet positions and a role in government. Aside from the basic problem of the exclusion of Africans, Botha's plan essentially maintains the concept of racial divisions, rather than promoting nonracial government, and also maintains the dominant position of whites.

In addition to launching initiatives in the three key areas of trade unions, the status of blacks in the white urban areas, and governmental structure, the Botha government has also undertaken or proposed a number of other changes. There have been moves to widen the administrative powers of the community councils set up in the African townships in white areas. Compulsary education for black children was begun on a limited basis in several urban areas in January 1981 (for most black children it remains neither compulsory nor free). A new study on Bantustan "consolidation" was launched. Botha implied that more land might be allocated to the Bantustans, saying that he did not regard the 1936 Land Act (by which the white government appropriated 87 percent of the country for whites) as a "holy cow." There has also been further relaxation of the laws segregating public facilities, and permission for "multinational" (i.e., racially mixed) sports events has been granted selectively—in response to the pressure of international protests and boycotts. Allocations for black housing and other public works has been substantially increased, but still lag far behind basic needs.   In analyzing the impact of the new dispensations offered by Botha, several observations can be made. The measures to allow black workers to move into semiskilled and skilled positions and into apprentice and training programs have been prompted by economic pressures. This outlook was expressed in the reports of the Wiehahn Commission on Labor Legislation and the Riekert Commission on Manpower Utilization. These reports, presented in 1980, underlined the costs to the white economy and the threat to the survival of capitalism in South Africa of the restrictions on the advancement of black workers. A recent study at the University of Witwatersrand[19] has shown that over the past three decades the over-all ratio of black workers to white workers has remained roughly constant (75 percent black and 25 percent white), but whereas the number of black workers in mining and agriculture, the traditional employers of large numbers of unskilled workers, has not increased, the number and ratio of black workers in other sectors, such as manufacturing, have increased significantly. This has not, however, eased the growing need for skilled workers in manufacturing caused by the small number of whites available and the prohibitions against black advancement. Employers have compensated by various means: recruiting white immigrants, using more capital-intensive production (i.e., mechanization), "job fragmentation" (breaking down more skilled "white" jobs into component tasks that are then assigned to low-paid black workers), or simply shifting job titles to let black workers do more skilled work without the title and for less pay. These tactics have, however, failed to meet the rising demand for more skilled workers. And as the percentage of white workers in industry is projected to drop from 16 percent in 1980 to only 7 percent by the turn of the century, there is no prospect that the situation will ease. These were the circumstances that prompted the Botha government, despite the opposition of traditional Nationalist constituencies, to align with business in allowing black workers to begin moving into more skilled positions.

The increasing importance of black workers—for their skills and not their numbers alone—has brought a great resurgence of black trade-union mobilization. This has been part of the wider pattern of black opposition that has developed since Soweto. Black trade unionism in South Africa began in the 1920s. After decades in which black trade unions flourished and were then decimated by government repression, the South African Congress of Trade Unions was established in 1955. By 1961, SACTU, with ties to the ANC, had thirty-five affiliated unions having 53,000 members, but within a few years it had been driven into exile. Virtually all of its organizers had been detained, and five SACTU activists had died in police custody. In 1972-73 spontaneous strikes by some hundred thousand black workers in the Durban area marked the beginning of renewed trade union activity, and it has continued to grow. Although black unions now represent only about 10 percent of the black industrial work force and 3 percent of black urban workers, they have begun to emerge as an important force on the South African scene. According to official figures, by the end of 1981 about 262,000 black workers were members of mainly black unions, while another 98,000 were members of "parallel" unions (the segregated branches of white unions), many of them against their will because of closed shop agreements.[20] The increasing activism of black workers has been reflected in the number of strikes (nearly all of them "illegal") and worker-days lost by companies. Again, according to official figures: in 1979 there were 101 strikes and 67,000 worker-days lost; in 1980 there were 207 strikes and 175,000 worker-days lost; and in 1981 there were 342 strikes and 226,500 worker-days lost.[21]

The largest black trade union organization is the Federation of South African Trade Unions (FOSATU), a national federation formed in 1979. As of the end of 1981, FOSATU had ten union affiliates and a membership of 95,000. The Confederation of Unions of South Africa (CUSA) is made up of eight unions having some 45,000 members. Both these federations have concentrated on labor relations issues rather than wider political protests against apartheid. In addition, there are a number of important independent unions: among these are the South African Allied Workers Union (SAAWU), based in East London; the General Workers Union, the major black union in Cape Town and the Western Cape; the African Food and Canning Workers Union, one of the oldest black unions and a former SACTU affiliate; the Black Municipal Workers Union, based in Johannesburg; and the Motor Assembly Components Workers Union of South Africa operating in Port Elizabeth. Of these unions, the SAAWU and the Motor Assembly Workers have stressed wider political issues.

In 1980 some ten thousand black workers in Johannesburg, members of the Muncipal Workers Union, went on strike for higher wages (their pay was approximately $43 a week) and for recognition of their union. After almost two months, the city government fired those workers who refused to return to work. More than 1,265 men refused and were summarily sent back to the Bantustans. The union's president was arrested under the Sabotage Act. In September 1982 nearly four hundred black dock workers, members of the General Workers Union, were dismissed by the state-owned Transport Services and threatened with expulsion to the Bantustans for staging a slowdown in an effort to win union recognition. The most protracted labor disputes have been an ongoing series of strikes and protests by the National Automobile and Allied Workers Union, a main FOSATU affiliate, against various auto companies in the Port Elizabeth area over wages and other issues.There were 56 shutdowns between early 1981 and early 1982 at the Volkswagen plant, as well as strikes at Ford and General Motors. Significantly, the gold-mining industry has also been hit by workers' unrest. (There have been no unions allowed for blacks in the mines since the great 1946 strike; and since most black mine workers are migrants, unionization is difficult.) After thousands of miners erupted in violent protest over wages in July 1982, police units were called in; ten workers were killed and more than a thousand were expelled to the Bantustans by the mining companies.[22]

The new legislation on trade unions must be interpreted in light of increasingly militant black labor. On the one hand there has been pressure for government recognition from companies who have come to see the black unions as a reality that must be dealt with if there is to be stability in the work force. However, the new legislation goes beyond simply extending recognition to the black unions: the goal is clearly to try to monitor and control them. This was stated openly by Manpower Minister Fanie Botha. He told a white audience, "We are registering black trade unions in order to control their activities."[23] For this reason some black unions, the more politically oriented ones, have decided not to register with the government, and even those which have registered have maintained their activitist policies. Behind the new legislation is the power of the police. As one correspondent has noted, "It is nearly impossible to have a legal strike in South Africa, because the legal machinery for getting one authorized is designed to minimize the chances of it ever occurring."[24] When workers strike illegally, the police routinely move in to break up the workers' meetings and rallies, and there is always the threat of expulsion to the Bantustans.

Beyond the repression against strikers, the Security Police have targeted the more politically oriented unions, particularly the SAAWU, for alleged links with the ANC. In February 1982 Dr. Neil Aggett, a white official with the African Food and Canning Workers Union, was found hanged in his cell at Security Police headquarters in Johannesburg. He had been detained without trial since the previous November, and was the first white to die in these circumstances. To honor him two hundred thousand black workers stopped work for a half hour on the day of his funeral. According to the South African Institute of Race Relations more than three hundred union members were detained without trial under security laws in 1981; ten union officials have signed affidavits charging they were beaten, tortured, or suffered other abuse while under detention.[25]

Despite the police repression and the government's bureaucratic efforts to control the black trade unions there is no doubt that black urban workers have gained job advancement and higher wages because of the need for their labor and because of their militancy. Still, they lag far behind white workers. The average wage of black workers in manufacturing is currently 30 percent of the average wage of whites, whereas ten years ago the figure was 20 percent. Yet in cash terms the gap has widened: white workers earned $3,000 more annually in 1970 and $7,700 more in 1979.[26] Above all, even the most advanced black worker (supervisor, manager, professional, or trader) is still subject to the maze of apartheid laws. Nevertheless, in comparison to the great majority of black workers, those who have been in a position to gain from the new opportunities in the urban economy have become an increasingly privileged stratum. Most of these better-off workers are those who have gained "section 10" authorization to reside in white areas, since employers are reluctant to provide training and more skilled positions to migrant or "illegal" workers. For the roughly 80 percent of black workers and their families who are not "insiders," the Botha government's policies on the pass laws and residency have hardly amounted to liberalization. Instead, they have served to sharply reinforce the pattern of divisions among black workers created over the decades by the white government's control of black labor.

Within this pattern created by apartheid the most impoverished strata are the Africans living in the Bantustans—now slightly more than half of the total African population. In 1960, out of an African population of 12.5 million, 40 percent lived in the Bantustans. By 1980 the African population had risen to 21.5 million, and 54 percent, or 11.6 million, resided in the Bantustans. And of these, 3.5 million had been forcibly removed from white areas by the white government; and an additional number of up to 2.0 million are still liable to removal if apartheid plans run their course.[27] Given the overcrowding and poverty in the Bantustans, African workers have no alternative but to register with the government labor bureaus for work as migrants in "white" South Africa. Migrants are assigned to various labor categories, such as agriculture, mining, laborers for the government, domestics in white homes, or workers in industry and businesses. They are given the roughest, lowest-paid work and have little chance for advancement, and once they are assigned to a labor category—which is stamped into the passbook that must be carried by law—changing to another is very difficult.

The alternative to work as a migrant under government control is work as an "illegal," scouting out hand-to-mouth jobs in the black townships or finding menial, low-paid work with no security with a white employer willing to risk a government fine. Although illegal workers are liable to imprisonment and expulsion to the Bantustans if caught, the level of poverty in the Bantustans is so severe that tremendous increases in earnings can be gained by illegal workers, even if they are caught and must go to prison. This was documented in a study at the University of South Africa which showed, for example, that a person from the Ciskei who worked illegally in Pietermaritzburg for three months and spent nine months in jail after being caught would still gain a 234 percent increase in income over what he could earn by staying in the Bantustan for the year. The gains are shown in Table 7-1.[28]

Within "white" South Africa the largest and lowest paid stratum of workers has been those on white farms. The number of Africans living in white rural areas has dropped from 30 percent of the African population in 1960 to 20 percent in 1980, but with the population increase there are still 4.3 million Africans in these areas, while there are now

TABLE 7-1

PERCENT INCREASE IN LIVING STANDARD

BANTUSTAN: URBAN AREA:	CISKEI Pietermaritzburg	LEBOWA Johannesburg	BOPHUTHATSWANA Pretoria
9 months work/ 3 months jail	703%	255%	85%
6 months work/ 6 months jail	424%	170%	57%
3 months work/ 9 months jail	234%	85%	29%

only 60,000 white farmers.[29] Like migrant workers from the Bantustans, Africans born in white rural areas have great difficulty in trying to change from the almost castelike status of agricultural laborer that is stamped in their passbook to other areas of work. To do so they must have the permission of their white farmer or the government, and the alternative work is usually migrant labor in the mines or, if available, in urban areas.

Traditionally, the black farm worker has not received a cash wage, only a food ration, a place to live with his family, and land for cultivation and grazing. This system of labor tenancy was to have been phased out after 1969, and it was declared illegal in 1981. Farm workers are now supposed to receive cash wages. Yet the feudal-like conditions of labor tenancy, with black farm families living at the bare subsistence level on white farms, remain widespread. The longer-term effects of the new system will, however, be to force more African families into the Bantustans as white farmers mechanize for more productivity, with fewer, more skilled workers paid regular wages, and as the government continues to remove "black spots" (numerous black freeholds in white areas originating before the 1936 Land Act) and black "squatters" on white farm lands.

The most privileged—or least disadvantaged—African workers are, of course, those with Section 10 status; they are authorized to live in the segregated townships outside white urban areas. As noted, the Nationalist government has pressed hard to limit the numbers in this category by promoting the migrant labor system, so that it is now mainly the children of current "insiders" who are added to their ranks. The Section 10 designation is not a right, but a privilege granted by the white authorities. It may be rescinded by the white bureaucracy. All Africans in white areas, either urban or rural, are classified according to Bantustan "nationality" by the government and are liable to removal there. Section 10 status is given only to individuals, not families, so that if a worker's spouse or children are not qualified, they may not stay in white areas.

The new legislation proposed by the Botha government in 1982 would provide some added security to Africans authorized to remain in white areas by classifying them as "permanent urban residents," although the urban residents are still considered nationals of the Bantustans. Like the measure providing for recognition of black trade unions, this step is a recognition of the needs of business for a more stable black work force having better training and greater skills. But the other side of this modest liberalization in regulations is the harsh new policy designed to force the "illegals" out of the white urban areas. Minister of Cooperation and Development Koornhoff vowed to "declare war" on blacks violating the pass laws.[30] In 1980, when the Botha government instituted a fine of up to R500 against employers caught employing unregistered workers, an office of the Black Sash, a women's group opposing apartheid, described the impact among the Africans affected:

> Never in the sixteen years since this office was opened have we experienced such anger expressed by black people or such a sense of impending catastrophe. Never have we felt more urgently the need to try to communicate to white South Africans the realities of what is happening. . . .
> Until this year people have been able to find illegal work and so have survived. Now, for the first time in all our experience, we have no hope and no comfort to offer the unregistered and the endorsed out. Always before, we, and they, have known that they would be able to go on somehow even if it meant arrest and imprisonment from time to time. All hope has now been removed and when you take hope away all that is left is rage and anger, bitterness and hatred.[31]

The new legislation proposed in 1982 would increase the maximum fine against employers tenfold, to R5000, and create a nighttime curfew barring unauthorized blacks from white areas (and the black townships in white areas) and impose heavy penalties for violations. These measures seek to make enforcement of apartheid ironclad by imposing intimidating penalties on those who would either employ unregistered workers or provide accommodations for them or their family. They are, as well, proposals that reflect the security concerns of the Total Strategy, in that they would make it harder for guerrillas who have found shelter in the Bantustans to move to strategic urban areas.

The new constitutional proposals announced by Botha appear to offer South Africans of mixed race and to Indians a new political status, seemingly almost on a plane with that of whites, i.e., seats in the parliament (though in segregated chambers) and representation in the cabinet and on a Presidential Council having expanded powers. Though details of such a plan remain unclear, the underlying assumption of the Botha proposals has been that parliamentary roles of the racial groups would involve only their immediate concerns; the people of mixed race and the Indians would gain a voice in handling their own affairs, though limits would be set by the national policies determined by whites. Botha's proposals affecting the political structure involve no change in other aspects of apartheid, particularly the Group Areas Act, which enforces the residential segregation by which the people of mixed race and the Indians have been restricted to assigned areas and removed from white areas.

The political status of the people of mixed race and the Indians has been a question mark under apartheid: these people do not have large separate areas, such as the Bantustans, that the Nationalist government might seek to convert into "independent" countries. The Botha proposals represent an effort to draw these communities away from their developing political alliance with the African majority. This again has direct strategic significance, since Defence Force leaders have wanted to start compulsory military service for both racial groups. That would be difficult to implement without an attempt at some kind of new political dispensation. The other significant aspect of the Botha proposals is the creation of the position of president with wide powers over those of parliament—the "de Gaulle option" that military leaders had been advocating. It would enable a president to run the country without the checks and the scrutiny of the parliamentary process, limited as they have been. The immediate goal would be to overcome the parliamentary opposition to Botha's Total Strategy from all quarters.

In addition to the various measures taken or proposed on black issues, the Botha government also established judicial commissions to report on the news media and on security legislation. The commissions' reports were presented to parliament in February 1982. The report on the media echoed the terminology that has been used by military leaders to justify the Total Strategy: it described a "total onslaught" of externally organized propaganda being mounted against South Africa, orchestrated from the Soviet Union. The strategy said to be pursued by the Soviets is to operate "by using proxy forces, such as the South African Communist Party, the ANC, and the PAC to conduct revolutionary war in order to neutralize Western Europe by denying it access to strategic minerals and oil, before finally tackling the U.S.A."[32] Aligned with the Soviet onslaught in this view are Western liberalism, as exemplified by the *New York Times* and the *Washington Post*, and the third world, operating through the United Nations and the Organization of African Unity, the World Council of Churches, and even the multinational corporations. The goal of this onslaught is, in the words of the commission, "nothing less than the political and moral subversion of the white man and his replacement by a black majority government" with either a "radical-socialist or liberal-democratic welfare-capitalist" system. The report uses a bizarre combination of biblical and scientific jargon to suggest how white South Africa must meet this onslaught, which threatens to subvert the media on every level:

> When entering the lists against such a daunting adversary so fearfully armed, the nonproductive and distorting glasses of unrealistic truthfulness [sic] must be exchanged for the clear visor of realistic vision and resolute thought. . . .
>
> Conduct, utterances and other matters generating perceptions are consequently of equal importance and must be handled in the knowledge of their vast potential for good and evil. . . .The time has come to gird our loins for the struggle and to clear our domestic decks of the damaging perception-breeding impedimenta.[33]

In spite of its apocalyptic visions of a global propaganda onslaught being waged against white South Africa, and suggestions that wider censorship is needed, the 1,367-page report actually offered no sweeping recommendations for government controls on the media, perhaps because the government's censorship powers are already considerable. The report did propose that an official body be formed to register journalists. That appeared to be a kind of warning to black journalists, the South African Council of Churches, and the English-language press that the government could intensify pressures against them.

A commission appointed to report on security legislation did not, as had been expected, propose major revisions or consolidation of the large corpus of security laws created by the Nationalists over three decades. The commission endorsed the police's power under the Terrorism Act and other laws to detain people indefinitely without charge or trial, but in light of the continuing pattern of deaths of political detainees and repeated charges of torture and abuse, the commission suggested the appointment of an inspector to monitor those held in detention. The commission also suggested that several security laws be revised to eliminate the possibility of double jeopardy on political charges and that the provision of the Terrorism Act under which defendants are assumed guilty unless proven innocent without reasonable doubt be relaxed: defendants would have only to prove their probable innocence.

The changes and the proposals for change that have been developed under the Total Strategy have been presented to white South Africans as a strategic necessity, with the warning that they must be ready to "adapt or die." Although the Botha government's programs are designed to preserve white supremacy, there is still considerable reluctance among whites to accept any change in the status quo.

In 1978 the Arnold Bergstraessen Institute of West Germany released the results of opinion polls taken among white and black South Africans. The director of the survey concluded that the opinions were so divergent that "while peaceful change was possible, it was highly improbable."[34] While 83 percent of the black South Africans polled in major urban areas said they wanted a system of one man, one vote in a unitary, multiracial state, 74 percent of the whites questioned declared they were prepared to fight to "maintain South Africa as they know it today." Only 33 percent were prepared to accept even some form of federation based on racial divisions which would permit a black voice at the central government level. On other issues whites expressed the following attitudes: 9 percent would permit interracial marriage, 13 percent would permit residential integration, 33 percent would allow integration on buses, 37 percent would allow blacks to supervise whites on the job, 52 percent would allow blacks to work in all occupations, 61 percent would allow integrated elevators, and 75 percent would allow equal pay for equal work.

A 1979 opinion survey among whites in East London and towns in the eastern Cape (an area of relatively moderate attitudes among whites), taken in connection with the granting of "independence" to the Ciskei Bantustan, revealed some highly contradictory views, but a generally strong resistance to basic changes.[35] Eighty-one percent of the whites polled felt that the "independent" Bantustans offered Africans "a healthy opportunity to develop along their own lines," and 59 percent felt that the rest of the world would ultimately recognize them and the merits of the policy. However, a majority of whites also felt that the Bantustans would become hostile black areas breeding conflict and terrorism and favored some form of continued federation with white South Africa rather than complete independence. Although only 22 percent of the whites would refuse under any circumstances to live in a black state (i.e., a Bantustan, not South Africa as a whole), fewer than a third accepted various concrete proposals for doing so with various guarantees and incentives suggested.

In light of these polls, the major split in the National party that developed over Botha's policies is not surprising. The showdown came in February 1982 over the issue of the constitutional proposals that were to be presented by Botha's Presidential Council. Botha had made clear his readiness to initiate "co-responsibility" and "power-sharing" with South Africans of mixed race and Asians, while Dr. Andries Treurnicht, the leader of the Transvaal branch of the National party and Botha's minister of state administration, opposed these initiatives as opening the door to racial integration and the loss of "white self-determination." Botha forced a confrontation in the National party's Transvaal branch's provincial committee, and when he won decisively, he expelled Treurnicht and fifteen supporters from their positions. Treurnicht then formed a new party, the Conservative party of South Africa, and drew an enthusiastic crowd of seven thousand white supporters (larger than any turnout for Botha) to the party's first convention in Pretoria. At the meeting Treurnicht spelled out the credo of his party: "We reject the idea of an open society, and we oppose all political pressure to enforce integration in the social and political spheres and to bring about multiracialism in South Africa."[36]

Among *verligte* Afrikaners (including members of Botha's cabinet) there has been strong suppport for Botha against the far right, but impatience at the slow pace of the promised changes. *Verligtes* have promoted the expectation that once the process of change is underway, some kind of political and territorial settlement could be worked out with Africans that would provide more land to the Bantustans and a political role for urban Africans similar to that offered to people of mixed race and to Indians. It would be a plan that would modify apartheid, but keep the great majority of Africans as Bantustan foreigners and allow whites the dominant role among people of mixed race, Indians, and urban Africans. Chief Buthelezi, with his tribal orientation, his antagonism to the ANC, and his strong support for South African capitalism, has been seen by some as the kind of important African figure with whom a deal could be struck.

Significant segments of the Afrikaner press have become platforms for *verligte* views.Ton Vosloo, editor of *Beeld* (Reflection), the most influential Afrikaans paper, has suggested that the Botha proposals for South Africans of mixed race and Indians could eventually be widened to include urban Africans. Despite the government's constant invocation of the "total onslaught" being promoted by the Soviets with the ANC as their proxy, he has written that the ANC is the "National party of black nationalism" and represents a force that would have to be accommodated.[37] *Beeld* also published an article by an Afrikaner academic which advocated negotiations with the ANC. An article in another paper, *Die Vaderland*, ridiculed the government's standard charge that SWAPO is a Communist movement, and indicated that "nationalism cannot be squashed, even if you jail a nation's leaders, shoot them, or ban its organizations."[38]

Commenting in an interview on the political situation of the Botha government in mid-1982, Vosloo said that if it was successful in persuading people of mixed race and Indians to agree to the new constitutional proposals and was able to achieve a Namibian settlement that was "acceptable" to most white South Africans, then the pace and direction of change would be well established, and the Botha government and the Total Strategy would be secure as the central political force among whites. These views appear valid, but neither condition seems likely to be fulfilled readily. Opposition to the constitutional plan among people of mixed race and Indians remains strong, and what most South African whites want in Namibia—a Cuban withdrawal from Angola and

SWAPO kept from winning political power—has been beyond South Africa's power to enforce, even with backing from the Reagan administration.

The Progressive Federal party has scored electoral gains in recent years but has no prospects of challenging the Nationalists for power. The Progressives have called for a national convention of all racial groups and advocate a new constitution that will provide for a decentralized, federal structure with a universal franchise and a single national assembly and safeguards for minority rights. The plan offered by Chief Buthelezi for a new provincial structure for Natal and KwaZulu is an example of the approach of the Progressives. In 1981 Harry Oppenheimer, chairman of the Anglo-American Corporation, who has been a major backer of the Progressives, raised the spectre of revolution in South Africa within five years unless major steps toward "power-sharing" were taken and for the first time advocated that the country adopt a system of one-man, one vote. Oppenheimer was among the signers of the Buthelezi report. Oppenheimer's criticisms of government policies reflected Botha's failure to win sustained support for his Total Strategy among the English-speaking business sector as he had set out to do during his first year in power. In this situation the Progressives, along with the English-language press, continue to voice some black grievances and offer whites an alternative to Nationalist politics.

The new Afrikaner elite represented by the Botha government—military and business leaders—has attempted to provide, through the Total Strategy, a solution enforced by military power to the political crisis generated by black resistance to apartheid and the country's related economic problems. The new, powerful position of president that is proposed as a part of the new constitutional structure represents the culmination of this effort to reorient South Africa's white politics. It would mean not only installing a president with a seven-year term of office and powers superseding those of the parliament, but also, assuming the presidency was in the hands of Botha or one of his supporters, that the administrative structure set up to implement the Total Strategy would remain in place. Botha and his military supporters have stressed that the changes thay have wanted to promote in order to save white South Africa involve turbulent and difficult adjustments, which has meant continual military mobilization for guerrilla conflict within the country for the war in Namibia, and for covert and overt strikes against the frontline states.

But while the Botha government wants to install a Gaullist system, there is no Gaullist figure on the South African scene. Neither Botha nor General Malan has been able to generate broad popular support among whites, not to mention the black majority. The increasing strength of the far right, as reflected in the formation of the Conservative party, indicates the difficulty for Botha and his Total Strategy in attracting substantial support from the traditional Nationalist constituencies: white workers and the middle class, farmers, civil servants, and the lower echelons of the military. A number of English-speaking South Africans are now joining Afrikaners in these categories. This makes it uncertain that the presidential proposals will be accepted by the white parliament. There appears every possibility that the far right will score electoral gains in parliament at the expense of the Nationalists. Thus, even though the goal of the Total Strategy has been to restructure apartheid to safeguard white domination, in the near term white politics will be marked by heavy infighting between Botha's Nationalists on the right and the Conservatives and their allies on the far right. And this means that South Africa will remain a country at war. The process of militarization will continue.

8 The Crisis in American Policy

A FEW WEEKS AFTER TAKING OFFICE, Ronald Reagan set the tone of his administration's policies on South Africa in a television interview. He said there had been "a failure" in the United States to "recognize how many people, black and white in South Africa, are trying to remove apartheid and the steps that they've taken and the gains they've made." He continued:

> As long as there's a sincere and honest effort being made, based on our own experience in our own land, it would seem to me that we should be trying to be helpful. Can we abandon a country that has stood beside us in every war we've ever fought, a country that strategically is essential to the free world? It has production of minerals we all must have and so forth.
>
> I just feel that, myself, that here, if we're going to sit down at a table and negotiate with the Russians, surely we can keep the door open and continue to negotiate with a friendly nation like South Africa.[1]

The President's remarks were well received by the Nationalist government and by its conservative friends in the United States, but they drew criticism from many other quarters. It was pointed out that during World War II a number of Nationalist leaders held pro-Nazi views. Harsh repression of opponents of apartheid has continued, while evidence of a "sincere and honest effort" to remove apartheid by the Botha government has not been convincing. How strategically essential is South Africa to the West? And is this interest best served by friendly ties with the Nationalist government? A few weeks before Reagan's comments, South African forces had attacked ANC members living in Mozambique, killing twelve. The President's friendly approach clearly legitimated Pretoria's aggressive raid. Within days after Reagan spoke, five top South African intelligence officials, among the closest advisors to Prime Minister Botha, visited the United States and met with Pentagon and National Security Council officials, as well as UN ambassador Jeane Kirkpatrick and members of Congress.[2] The State Department said a mistake had been made in giving the South Africans visas, but the visit was an evident sign that the administration looked favorably on the Nationalist government.

An inside picture of the new Reagan policies emerged at the end of May 1981 when State Department documents were leaked and made available to the *Washington Post* by TransAfrica, a national black lobbying organization in Washington. The documents, whose full texts are given in Appendix C, reflect the policies being pursued by the Reagan administration and indicate the stance being taken by the South Africans as well.

The first document, chronologically, is a "Memorandum of Conversation" that summarizes the first formal meeting between the Reagan administration and South African officials. Two days of discussions had been held in Pretoria in mid-April 1981 between Assistant Secretary of State for African Affairs Chester Crocker, South African Foreign Minister Roelof ("Pik") Botha and Defence Minister Magnus Malan. The memorandum indicates agreement on the central problem of stemming Soviet influence and involvement in southern Africa, with the discussion focusing on Namibia and Angola. The South Africans insisted that they would only accept "an anti-Soviet black government" in Namibia. They described the United States as "soft on SWAPO," and said that they would prefer to have the Namibia war continue rather than face a SWAPO election victory in a settlement. A SWAPO victory would mean a "Soviet flag in Windhoek," the South Africans claimed, and was part of a Soviet plan to conquer South Africa. The South Africans asserted that their Namibian forces could defeat SWAPO and implied that the United States should do its part by backing UNITA in Angola and applying pressure to force the Cuban troops out to topple the MPLA government.

Assistant Secretary Crocker argued against the South Africans' hardline approach. The continuing war in Namibia would bring greater Soviet involvement, he said; the way to avoid this would be a settlement under UN aegis engineered with constitutional guarantees and election procedures to circumscribe SWAPO's powers in the future government. This should be coordinated with a effort to promote the withdrawal of Cuban troops from Angola and to seek reconciliation between the MPLA government and UNITA by "playing on divisions in the MPLA." Crocker's over-all appeal to the South Africans was that with a settlement in Namibia and evidence of reforms underway in South Africa, the United States could "include South Africa in its general security framework."

The other four documents relate to Botha's visit to Washington, D.C., the following month, when he became the first government leader from Africa to meet with President Reagan. The only document that does not center on Namibia is a South African position paper dealing with relations between the United States and South Africa on nuclear matters. In this the South Africans requested that the United States drop its objections to the supply of enriched uranium by France to South Africa's new nuclear plant at Koeberg. They denied having tested a nuclear device, but argued that while "threatened by the USSR," they would not sign the Nuclear Non-Proliferation Treaty (NPT). (The United States has been calling for this since the Ford administration suspended nuclear ties in 1976).

A one-page memo to Chester Crocker, dated May 13, 1981, summarizes a meeting of the Western Contact Group on Namibia, in which it was agreed that during Botha's visit the United States should try to see whether the South Africans were ready to "move forward toward a restructured, internationally acceptable settlement"—without getting into delicate details.

A toast, offered by Secretary of State Alexander Haig at a luncheon for Pik Botha, exemplified the new friendly tone of the Reagan policies. Haig said that "good relations" with South Africa were a "goal high on the agenda of this administration," and he concluded: "Let this be the new beginning of mutual trust and confidence between the United States and South Africa, old friends, like Minister Botha, who are getting together again."

The "Scope Paper" prepared by Chester Crocker for Secretary of State Haig for his meeting with Pik Botha offers a clear statement of the aims of American policy and reveals the administration's views on the situation in southern Africa. The initial summary stated that the United States and South Africa "are at a crossroads of perhaps historic significance" with the opportunity for a new, positive relationship, but that a settlement must be achieved in Namibia as a "crucial first phase." In his conclusion, Crocker stressed to the South Africans that "a Russian flag in Windhoek is as unacceptable to us as it is to you." He argued that the right kind of settlement could "foreclose opportunities for the growth of Soviet influence in southern Africa and. . .contribute to the leverage we need to produce a withdrawal of Soviet/Cuban military forces from Angola."

Crocker warned Haig that "we cannot be excessive in what we suggest" to the South Africans in terms of rewards for cooperation on Namibia; he indicated that the United States had to adhere to the arms embargo, for example. But he said, "We can, however, work to end South Africa's polecat status in the world and seek to restore its place as a legitimate and important regional actor with whom we can cooperate pragmatically. You will also need to respond with an *artful combination of gestures and hints*."

The first example of "gestures and hints" was the initiation of training in the United States of a racially mixed contingent of the South African Coast Guard. Others included an easing of the Carter administration's export restrictions, allowing the sale of medical supplies and anti-hijacking metal detectors to the South African police and military, and an increase in the number of exchanged military attachés, which had been decreased by Carter.[3] The final points of the paper indicated that the goal of the discussions was to determine whether, in light of the new positive approach offered by the Reagan administration, the South Africans were ready to move seriously toward a Namibia settlement along the lines proposed.

Crocker was solicitous of the South Africans. He agreed with their assertions that past U.S. policies had been "soft" on the Soviets, and vacillating, as in the American disengagement during the Angola invasion of 1975-76, and inconsistent during the Carter administration. But he did not accept the South African's hardline stance that they were able to "go it alone" in the region. He referred ironically to Pik Botha's "familiar 'Africa is dying / Soviet onslaught against South Africa' speech" and warned Haig that he might be "subjected to Pik's rhetoric." The intent of Crocker's policies was to achieve cooperation with South Africa. He was offering better relations with the United States and a proto-alliance to control the future of the region. From his perspective he was appealing at once to the Nationalist government's and to white South Africa's best interest. In return for their cooperation with American strategies, he was willing to provide them with a protective umbrella, making them the junior partner of a global superpower.

As the documents indicate, Chester Crocker is the key person shaping the Reagan policies toward southern Africa. His background includes a doctorate in political science from Johns Hopkins University, where his dissertation dealt with the role of the military in African politics. Crocker subsequently worked on the staff of the National Security Council during the Nixon administration, working under Henry Kissinger from 1970 to 1972. He became well acquainted with Kissinger's deputy at the time, Alexander Haig. Although Crocker was not involved in formulating the policy options on southern Africa contained in National Security Study Memorandum 39 (NSSM 39), he did work with the National Security Council during the period when the secret "tilt" in favor of the white regimes in southern Africa was being implemented. He reportedly played an important role in the decision that allowed American importation of Rhodesian chrome despite United Nations sanctions. He was also said to have been politically and socially close to the lobbyists for the Rhodesian regime and to the South Africa Foundation.[4] After serving in the Nixon White House, Crocker moved to the Center for Strategic and International Studies at Georgetown University, where he became director of African studies. During the 1980 presidential campaign, he became an advisor to George Bush and was made chairman of the Africa subcommittee of the Republican National Committee's foreign policy group. After the nomination of Ronald Reagan, he became the head of Reagan's African working group for the campaign. After Reagan's election Crocker was nominated assistant secretary of state for African affairs, and with experience on African issues not widespread in the administration, he has clearly been in charge of shaping policy.

President Reagan's lack of experience in foreign affairs is well known. Prior to his election in November 1980, he had rarely commented on affairs in southern Africa. What little he did say indicated that his central concern was Soviet encroachment in the region. In 1976 he had criticized the idea that the elimination of racial injustice was the crucial issue in Africa, saying, "The African problem is a Russian weapon aimed at us."[5] He also criticized the suspension of American support for the FNLA/ UNITA in Angola. In 1978 he decried Soviet support for Rhodesian "terrorists"; the Soviets were out to gain control of southern Africa's mineral riches, he said.[6] During the 1980 presidential campaign he told the *Wall Street Journal* that he favored supplying arms to UNITA and *Jet* magazine that the problems in South Africa are "not so much racial as tribal."[7] Thus Reagan's personal views on southern Africa are those of the far right.

Though seen as an administration moderate, Secretary of State Haig had views on Africa that were also hardline, seeing Africa in term of U.S. confrontation with the Soviets. Haig urged in Congressional testimony in 1979 that NATO's military "shield" should be extended to cover southern Africa and warned of the danger of the Soviets' gaining control of southern Africa's mineral wealth.[8] In January 1981 he trumpeted the central theme of the new administration's foreign policy when he announced that the effort to stop Soviet-backed "international terrorism will replace human rights" as a main goal in U.S. policy.[9]

Confirmation of Chester Crocker's nomination as assistant secretary of state for African affairs was held up for more than four months. Ultraconservative Senator Jesse Helms proclaimed that Crocker's positions deviated from the administration's true views on Africa, and accused Crocker of wanting to force South Africa to turn Namibia over to SWAPO, of supporting the Marxist policies of the Mugabe government in Zimbabwe (which had gained power through "terrorism"), and of failing to give full support to UNITA in Angola to oust the MPLA government. But when the vote was finally taken, Crocker won easy approval. Crocker came to his new position with the direction and rationales for his policies already amply spelled out. The background to the policy of "constructive engagement" in southern Africa which he has promoted has been readily available in a number of articles and statements put out in recent years.[10]

Crocker has contrasted the policies of "constructive engagement" he advocates with those of previous administrations. During the Nixon-Ford period the United States had quietly tilted in favor of the white regimes in southern Africa, an approach that was consistent with the conservative stance of both administrations. While this policy was never spelled out publicly, in general it followed the approach outlined in "option two" of a study on policy options in southern Africa prepared in 1969 at the request of Henry Kissinger in National Security Study Memorandum 39 (NSSM 39). The secret study was leaked to the press several years later. The premise of option two stated:

> The whites are here to stay and the only way that constructive change can come about is through them. There is no hope for the blacks to gain the political rights they seek through violence, which will only lead to chaos and increased opportunities for the communists. We can, by selective relaxation of our stance toward the white regimes, encourage some modification of their current racial and colonial policies and through more substantial economic assistance to the black states. . .help to draw the two groups together and exert some influence on both for peaceful change.[11]

This policy of "communication" with the white regimes collapsed in 1974 with the coup in Portugal by army forces disillusioned by a decade of colonial war in Africa. Kissinger (still smarting from the fall of the South Vietnamese regime the year before) saw the political divisions in Angola as part of the U.S. global struggle with the Soviets rather than as a situation that could be resolved among Africans. He approved the covert CIA program to back UNITA/FNLA against the MPLA. This brought another major setback for his policies when the CIA operation and its cooperation with South Africa was exposed, Cuban and Soviet aid enabled the MPLA to gain the upper hand in the conflict, and the U.S. Congress passed the Clark amendment barring further U.S. funds for military support of groups fighting in Angola. Despite strenuous objections by Kissinger, Congress rejected the administration's policy for failure to seek public diplomatic and political solutions in Angola and its initiation of covert conflict that involved links with South Africa.

Kissinger tried to regain the initiative in southern Africa by announcing in a speech in Lusaka in April 1976 a new U.S. approach that urged "a clear evolution toward equality of opportunity and basic human rights for all South Africans"[12] and called on South Africa to support a rapid settlement in Rhodesia and set a timetable for ending its illegal occupation of Namibia. He tried to engineer a Rhodesian settlement, pressuring South Africa and putting U.S. and South African pressure on the Smith regime. But although Smith was forced to announce that he would negotiate the transition to majority rule, the talks broke down by the end of 1976 and Kissinger had been removed from the scene with the victory of Jimmy Carter in the U.S. presidential election.

Kissinger's new policies reflected the dramatic changes in southern Africa since the NSSM 39 study had been prepared. Far from being firmly entrenched, white power was crumbling. Instead of being an area which (in the conservative view) required only quiet support for the white regimes and no significant policy initiatives to protect American interests, southern Africa was suddenly a global hot spot. His new policy indicated that Kissinger felt that urgent efforts were needed to promote pro-Western settlements in Rhodesia and Namibia and reforms in South Africa in order to head off the more radical, Soviet-supported liberation movements. His approach, however, was still oriented toward dealing mainly with the whites holding power, as he did not set up effective contacts with ZANU, ZAPU, or SWAPO, or with key presidents of the frontline states. Nor did he pause in his diplomatic shuttling to even comment on the Soweto uprising that was shaking South Africa.

The Carter administration came to office committed to offering a new orientation toward southern Africa, shaped particularly by UN ambassador Andrew Young. There would be an effort to build stronger contacts with blacks (including the frontline states, the liberation movements, and blacks in South Africa) as the vast majority in the region and the initiators of change. The black struggle for freedom was not viewed as a destabilizing threat to American interests, but instead as a cause with which the United States could support (though not militarily). Africa as a whole would be dealt with not as a part of the global rivalry with the Soviets, but in terms of its own realitites. Andrew Young in particular indicated that Soviet and Cuban involvement in Africa, including support for the liberation movements in southern Africa, was not seen as a threat to either the United States or Africa. African nationalism was seen as a fundamental political value that would always assert its way over foreign influence, whether that of the Soviets or the West, though it was seen as harmonious with Western interests. It was felt that once freedom was won, even Marxist movements backed by the Soviets would turn to America and the West for investments, trade, loans, and technical aid needed for development and would not remain politically tied to the Soviets.

Kissinger had indicated that the United States, in exchange for South African cooperation on settlements in Namibia and Rhodesia, would not push for immediate steps toward dismantling apartheid. The tone of the Carter approach was indicated when Andrew Young agreed with a newsman's characterization of the South African government as "illegitimate" (though this was retracted by the State Department).[13] When Vice-President Walter Mondale met with Vorster in May 1977 to discuss U.S. policies, he said that South Africa must take steps toward "full political participation by all citizens of South Africa," and in a widely noted response to a question indicated that this meant the same as "one person, one vote." [14] The Carter administration was expressing opposition to apartheid and sympathy with black hopes at a time when South Africa was still shaking from student protests and police repression. But both Carter and Young opposed pressuring South Africa with economic sanctions and efforts to have American corporations withdraw their investments, arguing instead that American investment could play an important role in promoting change.

If the Vorster government had been wary of Kissinger's new policies, it reacted with anger to Carter's, and relations were soon strained. The United States warned South Africa not to carry out a nuclear weapons test after apparent preparations in the Khalahari Desert were sighted by a Soviet satellite in August 1977. Then, after the death of Steve Biko and the detention of Black Consciousness Movement leaders, the United States backed the mandatory arms embargo against South Africa passed by the UN Security Council in December 1977, and in 1978 barred the sale of all goods to the police and military. The Carter administration also maintained a suspension on nuclear dealing with South Africa pending, under terms of legislation passed in 1976, South African acceptance of the Non-Proliferation Treaty barring the development of nuclear weapons. Despite diplomatic initiatives by the United States there was no real progress toward settlements in Namibia and Rhodesia.

But by 1978 the accent of the Carter African policies suddenly shifted under the influence of national security advisor Zbigniew Brzezinski and domestic and international criticism for not standing up to the Soviets. Carter began warning about Soviet and Cuban activity in Africa (i.e., in Angola and Ethiopia), and Brzezinski urged Congress to repeal the Clark amendment to allow U.S. military aid to UNITA to bog the Cuban forces down in Angola. When former Katangese gendarmes from Zaire living in Angola launched their second attack in less than a year, in May 1978, against Zaire's mineral-rich Shaba province in a bid to topple President Mobutu, Carter charged it was a Cuban conspiracy. U.S. Air Force planes helped transport French and Belgian troops to Shaba to rescue Europeans and repulse the invaders. But Cuba said it had tried to stop the invasion, and Carter could offer no proof of his charges. By the following month the Carter policies veered again, this time seeking better relations with Angola, and this produced an Angolan-Zaire non-aggression pact and Angolan cooperation for American initiatives on Namibia.

With little progress being made on Zimbabwe and Namibia settlements, the United States began softening its stance toward South Africa in an effort to gain cooperation. Carter reportedly offered newly installed Prime Minister Botha an invitation to Washington if he would cooperate on a Namibia settlement. The administration also resisted efforts in

Congress and at the United Nations to impose economic sanctions against South Africa. It was soon evident that the 1977 arms embargo was badly weakened by wording the United States, Britain, and France had insisted on. Moreover, the Carter administration was responsible for failure to stop and then vigorously prosecute the 1977-78 deal by the Space Research Corporation supplying South Africa with a highly advanced 155-mm howitzer system and some 60,000 shells. This was the most serious of a number of violations and evasions of the embargo, yet the Carter administration insisted that the embargo was being strongly enforced and represented significant pressure on Pretoria.

Although the Gulf Oil Corporation operations in Angola were providing the government with a major part of its foreign exchange earnings (as it had under the Portuguese), showing that mutually beneficial ties between the United States and Angola were already in effect, the Carter administration refused to take the key step of extending diplomatic recognition to Luanda. This was because of the Cuban forces remaining there, the issue that had set off Carter's ire and which remained a big conservative issue in the United States and with South Africa. Yet the demand for the withdrawal of Cuban forces as a condition for recognition has been basically unfair, since the Cubans came as a result of covert American and South African military aggression against the MPLA. With South Africa continuing its attacks from Namibia and support of UNITA and the Carter administration having lobbied to resume support as well, the MPLA government could justify the continuing Cuban presence by the absence of guarantees of nonaggression by the United States and South Africa.

Recognition of the MPLA government of Angola by the United States could have defused the Cold War tensions surrounding the situation there and been an added form of pressure on South Africa for a Namibia settlement. But the Carter administration did not take this step. Nor were there efforts to try to curb the Botha government's military escalation in Namibia and growing intervention in Rhodesia.

However, with protests and pressures mounting from African and Commonwealth countries, the Thatcher government in Britain and the Carter administration resisted right-wing pressures to recognize the internal settlement in Rhodesia that had installed Bishop Muzorewa as prime minister. It was a decision that also recognized the military strength and political legitimacy of the Patriotic Front. This set the stage for the Lancaster House settlement and elections that brought an end to the war and produced Zimbabwean independence in 1980. It was a major success for the Carter policies in Africa. Not surprisingly, South Africa reacted by in effect putting negotiations on Namibia on hold to await the outcome of the 1980 U.S. elections, which brought Ronald Reagan to the White House.

From this review of U.S. policy comparisons can be made with the analyses and policies put forth by Crocker. One key assumption made by Crocker is that while increasing political conflict and violence in South Africa can be expected, "the balance of coercive power remains overwhelmingly in favor of the whites, and the outcome of violent challenges remains entirely predictable."[15] Thus whites are seen to hold the intitiative in South Africa, and the United States should shape its policies accordingly. There is a strong echo here of the premise of "option two" of NSSM 39. In contrast, the Carter administration, coming into office just after the collapse of Portuguese colonial rule and the Soweto upheaval, saw white power fading and the initiative in black hands.

But the region is no longer as stable as "option two" had assumed, and though claiming that South African whites are firmly entrenched, Crocker also sees southern Africa as dangerously threatened by intervention by the Soviets and the Cubans, and also sees significant Western interests (sources of strategic minerals, shipping lanes around the Cape, and trade and investment) at stake. Unlike the South African regime and its hard-line conservative supporters abroad, however, Crocker acknowledges that problems in the region have their roots in colonial and racist rule; they are not caused by the Soviets. But he argues that the Soviets have been illegitimately exploiting this situation through active military intrusion in the area. Related to this concern is his assertion that South Africa is "a part of the West"[16] and that South African and Western interests together extend throughout the whole of southern Africa.

Until the period of sudden hysteria at the time of the second invasion of Shaba province, the Carter approach did not regard Soviet military aid to the liberation movements as a big threat to Western interests. Nor, initially, was there great concern about the Cuban presence in Angola. Andrew Young referred to the Cubans as "a stabilizing influence" in Africa, presumably because they discouraged South African attacks on Angola.[17]

The dramatic unfolding of Zimbabwean independence and the victory of Robert Mugabe were seen by the Carter administration as a great vindication of their policies. ZANU had, in fact, been at odds with the Soviets, and it quickly tempered its socialist orientation with pragmatic, Western-oriented policies. The initial Carter policies (those of Young in particular) did not see southern Africa as "part of the West," as a zone automatically in the Western sphere of influence, but rather as an area that would be shaped by African self-determination. On this basis it was felt that a free southern Africa could naturally have close relations with the West based on common economic attitudes and interests.

In contrast, Crocker was critical of this hands-off, laissez-faire approach, for it appeared to leave the vital interests of the United States essentially in the hands of the liberation movements in the vague expectation that they would naturally turn away from their Soviet, Chinese, or other backers and seek close ties with America. In the case of Zimbabwe, Crocker criticized the Carter administration for favoring the Patriotic Front, for condemning the "security measures" of the Rhodesian regime while being reluctant to criticize "civilian atrocities" by guerrillas, and for giving the Rhodesian internal settlement short shrift.[18] He charged that the low-key Carter approach had given the Patriotic Front "a virtual veto" over the settlement process and had "helped to write the scenario in which militant guerrillas gained power through Western democratic forms."[19] Crocker had advocated a different scenario in 1978, evidently aimed at keeping as much power as possible out of the hands of the Patriotic Front. He urged Britain and the United States to act decisively to set up an "interim all-parties administration" in Rhodesia, before any elections and with or without the agreement of the Patriotic Front, in order to transfer power to a "broad group of nationalists."[20]

Crocker has therefore advocated the policy of "constructive engagement" in southern Africa whereby the United States would actively assert its influence in the direction of evolutionary change. The United States, he believes has to pursue this active, engaged policy in order to preempt the forces of both reaction and revolution that could produce violent, revolutionary upheaval that would threaten the future of the region and United States interests there. Operating on the assumption that the whites hold commanding power in South Africa, Crocker has criticized what he sees as the hypocrisy of the Carter administration's verbal attacks on apartheid that were combined with limited and ineffectual pressures. To close this "credibility gap" Crocker has moved to loosen pressures on South Africa and adopt more open, friendly relations with the Nationalist government.

While he has rejected the Bantustan "independence" program of apartheid, Crocker opposes the demand for a specific political blueprint (particularly a one man, one vote system) for the country and insists that the United States will not "choose between black and white" in South Africa.[21] To Crocker, the key to change in South Africa is the Botha government, which has announced policies for reform. He admits that there is no thought now among whites of surrendering their control, but he sees the country as entering a period of "open-ended reform" in which there will be black-white contestation, sometimes violent, in many areas. This could lead to the attainment of real black political power and a nonracial system. He acknowledges that the ANC "has legitimacy for many, if not most, politically aware blacks at the symbolic level as a unifying umbrella for nationalist activity."[22] But he says that the white government can hit back hard at guerrilla attacks from inside the country or at neighboring countries, and can contain violent disorders and "terrorism." Crocker is proposing therefore that the United States work actively among whites and blacks to promote moderate change, and he focuses on the ability of the white government to manipulate this, saying that "the way white leadership plays its cards will help shape the question of who sits at future bargaining tables and under what circumstances. . . .Autocratically imposed reform *could* become a part of a process leading at a future stage to compromise and accommodation between freely chosen representatives of all major groups."[23]

Linked to this scenario for South Africa is a view of how the United States can shape developments in the region. Here again Crocker wants a policy of active "engagement." The goal is to curb Soviet activities and influence and to continue the economic integration of the region with South Africa. To accomplish this he advocates that the United States should be ready to provide substantial economic aid to African states, including pragmatically oriented Marxist governments. Similarly, military aid should be provided to friendly states under certain circumstances. The economic aid would yield political leverage; the military aid would allow the frontline governments to keep a tighter control of anti-South African guerrilla groups on their soil. Possibly it would also discourage and lessen the need for South African military attacks on such guerrilla groups. In the "Scope Paper" prepared for Secretary Haig, Crocker indicated that, if a Namibia settlement could be achieved, "The new situation we envision in southern Africa would entail mutual recognition of the principles of inviolability of borders and noninterference in internal affairs in the states of the region."

Crocker presents his strategy as attempting to deal with the realities of the conflicts in southern Africa in a way that takes into account the interests of whites and blacks there and of the United States. He orients his strategy to the reform efforts of the Botha government and the various elements of *verligte* Afrikaner nationalism which it represents, particularly the leadership of the Defence Force. He has insisted that, through positive incentives for change rather than negative pressures, cooperation can be gained from the Botha government.

During the first year of the Reagan administration Crocker used various moves to indicate that the United States would reward a South African commitment to an American-orchestrated Namibia settlement, as well as reforms in apartheid and the upgrading of black institutions. Visas were allowed for visits to the United States by high-ranking military and police officials. The exchange of military attachés was normalized (after expulsions during the Carter era), and the United States agreed to have both countries increase the number of consulates. The sale of anti-hijacking security equipment for use in South African airports was permitted, and a racially mixed group of four South Africans was allowed to attend a U.S. Coast Guard training course. These gestures were followed by more significant moves: the relaxation of the restrictions imposed by the Carter administration that had banned virtually all American exports to the South African military and police (see Chapter 5). Thus while holding to the terms of the 1977 arms embargo, the United States is allowing South Africa and its police and military access to an array of strategic equipment. In 1982 the International Monetary Fund approved a $1.1 billion loan to South Africa with the support of the Reagan administration, despite protests by African countries, at the United Nations, and by anti-apartheid groups.

The Crocker strategy thus supports the combination of political reform in South Africa backed by carefully managed military organization—and muscle. In Congressional testimony in 1980 Crocker argued against calling upon the white government to scrap its security laws, saying it might be better to push for improved conditions and procedures "without expecting now that this embattled state disarm itself."[24] He has indicated that he looks favorably on the South African Defence Force, saying it should not be viewed as an "instrument of domestic brutality or as the rogue elephant of southern Africa." Referring to its potential as a "lobby of modernizing patriots," he suggested that the country might move toward a system "patterned on Gaullist France."[25]

What is one to conclude about the impact of U.S. policy in southern Africa under Crocker's "constructive engagement" approach? Although he insists that the United States "cannot endorse a system that is racist in purpose or effect,"[26] his policies in fact legitimate white power and control over change. His expressions of support for the South African police and military are the most significant sign of this. Given the increasingly prominent role of the military within South Africa, the harsh military grip on Namibia, and the growing pattern of aggression in the region, it would be hard to say that either the black majority in South Africa or the people of the frontline states share Crocker's sanguine view on the South African military. To suggest that the military leaders could be "modernizing patriots" supporting a South African brand of Gaullism is an indication that Crocker, through his preoccupation with the Afrikaner minority, is blind to the fact that the mission of the South African military is to safeguard white rule. Similarly, Crocker's assertions that the Botha government has begun open-ended change ignore the fact that Botha and his military leaders have plainly declared that they are urgently promoting change in order to insure that white control is secured.

Crocker calls black politics an "increasingly complex puzzle": black South Africans, he claims "are increasingly aware of the grossly discriminatory effects" of apartheid rule, and the United States can offer blacks help to strengthen their "capacity. . .to participate in shaping a changing system."[27] But the implication here is that blacks are only *now* beginning to oppose white domination, that they lack the ability to participate in politics, and that there is confusion among blacks about their political goals. This picture of black politics in South Africa is limited and distorted and wrong.

Although Crocker acknowledges the legitimacy and wide appeal of the African National Congress among black South Africans, the thrust of his strategy is to defeat it. He argues that, if the ANC were legalized, "a grand coalition" might take shape around it. But he does not therefore advocate legalizing the ANC, which would be a major move toward a peaceful solution. Instead, Crocker says the government is justified in retaining its security apparatus. So long as the ANC remains outlawed, a variety of internal black groups could be permitted to gain strength, and black unity around the ANC could thus be splintered.[28] He acknowledges that the white government has enormous powers to punish the black communities within South Africa and to assault the frontline states if they provide aid to guerrillas, but he has moved nonetheless to end American criticism of such domestic repression and foreign attacks. He has worked toward a strategic alliance with South Africa, and, while declaring United States adherence to the United Nations arms embargo, has provided moral and material support for the South African police and military.

Crocker asserts that white rule is strongly entrenched, but, paradoxically, warns that criticism by the United States or the implementation of economic sanctions or other pressures could trigger sudden "destabilization." In an analysis of the Defence Force, he has indicated that the effectiveness of the military could be undermined if whites lose their belief in the "rectitude" of their stand.[29] Thus a major goal of Crocker's policies is to reassure whites of American sympathy and support. Crocker grants legitimacy to the white monopoly on the use of armed force and violence and is opposed to armed black resistance to white oppression. While he insists that the United States will not "choose between black and white" in southern Africa, he in fact supports change controlled by whites. As one Africa specialist has noted, Crocker's formulation is

the first time the United States ever articulated a policy of neutrality on racial oppression to rationalize a policy of strategic alliance. If we cannot be "for" or "against" whites or blacks as such, we can be for black claims of equality and against white policies of oppression—a critical distinction. To be neutral on apartheid and toward the parties that are fighting against it, as the Reagan administration advocates, is to turn a blind eye to the deep-seated rage and revolutionary potential that are building up in South Africa, to be indifferent about the principles upon which our own society is built, and to display a contempt for international opinion as a whole.

. . .Constructive engagement lends respectibility to a system totally unworthy of respect, makes a mockery of our protestations of abhorrence of apartheid, and gives license to South Africa to proceed as it wishes.[30]

Crocker's regional approach also appears to be defective. He wants to eliminate Soviet and Cuban military involvement in southern Africa, but as long as there is no settlement in Namibia and no real progress in eliminating apartheid in South Africa, Soviet aid to the guerrillas and to the frontline states will be seen by black Africans as legitimate. Crocker has indicated that South Africa is justified in carrying out preemptive attacks and destabilization against the frontline states if they allow an active presence by the ANC or other opposition forces from South Africa. And he opposes the programs adopted by the frontline states in an effort to gain economic and logistic independence from South Africa.

Although the offer of aid to the frontline states is a positive incentive, the Reagan policies are not all "carrots." There is also the stick: the administration has made a strong effort to unleash the CIA, and it has sought to repeal the Clark Amendment, which blocks covert or overt military aid to forces operating against the government of Angola. (That move was narrowly rebuffed in Congress.) UNITA leader Jonas Savimbi has claimed, however, that he is getting American support despite the Clark Amendment.[31] The history of U.S. involvement in covert activities in Angola is liable to increase the wariness of other frontline states to the Crocker policies.

Ironically, it appears that the Botha government will also be hesitant to embrace the new American strategies. Afrikaner history was molded by resistance to the economic liberalism and political reformism of an earlier global superpower, Britain, and it is unlikely that an Afrikaner government will jump at the U.S. offer to be, in effect, a junior ally in its own region. Crocker is courting the Botha government with assurances of American goodwill and apologies for past weakness and vacillation. But the Nationalists are likely to take the "carrots" offered by the United States and to ask for more, while keeping to their own strategies. The South African priority is white "survival" through domination, and the stance remains hardline; in short, the South Africans do not follow the agenda set by the Reagan administration. Despite Crocker's claims as the Reagan administration was taking office that the United States has recovered from the post-Vietnam war syndrome and that the new administration is a reliable partner having a strong popular mandate, the South Africans must be aware that there has been considerable disorganization and disarray within the Reagan administration over foreign policy.

Chester Crocker has argued that his policies represent a centrist approach to southern Africa. But the centrist position was, in fact, preempted by others only a few months after the Reagan administration came to office, in *South Africa: Time Running Out*,[32] a major report organized and funded by the Rockefeller Foundation, carried out by an eleven-member Study Commission on U.S. Policy Toward Southern Africa. Copies of the 500-page book were distributed to Congressmen, government officials, corporations, organizations concerned with international affairs, and the news media. Crocker was one of the consultants to the study, and he contributed the draft chapter on South Africa's military forces. Although the commission's conclusions cited U.S. interests as similar to those Crocker mentions in his work on U.S. policy and touches on many similar themes, the policies it advocated for the United States differ. The commission urged increased pressures for change on the South African government rather then rewards or inducements, and it opposed moves toward making South Africa a strategic ally. It advocated a tightening of the arms embargo and an end to nuclear dealings and that there be no expansion and no new investments by American corporations in South Africa.

The commission suggested two general scenarios for South Africa's future. The first scenario envisions a situation somewhat similar to one seen by Crocker, of a *verligte* Nationalist government initiating reforms and successfully suppressing guerrilla attacks, leading to the emergence of a multiracial, decentralized government. The commission hoped to promote this end. In the second scenario, hardline *verkrampte* policies and an absence of reforms lead to a destructive, prolonged regional conflict ultimately won by guerrilla forces with the aid of the Soviets. Although *Time Running Out* had an insightful chapter on black politics—it highlighted the central importance of the ANC—the commission's conclusions did not really reflect this understanding. It called upon American officials to maintain greater contacts with the ANC's external leaders, but stressed that the United States should give substantial support only to black groups inside the country. Implicitly, it accepted the idea that a reformist white government could defeat ANC guerrillas. And it said, in reference to the second scenario, "Since the ANC would probably have had a major part in the struggle, a close relationship with the Soviet Union, East Germany, and Cuba would probably be expected."[33] This views the United States as inevitably at odds with the ANC, and the ANC as having close ties only to the Soviets and its allies. Since the commission accepts the legitimacy of the ANC cause, this conclusion is unfortunate. The commission might have formulated ways for the United States to build bridges to the ANC instead of accepting Cold War considerations as inevitable. This failure of the commission is all the more pronounced when it is realized that even prominent Afrikaner papers have speculated on the need for the white government to talk with the ANC in the future.

But despite these failings, the commission's recommendations of increased pressure on South Africa is significant. Given the commission's rather diverse makeup and its goal, which was to present practical, centerist policy proposals, one might have expected a report of the "lowest-common-denominator" variety. Moreover, the report invalidates Crocker's claim to represent a centrist position. This, in turn, could provide Pretoria with an incentive to be more receptive to Crocker's policies, for, as he himself argues, they could provide their "best shot" at an aboveboard working alliance with the United States.

The key questions remain unanswered: Will there be a settlement in Namibia? And what changes will be made in South Africa? Crocker's bias toward the Nationalist government might produce desired results, but it might also fail to satisfy Pretoria and make it impossible for SWAPO, the frontline states, and black South Africans to accept United States "engagement." The clear danger of the Crocker policies is that they legitimize white power and lend support to it in very real and strategic ways.

Some of the elements of an alternative American stance on southern Africa, one giving positive support to the cause of black freedom, were present in the policies of an early phase of the Carter administration. These embodied a basic attitude that the black majority in Namibia and South Africa will overcome oppression and a refusal to see the region as a Cold War battleground with the Soviet Union. There were areas where the Carter policies were not sufficiently strong. The 1977 arms embargo had significant weaknesses, and these loopholes needed to be closed. U.S. enforcement of the embargo must be strengthened. The Carter administration regarded U.S. corporate investment in South Africa as an agent of change and resisted calls to impose economic sanctions against South Africa. Now, with South Africa still resisting a Namibia settlement and carrying out a campaign of regional aggression and destabilization, sanctions are needed. There will be no easy or fast resolution to the southern African crisis, but it is urgent that the United States reorient its policies to cut ties with the structure of white domination and to support the black struggle for freedom.

The most recent comprehensive statement of Reagan administration policies on southern Africa was presented by Undersecretary of State for Political Affairs Lawrence Eagleburger in a speech in June 1983.[34] In style and substance the speech appeared to be the work of Chester Crocker. It was presented at a time when, after two years of "constructive engagement" by the United States, South Africa still illegally occupies Namibia, has carried out a widening campaign of aggression and destabilization against Angola and the other frontline states, and has faced spreading guerrilla attacks by the ANC within its borders. In this context, the Eagleburger speech was a broad restatement of administration goals and a defense of its approach against increasing criticism from African countries and at home.

The speech put both the Namibia issue and the problem of change in South Africa within the context of the need for regional security and co-existence in southern Africa. In both cases it was asserted that the South African government must have assurances of regional security as a pre-requisite for proceeding on a positive course. Thus Angola had to agree to remove Cuban forces there before South Africa could be expected to proceed with a Namibia settlement. Similarly, it was indicated that the frontline states had to curb the ANC and other opposition activity if Pretoria was to end its attacks and destabilization. And only under such circumstances, it was claimed, could basic change away from apartheid be expected from Pretoria.

On Namibia, therefore, Eagleburger maintained the U.S. insistence on tying South Africa's implementation of the UN independence plans to the withdrawal of Cuban forces from Angola. He did state that South Africa must leave Angola's southern provinces and Namibia. But by saying that "Angola can act to make such steps possible" by "assuring" the departure of Cuban forces, the burden is placed on Angola to act first. Yet the fundamental issue in the Namibia problem is South Africa's illegal occupation of the territory; it is obligated to withdraw without preconditions. The Carter policies had suggested that a Cuban with-drawal from Angola was desirable, and that it could be attained through a Namibia settlement. The Reagan approach has reversed this propo-sition. Moreover, Reagan has endorsed the South African claim that the Cubans pose a major security concern without any explanation or jus-tification. Yet it was South African (and American) intervention in An-gola in 1975 that prompted Cuban involvement. South Africa has repeatedly attacked Angola, and it controls a large area in the south. South Africa claims the Cuban presence intimidates and threatens Na-mibians, yet its own forces are vastly stronger than the Cubans'.

In extensive diplomatic contacts since the end of 1982, the United States has apparently offered Angola diplomatic recognition, improved economic ties, and, probably, other arrangements if it will come to terms with UNITA. But these incentives must be viewed in light of the great pressures that Angola faces if it does not go along with the Crocker policies. The United States and South Africa can blame it for the Namibia impasse. The war will continue, taking a rising toll in Namibian and Angolan lives. Angolan president Jose Eduardo dos Santos charged in November 1982 that South African attacks had caused $10 billion in damages to his country since 1975,[35] and this figure will surely rise.

In April 1983 a coalition of twenty-four national organizations (including black, civil rights, religious, and trade-union groups) issued a sharply critical report on what was described as the Reagan administration's "uneven diplomacy" on Namibia and urging an end to its alignment with South Africa.[36] But the Eagleburger speech signaled a continuation of this approach. Thus U.S. envoys have carried out extensive consultations with South Africa, while the United Nations (the lawful authority in the territory), SWAPO, the frontline states, and even other members of the contact group have often been left out or given prearranged proposals. Constitutional principles and election procedures elaborated by the United States have been proposed as concessions to Pretoria and impositions on SWAPO. The principles actually impinge on the Namibian right to self-determination, since they lay down governmental guidelines that the Namibians should formulate for themselves. Finally, the whole thrust of the Crocker diplomacy has been to push the Namibia problem further and further from its place as an international legal issue under the authority of the United Nations toward a position as a piece in the U.S. strategic plans for southern Africa and global confrontation with the Soviets.

On the issue of regional conflict, Eagleburger compared the situation to the Middle East, stating that "unless there is peace and stability in southern Africa, it will prove impossible to encourage essential change in South Africa." This stands as a warning to the frontline states that the United States will not pressure South Africa into halting preemptive attacks and destabilization so long as ANC attacks continue. It also seeks to place responsibility for change in South Africa on the frontline states. Though the Reagan administration professes concern about regional violence, it does not cite South African racism and repression as its root cause.

Eagleburger criticized apartheid as "morally wrong" and cited some of the fundamental abuses of the system. To promote change he declared U.S. support for the programs undertaken by the Botha government, particularly the new constitutional proposals, and announced that the administration "supports those inside and outside of the government of South Africa who are committed to peaceful change." This policy must be viewed in light of the polarization and conflict now underway in South Africa. Despite the massive program of militarization and the Total Strategy and the regime's record of violence and aggression, the claim is made that constructive change is underway. It is particularly hard to see how the Reagan policies, the most significant measures of which have been a series of relaxations in the regulations enforcing the arms embargo, can be seen to support peaceful change.

What are the alternatives to current U.S. policy? And are there prospects of implementing them given the extent of American holdings in

South Africa? The United States now has nearly $3 billion in direct investments in South Africa; if bank loans and other indirect investments are added, then the total figure for all forms of U.S. capital invested in some way in South Africa is more than $9 billion.[37] The Eagleburger speech stated that the call for withdrawal of American investments in South Africa is based on "no discernible philosophical or policy premise" and would "undo an avenue of positive effort." These assertions are not valid. The call for corporate disinvestment is based on the fundamental fact that to operate in South Africa means to operate under the laws of apartheid, to serve white interests, to do business with the South African government, and in some cases to provide direct support for the government in strategic fields. Protests against investments in and trade with South Africa are thus aimed not simply at symbolic ties with apartheid, but also at very direct forms of collaboration with the structure of racial repression.

South Africa's defiance of international law and its brutal war against the people of Namibia demand a strong response by the international community. South Africa's efforts to crush black resistance to apartheid have spread conflict throughout the region. South Africa is at war, and strong counterpressures are urgently needed if these escalating conflicts are to be turned toward peaceful resolutions. The use of economic sanctions, especially a comprehensive oil boycott, is one major way to apply pressure to South Africa. Just as important are measures to strengthen the terms of the arms embargo and assure its enforcement by individual countries. A wide range of other actions can be taken to isolate the Nationalist government and lend support for the liberation movements and those resisting South African racism. There will be no easy or fast resolution to the crisis in southern Africa, but it is urgent that the United States reorient its policies to cut ties with apartheid and to support the black struggle for freedom.

The Freedom Charter

(Adopted at the Congress of the People, Kliptown, South Africa, on 26 June 1955.)

We, the People of South Africa,
declare for all our country
and the
world to know:

That South Africa belongs to all who live in it, black and white, and that no government can justly claim authority unless it is based on the will of all the people; that our people have been robbed of their birthright to land, liberty and peace by a form of government founded on injustice and inequality;
that our country will never be prosperous or free until all our people live in brotherhood enjoying equal rights and opportunities;
that only a democratic state, based on the will of all the people, can secure to all their birthright without distinction or colour, race, sex, or belief;
And therefore, we the people of South Africa, black and white together—equals, countrymen and brothers—adopt this Freedom Charter. And we pledge ourselves to strive together, sparing neither strength nor courage, until the democratic changes set out here have been won.

The people shall govern!

Every man and woman shall have the right to vote for and to stand as a candidate for all bodies which make laws;
All people shall be entitled to take part in the administration of the country;
The rights of the people shall be the same regardless of race, colour or sex;
All bodies of minority rule, advisory boards, councils and authorities shall be replaced by democratic organs of self-government.

All national groups shall have equal rights!

There shall be equal status in the bodies of state, in the courts and in the schools for all national groups and races;
All people shall have equal right to use their own languages, and to develop their own folk culture and customs;
All national groups shall be protected by law against insults to their race and national pride;
The preaching and practice of national, race or colour discrimination and contempt shall be a punishable crime; All apartheid laws and practices shall be set aside.

The people shall share in the
country's wealth!

242

The national wealth of our country, the heritage of all South Africans, shall be restored to the people;
The mineral wealth beneath the soil, the banks and monopoly industry shall be transferred to the ownership of the people as a whole:
All other industry and trade shall be controlled to assist the well-being of the people;
All people shall have equal rights to trade where they choose, to manufacture and to enter all trades, crafts and professions.

The land shall be shared among
those who work it!

Restrictions of land ownership on a racial basis shall be ended, and all the land redivided amongst those who work it, to banish famine and land hunger;
The state shall help the peasants with implements, seed, tractors and dams to save the soil and assist the tillers;
Freedom of movement shall be guaranteed to all who work on the land;
All shall have the right to occupy land wherever they choose;
People shall not be robbed of their cattle, and forced labour and farm prisons shall be abolished.

All shall be equal before the law!

No one shall be imprisoned, deported or restricted without a fair trial;
No one shall be condemned by the order of any Government official;
The courts shall be representative of all the people; Imprisonment shall be only for serious crimes against the people, and shall aim at re-education, not vengeance; The police force and army shall be open to all on an equal basis and shall be the helpers and protectors of the people; All laws which discriminate on grounds of race, colour or belief shall be repealed.

All shall enjoy equal human rights!

The law shall guarantee to all their right to speak, to organise, to meet together, to publish, to preach, to worship and to educate their children;
The privacy of the house from police raids shall be protected by law;
All shall be free to travel without restriction from countryside to town,
from province to province and from South Africa abroad; Pass Laws, permits and all other laws restricting these freedoms shall be abolished.

There shall be work and security!

All who work shall be free to form trade unions, to elect their officers and to make wage agreements with their employers;
The state shall recognise the right and duty of all to work, and to draw full unemployment benefits;
Men and women of all races shall receive equal pay for equal work;.
There shall be a forty-hour working week, a national minimum wage,
paid annual leave, and sick leave for all workers and maternity leave on full pay for all working mothers;
Miners, domestic workers, farm workers, and civil servants shall have the same rights as all others who work;
Child labour, compound labour, the tot system and contract labour shall be abolished.

The doors of learning and of culture
shall be opened!

The government shall discover, develop and encourage national talent for the enhancement of our cultural life; All the cultural treasures of mankind shall be open to all, by free exchange of books, ideas and contact with other lands; The aim of education shall be to teach the youth to love their people and their culture, to honour human brotherhood, liberty and peace;
Education shall be free, compulsory, universal and equal for all children;

Higher education and technical training shall be opened to all by means of state allowances and scholarships awarded on the basis of merit;
Adult illiteracy shall be ended by a mass state education plan; Teachers shall have all the rights of other citizens;
The colour bar in cultural life, in sport and in education shall be abolished.

There shall be houses,
security and comfort!

All people shall have the right to live where they choose, to be decently housed, and to bring up their families in comfort, and security;
Unused housing space to be made available to the people;
Rent and prices shall be lowered, food plentiful and no one shall go hungry;
A preventive health scheme shall be run by the state;
Free medical care and hospitalisation shall be provided for all, with special care for mothers and young children;
Slums shall be demolished, and new suburbs built, where all have transport, roads, lighting, playing fields, creches and social centres;
The aged, the orphans, the disabled and the sick shall be cared for by the state;
Rest, leisure and recreation shall be the right of all;
Fenced locations and ghettoes shall be abolished, and laws which
break up families shall be repealed;
South Africa shall be a fully independent state, which respects the rights and sovereignty of nations.

APPENDIX B

A Listing of 1978-79 Secret Information Department Projects

On April 11, 1981, the Johannesburg *Star*, in a story on the Information Department, listed the secret projects budgeted for the 1978-79 fiscal year, the last year of the Mulder-Rhoodie program. The *Star* vouched for the authenticity of the listing; some projects had been discussed in the Erasmus Commission reports, and many had been mentioned by Rhoodie in interviews. Foreign Minister Botha claimed that only five of these projects were still active, although the Erasmus Commission had recommended continuing sixty-eight secret projects. The *Star* deleted some names and details from the projects when it was unable to establish they were still active. The total budget for the year was R14.8 million ($17.76 million). The largest single project was $7.76 for the *Citizen*, but this was so secret that it was not on the budget list. (NOTE: Projects marked with an asterisk had not been previously described.)

INFORMATION DEPARTMENT PROJECTS   *1978/79*

G.2	African comics projected in SA and SWA.	R400,000
G.2A	Publication of monthly journal "Hit" and supplement	1,000
G.2E	Purchase and expansion of "Drum Weekend" (Nominal)	1,000
G.2G	Purchase costs for the establishment of a black newspaper	1,000
*G.5 &		
G.16D	Germany and fellow workers.	13,000
G.6	Club of Ten, London	300,000
G.7	Committe for Fairness in Sport	150,000
G.8A	Don de Kiefer and Associates, Washington	250,000
G.8B	Liaison program in Latin America	20,000
G.8C	Liaison program in Germany	470,000
G.8D	Liaison program in Germany	215,000
G.8E	Special Jewish liaison program in USA, especially with regard to Senators and academics.	20,000
G.9	External news bureau	30,000
G.10	Special covert advertisements eg via To the Point and Business Week	100,000

245

G.11A & 11B	Ad hoc church actions. NGK special overseas action program	60,000
G.11C	Christian League of SA and actions in Britain and US	320,000
G.11D	Church actions in Germany	—
G.12	African Development magazine in London for Southern and East Africa.	—
G.14	Cover opinion surveys and market analyses.	—
*G.15	African-American Affairs Association in New York	10,000
G.16A	Ad hoc secret co-workers.	25,000
G.16F	Publishers, London	6,000
G.16H	Special news bureau in Nairobi for Africa news (van zyl Alberts)	20,000
*G.16K	in France	—
G.16L		6,000
*G.16M	in the Netherlands.	—
G.16N	in France	—
*G.16O	in London	—
G.16P	in the Netherlands	500
G.16Q	Gary Player (nominal)	1,000
G.17A	Bantu Films Production	500,000
G.17B	Distribution of films to black population	500,000
G.18	Case Studies in Human Rights—central manuscript	50,000
G.19	Institute for the Study of Plural Societies	100,000
G.20A	Special conferences in U.S.	150,000
G.20B	Special conferences in Germany	60,000
G.20C	Special conferences in South Africa	1,000
G.20D	Special conferences in London	1,000
G.20G	Special conferences in Frankfurt	1,000
G.20H	Ad hoc contributions for special conferences which must still be arranged.	
		75,000
G.21A	La Monde Moderne, France	30,000
G.21D	France Eurafrique—Monthly journal	—
G.21F	University Libre magazine in Paris	13,000
*G.22	A guarantee for books about South Africa worldwide	200,000
*G.23	Production companies in Switzerland	200,000
G.25	To the Point	1,300,000
G.26A	Front organizations: Ad hoc—aksies.	—
*G.26B	NZAW	19,000
*G.26C	Society, London	6,000
*G.26D	OESAC—Austrian Action	5,500
G.26E	AGNETA (Sweden)	12,000
G.26F	Plural Studies Journal in the Netherlands	21,000
G.26G	Foundation Control Centre, the Netherlands	13,000
*G.26H	Israel-South African Chamber of Commerce	11,000
G.26J	Centre for International Politics, Potchefstroom (SA)	25,000
G.26K	Institute for Strategic Studies, University of Pretoria	10,000
G.26L	German South African Association, Germany	105,000
G.26M	Institute for African Studies	4,000
G.26N	Netherlands South African Assoc. visits to the Netherlands.	7,000
G.26O	Japanese-South African Association, Tokyo	5,000
*G.26P	Foundation, London	—
G.26R	Human Rights Research Institute, South Africa.	—
G.27	Legal actions in the U.S. Britain, Netherlands and Germany	70,000
*G.28	Salary, Travelling & Subsistence.	45,000
*G.29	Co-worker in Israel	42,000
G.30	Anonymous coworkers	25,000
G.31	Ad hoc travel and subsistence of officials and other visitors.	100,000
G.32	Foreign guests of front organizations	200,000
G.33	Purchase of special equipment eg tape recorders, telephone scramblers, etc.	
		5,000

G.34A	Valiant Publications—book publishing company. S.African firm publishing and distributing conservative literature.	160,000
G.34D	Book publisher, France	5,000
G.34E	S.A. Freedom Foundation	130,000
G.35	Special SWA actions against Swapo.	20,000
G.36	Special secret administration costs (nominal)	2,000
G.42	Emergency Fund	—
*G.43	Communal actions together with the Israeli Government (nominal)	5,000
G.44A	Ad hoc contributions for pro-South African actions	—
G.44B	French South African Association, Johannesburg and Paris.	100,000
G.44C	S.A. Railways re To the Point	12,500
*G.44E	Satoer for providing cover for operations of in Israel.	12,000
G.44G	French South Africa Association's actions in France	20,000
G.45	Foreign Affairs association. (Academic study organization, organized seminars as well as publishing academic papers).	153,000
*G.47	Operations in Far East	5,000
G.48	British Parliament members' visit to S.A.	10,000
G.52	Guard: London	120,000
*G.61	Special radio cassette programs in African countries (nominal)	5,000
G.62	Political studies and evaluation in Africa	5,000
G.65	Thor Communicators—upkeep costs of company and replacement by Homerus Finance Corp. for channeling of funds to foreign countries (single).	6,000
G.73	Management budget for British, French and S.A. operations, including offices in Johannesburg, Paris and London.	200,000
G.75	Prescon Business News-Financial news service to the world.	37,000
*G.76	Americans Concerned for South African Operations in the USA	50,000
G.77	Internal actions in the black residential areas.	25,000
G.78	External news-picture service	1,000
*G.79	Ad hoc printing and distribution, e.g., Rotarians & Lions	25,000
G.80	Special bursary programme for foreigners tied in with. . .Ian Player.	30,000
*G.81	Confidential French newsletter	1,000
G.82	S/project (.) Berlin	28,000
G.83	International article service (nominal)	10,000
G.84	Letter writing campaign in different countries	500
G.85		
G.86	Special research program re The World, the Rand Daily Mail and other projects	1,000
G.87	Action program in Rhodesia for the benefit of moderate political parties (a one-shot program)	400,000
*G.88	Association British (60,000 members)	200,000
G.89	Purchase of Investors Review, London and extension program	—
*G.90	Senate actions via Jewish groups	30,000
*G.91	Purchase of journals in France (passports from the Bureau).	—
*G.92	Purchase of French municipal journals (two cabinet ministers)	—
*G.93	Establishment of the Atlantic Council branch for South Africa as well as the establishment of the head office in London and branch office in USA.	280,000
G.94	Actions in Scandinavia	10,000
G.95	Special action program for trade unions in Britain, Germany, Belgium and the US (nominal)	1,000
G.96	Purchase of special space in newspapers and magazines in Europe, Australia and US by means of the so-called "sailor" system whereby sympathetic journalists are involved (nominal)	1,000
*G.97	Special movie programs, eg, the movie of Dr. Beurt SerVaas of the Saturday Evening Post about South Africa (nominal)	

APPENDIX C

The Crocker Documents on South Africa

MEMORANDUM OF CONVERSATION

PARTICIPANTS: *South Africa*:

Foreign Minister Pik Botha
Defense Minister Magnus Malan

U.S.:

Assistant Secretary-designate Crocker
Alan Keyes, S/P

DATE & PLACE: April 15/16, 1981, Pretoria

SUBJECT: Discussions with SAG

COPIES TO: AF, IO-McElhaney, S/P-Keyes, AF/S

US-Africa Relations:

Botha opened first day's discussion by expressing unhappiness over what SAG perceives as backsliding by Administration from view of South Africa taken during U.S. presidential campaign. Reagan campaign statements produced high expectations in South Africa. But, administration, in response to views of allies, such as UK and Germany, and to influence of State Department professionals, has disappointed SAG expectations. USG handling of visit by military officers example of this. Botha raised issue of trust, referring to earlier "McHenry" duplicity on issue of SWAPO bases.

However, he affirmed that it means a great deal to SAG to have good relations with U.S. and that SAG understands U.S. problems in maintaining friendly relations with black African states. To begin second day's discussion, Crocker noted that, though he hadn't come to discuss South Africa's internal affairs, it was clear that positive movement domestically would make it easier for the U.S. to work with SAG. U.S. ability to develop full relations with SAG depends on success of Prime Minister Botha's program and extent to which it is seen as broadening SAG's domestic support. "Pik" Botha cautioned against making success of P. W. Botha's program a condition of U.S./South African relations. Crocker responded with view that this is not a condition but reflects U.S. desire to support positive trends. In response Pik Botha went more fully into reasons for deep SAG distrust of U.S. Botha reiterated view that, as result of pressure from African states in UN, and influence of State Department, USG has backed away from initial recognition of importance of its interests in southern Africa (read South Africa). He doubted whether, given domestic

248

pressures and views of such African states as Nigeria, U.S. could continue any policy favorable to South Africa, which would not provoke constant criticism.

In response, Crocker replied that present Administration would have more backbone in face of pressure than previous one. U.S. has many diverse interests and responsibilities, but will stand up for what we think right. Our objective is to increase SAG confidence.

Toward end of discussion, in context of Angola issue, Botha again came back to question of trust. He said he is suspicious of U.S. because of way U.S. dropped SAG in Angola in 1975. He argued that SAG went into Angola with USG support, then U.S. voted to condemn in UN. Cited many examples of past USG decisions that didn't inspire confidence -- Vietnam, Iran, USG failure to support moderate governments in Africa, while aiding those with leftist rhetoric. Alluding to Chad, Botha asserted that African leaders became so desperate for help against Qadafi that one even approached SAG privately, a last resort, to ask for help. Botha admitted that SAG can't yet pass judgement on present Administration. He pleaded for consistency, "When we say something, let's stick to it."

Crocker addressed trust issue, saying that new Administration is tired of double think and double talk. Despite rocky start in US/SAG relations, improvement is possible. Reagan election victory represents enormous change in US public opinion on foreign policy reversing trend of post-Vietnam years.

SAG View of Regional Situation:

During the first day's session Botha discussed at length situation in southern Africa and Africa at large. He cited economic, food and population problems to support view that Africa is a dying continent because Africans have made a mess of their independence. Botha asserted belief that cause isn't race, but fact that new nations lack experience, cultural background, technical training.

Referring to South African past experience in helping and training blacks in neighboring states, Botha discussed the need for peaceful co-existence between South Africa and its neighbors. Until they recognize they're making a mess of their independence, South Africa can't help them. South Africa is willing to help those who admit they need its help.

On this basis Botha presented vision of southern Africa's future, in context of "Constellation of States" concept. He appealed for USG support for South Africa's view of region's future, involving a confederation of states, each independent, but linked by a centralizing secretariat. SAG doesn't expect U.S. support for apartheid, but it hopes there will be no repeat of Mondale's "One man, One Vote" statement. SAG goal is survival of white values, not white privileges.

Botha argued that central issue in southern Africa is subversion. Noting that what ANC does, South Africa can do better. Botha stressed need for agreement on non-use of force. If region starts to collapse, fire will spread, there will be no winners. This is not meant as threat, but simply stating facts. Botha emphasized view that if you kill the part of Africa containing people who can do things, you kill whole of Africa.

Asked about U.S. view of the importance of southern Africa, Crocker summarized U.S. regional interests in context of its global responsibilities. He emphasized U.S. desire to deal with destabilization threats worldwide by going to their sources, using means tailored to each source and region involved. Crocker made clear that in Africa we distinguish between countries where Soviets and Cubans have a combat presence, and those whose governments espousing Marxism for their own practical purposes. He stressed that top U.S. priority is to stop Soviet encroachment in Africa. U.S. wants to work with SAG, but ability to deal with Soviet presence severely impeded by Namibia. Crocker alluded to black African view that South Africa contributes to instability in region. Said he agrees with this view to extent SAG goes beyond reprisal. Putting fear in minds of inferior powers makes them irrational.

Namibia/Angola Issue

Malan raised topic of Angola during first session. He asked about a supposed U.S. plan for an all-Africa force to replace the Cubans in Angola. Crocker responded that he was aware of no such plan, except perhaps as a symbolic gesture. Views were exchanged on the character of the MPLA Government, with the South Africans firmly asserting its domination by Moscow, while Crocker suggested a more nuanced view, allowing for several factions within the MPLA varying in ideological commitment and character. Discussion touched briefly on the nature of SWAPO. Botha alluded to the view that Nujoma is a "Bloody Thug."

Malan flatly declared that the SAG can't accept prospects of a SWAPO victory which brings Soviet/Cuban forces to Walvis Bay. This would result from any election which left SWAPO in a dominant position. Therefore a SWAPO victory would be unacceptable in the context of a Westminster-type political system. Namibia needs a federal system. SAG does not rule out an internationally acceptable settlement, but could not live with a SWAPO victory that left SWAPO unchecked power. Botha asserted that Ovambo dominance after the election would lead to civil war.

Crocker addressed these concerns saying USG recognized need to build South African confidence and security. Malan interposed with the view that it is the local people in Namibia who need security, and SAG could accept SWAPO victory only if their security is provided for. SAG can't dictate to local parties. Crocker remarked upon need to negotiate with governments, which ultimately means that parties can't have veto power. In response Botha gave eloquent rendition of SAG's problem in dealing with the internal parties. These parties fear secret plot to install SWAPO government. SAG doesn't wish to entrench white privileges but some confidence-building measures needed. Discussion briefly explored constitutional issues. South Africans asked who would write a constitution. Crocker alluded to idea of expert panel.

SAG sees Savimbi in Angola as buffer for Namibia. SAG believes Savimbi wants southern Angola. Having supported him this far, it would damage SAG honor if Savimbi is harmed. Second round of discussions went into greater detail on Namibia/Angola questions. Malan declared SAG view that Angola/Namibia situation is number one problem in southern Africa. Angola is one place where U.S. can roll back Soviet/Cuban presence in Africa. Need to get rid of Cubans, and support Unita. Unita is going from strength to strength, while SWAPO grows militarily weaker.

In his response Crocker agreed on relation of Angola to Namibia. USG believes it would be possible to improve US/South African relations if Namibia were no longer an issue. We seek a settlement, but one in our interest, based on democratic principles. Our view is that South Africa is under no early military pressure to leave Namibia. The decision belongs to SAG, and ways must be found to address its concerns. USG assumes Soviet/Cuban presence is one of those concerns, and we are exploring ways to remove it in context of Namibia settlement. We agree that UNITA is an important factor in the Angolan situation. We believe there can be no peace in Angola without reconciliation between UNITA and MPLA. We see no prospect of military victory for UNITA. Must achieve achieve movement toward reconciliation by playing on divisions in MPLA. With regard to Namibia, USG assumes that constitution is an important issue, which must be resolved before elections. The constitution would include guarantees for minority rights and democratic processes. We have said we believe SCR 435 is a basis for transition to independence for Namibia, but not for a full settlement. We wish to meet SAG concerns, while taking account of views on other side. We cannot scrap 435 without great difficulty. We wish to supplement rather than discard it.

Malan took up Namibian question, observing that internationalization of the issue posed greatest difficulty. He alluded to tremendous distrust of UN in South Africa. He questioned inclusion of South Africa and Front Line states in the quest for a settlement, asserting that SWAPO and the internal parties should conclude it. He agreed on the need for a constitution. But 435 can't work. The longer it takes to solve the Namibia question, the less

South African presence will be required there. We will reach a stage where internal forces in Namibia can militarily defeat SWAPO.

Malan's remarks set stage for Botha to discuss SAG view of SWAPO. Botha noted that SAG thought it was important to U.S. to stop Soviet gains. But if you say SWAPO not Marxist, you move in same direction as previous administration. SWAPO's people are indoctrinated in Marxism every day. Savimbi considers SWAPO universally Marxist. SAG's bottom line is no Moscow flag in Windhoek. If U.S. disagrees, let sanctions go on, and get out of the situation. South Africa can survive sanctions. Eventually South Africa can get support of moderate black African states. Better to start US/SAG relations with lower expectations, than to disagree angrily later. At moment, U.S. doesn't believe SAG view of SWAPO; you're soft on SWAPO. SAG appreciates U.S. firmness against Soviets, Botha continued. Even Africans now see you assuming leadership. But SAG worried that USG is moving toward Namibia plan SAG cannot understand. As with Kissinger attempt on Rhodesia, it will be difficult to get consensus, especially with so many parties involved. SAG tried one-on-one approach with Angolans, but Geneva meetings sidetracked effort. SAG has tried Angolans several times. Each time there is progress, but then something intervenes. We're convinced Moscow controls present government in Angola. We're convinced SWAPO is Marxist. Nujoma will nationalize the whole place, and cause upheaval and civil war, involving South Africa. We will have to invade Namibia, and other countries as well. We are pleading for you to see the dangers of a wrong solution in Namibia. It would be better to have a low-level conflict there indefinitely, than to have a civil war escalating to a general conflagration. If Nujoma governs as an Ovambo, the Hereros will fight. Also, Nujoma made promises to Soviets. Defectors from SWAPO have revealed their plan to SAG--first Namibia, then Botswana, Lesotho, and Swaziland, followed by the final attack on South Africa. SAG can't ignore this reality. We wouldn't justify that to our people. South Africa is a democracy as far as white voters are concerned. Even black leaders can criticize the government. South Africa has freedom, and can have more, but survival is the prerequisite. The BLS leaders agree with us. Even some Front Line leaders see the danger. We have twice saved Kaunda's life.

The situation is not what you think. You think in global terms; we're not a global power. We must safeguard our interests here. Not just white interests. We see the necessity of avoiding black-white polarization. But we see it as an ideological struggle. Developed moderate blacks are not communists. They will engage with us in common effort against communism. When whites see blacks as allies, whites will move away from discrimination. With more distribution of economic goods, more blacks will join us. But if we all come under Moscow's domination, that's the end.

Crocker addressed Botha's expressed fears and concerns by first accepting the premise that Soviet domination is the danger. But U.S. believes best way to avoid that danger is to get Namibia issue behind us. As long as issue subsists, we cannot reach a situation where U.S. can engage with South Africa in security, and include South Africa in our general security framework. If Namibia continues, it will open South/Central Africa to the Soviets. Simmering conflict in Namibia is not acceptable. The ideas U.S. has in mind don't include Soviets in Windhoek. We believe we can get the Soviets out of Angola, and provide a guarantee of security whether Nujoma wins or not.

Botha said this is the nitty-gritty. Without Soviet support, others won't accept Nujoma's rule. To satisfy others we need a political solution. Crocker agreed that a political solution is needed. Botha stressed the need to consult with leaders in Namibia. If U.S. can gain their confidence, and SWAPO's, and talk about minority rights, progress is possible. People in Namibia are concerned about property, an independent judiciary, freedom of religion, the preservation of their language and the quality of education under the present system, discrimination has been abolished by law, though it continues in practice. There is also the problem of the white ethnic Legislature vs. the black majority Council of Ministers.

Crocker said that U.S. understands concern with constitutional rights. U.S. has inherited a situation with many parties but we must build a consensus in Africa that we are serious and not just delaying. We believe a Lancaster type conference won't work. We see a panel of experts, consulting all parties, writing a constitution, and then selling it through the Contact Group. With SAG's help, we could sell it to the internal parties. Botha referred to reports of a French constitutional plan. He said that he's against multiple plans. Botha stressed need for U.S. leadership, and emphasized need for U.S. to consult with internal parties in Namibia. He discussed SAG relations with internal leaders, and need to avoid leaving them in lurch in order not to be discredited with other moderate leaders in Africa. He tied this to possibility of SAG cooperating with moderate African states to deal with economic development problems. Botha concluded by saying that SAG doesn't want to let Namibia go the wrong way; that's why South Africa is willing to pay the price of the war. We pray and hope for a government favorably disposed to us. The internal parties don't want us to let go until they have sufficient power to control the situation. We want an anti-Soviet black government.

Following the substantive discussion, Botha conveyed to Crocker written communications from the heads of Bophuthatswana and Venda. He explained that their ambassadors wanted to deliver the messages in person, but Botha decided to convey them to avoid appearance of trying to force U.S. hand. Then question of invitation to Botha to visit U.S. in May was discussed. Crocker stressed need for SAG to decide cooperation with U.S. was worth it before accepting invitation. Botha resisted setting any conditions for visit, and said he would prefer not to come if conditions are set. Crocker said there were no conditions, just a question of clarifying the spirit in which the visit would take place. Botha ended the discussion by noting that he would inform internal parties about discussion immediately. He said he would tell Prime Minister Botha that SAG should explore question of constitution before an election in Namibia. He noted that a referendum on the constitution rather than constituent assembly elections, would make matters easier.

SECRET

Washington, D.C.
14 May 1981

SOUTH AFRICAN—UNITED STATES NUCLEAR
RELATIONS

INTRODUCTION

1. South African - United States nuclear relations date back to just after the second World War when the Western Allies, and in particular the United States, were in dire need of uranium for their military programmes.

In collaboration with the Combined Development Agency (CDA), South Africa developed its uranium industry to supply uranium under contract to the CDA free of safeguards. These contracts expired in the late sixties when our production reached a level of over 3,000 tons per annum. At that time the United States also placed an embargo on foreign imports of uranium to the States.

2. An Agreement for Cooperation on the Peaceful Uses of Atomic Energy with a duration of 10 years was concluded with the US in 1957. Under this Agreement the US undertook to sanction the supply of the SAFARI research reactor to South Africa and to meet the fuel requirements for this reactor under a bilateral US-SA safeguards agreement. The 1957 Agreement for Co-operation was subsequently reviewed, amended and renewed in 1962, 1967 and again in 1974. (The 1962 amendment permitted the rental of HEU for SAFARI in addition to the purchase thereof by South Africa. The agreement was renewed in 1967 for a further 10 years after South Africa had on the insistence of the USA given assurances on its policy with regard to uranium sales. The trilateral safeguards agreement between the USA, South Africa and the IAEA was also amended to ensure the continued application of safeguards after expiry of the US-SA agreement.)

In 1974 the agreement was extended from 20 to 30 years, that is until 2007, and also to provide for the supply of separating working units by the United States for the life of the proposed Koeberg reactors (that is for 25 years after 1982).

In terms of this arrangement a contract for enriched uranium for the Koeberg reactors was concluded with ERDA, which was later transferred to DOE.

It must be emphasized that the 1974 agreement as well as the DOE supply contracts only provided for IAEA safeguards on such facilities and on the fuel to be transferred to South Africa by the USA.

These agreements and safeguards arrangements were and are still diligently honoured by South Africa.

3. During the latter half of 1976 it became clear to South Africa that it would become increasingly difficult to obtain fuel for its research reactor (SAFARI) from the US. Although the US never refused the required export permit for a batch of fuel, at that time on order and paid for by South Africa, unacceptable delays were experienced resulting in the cancellation of the order by South Africa when it became evident in 1977 that the delivery of the fuel would not be allowed by the previous US Administration.

4. In June of 1978 discussions took place in Pretoria on nuclear relations between the US and South Africa. During these discussions it became abundantly clear that the US would not supply the fuel in question unless South Africa acceded to NPT and subjected all its nuclear facilities and activities to international safeguards. More restrictive conditions were thus imposed unilaterally by the US after the conclusion of the contract.

5. South Africa has repeatedly stated that it will observe the principles of the NPT and also indicated that it was in principle not opposed to accession to the NPT if its basic requirements could be met.

6. Subsequent discussions to those in June 1978 revealed that even if South Africa should accede to the NPT, the US would find it difficult to provide South Africa timeously with the enriched uranium for Koeberg. South Africa was also prevented, through US intervention, from obtaining fuel from any other source unless it accepted the conditions unilaterally imposed on South Africa by the US.

THE PRESENT POSITION

7. Koeberg is scheduled for initial fuel loading in March 1982, and as no firm undertaking for the supply of enriched uranium could as yet be obtained, the chances are that the scheduled start-up of Koeberg would be seriously delayed at great cost to South Africa.

THE SOUTH AFRICAN POSITION

8. (i) As has been indicated in the past, South Africa is not in principle opposed to the NPT, provided that its *basic requirements* can be met.
   (ii) As in the past, South Africa will continue to conduct and administer its nuclear affairs in a manner which is in line with the spirit, principles and goals of the NPT.
   (iii) South Africa's nuclear programmes are geared to the peaceful application of nuclear energy and at no time has she tested a nuclear device.

9. It must be realized that South Africa is threatened by the USSR and its associates and by certain African countries with Soviet support and encouragement. South Africa has no hope of any assistance from the UN in case of attack. On the contrary, it is continually being threatened with action under Chapter VII of the Charter of the United Nations. While this state of affairs continues South Africa cannot in the interest of its own security sign the NPT and thus set the minds of its would-be attackers at rest, allowing them to proceed freely with their plans against us.

WHAT SOUTH AFRICA REQUESTS

10. (a) That the United States Government give an that export permits will be issued for delivery of enriched uranium to France;
    (b) if the US feels it cannot supply the enriched uranium through France timeously for the Koeberg reactors in present circumstances, the US makes it known to France that it would not insist on the conditions that it imposed unilaterally on South Africa after the signature of the original supply contracts if France were to supply the fuel, and
    (c) DOE agrees either to cancel the present contract for the supply of enriched uranium to ESCOM at no cost, or DOE agrees to postpone execution of the contract at no cost until such time as an agreement can be reached between the United States and South African authorities which would permit the United States to resume deliveries of fuel to South Africa.

WASHINGTON DC
14 May 1981

TOAST

Minister Botha, Mrs. Botha, Ladies and Gentlemen:

Recent elections have opened new horizons for both our countries. The peoples of the United States and South Africa have given our governments a clear mandate to seek a new beginning at home and abroad. The Reagan administration has accepted this challenge and welcomes the opportunity to improve relations between the United States and South Africa.

Good relations are a goal that must be set and worked towards. We have put this goal high on the agenda of this administration. We approach this task in a spirit of friendship and conciliation. In our relations with you we will not overemphasize the differences between us, nor underemphasize the ties that bind us together. We will speak directly to you of our concerns. We will also share with you the burdens now confronting us as we seek peace, justice and stability in the world and especially in southern Africa. Most importantly, South Africa can rely on our determination and backbone as leader of the free world.

I believe our talks today have laid a basis for moving forward constructively to resolve outstanding issues in the southern African region, including Namibia. We are determined to do our part to achieve a settlement in Namibia which will meet the interests of all of its people and will promote genuine independence and democracy there. While our choices will be difficult, we must move boldly down this path together.

Let us then build on these shared interests and let us talk as friends of the differences between us. Most importantly, let this be the new beginning of mutual trust and confidence between the United States and South Africa, old friends, like Minister Botha, who are getting together again.

May we now drink to friendship and cooperation between the United States and South Africa.

May 13, 1981

TO: AF - Chester A. Crocker
FROM: AF/S - Paul J. Hare
SUBJECT: Your Meeting with the Secretary Wednesday, May 13 4:00 P.M.

You may wish to add to your checklist a brief account of the May 12 Contact Group meeting. Everyone seemed to agree that in the Pik Botha visit we should be aiming at getting a better understanding of whether South Africa would be willing to move forward toward a restructured, internationally acceptable settlement. In particular, however, our interlocutors are:

—very leery of holding out the prospect to the SAG that we are willing to change UNSCR 435. They feel that will induce South African creativity, in particular an reinvigorated SAG assault on UNTAG which they see as the guts of 435. Part of the problem is semantical, i.e., they assent we should describe our efforts as attempts to "complement" rather than to "change" 435.

—generally reluctant to get involved in a fullblown constitution. The Canadians (at least Paul La Pointe) are in the lead on this issue claiming that a set of principles is sufficient. La Pointe's argument lacks logic and merit.

—in agreement that guarantees will need to be explored. Nevertheless, we are all certain that this is an especially delicate issue in which too much clarity on points such as Walvis Bay and enforceability are not desirable and should certainly not be discussed with the South Africans at this stage of the process.

Drafted:AF/S:RCFrasure:mo

TO: The Secretary
FROM: AF - Chester A. Crocker
SUBJECT: Your Meeting with South African Foreign Minister Botha, 11:00 a.m., May 14, at the Department—*Scope Paper*

SUMMARY:

The political relationship between the United States and South Africa has now arrived at a crossroads of perhaps historic significance. After twenty years of generally increasing official U.S. Government coolness toward South Africa and concomitant South African intransigence, *the possibility may exist for a more positive and reciprocal relationship between the two countries based upon shared strategic concerns* in southern Africa, our recognition that the government of P. W. Botha represents *a unique opportunity for domestic change,* and willingness of the Reagan Administration to deal realistically with South Africa. *The problem of Namibia,* however, which complicates our relations with our European allies and with black Africa, *is a primary obstacle to the development of a new relationship* with South Africa. *It also represents an opportunity* to counter the Soviet threat in Africa. We thus need Pretoria's cooperation in working toward an internationally acceptable solution to Namibia which would, however, safeguard US and South African essential interests and concerns.

I. OBJECTIVES

—To tell the South Africans that we are willing with them to open *a new chapter in our relationship* based upon strategic reality and South Africa's position in that reality and the continued explicit commitment of P.W. Botha's government to domestic change.

—To make clear to the South Africans that we see the continuation of *the Namibia problem as a primary obstacle* to the development of that new relationship and that we are willing to work with them toward an internationally acceptable settlement which will not harm their interests.

II. PARTICIPANTS:

US	SOUTH AFRICA
The Secretary	*Foreign Minister Botha*
Under Secretary Stoessel	*Brand Fourie*
Assistant Secretary-	*Ambassador Sole*
Designate Crocker	*Ambassador Ecksteen*
Assistant Secretary Abrams	

III. SETTING

The discussions with the South Africans will cover *three discrete areas: Namibia, US-South Africa nuclear cooperation and general bilateral issues.* Pik Botha may touch on each of these during his 15 minutes in private with you. Botha will probably weave these questions into an overview of southern Africa regional issues delivered in terms of his familiar "Africa is dying/Soviet-onslaught-against South Africa" speech. The expanded meeting with you and the working luncheon will focus specifically on Namibia. OES Assistant Secretary Jim Malone will conduct separate discussions with Brand Fourie on the nuclear issue. I will also conduct a separate discussion with Fourie on our bilateral relations with reference to the several specific issues now pending between us. *This format will permit you to focus on the Namibia issue.*

Our dialogue with South Africa over the possibility of a new and more balanced relationship began with my visit to Pretoria last month. As I reported to you from my meetings with Pik Botha and Defense Minister Magnus Malan, *I found the South Africans to be in a testy mood.* The substantial amounts of misinformation and disinformation which had appeared in the press since the November election had, I suspect, acted to bring to the surface ingrained distrust. *The South Africans are deeply suspicious of us, of our will, from the 1975-76 experience* and the Carter period. They claim that they can go it alone in the region--an attitude which is partly bluster, partly an opening bargaining position with us.

South African truculence (which can be coated with great charm) is compounded by the fact that, as an international pariah, the country has "had no meaningful, balanced bilateral relations in recent memory". Thus, the South Africans deeply resent being treated as an embarrassment and are not used to the give-and-take of pragmatic relations. If the South Africans still want to vent their frustrations, I fear you will be subjected to Pik's rhetoric. Thus, it is in your interest to take control of the meeting from the beginning.

IV. *DISCUSSION OF OBJECTIVES:*

1. *To tell the South Africans that we are willing with them to open a new chapter in our relationship based upon strategic reality and South Africa's position in that reality* and the continued explicit commitment of P. W. Botha's government to domestic change.

You will need to make it clear to Pik that *we share the South African hope that,* despite political differences among the states of southern Africa, *the economic interdependence of the area and constructive internal change within South Africa can be the foundations for a new era of cooperation, stability, and security in the region. We also share their view that the chief threat to the realization of this hope is the presence and influence in the region of the Soviet Union and its allies.*

You will also need to make it clear to Pik that *we are not willing to be manipulated by them* or to act as a smokescreen for their actions and misadventures with their neighbors. We must make it clear to the South Africans that *we have a role in rebuilding stability in southern Africa,* that is a shared goal they cannot reach without us, and they cannot go it alone. Our shared objectives require that our diplomacy have a chance to operate and our interests be observed as well as theirs. *We cannot afford to give them a blank check regionally.* Moreover, SAG intransigence and violent adventures will expand Soviet opportunities and reduce Western leverage in Africa. In turn, they may complain about our performance in the past and voice doubts about our constancy and reliability in the future.

TALKING POINTS

—WE WANT TO OPEN A NEW CHAPTER IN RELATIONS WITH SOUTH AFRICA.

—WE FEEL THE NEW RELATIONSHIP SHOULD BE BASED UPON OUR SHARED HOPES FOR THE FUTURE PROSPERITY, *SECURITY AND STABILITY OF SOUTHERN AFRICA,* CONSTRUCTIVE INTERNAL CHANGE WITHIN SOUTH AFRICA AND OUR SHARED PERCEPTION OF THE ROLE OF THE SOVIET UNION AND ITS SURROGATES IN THWARTING THOSE GOALS.

—WE CAN FORESEE COOPERATING WITH YOU IN A NUMBER OF WAYS IN OUR EFFORTS TO REESTABLISH REGIONAL STABILITY.

—US/SOUTH AFRICAN COOPERATION IS INDISPENSABLE FOR THE SUCCESS OF THOSE EFFORTS. FAILURE TO COOPERATE WILL ENCOURAGE FURTHER SOVIET GAINS, AND JEOPARDIZE THE INTERESTS OF BOTH OUR COUNTRIES.

—*WE WILL NOT ALLOW OTHERS TO DICTATE WHAT OUR RELATIONSHIP WITH SOUTH AFRICA WILL BE* AS EVIDENCED BY OUR RECENT VETO OF SANCTIONS. BUT JUST AS WE RECOGNIZE YOUR PERMANENT STAKE IN THE FUTURE OF SOUTHERN AFRICA, SO YOU MUST RECOGNIZE OUR PERMANENT INTEREST IN AFRICA AS A WHOLE.

—*WE MUST CONSIDER THESE INTERESTS IN OUR SOUTHERN AFRICAN POLICY AND EXPECT YOU WILL TAKE THEM INTO ACCOUNT IN YOUR DEALINGS WITH US.* THIS WILL REQUIRE RESTRAINT AND GOOD WILL BY ALL PARTIES. WE CANNOT CONSENT TO ACT AS A SMOKESCREEN FOR ACTIONS WHICH EXCITE THE FEARS OF OTHER STATES IN THE REGION, AND ENCOURAGE IMPRACTICAL, EMOTIONAL RESPONSES TO REGIONAL PROBLEMS.

—ALTHOUGH *WE MAY CONTINUE TO DIFFER ON APARTHEID,* AND CANNOT CONDONE A SYSTEM OF INSTITUTIONALIZED RACIAL DIFFERENTIATION, *WE CAN COOPERATE WITH A SOCIETY UNDERGOING CONSTRUCTIVE CHANGE. YOUR GOVERNMENT'S EXPLICIT COMMITMENT IN THIS DIRECTION WILL ENABLE US TO WORK WITH YOU.* YOU MUST HELP TO MAKE THIS APPROACH CREDIBLE. YOU ALSO SHOULD RECOGNIZE THAT THIS PERIOD REPRESENTS *YOUR BEST SHOT,* A RARE OPPORTUNITY, BECAUSE OF OUR MANDATE AND OUR DESIRE TO TURN A NEW LEAF IN BILATERAL RELATIONS.

—THE NEW SITUATION WE ENVISION IN SOUTHERN AFRICA WOULD ENTAIL

MUTUAL RECOGNITION OF THE PRINCIPLES OF INVIOLABILITY OF BORDERS AND NON-INTERFERENCE IN INTERNAL AFFAIRS IN THE STATES OF THE REGION.

—*OUR COOPERATIVE RELATIONSHIP WOULD ALSO RECOGNIZE THE KEY ECONOMIC ROLE PLAYED BY SOUTH AFRICA IN THE REGION* AND THE MAJOR CONTRIBUTIONS WHICH COULD BE MADE BY SOUTH AFRICA TO COORDINATED REGIONAL ECONOMIC DEVELOPMENT.

—I UNDERSTAND THAT IN A SEPARATE MEETING HERE YOU WILL BE DISCUSSING PRACTICAL STEPS WE CAN UNDERTAKE TO BEGIN THE PROCESS OF IMPROVING OUR BILATERAL RELATIONS.

2. *To make clear to the South Africans that we see US/SAG cooperation in resolving the Namibian problem as the crucial first phase of our new relationship and that we are willing to work with them toward an internationally acceptable settlement which will safeguard their interests and reflect our mutual desire to foreclose Soviet gains in southern Africa.*

Namibia complicates our relations with our European allies and with black Africa, and the interests of South Africa with those states as well. *We cannot allow the South Africans to be disingenuous with us over Namibia. If they have no intention of pulling out* of the territory under circumstances reasonably acceptable to the international community at large, *we will want to opt out of the negotiation process* rather than be subjected to an endless, meaningless charade. Contrary to what Botha will argue, UN involvement will be necessary to gain international acceptance for a Namibia settlement. As he told Crocker in Pretoria, there is no point in fooling around, dissimulation or miscommunication.

Conversely, *if the South Africans cooperate:* to achieve an internationally acceptable settlement, *this will greatly facilitate efforts to deal effectively with the Soviet threat.* We need to convey our seriousness about this strategic choice. A relationship initiated on a cooperative basis could move forward toward a future in which South Africa returns to a place within the regional framework of Western security interests. *The South Africans will be anxious to explore the details of such future relationship. We cannot be excessive in what we suggest to them,* e.g., any implication that we can return to 1945 is unrealistic given firm international commitments such as the arms embargo. *We can, however, work to end South Africa's polecat status* in the world and seek to restore its place as a legitimate and important regional actor with whom we can cooperate pragmatically. You will also need to respond with *an artful combination of gestures and hints.* The gestures would include, as described in the attached paper, small but concrete steps such as the normalization of our military attache relationship.

TALKING POINTS:

—*THE CONTINUATION OF NAMIBIA AS A FESTERING PROBLEM* COMPLICATES OUR RELATIONS WITH OUR EUROPEAN ALLIES AND BEDEVILS OUR RELATIONS WITH BLACK AFRICA. IT COMPLICATES YOUR RELATIONS WITH THOSE COUNTRIES AS WELL AND PREVENT SOUTH AFRICA FROM IMPROVING ITS RELATIONS WITH ITS NEIGHBORS.

—AS YOU TOLD CROCKER IN PRETORIA, *THERE IS NO POINT IN DISSIMULATION OR MISCOMMUNICATION BETWEEN US.*

—*WE SHARE YOUR VIEW THAT NAMIBIA NOT BE TURNED OVER TO THE SOVIETS* AND THEIR ALLIES. A RUSSIAN FLAG IN WINDHOEK IS AS UNACCEPTABLE TO US AS IT IS TO YOU.

—WE BELIEVE THAT *A CAREFULLY CONCEIVED AND IMPLEMENTED NAMIBIA SETTLEMENT* WILL HELP TO FORECLOSE OPPORTUNITIES FOR GROWTH OF SOVIET INFLUENCE IN SOUTHERN AFRICA, AND CAN, *IN THE COURSE OF SUCH A SETTLEMENT, CONTRIBUTE TO THE LEVERAGE WE NEED TO PRODUCE A WITHDRAWAL OF SOVIET/CUBAN MILITARY FORCES FROM ANGOLA.*

—WE SEEK YOUR SINCERE COOPERATION IN DEVELOPING CONCLUSIVE CRITERIA FOR A SETTLEMENT WHICH LEADS TO A TRULY INDEPENDENT NAMIBIA, WHILE ENHANCING OUR EFFORTS AGAINST SOVIET ENCROACHMENT AND SAFEGUARDING THE INTERESTS OF U.S., SOUTH AFRICA AND ALL THE PEOPLE OF NAMIBIA.

—*THIS APPROACH CAN FACILITATE A DEEPENING OF OUR BILATERAL RELATIONS*

IN MUTUALLY BENEFICIAL WAYS. IT CAN ALSO BEGIN A PROCESS LEADING TO THE END OF INTERNATIONAL REJECTION OF YOUR COUNTRY AND GREATER ACCEPTANCE OF SOUTH AFRICA WITHIN THE GLOBAL FRAMEWORK OF WESTERN SECURITY.

—WE DID NOT INVITE YOU HERE TO SELL YOU SPECIFICS OF A NAMIBIA PLAN. RATHER *WE WANT TO EXPLORE THE DEPTH AND SERIOUSNESS OF YOUR INTEREST IN A SETTLEMENT.*

—WE ARE INEVITABLY BROKERS IN THIS EXERCISE. YOU MUST TELL US TWO THINGS (A) *WHETHER YOU ARE IN FACT PREPARED TO MOVE TO A SETTLEMENT NOW*, TO COMMIT YOURSELVES TO IMPLEMENT A REVISED PLAN ONCE WE PIN DOWN SPECIFICS; (B) *WHAT YOUR CONCLUSIVE LIST OF CONCERNS INCLUDES.* WE WILL MAKE OUR BEST EFFORTS TO MEET YOUR CONCERNS BUT YOU MUST RESPECT OUR ROLE AS BROKER AND THE CRUCIAL IMPORTANCE OF AFRICAN ACCEPTANCE.

—MY PEOPLE NEED TO BEGIN SHAPING REVISED PROPOSALS. OUR CREDIBILITY IS ON THE LINE. *WE NEED TO KNOW SAG'S AUTHORITATIVE POSITION.*

Notes

CHAPTER 1: FROM POLICE REPRESSION TO MILITARY POWER

1. *New York Times*, March 25, 1982. Estimates of the size of the South African Defence Force to 1979 are given in *The Apartheid War Machine* (London: International Defence and Aid Fund, 1980), p 41.

2. *Daily News* (S.A.), February 26, 1982.

3. Simon Jenkins, "The Great Evasion—South Africa Survey," *Economist* (U.K.), June 21, 1980, p. 8.

4. Quoted in the *Financial Mail* (S.A.), December 10, 1979, p. 138.

5. *Survey of Race Relations in South Africa, 1980* (Johannesburg: South African Institute of Race Relations, 1981).

6. *Financial Mail* (S.A.), June 16, 1978.

7. *Financial Mail* (S.A.), June 16, 1978.

8. "The Battle for South Africa," *CBS Reports*, September 1, 1978.

9. *Argus* (S.A.), June 21, 1978.

10. A summary of this incident is given in Dan Smith, *South Africa's Nuclear Capability* (Oslo: World Campaign Against Military and Nuclear Collaboration with South Africa, 1980), p. 9.

11. *Cape Times* (S.A.), July 7, 1978.

12. *Financial Mail* (S.A.), June 23, 1978.

13. John de St. Jorre, *A House Divided: South Africa's Uncertain Future* (New York: Carnegie Endowment for International Peace, 1977), pp. 24-25, quotes the *Newsweek* article (October 25, 1976) and provides a description of trends in National Party politics in that period.

14. *Natal Witness* (S.A.), August 25, 1977.

15. *Sunday Times* (S.A.), March 13, 1977; see also De St. Jorre, *A House Divided*, pp. 23-25.

16. De St. Jorre, *A House Divided*, p. 77, refers to the South African military's advocacy of sending more forces into Angola. Former South African Information Department Secretary Eschel Rhoodie's claims about risky military plans were made in an interview with *Elseviers* magazine (Netherlands), August, 1979, translated in *Facts and Reports*, Holland Committee on Southern Africa, August 31, 1979, pp. 25-26.

17. See John Seiler, "A Government Against the World," *Africa Report*, September-October 1979, p. 10, and De St. Jorre, *A House Divided*, pp. 79-81.

18. De St. Jorre, *A House Divided*, pp. 23-24.

19. *Star* (S.A.), October 22, 1978.

20. *Africa* (U.K.), November 1978, p. 60; *Rand Daily Mail* (S.A.), August 15, 1979.

21. John Fullerton, "South Africa: Day of the Generals," *NOW* (U.K.), October 5, 1979, pp. 23-24.

22. *Sunday Times* (S.A.), October 22, 1978.

23. *Christian Science Monitor*, July 8, 1979.

24. *Star* (S.A.), July 21, 1979.

25. *Cape Times* (S.A.), July 21, 1979.

26. House of Assembly, *Debates* (S.A.), April 23, 1979, column 4776.

27. *Rand Daily Mail* (S.A.), March 3, 1979: Senate *Debates* (S.A.), March 1, 1979, quoted in *Focus*, no. 25, November-December 1979, p. 15.

28. *Natal Witness* (S.A.), August 13, 1979.

29. *Rand Daily Mail* (S.A.), September 12, 1979.

30. Department of Defence, Republic of South Africa, *White Paper on Defence and Armaments Supply*, 1979, p. 1.

31. *Newsweek*, September 29, 1980.

32. South Africa, *White Paper on Defence, 1979*, pp. 24-25.

33. *Financial Mail* (S.A.), June 1, 1979.

34. Figures on failure to report for military service are from *House of Assembly Debates* (S.A.), February 17 and 22, 1979, cited in statement of the Committee on South African War Resistance (COSAWR), London, August 1979. See also "War Resistance: A Response to Apartheid Militarization," COSAWR, November 1979.

35. *Financial Times* (U.K.), July 3, 1978.

36. *Survey of Race Relations in South Africa, 1980* (Johannesburg: South African Institute of Race Relations, 1981), p. 205.

37. *Argus* (S.A.), May 29, 1979.

38. *Survey of Race Relations, 1981*, pp. 214-16.

39. *International Herald Tribune*, January 31, 1980, and March 15, 1980; *Guardian* (U.K.), October 21, 1980.

40. *New York Times*, July 16, 1980.

41. *New York Times*, February 16, 1982.

CHAPTER 2: THE BLACK STRUGGLE FOR FREEDOM

1. *International Herald Tribune*, June 3, 1980; *Le Monde*, June 3, 1980.

2. *Le Monde*, June 4, 1980.

3. Quoted in *Southern Africa*, July-August, 1980, p. 7.

4. Ibid., p. 21.

5. See Tom Lodge, "The African National Congress in South Africa, 1976-1982; Guerrilla War and Armed Propaganda" (Paper delivered at the annual conference of the African Studies Association, Washington, D.C., October 1983), p. 1 and fn 1, p. 15; *New York Times*, May 23, 1983.

6. *Focus* 44 (January-February 1983), pp. 11-12.

7. Glenn Moss, *The Wheels Turn: South African Political Trials, 1976-1979* (Geneva: International University Exchange Fund, 1979), p. 4.

8. Monica Wilson and Leonard Thompson, eds., *The Oxford History of South Africa*, 2 vols. (London: Oxford University Press, 1969), 1:232.

9. Ibid., 2:330.

10. Quoted in Mary Benson, *South Africa: The Struggle for a Birthright* (Harmondsworth: Penguin Books, 1966), p. 25.

11. Thomas Karis and Gwendolen Carter, eds., *From Protest to Challenge: A Documentary History of African Politics in South Africa*, 4 vols. (Stanford: Hoover Institution Press, 1972-77), 2:300.

12. H. J. and R. E. Simons, *Class and Colour in South Africa, 1850-1950* (Harmondsworth: Penguin Books, 1969), p. 575; Bernard Makhosezwe Magubane, *The Political Economy of Race and Class in South Africa* (New York: Monthly Review Press, 1979), p. 294, cites private estimates that hundreds of miners were killed.

13. Karis and Carter, *From Protest to Challenge*, 2:427.

14. Ibid., 3:115.

15. Ibid., 3:246.

16. Conversation with Thomas Karis, quoted in Ibid., 3:516.

17. African National Congress of South Africa, *ANC Speaks: Documents and Statements of the African National Congress, 1955-1976* [no place or date of publication] pp. 26-27.

18. Muriel Horrell, ed., *A Survey of Race Relations in South Africa, 1961* (Johannesburg: South African Institute of Race Relations, 1962), p. 52.

19. Karis and Carter, *From Protest to Challenge*, 3:671.

20. Ibid., 3:796.

21. LSM Information Center, *South Africa-ANC: Interview with Alfred Nzo* (Richmond, B.C., Canada: LSM Press, 1974), p. 20; Joe Slovo, "South Africa—No Middle Road," in Basil Davidson, Joe Slovo, Anthony R. Wilkinson, *Southern Africa: The New Politics of Revolution* (Harmondsworth: Penguin Books, 1976), pp. 185-96.

22. African National Congress, *ANC Speaks*, p. 189.

23. For background on the Black Consciousness Movement, see Baruch Hirson, *Year of Fire, Year*

of Ash (London: Zed Press, 1979) and Gail Gerhart, *Black Power in South Africa: The Evolution of an Ideology* (Berkeley: University of California Press, 1978).

24. Hirson, *Year of Fire, Year of Ash*, p. 201.

25. *Sechaba*, March 1980, pp. 7-8.

26. *Post* (S.A.), October 14, 1979.

27. Bruce D. Larkin, *China and Africa, 1949-1970* (Berkeley: University of California Press, 1971), pp. 186-93.

28. United Nations Development Program, "Assistance to Colonial Countries and Peoples During 1978," DP/362 March 23, 1979.

29. See *Africa Contemporary Record, 1976-77*, p. B816; ibid., 1977-79, p. B903; *Star* (S.A.), December 14, 1979.

30. *Rand Daily Mail* (S.A.), June 2, 1978.

31. *Sunday Times* (S.A.), November 12, 1978.

32. The expelled ANC members issued T. Bonga et al., "Statement on the Expulsion from the ANC (SA)," London, December 27, 1975. The ANC statement on the expulsion appeared in *Sechaba* 10, no. 2 (1976):40-43.

33. For background on the South African Communist party, see its quarterly journal, *African Communist* (London); A. Lerumo, *Fifty Fighting Years: The Communist Party of South Africa,1921-1971* (London: Ikululeku Publications, 1971); H. J. and R. E. Simons, *Class and Colour in South Africa, 1850-1950* (Harmondsworth: Penguin Books, 1969).

34. For comments on membership, see Simons and Simons, *Class and Colour in South Africa*, p. 505; Karis and Carter, *From Protest to Challenge*, 2:408; Joe Slovo, "South Africa—No Middle Road," p. 157; and *African Communist* 65 (second quarter, 1976):35.

35. Karis and Carter, *From Protest to Challenge*, 3:789.

36. Ibid., 3:678.

37. John S. Saul and Stephen Gelb, *The Crisis in South Africa, Monthly Review* (July-August 1981), p. 141.

38. Quoted in Washington Office on Africa, *Washington Notes on Africa* (Spring 1982), p. 6.

39. *Africa Report*, September-October 1981, p. 21.

40. *New York Times*, February 7, 1982.

41. United Nation Development Program, "Assistance to Colonial Countries and Peoples During 1978"; "Non-Governmental Organizations: Actions Against Apartheid" (Geneva: International University Exchange Fund, 1978).

42. ANC statement on the end of the International Year Against Apartheid, Lusaka, Zambia, March 21, 1979.

43. Study Commission on U.S. Policy Toward Southern Africa, *South Africa: Time Running Out* (Berkeley: University of California Press, 1981).

44. *New York Times*, February 7, 1982.

45. Barry Streek, "Black Strategies Against Apartheid," *Africa Report*, July-August, 1980.

46. *New York Times*, December 3, 1981.

47. *Africa News*, April 28, 1980.

48. *New York Times*, November 30, 1980.

49. *New York Times*, December 3, 1981.

50. *Africa News*, March 24, 1980.

51. *Rand Daily Mail* (S.A.), June 15, 1978; *Financial Mail* (S.A.), June 16, 1978.

52. George Philip Quail et al., *Ciskei Commission Report* (Silverton, South Africa: Conference Associates, 1980) p. 193.

53. *Africa News*, November 2, 1981 (based on a poll taken by the Johannesburg *Star*).

54. Lewis L. Gann and Peter Duignan, *South Africa: War? Revolution? Peace?* (Stanford: Hoover Institution Press, 1979).

55. David Halberstam, "The Fire to Come in South Africa," *Atlantic Monthly*, May and June, 1980.

56. Bob Hitchcock, "Guerrillas: Pretoria Shaken by Attacks," *New African*, September 1981, p. 46.

57. Heribert Adam, *Modernizing Racial Domination* (Berkeley: University of California Press, 1971).

58. Saul and Gelb, *The Crisis in South Africa*, pp. 102-49.

59. Tom Lodge, "The African National Congress in South Africa, 1976-1982," pp. 1, 14.

60. *New York Times*, August 18, 1981.

61. *Africa News*, November 24, 1980.

62. *African News*, November 1, 8, 1982, pp. 1-3.

CHAPTER 3: THE WAR IN NAMIBIA AND REGIONAL AGGRESSION

1. *Sunday Telegraph* (U.K.), March 22, 1981; Colonel Norman L. Dodd, "South African Operations and Deployments in South West Africa/Namibia," *Army Quarterly and Defence Journal* 110, no. 3 (July

1980): 291-300, cited in Onkar Marwah, "Namibia: A Strategic Assessment" (Paper delivered at the Seminar on the Military Situation in and Relating to Namibia, United Nations Council For Namibia, Vienna, June 8-11, 1982).

2. *New York Times*, March 24, 1982.

3. An overview of the Namibian economy is provided in UN Commission on Transnational Corporations, "The Activities of Transnational Corporations in the Industrial, Mining, and Military Sectors of Southern Africa" (E/C.10/51), March 22, 1979. United Nations, Council for Namibia,"Namibian Uranium" 1982, provides a summary of hearings on the issue held by the Council, July 7-11, 1980.

4. United Nations, Office of Public Information, *A Trust Betrayed: Namibia* (1974), p. 37.

5. This estimate was made in a UN research paper cited in the *Guardian* (U.K.), September 1, 1976. See also *The Apartheid War Machine* (London: International Defense and Air Fund, 1980), pp. 61-62.

6. A. J. Venter, writing in *Scope* (S.A.), "Special Forces Supplement," Part I, October 7, 1977, p. 12.

7. The reports following were cited in the United Nations, *Report on Namibia* (A/33/23 Add. 2), September 29, 1978.

8. Republic of South Africa, Department of Defence, *White Paper on Defence, 1977*, published as a supplement to *Paratus*, May 1977, pp. xiii-ix.

9. Cited in United Nations, *Working Paper on Namibia* (A/AC.109/L.1238), June 22, 1978.

10. *Cape Times* (S.A.), June 7, 1978.

11. *Apartheid's Army in Namibia* (London: International Defence and Aid Fund, 1982), p. 34.

12. Paul Wee, "Notes from Namibia—29 June 1979," *Bulletin of Episcopal Churchmen for South Africa* (New York), July 1979.

13. *Guardian* (U.K.), August 30, 1976.

14. H. Hunke and J. Ellis, *Torture: A Cancer in Our Society* (London: Catholic Institute for International Relations, in cooperation with the British Council of Churches, 1978), pp. 8-9.

15. Wee, "Notes from Namibia—29 June 1979."

16. The reports following are quoted in William Johnston, "The South African War Against the People of Namibia" (Paper delivered at the Seminar on the Military Situation in and Relating to Namibia, United Nations Council for Namibia, Vienna, June 8-11, 1982).

17. *Guardian* (U.K.), January 29, 1981.

18. *New York Times*, June 17, 1981.

19. *New York Times*, January 6, 1981.

20. Ibid.

21. John Stockwell, *In Search of Enemies* (New York: W. W. Norton & Co., 1978), p. 54.

22. Ibid., pp. 187-88.

23. *New York Times*, July 18, 1982.

24. *Focus* 17 (July 1978): 8; United Nations, Security Council (S/13473), July 27, 1979, p. 8.

25. *International Herald Tribune*, December 8, 1978.

26. *Le Monde*, November 29, 1979.

27. *Guardian* (U.K.), January 29, 1981.

28. Documentation from the International Commission of Inquiry meeting in Angola is provided in *Focus*, Special Issue No. 2, April 1981.

29. *Africa Confidential*, December 9, 1981.

30. René Lefort, "Le Pouvoir Noir au Zimbabwe,"*Le Monde Diplomatique* 314 (May 1980): 10.

31. *Southern Africa* 13, no. 5 (June 1980): 8.

32. John de St. Jorre, *A House Divided: South Africa's Uncertain Future* (New York: Carnegie Endowment for International Peace, 1977),pp. 73-74.

33. See Martin Bailey, *Oilgate: The Sanctions Scandal* (London: Coronet Books, 1979).

34. *Guardian* (U.K.), April 19, 1978.

35. "Muldergate: The Eschel Rhoodie Story," *Elseviers Magazine* (Netherlands), August 1979, translated in *Facts and Reports* (Holland Committee on Southern Africa) August 31, 1979, p. 25; Karen Rothmyer, "The South Africa Lobby," *Nation*, April 19, 1980, p. 498.

36. *New York Times*, December 23, 1979.

37. *New York Times*, April 23, 1979.

38. *Guardian* (U.K.), October 6, 1979; *New York Times*, December 1, 1979; Lefort, "Le Pouvoir Noir au Zimbabwe," p. 10.

39. *New York Times*, January 29, 1983.

40. *New York Times*, January 3, 1983.

41. *New York Times*, February 27, 1983.

42. Cited in *Africa News*, September 13, 1982.

43. *New York Times*, October 13, 1980; Allan Isaacman, interview with President Samora Machel, *Africa Report*, July-August 1979, p. 40.

44. *New York Times*, February 14, 1982.

45. *Washington Notes on Africa*, Winter 1981, p. 3.

46. *New York Times*, November 1, 1982.

47. *Africa News*, September 6, 1982.

48. *New York Times*, January 4, 1983.
49. *New York Times* April 22, 1982, and May 10, 1982.
50. *New York Times*, January 29, 1983.
51. *International Herald Tribune*, June 8, 1982.
52. *New York Times*, May 1, 1982.
53. Flora Lewis, "South Africa's Israel Mask," *New York Times*, January 28, 1983.
54. *New York Times*, January 23, 1983.
55. Interview with Joseph Lelyveld, *New York Times*, February 17, 1983.
56. Flora Lewis, "Pax Afrikaansa," *New York Times*, January 25, 1983.
57. Ibid.
58. *New York Times*, January 29, 1983.
59. *New York Times*, December 10, 1982.
60. *Africa News*, February 14, 1983.
61. *Focus* 44 (January-February 1983), pp. 1-2.
62. Cf. excerpts of a speech by Lawrence S. Eagleburger, Undersecretary of State for Political Affairs, June 23, 1983, in *New York Times*, June 24, 1983.

CHAPTER 4: SOUTH AFRICAN MILITARY, POLICE AND SECURITY FORCES

1. Republic of South Africa, Department of Defence, *Defence White Paper*, 1977; Supplement to *Paratus* (S.A.), May 1977, p. vii. (Cited hereafter as *Defence White Paper*,1977).
2. *Star* (S.A.), December 17, 1974, cited in Cynthia H. Enloe, "Ethnic Factors in the Evolution of the South African Military," *Issue* 5, no. 4 (Winter 1975): 23.
3. *Citizen* (S.A.), September 4, 1980.
4. Republic of South Africa, Department of Defence, *White Paper on Defence and Armaments Supply*, 1982.
5. Ibid., p. xiii; *Official Yearbook of the Republic of South Africa, 1979* (Johannesburg: Rensburg, 1979), p. 325; *The Apartheid War Machine* (London: International Defence and Aid Fund, 1980), pp. 19-33.
6. *Apartheid War Machine*, p. 20.
7. *House of Assembly Debates*, Questions and Replies, February 16, 1979.
8. *Apartheid War Machine*, pp. 32-35; John Prados, "Sealanes, Western Strategy and Southern Africa," in *U.S. Military Involvement in Southern Africa*, ed. Western Massachusetts Association of Concerned African Scholars (Boston: South End Press, 1978), pp. 66-70.
9. Bernard Marks, *Our South African Army Today* (Capetown: Purnell, 1977).
10. Al J. Venter, "Recce Commandos," *Soldier of Fortune* (U.S.), July 1978, p. 40.
11. *Apartheid War Machine*, p. 21.
12. *Sunday Tribune* (S.A.), April 24, 1979; *Paratus* (S.A.), June 1979, p. 38.
13. *Windhoek Observer* (Namibia), August 19, 1980, cited in "The South African Military Occupation of Namibia," mimeographed (London: Committee on South African War Resistance, January 1981), p. 11; Helmoed-Romer Hetlman, "SWATF," *Armed Forces* (S.A.), September 1980, pp. 8-11; *Cape Times* (S.A.), October 9, 1980.
14. United Nations Security Council, Supplementary Report of the Security Council Commission of Inquiry Established Under Resolution 496 (1981), S/15492, November 17, 1982, pp. 18-22.
15. *Observer* (London), September 28, 1980.
16. *Guardian* (U.K.), January 9, 1981.
17. *Financial Times* (U.K.), February 7, 1981.
18. Jennifer Davis, "South Africa's Secret War," *Southern Africa*, March-April 1981, pp. 18-19.
19. *Defense White Paper, 1977*, p.xii.
20. *The Military Balance 1981-82* (London: International Institute for Strategic Studies, 1980).
21. *International Herald Tribune*, April 25, 1979.
22. *Debates*, April 24, 1979, column 4850.
23. Leo Marquard, *The People and Policies of South Africa* (London: Oxford, 1962), p. 27.
24. *House of Assembly Debates*, April 20, 1979, columns 2894-95.
25. Cynthia H. Enloe, "Ethnic Factors," pp. 24-25.
26. *International Herald Tribune*, April 25, 1979.
27. *Rand Daily Mail* (S.A.), May 25, 1980; *Observer* (London), September 28, 1980.
28. *Survey of Race Relations* (1978), p. 55.
29. *International Herald Tribune*, April 25, 1979.
30. Ibid.
31. *Debates*, April 24, 1979, column 4812.
32. *Survey of Race Relations* (1978), p. 55.

33. Ibid., *Post* (S.A.), June 18, 1978.
34. *Focus* 8, January 1977, pp. 14-15; *Focus* 12, October 1977, p. 7; *Focus* 13, November 1977, p.15; *Focus* 15, March 1977, p. 15.
35. *Daily Dispatch* (S.A.), June 12, 1978.
36. *International Herald Tribune*, April 25, 1979.
37. *Survey of Race Relations* (1978), p. 55.
38. *Cape Times* (S.A.), July 7, 1978.
39. *Survey of Race Relations* (1978), p. 56.
40. *Financial Times* (U.K.), July 5, 1979.
41. *Star* (S.A.), July 12, 1979.
42. *House of Assembly Debates*, April 24, 1979, columns 4838-40; 1977 *Defence White Paper*, p. xvi.
43. *Survey of Race Relations* (1978) p. 5.
44. *House of Assembly Debates*, April 23, 1979, column 4750.
45. *House of Assembly Debates*, April 23, 1979, column 4740.
46. *Guardian* (U.K.), May 19, 1979.
47. *Financial Times* (U.K.), July 5, 1978.
48. *Citizen* (S.A.), July 17, 1979; *Rand Daily Mail* (S.A.), July 13, 1979.
49. *House of Assembly Debates*, April 24, 1979, column 4800.
50. *Financial Mail* (S.A.), June 1, 1979.
51. *House of Assembly Debates*, April 24, 1979, columns 4816 and 4846.
52. *House of Assembly Debates*, April 20, 1979, columns 2894-95.
53. *Star* (S.A.), September 23, 1978.
54. Republic of South Africa, Department of Defence, *White Paper on Defence and Armaments Supply, 1979* (Cape Town: Naval Printing Office, 1979), p. 5.
55. *Defence White Paper*, 1979, p. 16; *Debates* (Questions & Replies), April 21, 1979, columns 485-87.
56. *Survey of Race Relations* (1977), p. 90.
57. *Survey of Race Relations* (1978), p. 56.
58. Ibid.; *Graphic* (S.A.), June 23, 1978.
59. From *Wits Student* (University of Witwatersrand), cited in *Resister* 4 (Committee on South African War Resistance, London), pp. 9-10.
60. *Yearbook of the Republic of South Africa*, 1979, pp. 314-16.
61. *Survey of Race Relations* (1979), p. 105.
62. Ibid., p. 106; (1977), p. 105.
63. *Apartheid War Machine*, pp. 44-45.
64. *Survey of Race Relations* (1977), pp. 108-15; *Defence White Paper, 1977*, p. xiv.
65. *Survey of Race Relations* (1979), p. 106.
66. Ibid. (1977), p. 106; *Apartheid War Machine*, pp. 44-46.
67. *BOSS: The First Five Years* (London: International Defence and Aid Fund, 1975), p. 7.
68. Cited in *Work in Progress* (University of Witwatersand, Johannesburg), March 1979, p. 16.
69. *New African*, March 1980, pp. 17-18; September 1980, pp. 30-32.
70. *Political Imprisonment in South Africa* (London: Amnesty International, 1978), p. 9.
71. United Nations, Human Rights Commission, E/CN.4/1366, January 31, 1980, p. 80.
72. *Work in Progress*, pp. 17-18.
73. *Survey of Race Relations* (1978), pp. 15-16.
74. *Rand Daily Mail* (S.A.), June 7, 1978.
75. *Survey of Race Relations* (1978), pp. 70-71.
76. *Guardian* (U.K.), November 14, 1979; *Observer* (London), January 16, 1980.
77. Republic of South Africa *Government Gazette*, May 16, 1969, cited in *BOSS: The First Five Years*, p. 11.
78. *Potgeiter Report*, p. 34 cited in *BOSS: The First Five Years*, pp. 19-20.
79. *Rand Daily Mail* (S.A.), June 5, 1979.
80. *BOSS: The First Five Years*, pp. 29-31.
81. *Survey of Race Relations* (1978), p. 122.
82. *Rand Daily Mail* (S.A.), June 30, 1979.
83. *Observer* (London), December 30, 1979; January 6, 1980; January 13, 1980.
84. *Africa News*, April 7, 1980.
85. John Stockwell, *In Search of Enemies* (New York: W. W. Norton & Co., 1978), pp. 187-88.
86. *Update* (African-American Institute, New York), March 25, 1981, p. 1.
87. *Rapport* (S.A.), June 17, 1978, p. 1, cited in *Guardian* (U.K.), June 19, 1978.
88. *Observer* (London), February 4, 1979.
89. *Rand Daily Mail* (S.A.), November 19, 1979.
90. *Rand Daily Mail* (S.A.), November 15, 1979.
91. *Sunday Times* (S.A.), November 18, 1979.
92. *Africa News*, January 3, 1983.
93. *Financial Mail* (S.A.), March 20, 1981.
94. Ibid.

95. *New York Times*, May 10, 1982.
96. Ibid.
97. *BOSS: The First Five Years*, pp. 8 and 21.
98. *Defence White Paper, 1977*, p. viii; see also *Debates*, March 23, 1979, column 4793.

CHAPTER 5: ARMS FOR APARTHEID

1. *Financial Mail* (S.A.), April 7, 1981.
2. International Defence and Aid Fund, "The British Embargo on Arms for South Africa," London, 1968, pp. 8-9; Comité Francais Contre l'Apartheid, "Contribution au Dossier sur la Vente D'Armes à l'Afrique de Sud," Paris, n.d., p. 1. Statement on February 20, 1968, quoted in International Defence and Aid Fund, "The British Embargo on Arms for South Africa," p. 5.
3. United States, Mission to the United Nations: Press Release No. 4233, August 2, 1963, quoted in Sean Gervasi, *The United States and the Arms Embargo Against South Africa: Evidence, Denial, and Refutation* (Binghamton, N.Y.: Fernand Braudel Center, State University of New York at Binghamton, 1978), p. 7.
4. Listings of French weapons supplied to South Africa appear in annual editions of *The Military Balance* (London: International Institute for Strategic Studies) and *Yearbook of World Armaments and Disarmament* (Uppsala): Stockholm International Peace Research Institute [(SIPRI)]. On French rationales for its policies see Abdul S. Minty, *South Africa's Defense Strategy* (London: Anti-Apartheid Movement, 1971), pp. 2-4.
5. See Gervasi, *United States and the Arms Embargo*; Michael T. Klare and Eric Prokosch, "Getting Arms to South Africa," *Nation*, July 8-15, 1978; and Michael T. Klare, "South Africa's U.S. Weapon's Connections," *Nation*, August 4, 1979.
6. See annual editions of *The Military Balance* and *Yearbook of World Armaments and Disarmement*; see also *Arms to Apartheid, South Africa: A National Profile*, British Anti-Apartheid Movement, March 1981.
7. There has been an extended polemic between the West German Anti-Apartheid Movement (Bonn) and the German government on the issue of nuclear and military cooperation with South Africa. Recent publications are the government's *Fact vs. Fiction* (October 10, 1978) and the West German Anti-Apartheid Movement's *Reply* (Bonn, December 1979). See also "Legal Obligations and Possibilities of the Government of the Federal Republic of Germany. . ." a paper delivered at the International Seminar on the Arms Embargo Against South Africa of the United Nations Centre Against Apartheid, London, April 1-3, 1981, by the West German Anti-Apartheid Movement.
8. Maxwell J. Mehlman, Thomas H. Milch, and Michael V. Toumanoff, "United States Restrictions on Exports to South Africa," *American Journal of International Law*. 73 no. 4 (October 1979): Sean Gervasi, *The United States and the Arms Embargo Against South Africa*; Michael T. Klare, "South Africa's Weapon's Connections."
9. A description of Silvermine by a source sympathetic to the Nationalist government is provided in Ian Greig, *The Communist Challenge to Africa* (Surrey, England: Foreign Affairs Publishing Co., 1977), p. 35. See also Michael T. Kaufman, "Ports and Oil Spur Naval Buildup by U.S. and Soviet," *New York Times*, April 20, 1981, p. A12; John Prados, "Sealanes, Western Strategy, and South Africa," in *U.S. Military Involvement in Southern Africa*, ed. Western Massachusetts Association of Concerned African Scholars (Boston: South End Press, 1978), p. 61; and Wolff Geisler, "The Apartheid Regime of South Africa: NATO's Advocate Against Africa," mimeographed; translated from *Informationsdienst Südliches Afrika* (Bonn), January-March 1981, pp. 4-8.
10. *Observer* (London), May 19, 1974, cited in Prados, "Sealanes, Western Strategy, and South Africa," p. 69; Wolff Geisler, "The Apartheid Regime of South Africa," p. 7.
11. Abdul S. Minty, "The International Arms Embargo Against South Africa" (Paper presented by the Director of the World Campaign Against Military and Nuclear Collaboration with South Africa [Oslo, Norway] to the United Nations International Seminar on the Arms Embargo Against South Africa, London, April 1-3, 1981), pp. 1-2.
12. *Financial Mail* (South Africa), December 5, 1980.
13. *Paratus* (S.A.), March 1974.
14. Abdul S. Minty, *South Africa's Defense Strategy* (London: Anti-Apartheid Movement, 1971), p. 3.
15. *Financial Mail* (S.A.), May 25, 1979.
16. *Financial Mail* (S.A.), December 5, 1980; Republic of South Africa, Department of Defence, *White Paper on Defence and Armaments Supply, 1982* (Cape Town: Government Printers, 1982), p. 25.
17. *New York Times*, December 5, 1982.
18. Ibid.; *Financial Mail* (S.A.), May 25, 1979.
19. *Financial Mail* (S.A.), November 28, 1980); *Defence White Paper*, 1982, p. 25.
20. *Defence White Paper1979*, p. 24.

21. *Financial Mail* (S.A.) December 5, 1980.
22. Muriel Horrell, ed., *A Survey of Race Relations in South Africa, 1977* (Johannesburg: South African Institute of Race Relations, 1977), p. 86.
23. *Star* (S.A.), November 13, 1980.
24. *New York Times*, December 5, 1982.
25. Abdul S. Minty, *South Africa's Defense Strategy*, p. 6.
26. Chester A. Crocker, "Current and Projected Military Balances in Southern Africa," in Richard Bissell and Chester A. Crocker, eds., *South Africa into the 1980s* (Boulder, Colo.: Westview Press, 1979), p. 99; Signe Landgren-Backstrom, *Southern Africa: The Escalation of a Conflict* (Uppsala: Stockholm International Peace Research Institute, 1976), pp. 141-42.
27. *Reply* (Bonn: Anti-Apartheid Movement in the Federal Republic of Germany and West Berlin, 1979), p. 40.
28. Landgren-Backstrom, *Southern Africa*, pp. 129-38; *Yearbook on World Armaments and Disarmament, 1976*, pp. 246-47.
29. *Yearbook on World Armaments and Disarmament, 1979*; Klare and Prokosch, "Getting Arms to South Africa"; Langren-Backstrom, *Southern Africa*.
30. The report of the UN Centre on Transnational Corporations, "The Activities of Transnational Corporations in the Industrial, Mining and Military Sectors of Southern Africa" (ST/CTC/12), 1980, citing Landgren-Backstrom and other sources, indicates that South Africa is able to produce all components for the F-1 except the engines; but given the sophistication of these aircraft, this is unlikely: the comprehensive study by Chester A. Crocker, which included interviews with current and former Atlas Aircraft Corporation employees, indicates that the Mirages are *not* among the weapons in which South Africa has achieved high self-sufficiency and that their production involves local assembly of imported components. (See Study Commission on U.S. Policy Toward Southern Africa, *South Africa: Time Running Out* [Berkeley: University of California Press, 1981], p. 251, and Crocker, "Current and Projected Military Balances," in Bissell and Crocker, p. 100.) *The Military Balance, 1979-80* indicates substantial self-sufficiency achieved by South Africa in the production only of airframes for advanced aircraft, which would be Mirages.
31. *Financial Mail* (S.A.), February 16, 1979; ibid., Transport Supplement, March 30, 1979.
32. Landgren-Backstrom, *Southern Africa: The Escalation of a Conflict*, pp. 131-32.
33. Much of the information about the Space Research Corporation case has been provided by investigative journalists, including a November 1978 program on "Panorama" (BBC television in Britain), the WGBH/TV (Boston) program "Hot Shells: U.S. Arms for South Africa," January 1979, and a series of stories by reporters Sam Hemingway and William Scott Malone in the *Burlington* (Vt) *Free Press* in 1979-80. A summary report on the case has been prepared by James Cason for the Africa Fund, New York (1981); see also Michael T. Klare, "South Africa's Weapons Connections," and *Arms to Apartheid: A National Profile*, (London: British Anti-Apartheid Movement, 1981), pp. 6-7.
34. *Jane's Fighting Ships, 1980; Observer* (London), October 1980; *The Military Balance*, 1980-81; West German Anti-Apartheid Movement, *Reply*, p. 30.
35. *Financial Mail* (S.A.), April 17, 1981; *To the Point* (S.A.), June 1, 1979, p. 34.
36. *Jane's Weapons Systems*, 1981, p. 225.
37. *Newsweek*, September 29, 1980, p. 44.
38. *Jane's Weapons Systems*, 1982, p. 254.
39. *Rand Daily Mail* (S.A.), October 16, 1981.
40. Department of Defence, Republic of South Africa, *White Paper on Defence and Armaments Supply, 1979*, pp. 24-26.
41. *Financial Mail* (S.A.), May 25, 1979.
42. *New York Times*, December 5, 1982.
43. *Financial Mail* (S.A.), December 5, 1980.
44. *Guardian* (U.K.), December 5, 1973.
45. *Financial Mail* (S.A.), December 5, 1980.
46. *Financial Mail* (S.A.), May 25, 1979.
47. *Electronics and Instrumentation* (S.A.), January, 1979, quoted in Thomas Conrad, *Automating Apartheid: U.S. Electronics and Computer Support for South Africa's Apartheid Government* (Philadelphia: American Friends Service Committee, 1981), p. 18.
48. Conrad, *Automating Apartheid*, p. 19.
49. Ann Seidman and Neva Seidman Makgetla, *Outposts of Monopoly Capitalism* (Westport, Conn.: Lawrence Hill, 1980), pp. 160-61.
50. *Financial Mail* (S.A.), December 14, 1979.
51. Jennifer Davis, "General Motors in South Africa: Secret Contingency Plans in the Event of Civil Unrest" (New York: The Africa Fund, 1978).
52. *Financial Mail* (S.A.), January 23, 1981.
53. *African Business* (U.K.), August, 1979; *Financial Mail* (S.A.), March 6, 1981.
54. See Ronald W. Walters, "U.S. Policy and Nuclear Proliferation in South Africa," in Western Massachusetts Association of Concerned African Scholars, eds., *U.S. Military Involvement in Southern*

Africa (Boston: South End Press, 1978), pp. 172-76; and Dan Smith, *South Africa's Nuclear Capability* (Oslo: World Campaign Against Military and Nuclear Collaboration with South Africa, 1980), p. 8.

55. *Washington Post*, February 16, 1977.

56. *Star* (S.A.), January 6, 1978.

57. Dan Smith, *South Africa's Nuclear Capability*, pp. 17-18.

58. *Reply*, West German Anti-Apartheid Movement, pp. 13, 23, 104.

59. *Times* (London) and other press reports cited in Abdul S. Minty, *South Africa's Defense Strategy*, p. 5.

60. Martin Bailey and Bernard Rivers, "Oil Sanctions Against South Africa," United Nations Centre Against Apartheid, June 1978. See also "Oiltankers to South Africa" (Amsterdam: Shipping Research Bureau, March 1981).

61. Chester A. Crocker, *South Africa's Defense Posture: Coping with Vulnerability*, Washington Papers, No. 84 (Beverly Hills and London: Sage Publications, 1981), p. 46.

62. Ibid., p. 51.

63. *Washington Post*, April 6, 1981.

64. Letter of April 22, 1980, from the United States to the United Nations Security Council Committee on the Arms Embargo Against South Africa, cited in the Committee's report of September 19, 1980 (S/14179).

65. U.S., Congress, House, Subcommittee on Africa, *The Space Research Case and the Breakdown of the U.S. Arms Embargo Against South Africa*, Staff Study, March 24, 1982.

66. Transcript of "Dr. Gerald Bull," Canadian Television, W-5, March 22, 1981, pp. 14-15. Testimony of Undersecretary of State for African Affairs Richard Moose, April 30, 1980, in U.S., Congress, House, Committee on Foreign Relations, *U.S. Policy Toward Southern Africa, Hearings*, before the Subcommittee on Africa, House of Representatives, 96th Congress, 1st Sess., 1980, p. 31.

67. Quoted in Gervasi, *The United States and the Arms Embargo Against South Africa*, pp. 38-39.

68. U.S., Congress, House, Committee on International Relations, *United States-South African Relations, Hearings*, before the Subcommittee on Africa, House of Representatives, 95th Cong., 1st sess., 1977, p. 62, quoted in Maxwell J. Mehlman, Thomas H. Milch, and Michael V. Toumanoff, "United States Restrictions on Exports to South Africa," *American Journal of International Law* 73, no. 4 (October 1979):595.

69. William Safire, "The Carrington Shadow," *New York Times*, February 23, 1981.

70. Report of the U.N. Security Council Committee on the Arms Embargo Against South Africa, September 19, 1980 (S/14179), p. 10.

71. U.S., Congress, *United States-Southern Africa Relations, Hearings*, 1977, p. 59, quoted in Mehlman et al., "United States Restrictions on Exports to South Africa," p. 595.

72. Karen Rothmyer, "U.S. Motor Industry in South Africa," The Africa Fund, New York, 1978, p. 2.

73. Additional Questions Submitted by the Subcommittee to Assistant Secretary of State Moose and Responses Thereto, *U.S. Congress, U.S. Policy Toward Southern Africa, Hearings*, 1980, p. 744.

74. Testimony of Richard Moose in Ibid., p. 5.

75. Quoted in Additional Questions Submitted to Moose, ibid., p. 745.

76. *Newsweek*, September 29, 1980.

77. Geisler, "The Apartheid Regime of South Africa: NATO's Advocate Against Africa," p. 2.

78. Statement of Franklin D. Kramer, Principal Deputy Assistant Secretary of Defense for International Security Affairs, April 30, 1980, House Committee on International Relations, *U.S. Policy Towards Southern Africa, Hearings*, 1980, pp. 8-9.

79. Chester A. Crocker, "Current and Projected Military Balances in Southern Africa," pp. 71, 80.

80. Ibid.

81. Study Commission on U.S. Policy Toward Southern Africa, *South Africa: Time Running Out*, p. 249.

82. Ibid.

83. Chester A. Crocker, "South Africa: Strategy for Change," *Foreign Affairs*, Winter 1980, p. 346.

84. *International Herald Tribune*, July 22, 1981; *New York Times*, May 14, 1981

85. *New York Times*, March 21, 1982.

86. *Africa News*, February 14, 1983.

87. The cases are described in *Africa News*, September 27, 1982.

88. *Financial Times* (U.K.), August 18, 1981.

89. *New York Times*, May 8, 1982.

90. *New York Times*, December 14, 1981.

91. *Flight International*, July 27, 1981.

92. *New York Times*, February 12, 1982.

93. *The Times* (London), October 21, 1981.

94. These cases are described in "Arms to Apartheid South Africa: A National Profile," British Anti-Apartheid Movement, March 1981.

95. *Rand Daily Mail* (S.A.), February 26, 1982; September 9, 1982.

96. Ibid., October 16, 1981.
97. *New York Times*, December 27, 1982.

CHAPTER 6: THE PROPAGANDA WAR

1. *Sunday Express* (S.A.), June 10, 1979.
2. Ferry A. Hoogendijk, "Muldergate: The Eschel Rhoodie Story," *Elseviers* (Netherlands), August 1979. This four-part article is in fact an interview with Rhoodie by Dr. Hoogendijk, the editor of *Elseviers*. It was translated into English and reprinted in *Facts and Reports* 9, no. Q (August 31, 1979), pp. 18-31. References hereafter are to the English version, cited as "Eschel Rhoodie Story."
3. These events are summarized in Galen Hull, "South Africa's Propaganda War," *African Studies Review* 22, no. 3 (December 1979): 85-88.
4. *Guardian* (U.K.), March 16, 1979.
5. "Eschel Rhoodie Story."
6. Mervyn Rees and Chris Day, *Muldergate* (South Africa, Macmillan, 1980). This is a detailed journalistic account of the scandal.
7. *International Herald Tribune*, March 9, 1979; December 12, 1978.
8. *Supplementary Report of the Commission of Inquiry into Alleged Irregularities in the Former Department of Information*, RP 63/1979 (Pretoria: Government Printer, 1979), p. 43. Hereafter cited as *Erasmus Commission, Supplementary Report*.
9. *Sunday Express* (S.A.) June 10, 1979.
10. *Africa News*, October 6, 1980.
11. *Times* (London), November 25, 1980.
12. Hull, "South Africa's Propaganda War."
13. *International Herald Tribune*, March 12, 1979.
14. Karen Rothmyer, "The South Africa Lobby," *Nation*, April 19, 1980, p. 456.
15. Rees and Day, *Muldergate*, pp. 163-64.
16. *Erasmus Commission, Supplementary Report*, pp. 45-48.
17. Rothmyer, "South Africa Lobby," p. 458; *Rand Daily Mail* (S.A.), June 27, 1979.
18. Donald K. Thrasher and James G. Newland, Jr. "South African Story Involves SerVaas, 'Post,'" *Indianapolis Star*, March 23, 1980.
19. Ibid.
20. *Rand Daily Mail* (S.A.), June 27, 1979.
21. Thrasher and Newland, "South African Story."
22. "Eschel Rhoodie Story," p. 19.
23. *International Herald Tribune*, Mar. 12, 1979.
24. "Eschel Rhoodie Story," p. 29.
25. *Rand Daily Mail* (S.A.), June 29, 1974, cited in Julian Burgess, et al., *The Great White Hoax* (London: The Africa Bureau, 1977) p. 64.
26. Anthony Sampson, "The Long Reach of the Arms Men," *Observer* (London), April 26, 1979.
27. *Citizen* (S.A.) March 20, 1980.
28. *Africa News*, Oct. 6, 1980.
27. *Citizen* (S.A.), March 20, 1980.
28. *Africa News*, Oct. 6, 1980.
29. *Rand Daily Mail* (S.A.), July 8, 1980.
30. *Citizen* (S.A.) March 20, 1980.
31. Julian Burgess et al., *The Great White Hope* (London: The Africa Bureau, 1976), p. 31.
32. "Moon Shines on Apartheid," *Washington Notes on Africa* (Washington Office on Africa), Summer 1982.
33. *Rand Daily Mail* (S.A.), July 16, 1980; *Africa News*, October 6, 1980.
34. *Africa News*, December 15, 1980.
35. *Sunday Times* (S.A.), November 5, 1978.
36. *Erasmus Commission, Supplementary Report*, p. 24; *Sunday Times* (South Africa), June 8, 1979.
37. *Africa News*, November 20, 1978.
38. *Sunday Times* (S.A.), November 5, 1978.
39. *Rand Daily Mail* (S.A.) October 30, 1978.
40. "Eschel Rhoodie Story," pp. 18-20.
41. *Rand Daily Mail* (S.A.), December 11, 1978.
42. "Eschel Rhoodie Story," pp. 21, 25.
43. *Rand Daily Mail* (S.A.), October 30, 1978; November 3, 1978.
44. Ibid.
45. "Eschel Rhoodie Story," p. 21.
46. *House of Assembly Debates* (Questions & Replies), May 2, 1979.

47. *Africa News*, December 11, 1979; *Southern Africa* 12, no. 1 (January 1979): 26.
48. "Eschel Rhoodie Story," p. 28, *Guardian* (U.K.), July 26, 1979.
49. *Southern Africa* 12, no. 4, p. 1.
50. *Sunday Express* (S.A.), August 5, 1979; *Rand Daily Mail* (S.A.), August 6, 1979; *Star* (S.A.), August 6, 1979.
51. *Sunday Times*, August 12, 1979.
52. "Eschel Rhoodie Story," p. 28.
53. Guardian (U.K.), July 26, 1979; "Eschel Rhoodie Story," p. 20.
54. "Eschel Rhoodie Story," pp. 29-30; *Africa News*, November 2, 1979, and November 6, 1978.
55. *House of Assembly Debates* (Questions & Replies), May 2, 1979.
56. Ibid.
57. Ibid.
58. "Eschel Rhoodie Story," p. 29.
59. Ibid., p. 19.
60. *Financial Times* (U.K.), March 21, 1979; *Sunday Times* (S.A.), November 5, 1978.
61. Quoted in July 1979 by the Gannett News Service, as reported in *Africa News*, July 24, 1979.
62. *Africa News*, July 24, 1979.
63. *Erasmus Commission, Supplementary Report*, p. 45.
64. *Erasmus Commission, Supplementary Report*, p. 46; *Rand Daily Mail* (S.A.) July 19, 1979.
65. *Rand Daily Mail* (S.A.), June 27, 1979.
66. *Erasmus Commission, Supplementary Report*, p. 46; *Sunday Times* (S.A.), June 16, 1979.
67. "Eschel Rhoodie Story," p. 20.
68. Karen Rothmyer, "Apartheid Trib," *Nation*, April 14, 1979; idem, "The McGoff Grab," *Columbia Journalism Review*, November-December 1979.
69. Rothmyer, "The McGoff Grab."
70. The background information on the *Washington Times* is taken from "Moon Shines on Apartheid," *Washington Notes on Africa*.
71. Ibid.
72. Ibid.
73. *Rand Daily Mail* (S.A.), November 2, 1978; *Africa News*, November 20, 1978.
74. *Africa News*, April 13, 1979.
75. *Erasmus Commission, Supplementary Report*, pp. 46-47.
76. Rothmyer, "South Africa Lobby," p. 456.
77. Ibid.
78. Thrasher and Newland, "South African Story."
79. *International Herald Tribune*, March 26, 1979.
80. *Africa Report*, May-June, 1979, p. 24.
81. *International Herald Tribune*, March 23, 1979.
82. *Africa Report*, May-June, 1979, p. 24.
83. *Guardian* (U.K.), March 28, 1979.
84. *Southern Africa* 12, no. 4 (May 1979):10-11.
85. *Guardian* (U.K.), March 28, 1979.
86. *House of Assembly Debates* (Questions & Replies), May 2, 1979.
87. *Southern Africa* 12, no. 1 (January 1979):6.
88. "Eschel Rhoodie Story," p. 29.
89. *Southern Africa*, 12, no. 4 (May 1979):11.
90. "Eschel Rhoodie Story," p.28.
91. *Africa News*, March 30, 1979; *Observer* (U.K.), quoted in *Southern Africa* 12, no. 4 (May 1979):11.
92. *Erasmus Commission, Supplementary Report*, pp. 42-44; "Eschel Rhoodie Story," p. 25; *Guardian* (U.K.), December 11, 1978; *Financial Times* (U.K.), December 12, 1978; *Sunday Times* (S.A.), July 27, 1979.
93. *Southern Africa* 12, no. 4 (May 1979):11.
94. *Sunday Express* (S.A.), June 10, 1979.
95. *House of Assembly Debates* (Questions & Replies), May 2, 1979.
96. Burgess et al., *Great White Hoax*, pp. 85-87.
97. *International Herald Tribune*, March 23, 1979.
98. "Eschel Rhoodie Story," pp. 29-31.
99. *Cape Times.* (S.A.), December 13, 1978; *Rand Daily Mail* (S.A.), December 14, 1978.
100. "Eschel Rhoodie Story," p. 27.
101. *New African*, May 1979, p. 22.
102. *International Herald Tribune*, March 9, 1979, and December 8, 1978.
103. *Guardian* (U.K.), March 28, 1979; *Africa Report*, January-February 1979, p. 25.
104. *Southern Africa* 12, no. 1 (January 1979):14.
105. "Eschel Rhoodie Story," p. 24.
106. *Southern Africa* 12, no. 4 (May 1979):11

CHAPTER 7: THE TOTAL STRATEGY

1. A biographical sketch of Botha appeared in *Le Monde*, September 30, 1978.
2. "The Day of the General," *Financial Mail* (S.A.), September 5, 1980.
3. *Star* (S.A.), January 29, 1982.
4. Department of Defence, Republic of South Africa, *White Paper on Defence, 1977*, Supplement to *Paratus*, May 1977, p. ii.
5. Ibid.
6. *BOSS: The First Five Years* (London: International Defence and Aid Fund, 1977).
7. Department of Defence, Republic of South Africa, *White Paper on Defence and Armaments Supply, 1979*, p. 3.
8. John Seiler, "How PW Rules SA," *Sunday Times* (S.A.), August 19, 1979.
9. John Fullerton, "South Africa: The Day of the Generals," *NOW* (U.K.), no. 4, October 10, 1979, p. 22.
10. *Guardian* (U.K.), March 25, 1980.
11. *To the Point* (S.A.), October 10, 1979.
12. *Financial Mail* (S.A.), August 15, 1980.
13. *Daily Dispatch* (S.A.), June 16, 1979.
14. *New York Times*, August 4, 1979
15. *Rand Daily Mail* (S.A.), September 20, 1979.
16. Philip Mayer, "Class, Status, and Ethnicity as Perceived by Johannesburg Africans," in Leonard Thompson and Jeffrey Butler, eds., *Change in Contemporary South Africa* (Berkeley: University of California Press, 1975), p. 140.
17. *New York Times*, December 28, 1981.
18. *New York Times*, May 13, 1982.
19. *New York Times*, December 28, 1980.
20. Joseph Lelyveld, "Black Unions Are Making Imprint in South Africa," *New York Times*, August 10, 1982.
21. *Financial Times* (U.K.), February 20, 1981; *Financial Mail* (S.A.), February 5, 1982, cited in Sandy Boyer, "Black Unions in South Africa" (New York: The Africa Fund, 1982), p. 3.
22. For background on recent strikes, see Lelyveld, "Black Unions Are Making an Imprint," and Boyer, "Black Unions in South Africa."
23. *Africa Confidential* (U.K.), March 11, 1981, cited in Boyer, "Black Unions in South Africa."
24. Lelyveld, "Black Unions are Making an Imprint."
25. Ibid.
26. Joseph Lelyveld, "South African Growth Lets a Few Blacks Advance," *New York Times*, December 27, 1981.
27. Joseph Lelyveld, "Transient Workers in South Africa Face a Maze of Regulations," *New York Times*, December 28, 1981; *Africa News*, July 11, 1983.
28. *Financial Mail* (South Africa), October 12, 1979
29. Joseph Lelyveld, "On South African Farms, Feudal Attitudes Linger," *New York Times*, December 29, 1981.
30. *New York Times*, August 21, 1982.
31. The Black Sash, Johannesburg Advice Office, "Emergency Report," November 1979, reprinted in the newsletter of Episcopal Churchmen for South Africa (New York), Christmas 1979.
32. *New York Times*, February 7, 1982.
33. Ibid.
34. *Rand Daily Mail* (S.A.), June 15, 1978. The survey was published in West Germany: Theodor Hanf et al., *Sudafrika: Friedlicher Wandel?* (Kaiser-Grunewald, 1978).
35. Survey by L. Schlemmer, University of Natal, in George Philip Quail et al., *The Quail Report—Report of the Ciskei Commission* (Silverton, S.A.: Conference Associates, 1980), pp. 298-300.
36. *New York Times*, March 21, 1982.
37. *New York Times*, March 15, 1982.
38. Ibid.

CHAPTER 8: THE CRISIS IN AMERICAN POLICY

1. *New York Times*, March 15, 1981.
2. *New York Times*, March 15 and 24, 1981.
3. Testimony of Assistant Secretary of State for African Affairs Chester Crocker, U.S. Congress, House, Subcommittee on Africa of the Committee on Foreign Affairs, *U.S. Policy Toward Namibia: Spring*

1981, Hearings, 97th Cong., 1st sess., June 17, 1981, p. 15; *Washington Notes on Africa,* Washington Office on Africa, Winter 1981, p. 5.

4. Background information on Chester Crocker appeared in *Washington Notes on Africa,* Washington Office on Africa, Winter, 1980/81, pp. 1-2, and Summer, 1980, pp. 3-4.

5. Quoted in *Africa Report,* July-Aug., 1980, p. 4.

6. Ibid.

7. Quoted in *Washington Notes on Africa,* Washington Office on Africa, Summer, 1980, p. 4.

8. Cited in *Washington Notes on Africa,* Washington Office on Africa, Winter, 1980/81, p. 1.

9. Ibid., Summer, 1981, p. 4.; in House hearings in March, 1981 he repeated the same theme, saying the Soviets were training "literally thousands of third world embryo-terrorists" (*New York Times,* March 22, 1981).

10. Among recent articles and statements by Chester Crocker are the following:

"Current and Projected Military Balances in Southern Africa," in Richard E. Bissell and Chester A. Crocker, eds., *South Africa into the 1980's* (Boulder: Westview Press, 1979), p. 71-105.

Michael A. Samuels, Chester A. Crocker, Roger W. Fontaine, et al., *Implications of Soviet and Cuban Activities in Africa for U.S. Policy* (Washington, D.C.: Georgetown University Center for Strategic and International Studies, 1979)—a report sponsored by the Defense Department.

"South Africa as a Problem in U.S. Foreign Policy: Interests and Objectives," prepared statement and testimony for U.S. Congress, House, Subcommittees on International Economic Policy and Trade, on Africa, and on International Organization, *U.S. Policy Toward South Africa, Hearings,* 96th Cong., 2nd Sess., June 10, 1980, pp. 660-741.

"African Policy in the 1980's," *The Washington Quarterly,* Summer 1980, pp. 72-86.

"South Africa: Strategy for Change," *Foreign Affairs,* Fall 1980, pp. 323-351.

With Mark Greznes and Robert Henderson, "A U.S. Policy for the 80's," *Africa Report,* January-February 1981, pp. 7-14.

South Africa's Defense Posture: Coping With Vulnerability, Washington Papers, No. 84 (Beverley Hills and London: Sage Publications, 1981). [A revised version of a study prepared for the Study Commission on U.S. Policy Toward Southern Africa, used for Chapter 11 of *South Africa: Time Running Out* (Berkeley, Calif.: University of California Press, 1981).]

Testimony in U.S. Congress, House, Subcommittee on Africa of the Committee on Foreign Affairs, *U.S. Policy Toward Namibia: Spring 1981, Hearings,* 97th Cong., 1st Sess., June 17, 1981, 39 pp.

"Regional Strategy for Southern Africa," address before the American Legion, Honolulu, Aug. 29, 1981, U.S. Department of State, Bureau of Public Affairs, Washington, D.C., Current Policy, No. 308.

"Reagan's Africa Policy: Chester Crocker with Elise Pachter" (interview), *SAIS Review 3,* no. 3 (Winter/Spring 1983), pp. 83-97.

11. Mohamed A. El-Khawas and Barry Cohen, eds., *The Kissinger Study of Southern Africa: National Security Study Memorandum 39* (Westport, Conn.: Lawrence Hill, 1976), pp. 105-6.

12. Ibid., p. 189.

13. Quoted in Study Commission on U.S. Policy Toward Southern Africa, *South Africa: Time Running Out* (Berkeley, Calif.: University of California Press, 1981), p. 359.

14. Ibid., p. 360.

15. Crocker, "South Africa: Strategy for Change," p. 344.

16. Crocker et al., "A U.S. Policy for the '80s," p. 11; Crocker, "South Africa: Strategy for Change," p. 325.

17. Cited in Garrick Uttley, *Globalism or Regionalism? United States Policy Towards Southern Africa,* Adelphi Papers No. 154 (London: International Institute for Strategic Studies, 1979), p. 27.

18. Chester A. Crocker, "The Trouble with Our Rhodesia Policy," *Washington Post,* September 25, 1978.

19. Crocker et al., "A U.S. Policy for the '80s," p. 8.

20. Crocker, "The Trouble with Our Rhodesia Policy."

21. Crocker, "Regional Strategy for Southern Africa," p. 3.

22. Crocker, "South Africa: Strategy for Change," p. 343.

23. Ibid., p. 344.

24. Crocker, "South Africa as a Problem in U.S. Foreign Policy: Interests and Objectives," p. 695.

25. Crocker, "South Africa: Strategy for Change," pp. 337-38.

26. Ibid., p. 324.

27. Ibid., pp. 341-42, 349.

28. Ibid., p. 343.

29. Crocker, *South Africa's Defense Posture,* pp. 87-88.

30. Pauline H. Baker, "The Lost Continent?" *SAIS Review* 3, no. 1 (Winter-Spring 1983), p. 112.

31. *New York Times,* December 13, 1981; *Washington Post,* January 23, 1982.

32. Study Commission on U.S. Policy Towards Southern Africa, *South Africa: Time Running Out.*

33. Ibid., p. 407.

34. Lawrence S. Eagleburger, Under Secretary of State for Political Affairs, speech on U.S. policy in Africa, delivered June 23, 1983, excerpts in *New York Times,* June 24, 1983.

35. The figure was given in a speech on November 11, 1982, marking Angolan independence day, cited in *Focus* 44 (January-February 1983), p. 4.

36. *Namibia: The Crisis in United States Policy Toward Southern Africa* (Washington, D.C.: TransAfrica, 1983). See also a critical analysis of the legal and political issues by an expert on Namibia: Elizabeth S. Landis, *Namibian Libreation: Self-Determination, Law and Politics* (New York: Episcopal Churchmen for South Africa, 1982), a report based on a paper delivered at the annual meeting of the African Studies Association, Washington, D.C., October 1982.

37. This total was calculated by James Cason of *Southern Africa Magazine*: it includes $2.85 billion in direct investment cited by the American ambassador to South Africa in a speech in February 1983, more than $3.5 billion in outstanding obligations cited by the U.S. Federal Reserve survey (June 1983), and $3 billion worth of South African gold-mining shares estimated to be held in the United States according to a 1981 report by a private South African brokerage firm.

Index

Abramson, David, 175, 184, 190, 191, 192
ACCESS (American Coordinating Committee for Equality in Sports and Society), 188
Adam, Heribert, 55
Aermacchi aircraft, 140
AFL-CIO, 56, 175, 187
African Food and Canning Workers Union, 211, 212
African Mine Workers Union, 27, 42
African National Congress of South Africa (ANC): 6, 15, 40-42, 46, 51-53, 83, 90, 94, 95, 128, 146, 235; history, 26-36, 40, 55; international support for, 38, 45, 46, 47, 91, 121; and S.A. Communists, 41-45; S.A. attacks against, 34; support for, in S.A., 47, 51, 54; underground and guerrilla operations, 9, 10, 21-23, 34, 35, 38, 40, 41, 48, 56, 57, 58, 60, 86; Youth League, 27, 28, 31, 44; Women's League, 30. See also Umkhonto we Sizwe
Afri-Comix, 176, 179
Afrikaners, 4, 5, 6, 7, 25, 37; history of, 24, 25
Afripix, 172, 184
Aggett, Dr. Neil, 56, 212
Alberts, Jan van Zyl, 170-73, 176, 179, 180
Allegany Ludlam Industries, 84
Allis-Chalmers, 145
Amax, Inc., 61
Anderson, Bill, 70
Anglo-American Corporation, 61, 122, 170, 220
Angola: 4, 39, 54, 107, 273; Cuban role in, 9, 14, 37, 76-79, 97, 229; and Namibia settlement, 68, 93, 96; relations with U.S., 221, 230, 239; and South African aggression, 14, 17, 59, 63, 73-76, 82, 86, 94; and South African invasion, 9, 11, 13, 18, 37, 64, 65, 77, 78, 185. See also Constructive engagement
Anti-Apartheid Movement (U.K.), 190
Apartheid: 4, 34, 47, 48, 56, 62; introduction of, 5, 6, 8, 9; pressure for modifications in, 5, 41, 45, 55, 95; under Total Strategy, 202, 203, 206, 215, 221
Armaments Corporation of South Africa (ARMSCOR): 18, 102, 106, 137, 138, 203; imports by, 136, 140, 141, 143, 144, 150; and private contractors, 138, 142-43; domestic production, 139; and self-sufficiency, 140, 142, 143, 144-45, 148-49; arms exports, 159, 160
Arms embargo, 15, 103, 148; weaknesses and nonenforcement of, 17, 18, 34, 95, 131, 132-37, 149, 150-59
Atlantic Council, 188
Atlas Aircraft Corporation (S.A.), 140, 141, 157
Azanian Peoples Organization (AZAPO), 49, 52, 53
Azanian Students Organization (AZASO), 49

Bailey, Martin, 147
Bank of America, 47, 177

Bantu (Urban Areas) Consolidation Act (1945), 206, 207
Bantustans: 19, 58, 84, 119, 122; and apartheid system, 5, 7, 8, 49, 205, 213; "independence" of, 8, 9, 101, 112; leaders and administrations, 48, 50
Barlow Rand, 138, 203
Barnard, Christian, 174-75, 187
Barnard, Lukas Daniel, 127, 128
Baron, Sydney S., 186, 187
Basutoland Congress, 90
Biko, Steve, 9, 37, 121, 135
Black Alliance, 49
Black Consciousness Movement: 9, 36, 41, 49, 50, 53, 121; contacts with ANC, 38, 40; and PAC compared, 36, 37
Black Consciousness Movement of South Africa (BCM/SA), 38
Black Municipal Workers Union, 211
Black Peoples Convention, 36
Black Sash, 215
Bophuthatswana, 17, 112, 176
Botha, Fanie, 212
Botha, Pieter W., 3-4, 8, 16, 17, 49, 59, 60, 67, 84, 85, 92-99, 111, 123, 129, 138, 140-42, 164, 222-23, 229; becomes prime minister, 13, 15; personal background, 198-99; and Total Strategy, 20, 130, 201-9, 213, 215, 220
Botha, R. F., 13, 15, 92, 154, 176, 223-25
Botha government, 15-20, 22, 58, 59, 76, 86, 93, 114, 128, 162, 163, 169, 172, 176, 182, 232, 236, 240; and Total Strategy, 202, 203, 205, 210, 217, 219, 221
Botswana, 60, 86-89, 91, 92, 94
Britain: 61, 64, 86, 103, 125; conquest in South Africa, 24, 25; and Rhodesian war, 82, 83, 85; and arms embargo, 132, 133, 136, 155, 156, 158; Department of Information programs in, 188-90, 192-93, 195
British Petroleum, 83, 147
Broederbond, 5
Brown, Jerry, 186
Brzezinski, Zbigniew, 229
Bureau of State Security (BOSS), 7, 9, 10, 12, 13, 14, 121, 123, 128, 130; in Vorster government, 124, 201; and British intelligence, 125; and CIA, 162, 166, 167; and propaganda programs, 179, 196, 197
Bush, George, 127, 226
Buthelezi, Gathsha: 48-53, 178, 219-20

Callahan government, 83, 135
Caltex, 83, 147
Carter, Jimmy, 12, 186, 229
Carter administration: 179; and arms embargo, 135, 150, 152, 153, 154, 157; policies in south-

ern Africa, 47, 50, 79, 83, 85, 127, 129, 228, 229, 230, 231, 232, 235, 238, 239
Center for International Politics, 177
Central Intelligence Agency: 19, 90, 132, 236; report on guerrilla conflict, 57-58; intervention in Angola, 77, 78, 79, 227; and Seychelles coup attempt, 92; collaboration with South Africa, 125, 126, 127; and Space Research Corporation, 150, 151; and Department of Information propaganda, 164, 165, 166, 184
Chemical Bank, 173
Christian League of Southern Africa, 174
CIA, see Central Intelligence Agency
Ciskei, 25, 48, 205
Ciskei Commission Report, 52
Citibank, 47
Citizen, 161, 162, 163, 164, 166, 170-72, 175, 178, 189, 195
Citizen Force, see South African Defence Force
Citizenship Amendment Bill (1978), 114
Civil Action program, 16, 17, 68, 105
Civil Defence Act (1977), 11, 116, 117
Clark, Dick, 153, 171, 185
Clark, Ramsey, 81
Clark amendment, 227, 229, 236
Club of Ten, 189, 19.
Coetsee, J., 16
Collier, Shannon, Rill and Edwards, 187
Coloured Labor party, 49, 111, 208, 209
Coloured Persons Representative Council, 112
Coloured people, see People of Mixed race
Committee for Fairness in Sport, 188
Committee on South African War Resistance (COSAWR), 18
Communist party of South Africa, 22, 27, 30, 35, 41, 42, 43. See also South African Communist party
Confederation of Unions of South Africa, 211
Conference of South African Students, 49
Congress Alliance, 30, 31, 32, 42, 51
Congress of Democrats, 29
Congress of the People, 28, 29, 30
Conservative party of South Africa, 218, 219, 220, 221
Consolidated Diamond Mines, 61
Constellation of states proposal, 202, 203
Constructive engagement policy, 75, 77, 93, 95, 96, 156, 226, 232-36, 238-40
Council for Scientific and Industrial Research, 100
Crocker, Chester A.: policies on southern Africa, 75, 82, 223-26, 231, 233-38, 240; on South African arms self-sufficiency, 148-49; on arms embargo, 154-56
Cuba, role of, in Angola, 9, 14, 37, 76, 78, 79, 97, 229

Dadoo, Yusuf, 35, 43
Daimler-Benz, 144
De Kieffer, Donald, 169, 187
De Kieffer Assoc., 187
De Villiers, Cas, 176
De Villiers, L. E. S., 187
Defence Act: (1957), 99, 102, 120; (1979), 110
Defence Advisory Board, 203
Defence White Papers: (1977), 10, 11, 13, 20, 64,

108, 113, 115, 117, 200; (1979), 17, 107, 142, 201; (1982), 100-1, 108, 115
Defiance campaign (1952), 28
Democratic Turnhalle Alliance, 66, 67, 68, 73, 96, 194
Department of Defence, South African, 15, 102, 167, 200
Department of Foreign Affairs, South African, 15, 167, 169, 174, 176, 190, 197
Department of Information, South African, 9, 13, 126, 127, 161-97
Department of National Security (DONS), 15, 123, 127. See also Bureau of State Security; National Intelligence Service
Department of Plural Relations, 122-23, 178
Diederichs, Nico, 166
Dos Santos, José Eduardo, 239
Drum International, 190, 191
Du Plessis, Willem, 129
Dube, John, 124
Dube, John Langalibalele, 26
Duignan, Peter, 55

Eagleburger, Lawrence, 238-41
Eaton Corporation, 145
Edwards, Ronnie, 110, 159
Edwards, Trevor, 73, 80-81, 106
Elseviers (magazine), 163, 173
Erasmus Commission, 124, 163, 165, 167, 170, 178, 180, 182, 183, 184

Federation of South African Trade Unions, 49, 211
Financial Mail, 12, 99, 113, 115, 129, 131, 143, 171
First, Ruth, 90, 125
Fischer, Abram, 43
Fluor Corporation, 21
FNLA, see National Front for the Liberation of Angola
Ford, Gerald, 78, 179, 184, 185
Ford administration, 127, 182, 227
Ford Motor Company, 144, 153, 177, 211
Foreign Affairs Association (S.A.), 175, 190
Foreign Affairs Research Institute, 193
Foundation for Social Studies, 194
France: in Western contact group, 64; arms sales to South Africa, 17, 18, 132, 133, 136, 140, 141, 142, 155, 158; nuclear cooperation with South Africa, 145, 146
Freedom Charter, 29, 30, 31, 35, 41, 43, 44, 45, 54
FRELIMO, see Mozambique Liberation Front
French-South Africa Society, 193
French-South African Chamber of Commerce, 193
French-South African Friendship Society, 193d
Frontline states, 17, 40, 46, 60, 69, 86, 87, 97, 131, 228, 233, 236, 240

Gann, Lewis, 55
Gelb, Stephen, 56
Geldenhuys, J. J., 111
Geldenhuys, M., 197
General Electric, 47, 144
General Electric Corporation, (U.K.), 144

General Laws Amendment Act (1963), 33; (1969), (1972),
General Motors Corporation, 47, 144, 153, 211
General Workers Union, 211
German Federal Republic: in Western Contact Group, 64, 67, 194; arms sales to South Africa, 133, 134, 141, 142, 155; nuclear cooperation with South Africa, 145, 146, 167; Department of Information propagana projects in, 190-91
German-South African Association, 190
Gervasi, Sean, 151
Global Communications, 180
Gqabi, Joe, 55, 88, 124
Group Areas Act, 28, 216
Guerrilla conflict: 10, 54; in South Africa, 11, 21-23, 38, 41; in Rhodesia, 34, 83, 85; in Namibia, 62, 64, 65, 66, 74, 77
Guerrillas, South African, see National Union for Total Independence of Angola; Mozambique Resistance Movement
Gulf Oil Corporation, 230
Haig, Alexander, 81, 224, 225, 226
Hain, Peter, 125
Haroun, Imam Adullah, 39
Hayakawa, S. I., 185
Helms, Richard, 165
Herero people, 61, 66
Heunis, Chris, 187
Himmelhoch, Ivan, 125
Hit (magazine), 176
Hoare, Mike, 91, 92, 129. See also Seychelle Islands
Holland Committee on Southern Africa, 47
Home Guards, 69, 71
Homerus Finance Corporation, 175
Hortors, Ltd., 175, 189, 190
Horwood, Owen, 203
Houphouet-Boigny, Felix, 197
Hull, Galen, 164

ICL Computers, 159
Immorality and Mixed Marriages Act, 28
Indemnity Act (1977), 119
Indian population of South Africa, 19, 25, 35, 109, 110, 215, 216, 219
Indian Reform party, 49, 111, 117
Industrial Conciliation Amendment Act, 206
Information Service of South Africa, 164, 167, 169. See also Department of Information
Inkatha, 49, 50, 51, 52, 53, 111
Institute for Strategic Studies, 177
Institute for the Study of Human Rights, 176
Institute for the Study of the Modern World (Paris), 193
Institute for the Study of Plural Societies, 177
International Commission of Jurists, 62
International Court of Justice, 60, 62, 63, 64
International Monetary Fund, 178, 234
International University Exchange Fund, 121
Isaacs, Henry, 39
Israel, 19, 93, 137, 142, 155, 156, 158, 197
Italy, arms sales to South Africa, 133, 137, 140, 142, 155

Jonathan, Leabua, 90
Jussen, Hubert, 171, 172

Kaunda, Kenneth, 91, 92, 129, 196
Khoikhoi people, 23, 24
Kirkpatrick, Jeane, 129, 223
Kissinger, Henry: 151; and Angola invasion, 77, 79, 185; and NSSM 39 policies, 155, 227, 228
Klue, Joseph, 128
Koornhof, Pieter, 49, 204, 205, 215
Kotane, Moses, 42, 44
Kruger, James, 10
Kruger, Paul, 25
KwaZulu, 17, 48, 50, 51

Labor in South Africa: black urban workers, 5, 211; "illegal" workers, 207, 213, 215; agricultural, 213, 214; migrant, 213; shortages, 204, 205, 210. See also Strikes; Trade unions
Labour party (U.K.), 33, 47, 125, 190
Labour Relations Act (1981), 206
Lancaster House settlement, 59, 82, 85, 230
Land Act (1936), 209
Lapchick, Richard, 188
Leballo, Potlako, 31, 32, 33, 38, 39
Lesotho, 33, 60, 86, 90, 91, 92, 94
Leyland Motors, 144
Liberal party, 125
Lloyd, C. J., 17
Lockheed Aircraft, 152
Lodge, Tom, 56
Lutheran World Ministries, 71
Luns, Joseph, 154
Lutuli, Albert, 28, 32, 51
Luyt, Louis, 170-71
MacBride, Sean, 81
McGivern, Arthur, 125
McGoff, John, 163, 165, 168, 171, 174, 176, 179, 180, 181, 182, 183, 185, 189
Make, Vusumzi, 39
Malan, D. F., 198
Malan, Magnus, 3, 13, 15, 19, 20, 84, 85, 92, 99, 129, 198, 199, 202, 204, 220, 223
Mancham, James, 195, 196
Mandela, Nelson, 27, 28, 30, 31, 32, 33, 34, 42, 44, 47, 50, 51, 52, 92
Manufacturers Hanover Trust, 47
Marais, Jaap, 94
Marais, Pieter G., 138, 140, 143
Maree, John, 138, 142, 203
Marks, J. B., 42, 43, 44
Matthews, Z. K., 28
Mdluli, Joseph, 40
Meany, George, 175, 187
Medische Kommittee Angola, 47
Military Balance, The, 108, 131, 151, 153
Military Intelligence, South African, 15, 23, 55, 92, 96, 123, 124, 127, 128-29
Military Police, South African, 122
Milner, Alfred, 25
Mmabatho Herald, 176
Mmusi, Peter, 95
Mobil Oil Corporation, 83, 147
Mobutu Sese Seko, 93, 196
Mofutsanyana, Edwin, 42
Mondale, Walter, 228

Moon, Sun Myung, 168, 181
Moose, Richard, 151, 153, 154
Morgan Grampian Publishing Group, 163, 189, 190, 192
Morogoro Conference, 34, 35, 41, 43, 44
Moss, Glenn, 23
Mostert, Anton, 162, 171, 183
Mothpeng, Zeph, 39
Motlana, Nthato, 50
Motor Assembly Components Workers Union of South Africa, 211
Mozambique, 4, 10, 11, 17, 54, 83-85, 92, 107; South African attacks on, 59, 60, 86, 89, 90, 94
Mozambique National Resistance (MNR), 60, 89, 90, 94
Mozambique Liberation Front (FRELIMO), 13, 37, 90
MPLA, See People's Movement for the Liberation of Angola
Mudge, Dirk, 66, 73
Mugabe, Robert, 54, 72, 82, 85, 87, 92, 203, 231
Mulder, Cornelius, 12-15, 127, 162, 163-64, 166-67, 176, 179-80, 184-85, 197
Muldergate, 163
Muldergate scandal, 13, 67, 161-67, 170-97. See also Department of Information
Munangagwa, Emmerson, 88
Muofhe, Tshithiwa Isaac, 48
Muzorewa, Abel, 54, 84, 87, 230
Muzorewa regime, 85, 203

Nama people, 61, 66
Namibia, 4, 9, 10, 15-17, 79, 194-95; and war, 11, 18, 54, 59, 72-75, 79, 86; settlement diplomacy, 14; South African occupation of, 59-69, 76; economy of, 61; and constructive engagement, 93, 96, 97, 223
Natal Indian Congress, 29, 49
National Automobile and Allied Workers Union, 211
National Front for the Liberation of Angola (FLNA), 77-81, 93, 106, 227
National Intelligence Service, 123-28, 129
National Key Points Act (1980), 19
National party, 4-8, 12, 13, 15, 20, 27. See also Botha government; Vorster government
National Security Study Memorandum 39, 155, 227, 228, 231
National Servicemen, see South African Defence Force
National Union of South African Students, 36
National Union for the Total Independence of Angola (UNITA), 60, 73, 77, 78, 79, 80, 81, 87, 97, 106, 182, 223, 227, 236
National Youth Organization, 40
Native Land Bill (1912), 26
Neto, Agostinho, 80
New Zealand, 134
News World, 181
Newmont Mining Co., 61
Nixon, Richard, 179
Nixon administration 127, 225, 227
Nkomo, Joshua, 54, 88
Nouvelle Société de la Presse, 190, 191
Nuclear Fuels Corporation (U.K.), 64

Nuclear Non-Proliferation Treaty, 145, 158, 224, 229
Nuclear technology, foreign assistance to South Africa, 11-12, 93, 126, 128, 134, 135, 136, 145, 146
Nuclear weapons in South Africa, 131, 145, 158
Nujoma, Sam, 62, 72
Nyawose, Petros, 91
Nzo, Alfred, 35

Odendaal Commission Report (1964), 62
Oppenheimer, Harry, 220
Opperman, Daniel J. J., 128
Orderly Movement and Settlement of Black Persons Bill, 207
Organization of African Unity (OAU), 39, 45, 46, 78, 178, 195

PAC, see Pan Africanist Congress
Pace, 172-73, 175
Pan Africanist Congress PAC), 6, 15, 31, 32, 33, 36, 37, 38, 39, 40, 41, 42, 44, 47, 52, 53
Panax Newspaper Corporation, 165, 176, 179, 180, 181, 182
Paratus, 21, 112, 117
Pass system: 5, 205; antipass campaigns, 27, 30, 32
Patriotic Front, 47, 54, 59, 84, 85, 89, 121, 230
Pegg, Stuart, 175, 190, 191, 192
People's Movement for the Liberation of Angola (MPLA), 9, 14, 37, 64, 75, 77-79, 93, 106, 223, 230
People of mixed race, 19, 24, 25, 35, 109, 110, 208, 215-16, 219
Perkins Diesels, 145
Philips Electronics, 144
Pieterse, Andre, 173
Player, Gary, 177
Plessey Electronics, 159
Pokela, John, 40
Police Amendment Act (1955), 120; (1979), 119
Political Imprisonment in South Africa, 121
Population Registration Act, 28
Poqo, 33, 38
Portuguese colonial empire, 4, 10, 39, 41, 59, 77
Potts, James, 78
Prescon Business, 177
Presidential Council, 208, 209, 218
Progressive Federal party, 110, 220
Propaganda, see Department of Information

QwaQwa, 49

Racal Electronics, 143
Railways, Harbours, and Airways Authority Police, 122
Reconnaissance Commandos, 103, 104, 106
Reagan, Ronald, 222, 226
Reagan administration: 47, 58, 74, 90, 129, 222; and "constructive engagement," 71, 75, 77, 81, 82, 93, 95, 96, 156, 222-26, 232-36, 238-40; and arms embargo, 149, 157
Rees, Mervyn, 163
René, Albert, 196
Rheinmetall, 141
Rhodes, Clarence, 181

Rhodesia: 4, 10, 14, 17, 72, 79, 195, 230; and South African intervention, 11, 14, 34, 59, 68, 82-85. *See also* Zimbabwe
Rhoodie, Eschel, 84, 127, 161, 162-97 passim
Rhoodie, Nic, 177, 194
Richard Manville, Inc., 195
Rio Tinto Zinc, 61
Rivers, Bernard, 147
Rivonia arrests and trial, 33, 34, 42, 44, 55
Roux, A. J. A., 146
Rusher, William, 182

Saager, Bruno, 189
Sabotage Act, 33, 211
Sacramento Union, 165, 180-83
SACTU, *see* South African Congress of Trade Unions
SADCC, *see* Southern Africa Development Coordination Conference
Saffir, Leonard, 181
San people, 23, 111
Saturday Evening Post, 165, 184
Saul, John, 56
Savimbi, Jonas, 81, 236
Scaife, Richard M., 165, 166, 180, 181
Sears, John, 169
Sebe, Charles, 48
Seme, P. Ka Izaka, 26
SenBank, 185, 186
Separate Representation of Voters Act, 28
SerVaas, Beurt, 165, 166, 171, 172, 184
Seychelle Islands, 91, 92, 106, 129, 195, 196
Shangaan people, 19, 110
Shannon, Thomas, 169
Sharon, Ariel, 93, 158
Sharpeville massacre, 6, 7, 9, 32, 132
Shaw, Fred, 174
Shell Oil (U.K.), 83, 147
Shreve, Gavin, 66
Sibeko, David, 39
Siemens Electronics, 144
Simon, William, 186
Simonstown Agreement, 132, 133
Sisulu, Walter, 27, 28, 31, 34, 44
Slovo, Joe, 22
Smathers, George, 169
Smit, Robert, 126, 178
Smith, Ian, 227
Smith regime, 59, 82, 83
Smoak, Marion, 169
Smuts, Jan, 5
Smuts government, 8, 27
Sobukwe, Robert M., 31, 32, 33, 38, 39, 50
South Africa Foundation, 225
South Africa: Time Running Out, 47, 237
South Africa, Union of, 5, 26, 120
South African Air Force, 23, 55, 102-3, 111
South African Airways, 195, 197
South African Allied Workers Union, 48, 211, 212
South African Army, 99, 102, 111
South African Associated Newspapers, 170, 171
South African Atomic Energy Board, 146
South African Bishops' Conference, 72
South African Coloured Peoples Organization, 29

South African Communist party, 42-45, 94. *See also* Communist party of South Africa
South African Congress of Trade Unions, 29, 44, 90, 210
South African Council of Churches, 52, 72, 217
South African Council of Sport, 49
South African Defence Force: 12, 16-18, 21, 22, 64, 65, 68, 71, 79, 88, 89, 91, 98, 102, 119, 201, 216, 234; Afrikaners in, 6, 98; compared, 107, 131; manpower strains, 19, 57; military policy, 99, 101; recruitment of blacks, 18, 69, 98, 109-12, 116, white women in, 11, 109, 112, 116. COMPONENTS: Air Commandos, 103, Cadets, 109-, 117-18; Cape Corps Service Battalion, 66, 77; Citizen Force, 16, 18, 64, 102, 107, 108, 109, 115-16; National Servicemen, 17, 59, 102, 107, 108, 109, 114; Permanent Force, 3, 18, 19, 59, 99, 107, 108, 113-14. *See also* South African Air Force; South African Army; South African Navy
South African Foreign Trade Association, 185, 186
South African Indian Congress, 28, 29, 35, 43
South African Indian Council, 208, 209
South African Institute of Race Relations, 212
South African Navy, 99, 102, 103, 111
South African Police, 48, 69, 71, 118-20
South African Security Police, 10, 15, 37, 40, 48, 52, 56, 69, 119, 120-22, 123, 124, 125
South African Student Movement, 36, 38
South African Students Organization, 36-38, 124
South African Women's Federation, 30
South Atlantic Treaty Organization, 134
South-West Africa, *see* Namibia
South-West African Peoples Organization (SWAPO), 9, 45, 47, 54, 59, 62-77, 79, 96, 97, 100, 119, 121, 128, 195, 240
South-West African Police, 69
South-West African Territorial Force, 59, 68, 69, 73, 104
South African Development Coordination Conference, 85, 87, 89, 91, 94, 204
Southern African Freedom Foundation, 173-74
Soviet Union, 86; and ANC, 11, 39, 45; and MPLA, 14, 77, 78, 79; South African view of, 42, 100, 216-17
Soweto uprising, 4, 9, 37-38, 40-41, 50
Soweto Committee of Ten, 49, 50
Space Research Corporation, 18, 134, 136, 141, 149, 150-51, 53
Sperry-Rand, 144
Springer, Axel, 171, 191
State Security Council, 137, 130, 200-1
STEAG, 133
Stockwell, John, 77, 126-27, 151
Strikes, 27, 28, 56, 63, 210, 211. *See also* Labor
Study Commission on U.S. Policy Toward Southern Africa, 47, 237
Sullivan code, 50
Sunday Express (S.A.:), 184, 193
Suppression of Communism Act, 28, 42
SWAPO, *see* South-West African Peoples Organization
Swazi people, 19, 110
Swaziland, 86, 91, 92
Sydney S. Baron Associates, 186, 187

Symington, James, 169
Tambo, Oliver, 27, 30, 31, 34, 35, 38, 44, 45, 47, 55
Tanzania, 89, 196
Terrorism Act (1967), 37, 38, 62, 71
Thatcher government, 85, 96
Thompson, Meldrim, 174
Thesaurus Continental Securities Corp., 180, 183, 188-89
Thloloe, Joseph, 40
Thor Communicators, 175, 179, 189
Thrope, Jeremy, 125
Tiro, O. R., 37, 124
Toivo, Herman ja, 62-63
Tolbert, W. R., 196
Total, 83, 147
To the Point, 171, 172, 184
Trials, 10, 23, 30, 34, 39, 42, 52, 57
Trade unions, 48, 56, 57, 210, 211, 212.
TransAfrica, 57, 128, 223
Transkei, 9, 25, 112
Transvaal Indian Congress, 27, 34
Treurnicht, Andries, 218
Trib, 181, 183
Tsongas amendment, 187
Tsumeb Corporation, 61
Tunney, John, 185, 186
Turnhalle Conference, 66
Tutu, Desmond, 52, 72, 205

Umkhonto we Sizwe, 22, 32, 33, 34, 42
Unification Church, 168, 181-83
Union of South Africa, 5, 26, 126
UNITA, see National Union for the Total Independence of Angola
United Nations, 45, 46, 60, 66; and Namibia, 62, 63, 67, 68, 76, 240. See also Arms embargo
United Nations Centre Against Apartheid, 136, 147
United Nations Commission on Human Rights, 121, 122
United Nations Council for Namibia, 62, 64
United Nations General Assembly, 46, 62, 63, 64, 66, 76
United Nations High Commissioner for Refugees, 67
United Nations Security Council, 8, 17, 34, 46, 63, 64, 75, 80, 81, 83, 129, 131; Arms Embargo Committee, 136, 152; Resolutions, 64, 132, 135, 136
United Press International Television News, 180, 181, 183
United States Agency for International Development, 90
United States Defense Intelligence Agency, 129
United States House of Representatives, Subcommittee on Africa, 156
United States National Security Council, 129
United States Securities and Exchange Commission, 183
United States Senate, Foreign Affairs Committee, 78; Subcommittee on Africa, 171, 185; Subcommittee on Security and Terrorism, 45

University Christian Movement, 36
Urban Areas Consolidation Act, 206, 207

Vaderland, 219
Valiant Publishers, 178
Van den Bergh, Hendrik, 7, 8, 13, 15, 78, 83, 120, 123-24, 163, 167, 170, 197, 201
Van der Westhuizen, P. W., 129
Van Tonder, Nils, 129
Van Wyck, Alexander, 123
Venda people, 19, 25, 110, 112, 205
Verwoerd, Hendrik, 7, 8
Verwoerd government, 123, 198
Vorster, J. B., 3, 8-16, 49, 50, 79, 83, 84, 92, 94, 120, 124, 127, 201, 205; and propaganda war, 161-67, 180-82, 196, 197
Vorster government, 7, 41, 64, 67, 78, 130, 201, 204, 228, 229
Vosloo, Ton, 219

Washington Star, 168, 180, 182, 183
Washington Times, 168, 181-83
Wee, Paul, 71
West Africa, 192
West German Anti-Apartheid Movement, 140, 142, 146
Western Contact Group, 64, 67, 80, 81, 224, 240
Westinghouse, 144
Westmoreland, William, 187
Whelan, James, 181-82
Wiehahn Commission on Labor Legislation, 209
Williamson, Craig, 121
Winter, Gordon, 125
Woods, Donald, 175
World Campaign Against Military Collaboration with South Africa, 136
World Council of Churches, 47, 62, 100, 174, 175, 191, 192
World Forum Features, 165
Writers Association of South Africa, 49, 173

Xanap, 176, 179
Xhosa people, 24, 25, 51
Xuma, A. B.,

Young, Andrew, 79, 228, 229, 2331

Zaire, 8, 77, 78, 79, 87, 93, 196
Zambia, 17, 34, 59, 60, 68, 83-94, 107, 196, 197
ZANU, see Zimbabwe African National Union
ZAPU, see Zimbabwe African Peoples Union
Zeitsman, C. F., 10, 41
Zimbabwe, 16, 54, 60, 72, 83, 86-90, 92, 94, 107, 203. See also Rhodesia
Zimbabwe African National Union (ZANU), 84, 87, 119, 231
Zimbabwe African National Union-Patriotic Front (ZANU-PF), 82, 85, 88
Zimbabwe African Peoples Union (ZAPU), 34, 83, 84, 87, 88, 119
Ziyang, Zhao, 40
Zulu people, 19, 24, 25, 50-51, 110-11